T0330326

Risk Management
in Commodity Markets

Risk Management in Commodity Markets:

From Shipping to Agriculturals and Energy

Edited by

Hélyette Geman

A John Wiley and Sons, Ltd., Publication

Other Wiley Editorial Offices

John Wiley & Sons Inc., 111 River Street, Hoboken, NJ 07030, USA

Jossey-Bass, 989 Market Street, San Francisco, CA 94103-1741, USA

Wiley-VCH Verlag GmbH, Boschstr. 12, D-69469 Weinheim, Germany

John Wiley & Sons Australia Ltd, 42 McDougall Street, Milton, Queensland 4064, Australia

John Wiley & Sons (Asia) Pte Ltd, 2 Clementi Loop #02-01, Jin Xing Distripark, Singapore 129809

John Wiley & Sons Canada Ltd, 6045 Freemont Blvd, Mississauga, Ontario, L5R 4J3, Canada

Wiley also publishes its books in a variety of electronic formats. Some content that appears
in print may not be available in electronic books.

Library of Congress Cataloging-in-Publication Data

Risk management in commodity markets : from shipping to agriculturals and energy / edited by Hélyette Geman.
    p. cm. – (Wiley finance series)
  Includes bibliographical references and index.
  ISBN 978-0-470-69425-1 (cloth : alk. paper) 1. Commodity exchanges. 2. Commodity futures. 3. Risk
  management. 4. Investment analysis. I. Geman, Hélyette.
  HG6046.R57 2008
  332.64′4–dc22

                                                                                   2008038613

British Library Cataloguing in Publication Data

A catalogue record for this book is available from the British Library

ISBN 978-0-470-69425-1

Typeset in 10/12pt Times by Laserwords Private Limited, Chennai, India
Printed and bound in Great Britain by Antony Rowe Ltd, Chippenham, Wiltshire

Contents

15 Case Studies and Risk Management in Commodity Derivatives Trading   255

Hilary Till, Premia Capital Management LLC

Preface

There has been lately a gigantic interest worldwide in the commodities space, energy in particular, as evidenced by the number of press editorials that are published on the subject. Commodity prices have been experiencing an unprecedented rise in the last few years and there is no sign, at the date of writing (July 2008), that we may revert to the levels of 2005 or 2006, not to mention those prevailing in the early 2000s which seem to belong to prehistory. Uranium prices went from $7 per pound in 2003 to $90, then $100 in early 2008, with 442 nuclear reactors in the world needing 180 million pounds of uranium, a number that is much larger than the current production. The LNG (Liquid Natural Gas) market is boiling at minus 160 Celsius degrees; Korean shipyards are delivering new carriers with increased capacity and, interestingly, some of the LNG tankers start being used as floating storage (hence, embedding a valuable optionality). Demand for metals, energy and cereals from Brazil and Russia, two of the fastest- growing economies, is undoubtedly pushing prices up, together with the one coming from the heavily populated India and China. As an example, between 2001 and 2005, China's demand for copper, aluminium and iron respectively increased by 78 %, 85 % and 92 %. As part of the expansion of the commodities universe, azuki beans, which used to be ignored in many parts of the world, are now a component of a number of commodity indexes into which gigantic amounts of money have poured lately. Energy prices, e.g., crude oil and coal, have witnessed an amazing increase these last two years, with a greater public awareness of "Peak Oil" or at least, the exhaustible nature of fossil energy. The West Texas Intermediate (WTI) crude oil, that had undergone a respite in price increase during the year 2006, resumed in 2007 its irresistible ascent to go over the symbolic threshold of $100 per barrel in early 2008. It went above $140/bbl in June and July, resulting in prices multiplied by more than 500 percent in less than four years, with – among other reasons – supply disruptions in Nigeria, a structural decline in production in Mexico and other countries.

Call options on crude oil with strikes of $100 or more were the subject of great attention when they appeared in New York in summer 2006. By May 2008, there were 21,000 outstanding contracts for the NYMEX December 2008 call options with a strike of $200/bbl. Their volume has more than quadrupled since the beginning of 2008, signalling that a number of market participants are betting that crude oil prices would hit $200 before the end of 2008, a possibility first mentioned by the US bank Goldman Sachs, a major player in the oil market. As another sign of changing times, US heating oil futures trading was interrupted for a short while on the electronic platform CME Globex, after prices struck the fluctuation limit of 25 cents, or 6.82 percent. This "limit up" move triggered the halt in the electronic trading of all energy contracts, including WTI crude oil and RBOB gasoline. This was the first shutdown since electronic trading began in 2006 and created confusion and concern among traders.

Since commodities are essentially denominated in dollars, the weakness of the "numéraire" currency has often been cited as a major explanation for the rise of commodity prices. Still, in constant dollars, average crude oil prices rose by 124 percent over the period 2002 – 2006; and the recent increase has been even steeper. At the beginning of April 2008, the secretary of the Organization of Petroleum Exporting Countries, which pumps 40 % of the oil world supplies, rejected requests for an increase in the cartel's crude output, saying that non-fundamental factors were to blame for current high prices. In fact, OPEC maintained its output at 29.67 million barrels per day at its last meeting in March 2008 and warned that there would be little OPEC could do if prices hit $200. With a forward looking perspective, the entire WTI crude forward curve has been trading over the level of $105 since the beginning of April 2008, with the long dated contract for December 2016 trading above $110, indicating a market consensus over $100 for a while.

The same tight market conditions across the spectrum of the three commodity classes – energy, metals and Agriculturals – are also unlikely to drastically improve in the near future, with land itself becoming rare and water insufficient, disruptions occurring in South African mines because of electricity shortages, geopolitical issues in a number of countries producing commodities and a world surge in demand. We can observe that these elements illuminate a property that did not used to be true, namely that the three commodity sub-asset classes are increasingly *correlated*, a property that we can certainly view as novel in the commodity markets. Hence, energy companies and agrifood business now need, like bankers and portfolio managers, to follow what is happening in the space of all commodities while deciding on the acquisition of new physical assets such as power plants, gas storage facilities, aluminium smelters or grain elevators. This is illustrated by the example of the private equity fund KKR acquiring the biggest utility in Texas.

One should remember that the history of commodities has been filled with booms, busts, seasonal volatility, weather events, geopolitical tensions and occasional attempts to "corner" the market, features that were reasonably acting as a deterrent for new entrants. Moreover, the physical constraints of delivery and storage make spot commodity trading difficult or impossible; transactions on commodity futures Exchanges can only be performed through a broker who is a member of the Exchange (hence, the gigantic success of the recently introduced ETFs (Exchange-Traded Futures), that are accessible to individual investors. All participating agents must keep in mind, however, that volatility swings reflect not only supply and demand concerns, but also the fact that these markets are sometimes dominated by large players, are often opaque, always directed by the long lead-time between a production decision and its actual viability. Trading volumes have also widely fluctuated over time: during the high inflation era of the 1970s, commodity futures trading exploded and the real estate sector boomed since bonds and stocks were generating a real return close to zero over a decade. The end of the 1970s commodity boom can be identified with the crash in 1980 of precious metals prices, when the famous squeeze of the silver market by the Hunt Brothers (who were holding at some point an estimated 50 percent of the global deliverable supply of silver) failed. Afterwards, there was a long period of nearly 20 years of stagnation in commodity prices, that some experts attribute to supply fundamentals and lower inflation.

Over the decades, commodities have essentially captured the attention of famous economists such as Keynes, Kaldor or Working and industrial organization researchers. They have generally been under-studied and certainly under-represented in finance literature. This book aims at filling part of this vacuum, and I express my gratitude to the experts, academics and practitioners, who agreed to contribute a chapter. Through the various chapters, a number of economic, geopolitical and modelling issues, all fascinating, were analyzed in a superb way.

Hélyette Geman

About the Editor

HÉLYETTE GEMAN

Hélyette GEMAN is a Professor of Finance at Birkbeck, University of London and ESSEC Graduate Business School. She is a graduate of l'Ecole Normale Supérieure in mathematics, holds a Masters degree in theoretical physics and a PhD in mathematics from the University Pierre et Marie Curie and a PhD in Finance from the University Pantheon Sorbonne.

Professor Geman has been a scientific advisor to major financial institutions and energy and mining companies for the last 18 years, covering the spectrum of interest rates, catastrophic risk, oil, natural gas, electricity, and metals. She was previously the head of Research and Development at Caisse des Dépôts. Professor Geman was the first president of the Bachelier Finance Society and has published more than 95 papers in top international finance journals including *the Journal of Finance, Journal of Financial Economics, Mathematical Finance*. She is a Member of Honor of the French Society of Actuaries. Professor Geman's research includes interest rates and catastrophic insurance, asset price and commodity forward curve modelling, hedge funds and alternative investments, as well as exotic option pricing for which she won the first prize of the Merrill Lynch Awards in 1994. Her work on catastrophic options and CAT bonds and book *Insurance and Weather Derivatives* (1998) received the AFIR (actuarial approach to financial risk) prize. Professor Geman was named in 2004 in the Hall of Fame of Energy Risk and received in July 2008 the ISA medal for sciences of the Alma Mater University of Bologna for the CGMY model, a pure jump Lévy process widely used in finance since 2002.

Her reference book *Commodities and Commodity Derivatives* was published by Wiley Finance in January 2005. Professor Geman is a Member of the Board of the UBS-Bloomberg Commodity Index.

About the Contributors

Carol Alexander

Carol Alexander is a Professor of Risk Management at the ICMA Centre, University of Reading, and Chair of the Academic Advisory Council of the Professional Risk Manager's International Association (PRMIA). She is the author of a new four-volume text on Market Risk Analysis and of the best-selling textbook Market Models, both published by Wiley. She has also been editor of and contributor to a very large number of books on finance and mathematics, including the multi-volume Professional Risk Manager's Handbook (McGraw-Hill, 2008 and PRMIA Publications). Carol has published over 100 academic journal articles, book chapters and books, the majority of which focus on financial risk management and mathematical finance.

Giovanni Barone-Adesi

Giovanni Barone-Adesi is Professor of Finance Theory at the Swiss Finance Institute, University of Lugano, Switzerland. After graduating from the University of Chicago, he taught at the University of Alberta, University of Texas, City University and the University of Pennsylvania. His main research interests are derivative securities and risk management. He is the author of several models for valuing and hedging securities. Especially well-known are his contributions to the pricing of American commodity options and the measurement of market risk. He advises several exchanges and other business organizations.

Svetlana Borovkova

Currently an associate professor of Finance at the Vrije Universiteit Amsterdam, Dr Borovkova has specialized in applying mathematical and statistical methods to problems within the finance and energy sectors. She is often consulted by major banks and energy trading firms, most notably for her work in derivatives pricing, futures trading and market modeling. She is a frequent speaker at international finance and energy conferences, such as the Bachelier Congress for Mathematical Finance and Energy Risk. Previously she held a position as assistant professor at Delft University of Technology and a trading analyst position in Shell Trading, London. She received her PhD in 1998 from the University of Groningen, The Netherlands, and Oregon State University, US, for analysis of nonlinear and chaotic time series, and MSc degrees in computer science and in mathematics from Moscow and Utrecht.

Wolfgang Bühler
Wolfgang Bühler holds the Chair of Finance at the University of Mannheim. He studied mathematics and economics at the Technical University of München and received his PhD and Habilitation degrees from the RWTH Aachen. Professor Bühler was a visiting professor at UCLA, the Stern School, and the Post Graduate School of Economics in Rio de Janeiro. He served as Associate Editor of *Management Science*, the *Review of Derivatives Research*, and the *European Finance Review*. His research interests include the theoretical and empirical analysis of capital markets, fixed income analysis, valuation of derivatives, management of market, credit, liquidity and commodity risks.

Julie Dana
Julie Dana is a Technical Specialist working in the World Bank's Agriculture & Rural Development Department in the Commodity Risk Management Group. She is an expert on commodity markets and risk management, with a focus on supply chain management, commodity hedging, insurance, and trade finance solutions. She has been with the World Bank for six years. Prior to joining the Bank she spent seven years working as a commodities trader in the private sector. At the World Bank, Julie's activities have focused on cotton, coffee, and grains sectors in Africa. For the past two years a large part of her work has focused on market-based solutions to food security problems in East and Southern Africa. She has a BA in English Literature/Political Science from Washington University in St Louis, and an MBA from the University of Denver with a focus on International Trade. Julie's work in Malawi during the food shortage of 2005–06 was part of an Emergency Response project which was awarded the World Bank's Africa Regional Award for Excellence.

Paolo Falbo
Dr Falbo is Associate Professor at the University of Brescia and teaches quantitative methods courses for economics and finance. He graduated from the University of Bergamo, where he also took his PhD in Finance. His research interests are mainly focused on integrated risk management of energy producers, real options modelling, and trading optimization on mean reverting markets. He acts as a referee for several scientific journals. Professor Falbo is a scientific and strategic advisor for major energy, financial and manufacturing companies.

Alexander Eydeland
Dr Alexander Eydeland is Managing Director at Morgan Stanley in charge of global commodities analytic modelling. His papers on risk management, scientific computing, optimization and mathematical economics appeared in a number of major publications and he lectured extensively on these subjects throughout the United States, Europe, and Japan. Dr Eydeland is a co-author (with K. Wolyniec) of the book "Energy and Power Risk Management". He holds a PhD degree in mathematics from Courant Institute of Mathematical Sciences.

Daniele Felletti
Daniele Felletti is a researcher at the University of Milano Bicocca. He holds a degree in Physics from the University of Milano and a PhD in Mathematics for Finance from the University of Bergamo. He studies integrated corporate risk, data analysis and multidimensional linear stochastic processes mainly applied to commodities and energy.

Roza Galeeva
Roza Galeeva is a Vice President at Morgan Stanley, Finance Division. She is responsible for models review and model control process across different businesses in North America.

She has comprehensive experience in both the academic field and the financial industry, in modelling energy derivatives and risk management, research in dynamical systems and teaches a variety of courses in mathematics. She has written numerous papers on chaotical dynamical systems and applications published in major journals. Roza Galeeva holds a PhD in Mathematical Physics from Moscow State University.

Christopher Gilbert

Christopher Gilbert is Professor of Econometrics at the University of Trento, Italy where he is Academic Director of the Doctoral Program in Economics and Management and Director of the TGDR (the Trento Group for Development Research). He also holds a part-time Chair in Economics at Birkbeck, University of London, where he teaches financial econometrics. Prior to moving to Italy in 2003, Gilbert was Professor of Finance at the Free University, Amsterdam. His previous university positions were at Queen Mary, University of London, Oxford University (where he was a fellow of Wadham College) and Bristol University. Professor Gilbert has written extensively on commodity market issues and on commodity and financial futures markets in academic and policy journals. He has particular expertise in the cocoa, coffee and cotton industries and in non-ferrous metals. He consulted to the Commodity Risk Management Group (CRMG) of the World Bank from its inception in 1999 to 2007. He has worked on both metals and soft commodity markets with Euronext-LIFFE, CRU International, the International Coffee Organization, the World Bank, the InterAmerican Development Bank, the International Monetary Fund, the European Commission and the FAO. He has also published extensively on the history and methodology of econometrics and on the political economy of global economic institutions.

Jiri Hoogland

Dr Jiri Hoogland is Vice President at Morgan Stanley in the global commodities analytic modelling group. His papers on scientific computing, physics, and financial mathematics have appeared in a number of major publications. He holds a PhD degree in theoretical physics from the University of Amsterdam.

Manolis G. Kavussanos

Professor Kavussanos holds a BSc and MSc (Economics) from London University and PhD (Applied Economics) from City University Cass Business School, London. He has held various academic posts at Cass Business School, including Reader in Shipping Economics and Finance. There, he launched and Directed the MSc in Trade, Transport and Finance until he joined Athens University of Economics and Business, as Professor of Finance, where he is also the Director of the MSc and PhD programs in Accounting and Finance and of the Research Centre for Finance. He has been visiting professor at Erasmus University; Antwerp University; LUISS University; Cyprus International Institute of Management; University of Piraeus; and Hellenic Open University. He has developed the area of risk analysis and management in shipping and is the author of the book "Derivatives and Risk Management in Shipping".

Paul R. Kleindorfer

Paul R. Kleindorfer is the Anheuser Busch Professor of Management Science (Emeritus) at the Wharton School of the University of Pennsylvania and Distinguished Research Professor at INSEAD, Fontainebleau. Dr Kleindorfer graduated with distinction from the US Naval Academy in 1961. He studied on a Fulbright Fellowship in Mathematics at the University of Tübingen, Germany (1964/65), followed by doctoral studies in the Graduate School of Industrial Administration at Carnegie Mellon University (Phd, 1970). Dr Kleindorfer's research had been focussed on risk management and pricing in several industries, including electric power, chemicals, and logistics.

Elisa Luciano

Dr Elisa Luciano is Professor of Mathematical Finance at the University of Turin, School of Economics, Research Fellow of ICER (International Center for Economic Research), Turin, Fellow of Collegio Carlo Alberto, Moncalieri, and Associate Fellow of FERC (Financial Econometrics Research Center), Warwick University, UK. She coordinates the Master in Finance Program of the University of Turin and is a Member of the Scientific Committee of the Doctoral School in Economics. She has been in charge of the Financial Engineering course at the Master in Finance of Bocconi University, Milan, as well as of Risk Management at l'École Normale Supérieure de Cachan, Paris (Mastère Specialisé Management Globale des Risques), and at l'École Supérieure en Sciences Informatiques, Université de Nice-Sophia Antipolis, France (DESS). At present she is Faculty Member of the IEL PhD program (Cornell University, Gent University, École Polytechnique and Turin University). Her main research interest is Quantitative Finance, with special emphasis on risk measurement and dependence modelling. She has published extensively in academic journals, including the *Journal of Finance*. She has published also in *Risk* and the Risk book series. She has co-authored a book in the Wiley Finance series and edited one for E.Elgar. She sits on the Editorial board of the *Journal of Risk* and acts as a referee for many international journals.

George Martin

George A. Martin is Managing Director at Alternative Investment Analytics, LLC (AIA); President of Symplectic Partners, LLC; Associate Director for the Center for International Securities and Derivatives Markets (CISDM) at the University of Massachusetts; a member of the Advisory Board of the Chartered Alternative Investment Analyst Association (CAIA) and Chair of its Structured Products Curriculum Subcommittee; and a member of the Editorial Board of the Journal of Alternative Investments. He has been active in the area of alternative investments for more than 15 years, including hedge funds, commodities and "alternative alternative" investments. Previously, he was a Research Fellow at the Brookings Institution. He has a B.A. and M.A. from Johns Hopkins University.

Jens Müller-Merbach

Jens Müller-Merbach works as Senior Risk Controller with BHF-Bank AG, Frankfurt, where his focus is on market and credit risk from financial and commodity derivatives. BHF-Bank provides clearing services on most energy exchanges across Europe and is the leading clearing member on the EEX. After finishing his studies in Germany and Sweden, Jens Müller-Merbach worked as a research assistant at the Chair of Finance, University of Mannheim. His research interests include the pricing and the risk management of electricity derivatives. He started his professional career as a quantitative analyst with DB Energie GmbH, the energy supplier for Deutsche Bahn AG.

Steve Ohana

Dr Ohana is a researcher and consultant in commodity risk management. After graduating his PhD under the supervision of Professor H.Geman, he joined the Commodity Finance Centre at Birkbeck, University of London, where he teaches quantitative methods in commodity nance in a Master of Financial Engineering. He applied his expertise in commodity portfolio optimization, econometrics of commodity markets, and commodity risk measurement for several energy companies, including Gaz de France, POWEO, Constellation Energy, Masefield). His current research interests include the comparison of dynamic optimization strategies in physical commodity portfolio management, the modelling of dependency and regime-switching in commodity prices, the modelling and pricing of disruption risk in commodity portfolios and the analysis of hedge fund strategies in commodity futures markets.

Craig Pirrong

Dr Pirrong joined the Bauer College faculty after teaching at the Michigan Business School, the Graduate School of Business of the University of Chicago, the Olin School of Business at Washington University in St. Louis, and Oklahoma State University. He worked in private industry for Lexecon, Inc. and GNP Commodities, and has also done consulting for OM, Warenterminbörse, Deutsche Terminbörse, Eurex, the Winnipeg Commodity Exchange, the New York Mercantile Exchange, the Chicago Board of Trade, the Chicago Stock Exchange, several electric utilities, and the FHLBB. Dr Pirrong has also testified in a variety of high profile cases involving derivatives, market manipulation, bankruptcy, and intellectual property. His research focuses on commodity price dynamics, the organization of financial exchanges (including the integration of clearing and execution); the economics of derivatives markets and risk management; and market manipulation. He has developed an innovative model for pricing and calibrating electricity derivatives. Dr Pirrong has authored over 30 articles and three books on a variety of finance and economics topics. He has a PhD, an MBA, and a BA from the University of Chicago.

Silvana Stefani

Silvana Stefani is Professor of Mathematics Applied to Economics and Finance, University of Milano Bicocca, Faculty of Economics. She is a graduate in Mathematics of the University of Milano. Her research includes modelling optimal production and hedging strategies in commodity and (conventional and renewable) energy markets, and discrete mathematics applied to complex systems. She has published numerous papers in international journals and has been scientific consultant for financial and energy institutions.

Richard Spurgin

Richard Spurgin is an Associate Professor of Finance at Clark University. He holds a Bachelors degree in Mathematics from Dartmouth College and a PhD in Finance from the University of Massachusetts. He has published over 30 articles in journals such as the *Journal of Derivatives* and the *Journal of Alternative Investments* and has assisted in the design of a number of alternative investment benchmark products including the Dow Jones Hedge Fund indices and the Bache Commodity Index. He currently serves on the editorial board of the *Journal of Alternative Investments* and the curriculum committee for the Chartered Alternative Investment Analysts Association. Professor Spurgin is also a founding principal of the consulting firm Alternative Investment Analytics LLC, and a founding principal of the investment management firm White Bear Partners LLC.

Hilary Till

Hilary Till is a co-founder of Chicago-based Premia Capital Management, LLC. She is also the co-editor of "Intelligent Commodity Investing", Risk Books (2007); and serves on the North American Advisory Board of the London School of Economics. Ms Till is also a

Research Associate at the EDHEC Risk and Asset Management Research Centre (France). Her research work on behalf of EDHEC-Risk has been cited in the Journal of Finance and as well as by the Bank of Japan, the European Central Bank, the Bank for International Settlements, the International Monetary Fund, and by the US Senate's Permanent Subcommittee on Investigations.

Richard S. J. Tol

Dr Richard S.J. Tol is a Research Professor at the Economic and Social Research Institute (Dublin) and the Professor of the Economics of Climate Change at the Vrije Universiteit Amsterdam. An economist and statistician, his work focusses on impacts of climate change, international climate policy, tourism, and land and water use. He is ranked among the 500 best economists in the world. He is an editor of *Energy Economics*. He has played an active role in international bodies such as the Stanford Energy Modeling Forum, the Intergovernmental Panel on Climate Change, the Global Trade Analysis Project, and the European Forum on Integrated Environmental Assessment.

Ilias Visvikis

Dr Ilias Visvikis holds a PhD in Finance from City University Cass Business School, London. He is elected as an Assistant Professor of Finance and is the Academic Director of the MBA is Shipping Program at ALBA Graduate Business School, Greece. He has lectured in several academic institutions and his research work, in the areas of finance and shipping, has been published in top international refereed journals and presented extensively in international conferences. Dr Visvikis held posts in the Central Securities Depository of Greece, in the derivatives market of the Athens Exchange, and in shipping companies in various departments. At the same time, he has provided consultancy services to private companies in the areas of finance and risk management.

Gary W. Yohe

Dr Yohe is the Woodhouse/Sysco Professor of Economics at Wesleyan University. His work has made him a leader in calling for a risk management approach to climate policy– an approach that was adopted last fall in the Synthesis Report of the Fourth Assessment Report of the Intergovernmental Panel on Climate Change (IPCC). Dr Yohe is a senior member of the IPCC which was awarded a share of the 2007 Nobel Peace Prize. Involved with the Panel since the mid-1990s, he served as Lead Author for four different chapters in the Third Assessment Report published in 2001. He also served as Convening Lead Author for the last chapter of the contribution of Working Group II to the Fourth Assessment Report and worked with the Core Writing Team to prepare the overall Synthesis Report for the entire assessment. He has also served as one of five editors of Avoiding Dangerous Climate Change.

1
Structural Models of Commodity Prices

Craig Pirrong

1.1 INTRODUCTION

The transparency of fundamentals in commodity markets (in contrast to equity or currency markets, for instance) holds out the promise of devising structural models of commodity price behavior that can illuminate the underlying factors that drive these prices, and which perhaps can be used to value contingent claims on commodities. There has been much progress on these models in recent years, but the empirical data show that real-world commodity price behavior is far richer than that predicted by the current generation of models, and that except for non-storable commodities, structural models currently cannot be used to price derivatives. The models and empirical evidence do, however, point out the deficiencies in reduced form commodity derivative pricing models, and suggest how reduced form models must be modified to represent commodity price dynamics more realistically. They also suggest additional factors that may be added to the models (at substantial computational cost) to improve their realism.

This chapter sketches out the current state of fundamental models of commodity markets. It starts with a taxonomy of commodities, and then proceeds to discuss models for storable and non-storable commodities, and structural models for each.

1.2 A COMMODITY TAXONOMY

Although the catchall term "commodity" is widely applied to anything that is not a true asset, it conceals tremendous diversity, diversity that has material impacts on price behavior and modeling.

The most basic divide among commodities is between those that are storable, and those that are not. The most important non-storable commodity is electricity (although hydro generation does add an element of storability in some electricity markets). Weather is obviously not storable – and it is increasingly becoming an important underlying in commodity derivatives trading.

Most other commodities are storable (at some cost), but there is considerable heterogeneity among goods in this category. Some are continuously produced and consumed, and are not subject to significant seasonality in demand; industrial metals such as copper or aluminum fall into this category. Some are continuously produced and consumed, but exhibit substantial

Craig Pirrong, University of Houston, Houston, TX 77204. Tel: 713-743-4466. Email: cpirrong@uh.edu

Risk Management in Commodity Markets: From Shipping to Agriculturals and Energy   Edited by Hélyette Geman

seasonality in demand. Heating oil, natural gas, and gasoline are prime examples of this type of commodity. Other commodities are produced seasonally, but there is also variation within the category of seasonally produced commodities. Grains and oilseeds are produced seasonally, but their production is relatively flexible because a major input – land – is quite flexible; there is a possibility of growing corn on a piece of land one year and soybeans the next, and an adverse natural event (such as a freeze) may damage one crop, but does not impair the future productivity of land. In contrast, tree crops such as cocoa or coffee or oranges are seasonally produced, but utilize specialized, durable, and inflexible inputs (the trees) and damage to these inputs can have consequences for productivity that last beyond a single crop year.

Fundamentals-based models must take these variations across commodities into account. Moreover, this cross sectional variation has empirical implications that can be exploited to test fundamental-based structural models.

1.3   FUNDAMENTAL MODELS FOR STORABLE COMMODITIES

In a nutshell, a fundamental model derives commodity prices as the equilibrium result of basic supply and demand factors. In contrast, a reduced form model merely specifies the dynamics of a commodity price (or a forward curve of commodity prices), usually in the form of a stochastic differential equation.

The Theory of Storage is the canonical fundamental commodity price model. Early versions of the theory of storage (due to Kaldor (1939) and Working (1949)) posit that commodity inventories generate a stream of benefits – a convenience yield – and that marginal convenience yield varies inversely with the level of inventories. This theory was devised to explain the fact that the forward prices of storable commodities are routinely below the spot price plus the costs of holding inventory until contract expiration. However, it is *ad hoc* and does not provide an equilibrium model of the determinants of the marginal benefit of inventory holding.

A more solidly grounded Theory of Storage is embodied in the rational expectations model of Scheinkman and Schectman (1983). In this model, a random amount of a commodity is produced every period, and competitive agents allocate production between current consumption and storage. The stored commodity can be consumed in the future. In a competitive market, the equilibrium storage decision maximizes the discounted expected utility of the representative agent. This decision depends on two state variables: current output and current inventories. In brief, agents add to inventories when production is higher than average (especially when current stocks are low) and consume inventory when production is lower than average (especially when stocks are high).

The constraint that storage cannot be negative has important pricing implications. When demand is low (and/or stocks are high) it is optimal for agents to hold inventory. In a competitive market, forward prices must cover the costs of storage in order to induce the optimal decision in these conditions, and the forward price will equal the spot price plus the cost of holding inventory to the next production date. When demand is very high and stocks are low, however, it is optimal to consume all inventories. Since storage links spot and futures prices, such a "stockout" disconnects these prices. Moreover, when it is not efficient to store, forward prices should punish storage by failing to cover by the costs of holding inventory. Indeed, if demand is sufficiently high, the equilibrium forward price during a tockout is less than the spot price. This is sometimes referred to as a "backwardation" r an inversion. Thus, in contrast to the *ad hoc* convenience yield theory, this version f the theory of storage provides a fundamentals-based, structural model of forward price tructures.

As is common with rational expectations models, Scheinkman-Schectman requires a umerical solution of a dynamic programming problem. That is, it cannot be solved in closed orm. However, since the problem is typically a contraction mapping, it is readily amenable) solution using standard recursive techniques. In the original Scheinkman-Schectman 1odel, the commodity is produced every period, and the production shocks are IID. Solu- ions to the dynamic program are computationally cheap when there is a single independent nd identically distributed (IID) demand shock. See Williams and Wright (1991) for detailed escriptions of the relevant numerical techniques.

Such a model is appropriate for a continuously produced commodity with IID demand hocks. The model implies that prices should be autocorrelated even when demand shocks re IID because storage links prices over time. When demand is low today, for instance, nore of the commodity is stored, increasing future supply and thereby depressing prices in ne future.

Deaton and Laroque (1992) perform empirical tests on the storage model with IID emand shocks using annual data on a variety of commodities encompassing all types f storables, including tree crops, grains, and continuously produced goods such as copper.)eaton-Laroque find that real-world commodity prices exhibit far more persistence than ne storage model can generate. Storage in the presence of IID demand shocks can pro- uce autocorrelations on the order of 20%, far below the 90% that Deaton-Laroque find. 1 later emprical work, these authors (Deaton-Laroque, 1996) attribute virtually all of the ersistence in commodity prices to autocorrelation in demand shocks.

The use of annual data and the homogeneous treatment of these commodities are prob- ematic given that the frequency of the storage decision is less than a year, and varies across nese disparate commodity types. Moreover, this approach disregards an important source f valuable price information: daily data on futures prices for various maturities that are vailable for a wide variety of commodities.

Exploitation of high frequency futures price data, and of the cross-sectional variation in ommodity characteristics, requires use of more sophisticated models. Pirrong (2006, 2007) xtends the basic Scheinkman-Schectman framework to include multiple, autocorrelated emand shocks for a commodity in which the frequency of the storage decision is the same s the frequency of production.[1] This is appropriate for continuously produced commodities uch as copper. Solution of such a model is substantially more computationally demanding lue to the curse of dimensionality common to dynamic programming models), but provides 1ore realistic characterizations of storage economics, and its implications for the behavior f commodity price structures. Moreover, given the solution of the storage problem, it is ossible to solve partial differential equations to determine the price of any forward contract /ith a maturity greater than the frequency of production.

This more complicated model can generate price behavior that mimics some of the features ocumented for industrial metals by Ng-Pirrong (1994). Specifically, in this model, spot rices are more volatile when the market is in backwardation (a signal of tight supply and

---

Routledge, Seppi, and Spatt (2000) and Deaton-Laroque (1996) also model commodity prices when demand is utocorrelated. Pirrong permits multiple demand shocks with differing persistence.

demand conditions), and the correlation between spot prices and forward prices (e.g., a three-month forward price) is near 1 when stocks are high and the market is at full carry, and is below 1 and decreasing in the amount of backwardation (and in inventories) when the market is in backwardation. These basic behaviors are documented in Ng-Pirrong, but the more complex model calibrated to match the behavior of prices in the copper market cannot duplicate other aspects of the Ng-Pirrong empirical dynamics. For instance, in Ng-Pirrong three-month forward prices are substantially more volatile (though less volatile than spot prices) when the market is in backwardation than when it is not; in the augmented storage model, in contrast, three-month forward price volatilities vary much more weakly with backwardation (and stocks). Moreover, the augmented storage model does a poor job at explaining the dynamics of more distant forward prices, such as 15 or 27-month copper prices. Even if one of the demand shocks is highly persistent (and nearly integrated), in the storage model the long maturity forward prices exhibit virtually no variability when the market is in backwardation, whereas real-world 15 and 27-month copper prices exhibit substantial volatility. Over such a long period, a current demand shock (even if highly persistent) has little power to forecast demand in the distant future, so in the model distant forward prices do not vary in response to demand shocks.

Other extensions of the model can capture market price behaviors that are otherwise puzzling. For instance, in 2005–2006 many market commentators, and even a committee report of the United States Senate, declared that the simultaneous increase in energy prices and inventories observed during that period was symptomatic of a disconnection between market fundamentals and prices, driven by speculative excess. Pirrong (2008) modifies the basic storage model to include stochastic volatility in the net demand shock to explain this seemingly anomalous behavior.

The intuition is quite straightforward. Inventory is largely held to smooth the impact of fundamental shocks. If these shocks become more volatile, it is optimal to hold larger inventories. When market participants perceive that fundamental volatility has increased, they rationally increase inventories. This requires a reduction in consumption and, con-comitantly, an increase in prices. Hence, the model predicts simultaneous increases in inventories and prices during periods of heightened risks; since the risks of hurricanes and geopolitically driven disruptions in energy production quite plausibly increased beginning in late-2005 (think Hurricanes Rita and Katrina; the Lebanon War; Iraq; turmoil in Nigeria, Venezuela, and other energy-producing regions), the model can explain the inventory and price movements that baffled so many market analysts.

Despite the modest empirical successes of the augmented storage model, empirical work that exploits the diversity of commodities points out difficulties with the received rational expectations version of the theory of storage. Specifically, Pirrong (1999), Osborne (2004), and Chambers and Bailey (1996) model seasonal commodities. In these models, storage decisions occur more frequently than production (as is realistic). Moreover (again realisti-cally), agents receive information about the size of the future crop prior to harvest. In this model, the state variables are the current demand shock, current inventories, and information about the size of the next harvest.

This model predicts that (a) well prior to the harvest, spot prices ("old crop" prices) should exhibit little correlation with "new crop" futures prices (i.e., futures with delivery dates immediately following the harvest), and (b) information about the size of the harvest should have little impact on spot prices but a big impact on new crop prices. These predictions obtain regardless of whether demand shocks are highly persistent. The intuition behind these esults is straightforward. Except under highly unusual circumstances (e.g., a large crop at he previous harvest and low demand, leading to high current inventories, combined with forecast of an extremely short upcoming crop), agents seldom find it efficient to carry positive inventory into the new harvest: why carry supplies from when they are relatively carce (right before the harvest), to when they are relatively abundant (immediately following he harvest)? Thus, storage cannot link "old crop" spot prices and new crop futures prices, nd information that relates to the size of the new crop is largely immaterial to the price of he old crop, as it affects neither the demand for the old crop (which is driven by demand p to the time of the harvest) nor its supply (which was established at the last harvest and subsequent storage decisions).

This model predicts the differential behavior of new crop and old crop prices even if, as Deaton-Laroque posit, demand is highly autocorrelated. Thus, examining seasonals prices t weekly (rather than annual) frequency can help determine whether high demand autocorelation is indeed the key factor in explaining the persistence of commodity price shocks.

In reality, however, there is a high correlation (typically between 90 % or higher) between old crop and new crop corn, wheat, cotton, and soybean futures prices, and both old crop nd new crop prices respond by about the same amount in the same direction to official orecasts of crop size. Thus, neither storage nor high demand autocorrelation can explain the behavior of seasonal commodity futures prices. This raises doubts about the reliability of the torage model. Pirrong (1999) discusses some possible factors that can explain the evident ntertemporal connections between old crop and new crop prices, including intertemporal ubstitution (ruled out in the basic storage model) and final goods production (e.g., soybeans are used to produce oil and meal, rather than consumed directly as the basic storage model ssumes). The former explanation is somewhat *ad hoc* and difficult to test. The latter is con-eptually rigorous, but increases the dimensionality of the dynamic programming problem, because it is necessary to add a state variable (final goods inventory) and solve additional quilibrium conditions (one each for the raw and final good markets). At present, the curse f dimensionality precludes sufficiently timely solution of the problem to permit rigorous mpirical testing.

In sum, fundamentals-based structural rational expectations models of storable commodi-ies shed some light on the behavior of commodity prices, commodity price forward curves, nd commodity price dynamics, but it is clear that these models are missing important fea-ures. The non-negativity constraint on storage that plays a central role in this type of model an shed light in a rigorous, equilibrium-based way on the reasons that (a) futures curves ometimes are in backwardation, (b) commodity price volatilities and correlations are time arying, and (c) volatilities and correlations covary with inventories and the slope of the orward curve. However, this type of model fails miserably in explaining why old crop and ew crop futures prices behave so similarly. Moreover, although it can closely mimic the behavior of spot prices (namely the evolution of spot price volatility over time), its ability o capture the dynamics of forward prices degrades rapidly with time to maturity. This last eature may reflect the fact that the model takes certain factors (namely productive capacity) s fixed, whereas in reality agents can invest in new capacity. The curse of dimensionality gain sharply constrains our current ability to investigate this possibility.

The basic storage model is clearly not ready for derivatives pricing prime time, due both o its empirical deficiencies, and the curse of dimensionality. However, it does shed serious oubts on the reasonableness of received reduced form models used to price commodity erivatives. These models typically assume constant volatilities, and for curve sensitive products (such as spread options or swaptions), constant correlations. The storage model, which at least captures some important aspects of commodity price determination, shows clearly that these assumptions are dubious (as does much empirical evidence).

1.4   NON-STORABLE COMMODITIES

Life is far easier when studying non-storable commodities, such as electricity, because the lack of storability makes it unnecessary to solve recursively a dynamic programming problem to determine the efficient (and competitive equilibrium) allocation of resources, and hence to determine the equilibrium evolution of prices. For a true non-storable, every instant of time is distinct from every other instant, and intertemporal connections only arise due to persistence in demand or supply shocks. If these shocks are Markovian, an assumption that does not do too much violence to reality, it is a straightforward exercise to determine the non-storables' spot price as a function of current supply and demand fundamentals, and given specification of the dynamics of these fundamentals, to characterize the dynamics of the spot price.

   This approach has been applied most frequently and successfully to the study of electricity markets by Eydeland and Geman (1998), Pirrong and Jermakyan (1999, 2008), and Eydeland and Wolyniec (2002). The basic approach in this research is to posit that the spot price of electricity depends on a small number of drivers, notably load (the demand for electricity), available capacity, and a fuel price (or a set of fuel prices). Each of these drivers evolves in a Markovian way. Moreover, especially when one considers load, an abundance of data makes it straightforward to determine empirically these dynamics. More specifically, the relevant supply curve of electricity (the relation between the spot price and load, conditional on the fuel price) is flat for low levels of load, but increases steeply as load nears available capacity. This supply curve implies that the dynamics of prices are time varying. When load is low, prices are low and exhibit relatively little variability, but when load is near capacity, prices can "spike" and exhibit extreme variability.

   Since (a) a relatively small set of well-behaved, observable factors explains a substantial fraction of the variability in power prices, and (b) no solution of a dynamic programming problem is necessary to determine the relations between the fundamental state variables and spot prices, for non-storables it is possible to use a fundamentals-based model to price deriva-tives. Both Eydeland-Wolyniec and Pirrong-Jermakyan do just that, although in slightly different ways. The key nettle that must be grasped in doing so is that the underlying state variables are not traded assets, and hence the market is incomplete.[2] Thus, any derivatives price depends on a market price of risk function that must be inferred from the prices of traded claims. This fact is emphasized explicitly in Pirrong-Jermakyan, who use inverse techniques to estimate the market price of risk, but it is implicit in the Eydeland-Wolyniec approach as well, and as a result their calibration techniques effectively determine model parameters in the equivalent pricing measure.

   The assumption of non-storability for electricity is quite apt for some markets, such as Texas, that are almost strictly fossil-fueled. The assumption is less realistic for other markets, such as Scandinavia, where hydro power is central; although electricity cannot be stored, water can be, and hence optimization in a hydro market requires solution of a dynamic

---

[2] Since electricity is not storable, and hence cannot be a proper asset, this problem cannot be avoided by going to a reduced form model that specifies the dynamics of the spot price.

rogramming problem. Non-storability is clearly apposite for other "commodities", most otably weather, that are definitely not storable.

The fundamentals-based models of non-storable prices are far preferable to reduced form nodels, particularly when pricing derivatives. Non-storables markets are inherently incomplete, so both structural and reduced form models must confront the problem of determining market price of risk. Moreover, non-storability results in extreme non-linearities – such s large spikes in power prices – that are very difficult to capture in reduced form models, but which are a natural feature of well-specified fundamental models because these on-linearities are a direct consequence of fundamental supply and demand factors. Reduced orm models also face difficulties in addressing the seasonality in many non-storables, vhereas this is not a problem for the structural models. Finally, fundamental models can nore readily handle the pricing of contingent claims with payoffs that depend on multiple actors (e.g., spark spread options, whose payoffs depend on load and fuel prices) because hese factors are built into the pricing model, whereas multiple reduced form models must e bolted together to price these claims.

1.5 SUMMARY

tructural models of commodity price behavior have improved our understanding of commodity price dynamics, but for storable commodities there is still a yawning gap between heory and evidence. The modern Theory of Storage has shown how inventory decisions n competitive markets subject to random demand shocks can influence the shape of commodity forward curves. However, this theory cannot mimic the richness of commodity price ehavior, especially for seasonal commodities and for long-dated forward contracts. These mpirical deficiencies and the curse of dimensionality hamper the utility of these models as erivative pricing tools. In contrast, structural models of non-storables' prices can capture alient features of non-storables' prices, and with sufficiently sophisticated techniques for xtracting information about market risk prices from the prices of traded claims, can be sed to price and hedge non-storable commodity contingent claims.

1.6 REFERENCES

hambers, M. and R. Bailey. (1996). A Theory of Commodity Price Fluctuations. *Journal of Political Economy* **104**, 924–957.
eaton, A. and G. Laroque. (1992). On the Behavior of Commodity Prices. *Review of Economic Studies* **59**, 1–23.
eaton, A. and G. Laroque. (1996). Competitive Storage and Commodity Price Dynamics. *Journal of Political Economy* **104**, 896–923.
ydeland, A. and H. Geman. (1998). Fundamentals of Electricity Derivatives, in R. Jameson, ed., *Energy Modelling and the Management of Uncertainty*. London: Risk Publication.
ydeland, A. and K. Wolyniec. (2002). *Energy and Power Risk Management: New Developments in Modeling, Pricing, and Hedging*. New York: John Wiley & Sons Inc.
aldor, N. (1939). Speculation and Economic Stability. *Review of Economic Studies* **7**, 1–27.
g, V. and C. Pirrong. (1994). Fundamentals and Volatility: Storage, Spreads, and the Dynamics of Metals Prices. *Journal of Business* **67**, 203–230.
sborne, T. (2004). Market News in Commodity Price Theory. *Review of Economic Studies* **7**, 133–164.

Pirrong, C. (1999). Searching for the Missing Link. Working paper, Washington University.

Pirrong, C. (2006). Price Dynamics and Derivatives Prices for Continuously Produced, Storable Commodities. Working paper, University of Houston.

Pirrong, C. (2007). Testing the Theory of Storage. Working paper, University of Houston.

Pirrong, C. (2008). Stochastic Volatility of Fundamentals, Commodity Prices, and Inventories. Working paper, University of Houston.

Pirrong, C., and M. Jermakyan. (2008). The Price of Power. Forthcoming, *Journal of Banking and Finance*.

Pirrong, C., and M. Jermakyan. (1999). Pricing Forwards and Options Using the Mesh-Based Partial Differential Equation Approach, in R. Jameson, ed., *Energy Modelling and the Management of Uncertainty*. London: Risk Publications.

Routledge, B., D. Seppi, and C. Spatt. (2000). Equilibrium Forward Curves for Commodities. *Journal of Finance* **55**, 1297–1338.

Scheinkman, J., and J. Schectman. (1983). A Simple Competitive Model of Production with Storage. *Review of Economic Studies* **50**, 427–441.

Williams, J., and B. Wright. (1991). *Storage and Commodity Markets*. Cambridge: Cambridge University Press.

Working, H. (1949). The Theory of the Price of Storage. *American Economic Review* **39**, 1254–1262.

2
Forward Curve Modelling
in Commodity Markets

Svetlana Borovkova and Hélyette Geman

2.1 INTRODUCTION

Commodity markets have been buoyant for the last few years and commodity spot prices continue (at the time of writing) to reach new record highs, driven by a strong world demand and a tight supply, very sensitive to political or weather events. Moreover, for more than a century, forward markets have been the main place of commodity trading as they allow investors to avoid the hurdles of physical delivery while getting the desired exposure to changes in commodity prices. Most examples in this chapter dedicated to the fundamental problem of forward curve modelling will be investigated in the setting of strategic energy commodities such as crude oil or natural gas. But the methodology identically applies to other commodity classes, either seasonal such as agriculturals or non-seasonal such as metals.

First we recall some elementary definitions around forward and futures contracts. *Forward contracts* are traded over-the-counter between two parties and the grade of oil, delivery point, exact amount and exact delivery date are specified at the time of writing the contract. In this respect they are different from *futures contracts*, which are standardized in terms of the grade, amount, delivery date and location. Energy futures are traded on exchanges such as the InterContinental Exchange (ICE) and New York Mercantile Exchange (NYMEX). For instance, most of the trading activity in oil markets takes place in futures and forward contracts, where the volume of trades is almost ten times higher than in the spot market.

Throughout the chapter, we will denote the futures or forward price on day t for maturity date T by $F(t, T)$ and the spot price on day t by $S(t)$. The forward curve prevailing on day t is the collection of futures prices $\{F(t, T)\}_T$ for all traded maturities $T = 1, 2, \ldots, N$.

In what follows, we will use indifferently the terminology futures or forwards. It has been known for some time (see Cox *et al.* (1985)) that, in the absence of credit risk, forward and futures prices are equal under non-stochastic interest rates. In commodity markets, interest rate risk plays a secondary role compared to the commodity spot price risk and will not be our first concern in this chapter (see Geman and Vasicek (2001) for the introduction of

Svetlana Borovkova: Vrije Universiteit Amsterdam.
Hélyette Geman: Birkbeck, University of London, and ESSEC
Svetlana Borovkova, corresponding author, Department of Finance, Faculty of Economics and Business Adminis-tration, Vrije Universiteit Amsterdam, The Netherlands. Email: sborovkova@feweb.vu.nl

Risk Management in Commodity Markets: From Shipping to Agriculturals and Energy   Edited by Hélyette Geman

stochastic interest rates in energy forward and futures contracts). From now on we will use terms "futures price" and "forward price" interchangeably.

For crude oil, futures for up to 84 months are traded on both the ICE and NYMEX, for oil products such as heating oil and gasoline up to 18 and 36 months respectively. The NYMEX recently started trading long-dated natural gas futures contracts, going up to 72 months ahead. More and more long-dated energy futures contracts are being traded today, resulting in the availability of longer forward curves.

The first-to-expire futures contract is usually referred to as the *front-month*, or *nearby* contract, and denoted by the letter M after the contract's name. The second nearby contract (next-to-front) is denoted by M+1, the next one M+2 and so on. On the first maturity date, the front-month contract expires and the next-to-front becomes the front-month contract. All other futures contracts shift by one position (M+2 becomes M+1 and so on) and a new contract is added. This shift is called the *rollover*. It plays a key role in the management of commodity indices as the roll yield may be a positive or negative component in the total return, depending on the shape of the forward curve. Given the billions of dollars that have been recently poured into commodity markets, the rolling activity has itself an impact on the volatility of the nearby futures. This in turn may induce a portfolio manager to invest the share of the index dedicated to a given commodity (e.g. crude oil) into more distant maturity forward contracts.

Futures markets such as the ICE and NYMEX provide the most reliable and liquid forward curves. However, sometimes it can be beneficial to use OTC forward prices for the construction of the forward curve. For example, in electricity markets this can be a better alternative, as futures contracts are either not traded on exchanges or are rather illiquid. Then it can be a complicated task to construct a smooth forward curve, indexed by regular maturities, from prices of irregularly spaced and complex forward contracts (which may be based for instance on average prices over a specified period). The example of such a forward curve construction is given in Benth *et al.* (2007).

Forward curves are of paramount importance in commodity markets, for several reasons. They provide information about the views of market participants, anticipated price trends and expectations about future supply and demand. Futures prices observed in liquid futures markets provide price discovery and are essential for daily marking to market existing portfolio positions as well as for risk management activities such as VaR calculations. Forward commodity prices influence storage, production and other strategic decisions in related industries such as oil refining or soybean processing. Finally, futures contracts provide the right way of calibrating derivatives pricing models under the risk-neutral probability measure, as they present a great liquidity, hence the market "view" one needs to capture.

The "Rational Expectation Hypothesis", discussed for a long time by famous economists (such as Keynes and Lucas), examines whether forward prices provide valid forecasts for spot prices in the future. However, the actual forecasting ability of futures prices in commodity and, in particular, in oil markets is rather poor. For example, if futures prices were right in predicting the spot price of oil then, according to the forward curves observed one and two years ago (February 2006 and 2007), the oil price in February 2008 should have been 67 $/bbl (while in fact, on 19 February 2008, it was over 100 $/bbl).

The spot price of a commodity is often considered as the most important factor driving the whole forward curve (see Gibson and Schwartz (1990), Schwartz (1997)). The influence of the spot price becomes greater as the futures contract approaches maturity, culminating in the following convergence property: on maturity date, the futures price must coincide with the spot price

$$F(T, T) = S(T). \tag{2.1}$$

This property follows from the absence of arbitrage and the possible occurrence of physical delivery of a commodity at the futures contract's maturity. However, there are markets where the spot price is rather opaque or unreliable (or completely non-existent, as is the case, for instance, in electricity markets). In such cases, the convergence property does not necessarily hold. It is also possible that the convergence does not take place smoothly as the maturity approaches (which is the case in, for instance, crude oil markets), but only on maturity date, when the futures price makes a sudden move to coincide with the spot price. These considerations, among others, may question the suitability of the spot price as the main driving factor of the forward curve. We shall return to this issue in Section 2.3.

Crude oil forward curves have traditionally been in one of these two shapes: backwardation, when the futures prices for short maturities are more expensive than those maturing later, or contango, which is the opposite situation. Figure 2.1 shows the NYMEX crude oil forward curve on 21 February 2008, when the market was in backwardation, and Figure 2.2 shows a contango forward curve observed on 28 February 2007.

Whether the market is in backwardation or in contango depends on the current price as well as inventory levels, transportation and storage costs, supply and demand equilibria, strategic and political issues and many other factors. A particular shape of the oil forward curve (backwardation or contango) is closely related to the notion of the so-called *convenience yield*, i.e. the benefit of holding a physical commodity over a futures contract (in the

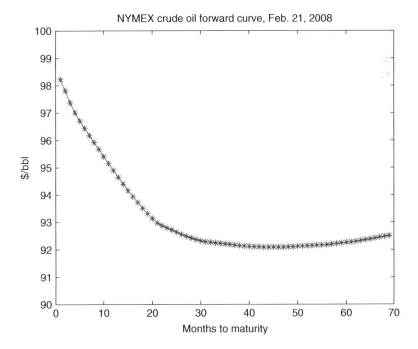

Figure 2.1   NYMEX crude oil forward curve, 21 February 2008

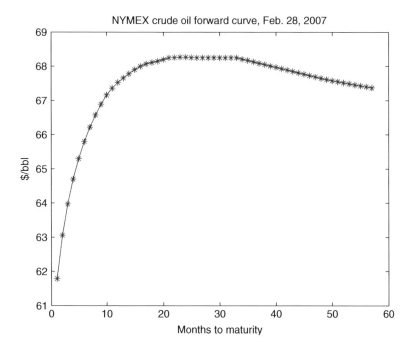

Figure 2.2 NYMEX crude oil forward curve, 28 February 2007

next section we will discuss the convenience yield in more detail). Backwardated forward curves arise when the benefit of holding a physical commodity (i.e. the convenience yield) is high and the interest rates and storage costs (representing together the "cost of carry") are relatively low. This happens, for instance, when there is a general perception of low availability of oil and instability of its supply. More generally, the shape of the forward curve summarizes perceptions of oil market participants about the current state and future developments of the global oil market, such as new fields discovery or new deep sea oil rig equipment.

As said before, oil forward curves have until recently always been in either backwardation or contango state, with a much more frequent situation of backwardation (see Gabillon (1995)), in agreement with the terminology "normal backwardation", introduced in the economic literature by Keynes. However, in 2005–2006 a hump-shaped forward curve was observed briefly (see Figure 2.3), which was probably caused by a massive arrival of hedge funds and other new investors into oil futures markets and the short-dated futures rollover strategies they employed.

Lastly, for seasonal commodities such as natural gas, electricity, or agricultural commodities, futures prices are largely governed by seasonal demand (as is the case for energy) or supply (for agricultural commodities). For those commodities, transportation or storage capabilities are limited, so the excess demand or supply shortage cannot be absorbed by transporting a commodity from a different part of the world with excess supply, or storing at times of plentiful supply and using it whenever necessary. This results in a high seasonal premium on futures contracts maturing during periods of high demand (such as winter, in

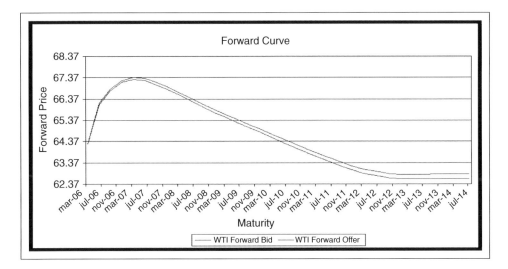

Figure 2.3   NYMEX crude oil forward curve, 7 March 2007

the case of natural gas) or low supply (such as before harvest, for agricultural commodities). This is illustrated in Figure 2.4, where a forward curve for natural gas in the UK is shown. Futures maturing in the winter (the time of high demand for gas in the UK) are clearly at a premium compared to those maturing in summer.

Most traditional methods of forward curve modelling, which we will review in Section 2.2, are unable to deal with this prominent seasonal feature observed in many futures markets. In Section 2.3 we describe the seasonal forward curve model which introduces the seasonal premium into futures prices and hence is able to capture seasonalities present in forward curves such as those shown in Figure 2.4.

The dynamic modelling of the forward curve (i.e. the description of its random movements over time) and the understanding of the main fundamental factors behind its evolution have been the subject of extensive research, both by practitioners and academics. A proper model of the dynamics of the forward curve is an essential input in most derivative pricing models, scenario simulation and risk management applications. A successful forward curve model should be able to match current observed forward curves, generate realistic forward curves containing empirically observed features and ideally should be able to extrapolate the forward curve beyond the longest observed maturity. Moreover, it should be easily and quickly calibrated to the market data. However, just as in case of the Treasuries yield curves, commodity forward curve modelling is a challenging task, due to the inherent multidimensionality of the problem and a non-trivial dependence structure across maturities. In contrast to interest rates, features such as seasonality may further complicate the modelling process.

In the next section we review several forward curve modelling approaches, before proceeding in Section 2.3 to the case of seasonal forward curves. Section 2.4 describes the application of the Principal Component Analysis to commodity forward curves. Section 2.5 introduces several forward curve indicators and Section 2.6 concludes.

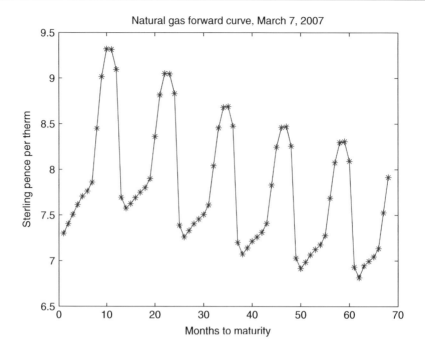

Figure 2.4   UK Natural gas forward curve, 7 March 2007

2.2   FORWARD CURVE MODELS FOR NON-SEASONAL COMMODITIES

Forward curve modelling approaches for commodities can be loosely classified into three main categories. The first one is a martingale-based approach, which models the dynamics of futures prices directly under the risk-adjusted probability measure, making use of the fact that futures prices are martingales under such a measure. One or possibly several risk factors driving the risk-neutral dynamics of the entire forward curve are usually assumed (resulting into so-called one-factor or multifactor models).

Another approach is a static arbitrage-based one, making use of the cash-and-carry arguments and describing the no-arbitrage relationship between the spot and futures prices. In the remainder of this section we shall review these modelling approaches in more detail.

Multifactor models such as described in Clewlow and Strickland (2000) are similar to the celebrated HJM approach for modelling the yield curve (Heath *et al.* (1992)), in that they directly model futures prices under the risk-neutral probability measure.[1] So the following representation is often considered:

$$\frac{dF(t, T)}{F(t, T)} = \sum_{i=1}^{n} \sigma_i(t, T) dW_i(t), \tag{2.2}$$

---

[1] As a futures contract does not require an initial investment, under Q its price remains constant on average and there is no drift term representing the average growth on the investment.

where n is the number of risk factors, $W_i(t)$, $i = 1, \ldots , n$ are Brownian motions representing sources of uncertainty and $\sigma_i(t, T)$ are volatilities associated with the risk factors
(possibly varying deterministically in time and maturity). The Brownian motions can be
correlated, but if the risk factors are derived using the Principal Component Analysis
(described in Section 2.4), then they are assumed uncorrelated. This approach focusses
on the martingale property of $(F(t, T))_{t\leqslant T}$ under Q, which is useful for derivatives pricing but not for trading strategies involving spot and forward positions, the most common
ones in a trading environment, as it says nothing about the actual evolution of the forward curves and hence cannot be calibrated to historical futures market data. We will
mainly concentrate in this chapter on the evolution of a forward curve under the statistical probability measure, as we are mainly interested in trading strategies in forward
contracts.

In the first approach, the main fundamental factors (sources of uncertainty) are rather
arbitrary (e.g., derived by the PCA) and do not always have a clear meaning. Alternatively,
more interpretable fundamental stochastic factors can be taken. For example, a popular
choice is to take the short-term and long-term price components (e.g. Lucia and Schwartz
(2002), Sorensen (2002)), which together determine the commodity's spot price:

$$S(t) = s(t) + X(t) + L(t), \tag{2.3}$$

where $X(t)$ and $L(t)$ are respectively the short- and long-term price components and $s(t)$ is
a possible (deterministic) seasonal component of the spot price. Then the futures prices are
obtained using the relationship

$$F(t, T) = E_Q(S(T) \mid \mathcal{F}_t), \tag{2.4}$$

where Q is the risk-adjusted probability measure and $\mathcal{F}_t$ is the information available up to
date t. To evaluate the expression (2.4), the dynamics of the fundamental factors under the
risk-adjusted probability measure Q should be specified. Usually such dynamics include the
market prices of risk (the spot price risk and convenience yield risk), which make these
models rather hard to calibrate, as market prices of risk are not observable. Moreover,
the forward curves derived from (2.4) using this approach usually do not match observed
forward curves, which is obviously a problem.

The static arbitrage approach is based on the no-arbitrage assumption and implies that
the futures price of a commodity (or any other asset) must be equal to the cost of acquiring
the physical commodity and carrying it until the future's maturity. For financial assets,
this means that the futures price must exceed the spot price by the interest accumulated
on the investment until the maturity date (minus eventual dividends, in case of stocks).
Physical commodities, unlike financial assets, cannot be stored without cost; hence, for
them, the cost of carry is also determined by the accumulated storage costs. However, these
arguments would imply that commodity forward curves should always be in contango, i.e.,
futures prices for longer maturities should always be higher than those for shorter maturities
and the spot price. In practice, this is rarely the case; in fact, the crude oil futures market
historically has been in backwardation approximately 75 % of the time. To cope with this
observation, the notion of *convenience yield* was introduced by Kaldor (1939) and Working
(1948). It is defined as the premium received by the owner of the physical commodity and

not accruing to the holder of a futures contract written on it. This concept leads to the famous cost-of-carry relationship:

$$F(t, T) = S(t)e^{[r(t)+c(t)-\tilde{y}(t)](T-t)}, \tag{2.5}$$

where $r(t)$ is the riskless interest rate on the date t, $c(t)$ is the storage cost (per unit of time and per dollar worth of commodity) and $\tilde{y}(t)$ the convenience yield, all continuously compound. Often, the convenience yield is defined net of storage costs: $y(t) = \tilde{y}(t) - c(t)$, in which case the cost-of-carry relationship becomes

$$F(t, T) = S(t)e^{[r(t)-y(t)](T-t)}. \tag{2.6}$$

In its early versions, the cost-of-carry relationship (2.6) included a constant or deterministic (but time-varying) convenience yield, such as in Brennan and Schwartz (1985). The next step was to define the convenience yield as a function of the spot price. More realistic versions of (2.6) (e.g. those in Gibson and Schwartz (1990), Litzenberger and Rabinowitz (1995)) included the convenience yield as a stochastic process. Some authors stressed a time-spread optionality embedded in the convenience yield (discussed in e.g. Routledge *et al.* (2000)). To emphasize this option-like feature of the convenience yield, it should be considered as a function of maturity T (or time to maturity $T - t$), as well as time t: $y = y(t, T)$, as suggested in Borovkova and Geman (2006). This representation is particularly useful in the case of seasonal commodities, as we show in the next section.

Obtaining a dynamic model for the forward prices from the cost-of-carry relationship (2.6) goes as follows. The spot price $S(t)$ and the convenience yield $y(t)$ are considered as the fundamental stochastic factors driving the forward curve's evolution. A stochastic model is assumed for the joint dynamics of $S(t)$ and $y(t)$ and then the corresponding dynamics for the futures prices is obtained by substituting the expressions for $S(t)$ and $y(t)$ into the cost-of-carry relationship (2.6). Sometimes the interest rate can be added as another fundamental factor, as in Miltersen and Schwartz (1998). The cost-of-carry relationship (2.6) holds under any probability measure, so for the purposes of derivatives pricing, the risk neutral dynamics of futures prices can be obtained from the risk-neutral dynamics of the fundamental factors.

None of the approaches described above is directly suited to modelling seasonal forward curves, often observed in energy and agricultural markets. One attempt has been made by Sorensen (2002) and Lucia and Schwartz (2002), who consider a seasonal component of the spot price that subsequently enters the expression for the forward prices in a rather opaque way. However, seasonality in forward prices obtained in this way does not match the empirically observed seasonal patterns present in the forward curve, especially the fact that the forward price's seasonality is a function of the contract *maturity* T and not so much of the current date t. In the next section we introduce an explicit modelling of maturity-related seasonalities in commodity forward curves. Ours is a two (or three) factor model, where the spot price is replaced by a more stable quantity and the convenience yield is considered net of deterministic seasonal effects.

2.3 THE SEASONAL FORWARD CURVE MODEL AND ITS EXTENSIONS

Forward prices of seasonal energy commodities such as natural gas and electricity are influenced by seasonal demand due to heating or airconditioning; agricultural commodities are influenced by seasonal supply (harvest). These constraints result into positive seasonal premia attached to calendar months of high demand or low supply. Furthermore, the commodity spot price can be unreliable or unavailable, so it is not always a good candidate to be the main fundamental factor driving the forward curve. In this section we explore these observations within the framework of the "seasonal forward curve model". In Section 2.3.1 we describe the original two-factor model proposed by Borovkova and Geman (2006) and apply it to seasonal energy commodities such as natural gas and electricity. In Section 2.3.2 we introduce an important generalization of the original model. In the generalized seasonal forward curve model, we introduce three stochastic factors, in order to allow for a trend in a seasonal forward curve.

2.3.1 Seasonal cost-of-carry model

For clarity of exposition, we will assume that the forward curve contains liquid maturities up to one year (12 months) or an integer number of years. We define the first fundamental factor as *the geometric average of the observed forward prices at date t*:

$$\overline{F}(t) = \sqrt[N]{\prod_{T=1}^{N} F(t, T)}, \tag{2.7}$$

where N is the most distant maturity and $N = 12 \times k$ ($k = 1, 2, \ldots$. This assumption assures that $\overline{F}(t)$ is a non-seasonal quantity, which is another advantage of using it instead of the (possibly seasonal) spot price.

Next, we define the seasonal premia $s(M)$, $M = 1, \ldots, 12$, attached to calendar months, as the collection of 12 long-term average premia with respect to the average forward price $\overline{F}(t)$. We assume that the vector $(s(1), \ldots, s(12))$ is deterministic and require that $\sum_{M=1}^{12} s(M) = 0$.

Finally, we write the *seasonal cost-of-carry model* describing the relationship between the prevailing forward price $\overline{F}(t)$ and the futures price $F(t, T)$:

$$F(t, T) = \overline{F}(t)e^{[s(T)-\gamma(t,T-t)(T-t)]}, \tag{2.8}$$

where the quantity $\gamma(t, T - t)$, defined by the relationship above, is called the *stochastic premium* at date t (as opposed to the deterministic seasonal premium $s(T)$), associated with the maturity T. We denote the *time to maturity* $\tau = T - t$ and write $\gamma(t, \tau) = \gamma(t, T - t)$, to emphasize that the stochastic premium γ is indexed by the time to maturity τ rather than the maturity date T (as is the case for the deterministic seasonal premium $s(T)$).

We define $s(T)$ for maturity T as follows: $s(T) = s(M)$ if the maturity T is in the calendar month M ($M = 1, \ldots, 12$). Note that, in this way, futures maturing in, for example February 2009 and February 2010, get the same seasonal premium $s(2)$ associated with the month of February. Furthermore, note that we define $s(M)$ as an absolute quantity (expressed in percentage) and not as a rate. This reflects that the seasonal premium does not accumulate with distant maturities, but is only associated with the calendar maturity month. In this way, the seasonal premium for the February contract is the same, be it the front month contract or the one maturing in a year's time.

To summarize, futures maturing in a particular calendar month can be either at a premium or a discount relative to the average level of the forward curve. This is a periodic, i.e., seasonal effect, which is associated with periods of high demand or low supply. This premium is summarized in the non-stochastic quantity $s(M)$, which can be consistently estimated from the historical data.

The quantity $\gamma(t, \tau)$, on the other hand, is a stochastic process in t, indexed by the time to maturity τ, and summarizes all deviations of the actual observed futures prices from the anticipated futures prices given by $\overline{F}(t)e^{s(T)}$. Its expected value is zero, since all systematic deviations of futures prices from $\overline{F}(t)$ are embedded in the seasonal premium $s(T)$. So we will model it by the Ornstein-Uhlenbeck process with zero mean. We call $\gamma(t, \tau)$ the *stochastic cost of carry*, or *stochastic premium devoid of seasonal premium*, for time to maturity τ. Factors influencing the function γ are, for example, levels of stocks, political news and events or unusual weather conditions.

The seasonal cost-of-carry model (2.8) is related to the traditional cost-of-carry models such as the one exhibited in Brennan and Schwartz (1985) and many other papers. To our best knowledge, it is the only model that uses the average forward price $\overline{F}(t)$ instead of the spot price $S(t)$ as the first state variable. Accordingly, the traditional convenience yield introduced by Kaldor (1939) in the Theory of Storage is replaced by the stochastic premium $\gamma(t, \tau)$. This stochastic premium can be seen as the "relative convenience yield" (with respect to its average across all maturities), net of the scaled seasonal premium:

$$y(t, T) - \frac{1}{N} \sum_{M=1}^{N} y(t, M) = \gamma(t, \tau) - \frac{s(T)}{\tau},$$

where $y(t, T)$ is the traditional convenience yield. The stochastic premium γ and the seasonal cost-of-carry model have the merit of being applicable to non-storable commodities such as electricity. For these commodities, the traditional cost-of-carry model and the convenience yield do not make sense, as the absence of storability prevents any cash-and-carry arguments (see Eydeland and Geman (1998)). Moreover, the seasonal cost-of-carry model does not imply any convergence, smooth or not, of the futures price to the spot price, a property that is unobserved in a number of commodity markets.

Another advantage of having the average forward price $\overline{F}(t)$ as the first fundamental factor is that it is a non-seasonal quantity by construction, and hence can be modelled by a stationary stochastic process of the model builder's choice, e.g., mean reverting or geometric Brownian motion, or including jumps. The quantity $\overline{F}$ gives a very good proxy for the overall level of the futures market, while being more visible and less unstable than the spot price. However, it can happen that, in forward curves spanning several years, the average forward price differs for different years ahead, as it reflects the market anticipation of the remaining reserves left at that time for exhaustible commodities such as copper, crude oil or uranium. Below we introduce an important generalization of the model, which deals with such issues.

Note that the convergence property of the futures price to the spot price (2.1) provides the following expression for the spot price within the seasonal cost-of-carry model:

$$S(t) = \overline{F}(t)e^{s(t)}. \tag{2.9}$$

Hence, if the spot price is not available in a particular market, the above relationship can be used to define a valuable proxy for the spot price.

Returning to the dynamics of the state variables, the stochastic premium can be arguably represented by an Ornstein-Uhlenbeck process with zero mean:

$$d\gamma(t, \tau) = -a^{(\tau)}\gamma(t, \tau)dt + \eta^{(\tau)}dW(t), \tag{2.10}$$

where the mean-reversion speed and the volatility parameters may differ per maturity T. In the above specification, the entire term structure of $\gamma(t, \tau)$ is driven by the same Brownian motion $W(t)$; however, more sources of uncertainty can be easily incorporated. The average forward price $\overline{F}(t)$ can be modelled by any appropriate diffusion process, uncorrelated to the process driving the term structure of $\{\gamma(t, \tau)\}_\tau$. For example, a mean-reverting process can be used, which is a popular choice for commodities. However, in recent years most commodities have experienced massive price increases. Geman (2005) argues that, in the case of crude oil prices, "mean-reversion is dead". This may be true for other commodities such as copper or uranium. In these cases, one can use other model specifications for $\overline{F}(t)$, such as a geometric Brownian motion or a mean-reverting process with a deterministic (or even stochastic) trend.

The seasonal cost-of-carry model (2.8) provides the relationship between the fundamental factors and the futures contracts prices. So the dynamics and the distributions of the futures prices can be obtained from the dynamics of the fundamental factors, by substituting them into (2.8). For example, the above specification (2.10) of $\gamma(t, \tau)$ and a mean reverting diffusion for the log-average forward price $X(t) = \ln \overline{F}(t)$

$$dX(t) = \alpha(m - X(t))dt + \sigma d\overline{W}(t) \tag{2.11}$$

lead to the following futures price dynamics:

$$d(\ln F(t, T)) = [\alpha(m - X(t)) + \gamma(t, \tau)(a^{(\tau)}\tau + 1)]dt \\ + \sigma d\overline{W}(t) - \eta^{(\tau)}\tau dW(t), [\tau = T - t.] \tag{2.12}$$

So in this case, the futures price $F(t, T)$ is lognormally distributed, with mean $\overline{F}(t)e^{s(T)}$ and the volatility term structure defined by

$$\delta(t, \tau) = \sqrt{\sigma^2 + (\eta^{(\tau)}\tau)^2}. \tag{2.13}$$

This is the description of the futures prices under the statistical probability measure P. For derivatives pricing, only the risk neutral dynamics are relevant. These are obtained by specifying the risk neutral dynamics of the fundamental factors and using again the equality (2.8). Now, under the risk neutral measure Q, futures prices are martingales, i.e., their drift is identically zero. This results into a restriction on the model parameters under Q, similar to the HJM condition (Heath *et al.* (1992)) on Treasury forward rates.

The seasonal premium and other model parameters can be estimated from the set of historical futures prices. The average forward price can be computed on any day t by formula (2.7) (as said before, it is essential that the futures prices up to one year or an integer number of years are included, in order to eliminate seasonal features). The seasonal premium associated with the month M is estimated according to its definition by

$$\hat{s}(M) = \frac{1}{n} \sum_{t=1}^{n} [\ln F(t, M) - \ln \overline{F}(t)], \qquad (2.14)$$

where n is the number of observations in the historical dataset and we include all futures expiring in the calendar month M (possibly for different years). The series of daily stochastic premia $(\gamma(t, \tau))_{t=1,\ldots,n}$ for all available times to maturity τ is computed as

$$\hat{\gamma}(t, \tau) = \frac{\ln(\overline{F}(t)/F(t, T)) + \hat{s}(T)}{\tau}. \qquad (2.15)$$

From the obtained series $(\overline{F}(t))_t$ and $(\hat{\gamma}(t, \tau))_t$, the parameters of the associated stochastic diffusion models can be estimated by, for instance the method of maximum likelihood.

Figure 2.5 shows the estimated seasonal premia for UK natural gas, electricity and heating oil futures. Our estimates are based on historical datasets of ICE futures prices from 2001 to 2004.

As expected, futures expiring in winter are at a premium with respect to the average price level, and summer futures at a discount. December gas futures are on average at a 28 % premium, December electricity futures are at 15 % premium. The seasonal premium for heating oil is generally smaller, and is at most 3 %. This reflects a wider availability of storage and transportation for heating oil. Note that similar products traded on the NYMEX may exhibit different seasonal premia, as those reflect the risk aversion of producers and speculators in each particular market to different types of events.

Figure 2.6 shows the volatility term structure of the stochastic premium $\gamma(t, \tau)$, for natural gas and gasoil. Note that it mimics the behavior of the futures prices volatility, which decreases for more distant maturities (the so-called Samuelson effect).

Figure 2.7 shows the realization of the natural gas and gasoil stochastic premium $\gamma(t, \tau)$, for $\tau = 2$, i.e. for two months to maturity. The mean of γ is indeed zero and the graph resembles a mean-reverting process.

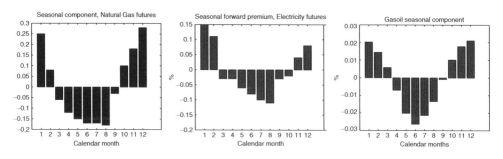

Figure 2.5 Natural gas, electricity and heating oil seasonal premia

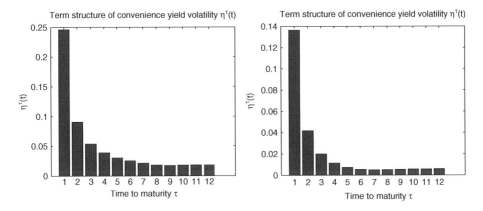

Figure 2.6   Volatilities of natural gas and gasoil stochastic convenience yields

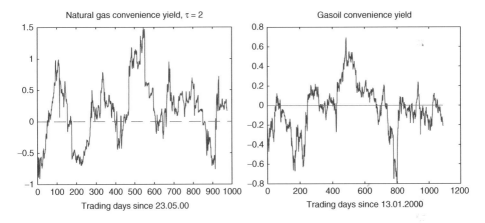

Figure 2.7   Natural gas and gasoil stochastic convenience yields, $\tau = 2$

Applications of the seasonal cost-of-carry model include the generation of realistic seasonal forward curves for risk management and scenario simulations. Moreover, this model can be used for extending the observed forward curves beyond the most distant liquid maturity, a necessary task in the valuation of physical assets such as gas storage facilities or refineries. The generalization of the model, introduced in the next paragraph, is particularly useful for this purpose. The formulation of the fundamental factors' risk neutral dynamics provides a unifying framework for pricing derivatives that depend on the entire forward curve, such as calendar spread options.

2.3.2   The generalized seasonal forward curve model

Recall that, above, we defined $\overline{F}(t)$ as the geometric average of all available forward prices or, in other words, $\ln \overline{F}(t)$ as the arithmetic average of all log-futures prices:

$$\ln \overline{F}(t) = \frac{1}{N} \sum_{T=1}^{N} \ln F(t, T), \qquad (2.16)$$

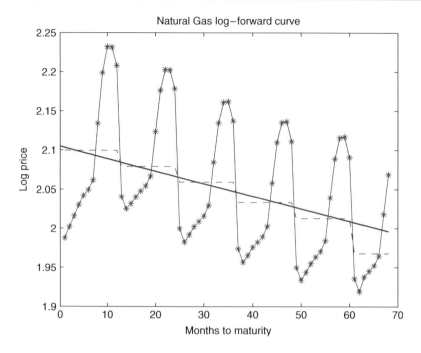

Figure 2.8   NYMEX Natural Gas forward curve, three factor model

where N is the longest traded maturity. In cases such as depicted in Figure 2.4, we can define the (geometric) average forward prices $\overline{F}_i(t)$ for each year i present in the forward curve as

$$\ln \overline{F}_i(t) = \frac{1}{12} \sum_{T=12(i-1)+1}^{12i} \ln F(t, T). \tag{2.17}$$

To obtain a multiplicative model similar to (2.8), we first go from forward prices to their logarithms, so we consider the log-forward curve $(\ln F(t, T))_T$. Figure 2.8 shows the logarithm of a forward curve of NYMEX Natural Gas futures, together with a collection of average yearly forward log-prices $(\ln \overline{F}_i(t))_i$. These average log-prices are highly correlated and move for a large part together, so defining them as separate fundamental stochastic factors does not really make sense, not to mention the increase in the problem's dimensionality. Instead, we suggest extending the number of fundamental factors by just one extra factor, in the following way.

Note that the collection $(\ln \overline{F}_i(t))_i$ defines a step function (in terms of maturities) approximating the logarithm of the forward curve. A more general way to approximate the overall shape of the log-forward curve on day t is to fit a least-squares straight line through all available forward log-prices:

$$X_T(t) = X_0(t) + \alpha(t)T, \tag{2.18}$$

where the parameters $\alpha(t)$ (slope) and $X_0(t)$ (intercept) are estimated on each day t by the ordinary least squares method. This straight line approximation is illustrated in Figure 2.8.

Note that equation (2.18) describes, at date t fixed, $X_T(t)$ as an affine function of the maturity T.

Denote $\overline{F}_0(t) = \ln X_0(t)$ and $\overline{F}_T(t) = \ln X_T(t)$. The relationship (2.18) implies that the overall shape of the forward curve is approximated by an exponential function given by

$$\overline{F}_T(t) = \overline{F}_0(t)e^{\alpha(t)T}, \tag{2.19}$$

where $\alpha(t)$ evolves randomly over time.

If the slope $\alpha(t)$ on day t is negative, then the forward curve is in overall backwardation, such as in Figure 2.4, where the seasonal premium is still clearly present. The positive slope parameter $\alpha(t)$ defines the contango forward curve shape. If the slope parameter is not significantly different from zero, then we are in the situation of the initial seasonal cost-of-carry model of the previous section, with the parameter $\overline{F}_0(t)$ being exactly the geometric average of the forward curve $\overline{F}(t)$.

The seasonal deterministic premia $s(M)$ $(M = 1, \ldots , 12)$ are now defined as *the average premia, expressed in %, in futures expiring in the calendar month M with respect to $\overline{F}_T(t)$ described in (2.19) and defining on day t the overall shape of the forward curve.*

The new formulation of the generalized seasonal cost-of-carry model is then

$$F(t, T) = \overline{F}_0(t)e^{\alpha(t)T + s(T) - \gamma(t, T-t)(T-t)}, \tag{2.20}$$

where $\gamma(t, \tau)$ is again the stochastic forward premium, defined by the relationship (2.20) above.

The slope $\alpha(t)$ and $\overline{F}_0(t)$ (or its logarithm $X_0(t)$, which is the intercept), defining together the straight line (2.18), are now the two new fundamental factors of our generalized seasonal forward curve model. The third one remains the stochastic premium $\gamma(t, \tau)$, defined by the relationship (2.20).

The two new fundamental factors $\overline{F}_0(t)$ and $\alpha(t)$ have a well-known interpretation, closely related to the Principal Component Analysis of the forward curve, described in Section 2.4. These factors reflect the *level and slope* of the forward curve on date t and contain most of the forward curve's variability. The remaining stochastic variation of the forward curve, in particular its curvature, is now summarized in the stochastic forward premia $\gamma(t, \tau)$. We postulate that all three fundamental factors are pairwise uncorrelated. Both $\overline{F}_0(t)$ and $\alpha(t)$ are uncorrelated to $\gamma(t, \tau)$ because the latter quantity accounts for unexpected shocks in the commodity market, such as extreme weather conditions or disruption in supply. Furthermore, we can view $\overline{F}_0(t)$ as being uncorrelated to $\alpha(t)$ (the slope of the affine function of maturity). The theory of normal backwardation ($\alpha(t)$ negative when $\overline{F}_0(t)$ high) appears to be essentially invalidated by the current commodity markets, as $\overline{F}_0(t)$ represents the current position held by many market participants, including new entrants, and the slope $\alpha(t)$ carries long-term views of the fundamental players.

The dynamics of the new fundamental factor $\overline{F}_0(t)$ can be specified by a model builder according to the observed empirical features deduced from historical data. For example, it can be a mean reverting process with a constant or increasing level of mean-reversion, or a Geometric Brownian motion. The slope $\alpha(t)$ and the stochastic premium $\gamma(t, \tau)$ should be modelled as Ornstein-Uhlenbeck processes mean reverting to zero. Since we continue to observe, including in the recent past, forward curves that change from backwardation to contango and vice versa, we believe that the choice for $\alpha(t)$ of Ornstein-Uhlenbeck process mean-reverting to zero is a reasonable one.

The fundamental factors' dynamics specifications lead to the dynamics of forward prices via the generalized seasonal cost-of-carry relationship (2.20). Portfolio strategies involving spot and forward positions will be devised using the representation under the real probability measure P. For the purposes of derivatives pricing, all dynamics should be specified under the risk-adjusted probability measure Q. Equation (2.20) can be viewed as written under the measure Q, hence any risk-neutral dynamics for the three fundamental factors imply the corresponding dynamics and distributions for the futures prices.[2] With these in hand, derivatives such as futures options or calendar spread options can be easily valued by a Black-Scholes-like approach or by Monte Carlo simulations.

2.4 PRINCIPAL COMPONENT ANALYSIS OF A FORWARD CURVE

Forward curve modelling is an inherently multivariate problem: there are as many variables (futures prices) as the number of traded futures contracts with different maturities (e.g., 72 for NYMEX Natural Gas futures). In applications such as risk management, considering them as separate (but correlated) risk factors is rather excessive since these futures prices move, for a large part, together. The well-known and powerful statistical multivariate technique of Principal Component Analysis allows us to concentrate only on a few main uncorrelated *linear combinations* (i.e. principal components) of the forward prices (which may represent the main risk factors), which together describe virtually all possible forward curves or their evolutions.

In studies involving a large number of observed variables, it is often convenient to consider a smaller number of linear combinations of these variables, which summarize their main features. *Principal components* are such uncorrelated linear combinations. There are as many principal components as original variables and, taken together, they explain all the variability in the original data. However, because of the way they are calculated, it is usually possible to consider only a few of the principal components, which together explain *most* of the original variation. The principal components are ordered according to their contribution to the variability of the data: the first component contributes more to the variability than the second one and so on. To visualize the principal components, the coefficients of these linear combinations (i.e. of the principal components) are used. They are called the *principal component loadings* and provide a convenient summary of the influence of the original variables on the principal components (or, equivalently, the response of each original variable to a change in the corresponding principal component), and thus a useful basis for interpretation.

A forward curve of practically any shape can be constructed by combining three simple shapes: the so-called *level, slope and curvature*. Consequently, the dynamic of the forward curve is mainly determined by the evolution of these three main factors: parallel shift of the entire forward curve, "tilting" of the forward curve and changes in its curvature. This was first established by Litterman and Scheinkman (1991) for the US government bond yields and subsequently applied to commodities by Cortazar and Schwartz (1994), who studied the evolution of copper forward curves. It turns out that, for non-seasonal commodities such as crude oil, the first three principal components of the historical futures price returns

---

[2] However, as said before, the martingale property of futures prices under the risk-adjusted probability measure leads to certain restrictions on drifts and volatilities of the fundamental factors under Q.

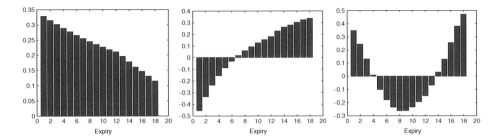

Figure 2.9 Loadings of the first three principal components, oil futures prices

correspond exactly to these three main factors: the level, slope and the curvature. This is shown in Figure 2.9, which depicts the loadings of the first three principal components for the historical returns of Brent oil futures prices for the first 18 maturities.

These first three principal components explain approximately 95 % of the original variation in the forward curves. Hence, they provide an excellent way of extracting most of the essential information and expressing it via a small number of factors. The economic interpretation of these factors is rather straightforward: for energy futures (and, to a lesser extent, for other commodities) a parallel shift of the forward curve is caused mainly by changes in global economy, political situation, and exploration techniques. A slope change is caused by changes in expected long-term price or by a change in the "convenience premium", or convenience yield, discussed above, on holding a physical commodity. The curvature of the forward curve is related to volatilities of futures prices, as well as long-term vs. short-term expectations on supply and demand.

Depending on a given application, the PCA can be performed either for historical futures prices or returns. For simulations or for generating trading indicators (discussed in Section 2.5), PCA is applied directly to the futures prices, as is done, for example, in Weron (2006) for simulating electricity forward prices. For risk management and derivatives pricing applications, the main risk factors and corresponding volatilities can be conveniently summarized by the principal components of the historical futures price returns. This significantly reduces the number of risk factors in futures portfolios and simplifies Value-at-Risk calculations. For applications of principal components in risk management for bond portfolios see e.g., Golub and Tilman (1997), Singh (1997), and Borovkova (2006) for commodity portfolios. In multifactor forward curve models (such as that of Clewlow and Strickland (2000), represented by the equation (2.2)), the first three principal components of the forward curve are taken to be the three fundamental factors, and corresponding volatility functions $\sigma_i(t, T)$ (suitably parameterized) are estimated from the historical data.

For seasonal commodities, the application and interpretation of the principal component analysis is not straightforward. PCA cannot be applied to historical forward curves directly (although many authors have attempted to do so): the resulting principal components will reflect the harmonics at the main frequencies present in the periodical pattern. As a result, many principal components might seem important in explaining the forward curve's variability (and not just the first three): for example, Koekebakker and Ollmar (2001) report that as many as 10 principal components are needed to adequately explain the electricity forward curve's variability, which is obviously a too high-dimensional problem. We would like to stress that this is caused by maturity-related seasonalities found in natural gas forward prices and volatilities.

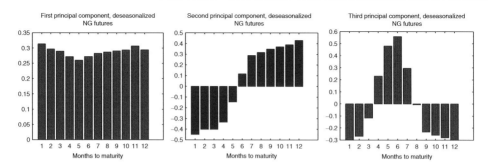

Figure 2.10   Loadings of the first three principal components, deseasonalized natural gas futures prices

One way to deal with prominent seasonalities when applying PCA to seasonal forward curves is to apply PCA separately to historical futures prices maturing in different seasons (an approach adopted in e.g., Tolmasky and Hindanov (2002)), or even separately for each maturity month (as in Blanco *et al.* (2002)). However, this results in over-parametrization. Alternatively, the historical forward prices and returns can be deseasonalized before applying the principal component analysis. For applications such as forward curve simulations, the seasonal premia ($s(M)$, $M = 1, \ldots , 12$) can be estimated in the way described above and the PCA applied to the deseasonalized historical forward prices $\tilde{F}(t, T) = F(t, T)e^{-\hat{s}(T)}$, where $\hat{s}(T)$ is the estimated seasonal premium corresponding to the maturity month T.

We applied PCA to the deseasonalized historical natural gas forward curves. The factors analogous to the level, slope, and curvature are clearly present, as Figure 2.10 shows.

For risk management and derivatives pricing applications, futures price returns should be also deseasonalized, since futures price volatility can also exhibit seasonal (maturity-related) patterns (for example, natural gas futures prices are more volatile for futures expiring in months of high demand, i.e. winter months in UK). This can be done by first estimating the seasonal component of the futures price volatility σ_M, $M = 1, \ldots , 12$ for all calendar maturity months, and then applying the PCA to the deseasonalized returns $\tilde{r}(t, T) = r(t, T)/\hat{\sigma}_T$, where $r(t, T)$ is day-t return on futures with maturity T and $\hat{\sigma}_T$ is the estimated seasonal volatility component corresponding to the maturity month T. Then the main risk factors extracted by the deseasonalized PCA can be subsequently used in portfolio risk analysis and derivatives pricing, in the same way as for non-seasonal commodities.

2.5   FORWARD CURVE INDICATORS

We presented above a detailed analysis of commodity forward curves and discussed the quantification of a forward curve's features by means of seasonal premia and principal components. However, in a trading environment there is often a preference towards expressing information in the form of technical indicators (such as e.g. Relative Strength Index). An indicator quantifies a certain feature of the spot or forward market by means of a single number, extracted from current market prices. Such indicators can be easily monitored on a daily or intra-day basis and used for developing trading strategies. There are many technical indicators developed for asset spot prices which are routinely applied to commodity spot prices. However, trading indicators obtained on the basis of forward prices are not that common. Here we discuss several such indicators and outline their potential use.

As we noted above, forward markets for non-seasonal commodities such as crude oil are mainly in two states: backwardation or contango. Whether the market is in backwardation or in contango depends on many fundamental factors. The depth of backwardation or contango (characterized by the steepness of the forward curve) or an anticipated switch from one state to the other is important for market participants: it influences their trading and production decisions. Hence, it is important to detect or forecast such a switch as early as possible. Often, the difference between futures prices with two closest maturities (the so-called *first intermonth spread*) is used for measuring the strength of backwardation or contango and for detecting changes in forward markets. Fundamentals of a commodity market are ultimately responsible for any changes in forward curves, so a change can be anticipated by studying the market fundamentals. In practice, however, traders are interested in working with indicators derived from the futures prices alone, such as the first intermonth spread. The first intermonth spread (or any other calendar spread) is rather inefficient as an indicator of an overall forward curve shape, as it uses only futures prices with two maturities, while many liquid futures prices are often available. Here we describe two change indicators that use the entire forward curve, i.e. all available futures prices. The first indicator measures the "strength" of the backwardation or contango market, i.e. the steepness of the forward curve. The second indicator is based on the principal component analysis. The application of these indicators to seasonal forward curves can reveal features normally obscured by dominant seasonal effects.

A forward market can be in backwardation or in contango for a prolonged period of time. A change from one state to the other is gradual and takes several days or even weeks. The change from backwardation to contango and vice versa is characterized by an intermediate stage of an almost flat forward curve. This observation is crucial in constructing the change indicators.

Denote $Y(t, T) = F(t, T + 1)) - F(t, T), T = 1, \ldots, N - 1$, the day-$t$ intermonth spreads, i.e. the differences in futures prices with consecutive maturities (N being the longest liquid maturity). The first candidate for the change indicator is

$$I_1(t) = \sum_{T=1}^{N-1} w_T Y(t, T), \qquad (2.21)$$

where $(w_T)_{T=1,\ldots,N-1}$ is a suitably chosen collection of weights. $I_1(t)$ measures the steepness of the forward curve on day t and the following three situations can arise:

1. $I_1(t) >> 0 \longrightarrow$ upward-sloping forward curve (contango);
2. $I_1(t) << 0 \longrightarrow$ downward-sloping forward curve (backwardation);
3. $I_1(t) \approx 0 \longrightarrow$ flat forward curve (intermediate market state), indicating a possibility of a change.

Futures prices are volatile and, in turn, so is the indicator I_1. Hence it can get close to zero solely as a result of a random shock. On the other hand, the transition between market states happens gradually. So only a persistent near-zero value of I_1 indicates a market change. Instead of the "raw" indicator I_1, therefore, we can use the moving average smoothed indicator $\tilde{I}_1$:

$$\tilde{I}_1(t) = \frac{1}{M} \sum_{i=0}^{M-1} I_1(t-i),$$

where M is a suitably chosen moving window size.

The purpose of the weights (w_T) is two-fold. First, they allow us to scale the intermonth spreads in the indicator (2.21) by their volatilities, to discount for liquidity-related effects. Second, it is possible to give more weight to futures prices with shorter maturities if we believe that the front end of the forward curve "drives" the whole curve. We suggest to take weights of the form:

$$w_T = \frac{\gamma^T}{\sigma(t, T)}$$

for some $\gamma \in (0, 1)$, where $\sigma(t, T)$ is the day-t volatility of the Tth intermonth spread, suitably estimated. The choice of γ for a particular commodity can be data-driven, by a variant of cross-validation on the basis of historical data. Applications to the oil futures prices have shown that values of γ in the range $0.8 \div 0.95$ perform quite well.

Another parameter to be chosen is the moving average window M. Choosing M too large leads to a late signal (oversmoothing), while choosing M too small results in the indicator being too noisy (undersmoothing). In practice, we have to balance these two factors. For example, one can use $\tilde{I}_1(t)$ for different values of M ("fast" and "slow" moving averages) at the same time.

The second indicator is based on the Principal Component Analysis of the forward curve. Recall that the three main movements of a forward curve are the parallel shift, "tilt" and the change in its curvature, represented by the first three principal components of the forward curve. When studying transitions from backwardation to contango and vice versa, we are interested in the movement of the second type, i.e. when the forward prices with short and long maturities move in the opposite directions. So the second principal component, corresponding to the "tilt" in the forward curve, can be used to construct a change indicator.

To get rid of the dominant parallel shift component, we first remove the average day-t forward price $\overline{F}(t)$ and consider $\tilde{F}(t, T) = F(t, T)/\overline{F}(t)$ (all $\tilde{F}(t, T)$ are scaled to have mean one, for any date t). Then the *first* principal component of $(\tilde{F}(t, T))_{T=1,...,N}$ corresponds to the slope of the forward curve, as shown in Figure 2.11, which depicts the first two principal components of $(\tilde{F}(t, T))_{T=1,...,N}$.

We define the principal component indicator by

$$I_2(t) = \sum_{T=1}^{N} L_T^{(1)} \tilde{F}(t, T), \qquad (2.22)$$

where $L_T^{(1)}, T = 1, ..., N$ are the loadings of the first principal component of $(\tilde{F}(t, T))_{T=1,...,N}$ (shown on the left plot in Figure 2.11). Note that the equation (2.22) defines a *projection* of the scaled forward curve $(\tilde{F}(t, T))_{T=1,...,N}$ on the first principal

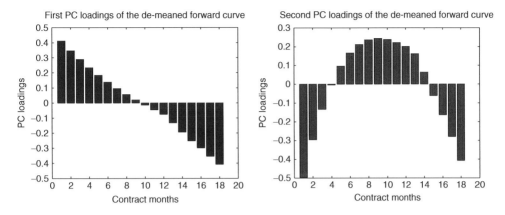

Figure 2.11 First two principal components of $(\tilde{F}(t, T))_T$

component. The corresponding moving average smoothed indicator is then

$$\tilde{I}_2(t) = \frac{1}{M} \sum_{i=0}^{M-1} I_2(t - i),$$

with a suitably chosen moving window length M.

Indicators I_1 and I_2 (and their moving average smoothed versions) can be computed daily and monitored for detecting a switch between backwardation and contango. Loosely speaking, values of indicators close to zero (i.e. in some critical ε-neighborhood of zero) signal a possible switch. A critical value of ε can be specified via the distribution (empirical or theoretical) of the indicators under the null-hypothesis of no change. Alternatively, simulation techniques called the *smooth stationary bootstrap*, introduced in Borovkova (2004), can be used to construct critical regions for the indicators.

For seasonal commodities, the most prominent feature of the forward curve is the maturity-related seasonality, summarized in the seasonal premia $(s(M))_{M=1,\dots,12}$. The *deseasonalized forward curve* $(F(t, T)e^{-s(T)})_T$ can exhibit features similar to backwardation or contango, or show deviations from the expected seasonal pattern. So for seasonal commodities, we define both indicators I_1 and I_2 in relation to the deseasonalized forward curve $(F(t, T)e^{-s(T)})_T$. More precisely, the weighted strength indicator $I_1(t)$ is defined again by (2.21), with $Y(t, T)$ being the intermonth spreads of the deseasonalized forward curve and with weights $(w(T))_T$ reflecting particular features of a commodity. For instance, the weights for a few shorter maturities can be chosen higher than all others, to reflect most significant deviations occurring in the front end of the forward curve. The principal component indicator is defined as the projection of the deseasonalized (and discounted by $\overline{F}(t)$) forward curve $\tilde{F}(t, T) = F(t, T)e^{-s(T)}/\overline{F}(t)$ on the first principal component of $(\tilde{F}(t, T))_T$.

These indicators can be used in the same way as for non-seasonal commodities, monitoring changes between an overall backwardation or contango state of the forward market, while still allowing for seasonalities. In markets where there is no significant slope in the forward curve (such as the case for shorter forward curves, e.g. for maturities up to 12 months), the expected deseazonalized forward curve should be approximately flat. Then both indicators (and, to a lesser degree, the projection of the forward curve on the curvature principal component) measure the forward curve's deviations from the flat shape. This means that values of the indicators far from zero (e.g., outside 95% confidence bounds around zero) indicate significant deviations of the forward curve from the expected shape given by the dominant seasonal component.

Figure 2.12 shows the Principal Component Indicator for the UK Natural Gas futures prices (01.04.01 01.04.08), together with its overall historical 95% confidence intervals around zero.

There are several periods when the indicator leaves its 95% confidence bounds. During these periods, there are significant deviations of the futures prices from the seasonal pattern. For example, around the 1500th observation (March 2007) the indicator values are very high, meaning that during this period a prominent backwardation shape was detected in the forward curve. Such extreme situations are clearly not persistent, so this information can be used for constructing profitable trading strategies.

Tracking the indicators for seasonal commodities can be useful for monitoring futures markets, detecting shifts in fundamentals or possible mispricing of some futures. Trading signals can be generated when the indicators exceed some pre-determined threshold, generated from either historical data or simulations. In the absence of delivery issues, a simple speculative trading strategy during periods of high (and positive) indicator values could be to sell futures with closer expiries, buy futures expiring later, and close all the positions as soon as the indicator returns inside the threshold bounds. The size of the future's positions can be made proportional to the principal component loadings. The risk exposure of such

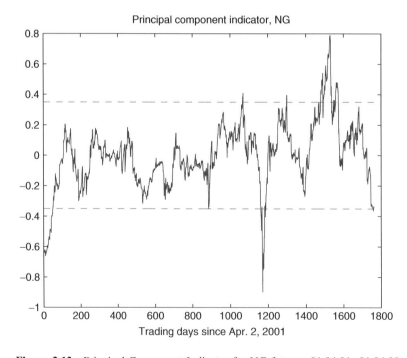

Figure 2.12   Principal Component Indicator for NG futures, 01.04.01–01.04.08

a trading strategy is due to calendar spreads and not to the outright futures prices, which leads to a quite low value-at-risk.

Other (possibly more sophisticated) trading strategies are feasible. For instance, one can also involve the curvature principle component, to actively trade in the middle of the forward curve (middle maturities), in addition to short and long maturities. Additionally, one can exploit autocorrelations present in the daily indicator series: a predictive model (such as an autoregressive one) can be fitted to the historical indicator series and used for forecasting. Generally, the forward curve indicators (together with the estimated seasonal premia) provide valuable information about the state of the futures market and economic fundamentals.

2.6 CONCLUSIONS

Forward curves are of paramount importance in commodity markets. They are essential for financial and physical asset pricing and production planning decisions as they provide information about anticipated price trends. Forward curves obtained from liquid futures markets are essential tools for marking portfolio positions to market and calibrating derivatives pricing models under the risk-adjusted probability measure. Dynamic modelling of forward curves is a challenging task for researchers and practitioners, due to the multi-dimensionality of the problem and particularly complex empirical features of forward curves observed in the markets.

Traditional cost-of-carry arguments are only partially successful in modelling energy forward curves. This is because, on the one hand, the spot price is not always a good image of the current market conditions and, on the other hand, a maturity-independent convenience yield fails to capture seasonal effects often present in energy forward curves. The seasonal forward curve model overcomes both limitations and is capable of capturing prominent characteristic features of seasonal forward curves. The generalized seasonal forward curve model introduced here incorporates the existence of non-seasonal trends in forward prices, while still preserving seasonalities. It is a three-factor model, both parsimonious and sufficiently rich to generate realistic forward curves.

2.7 REFERENCES

Benth, F.E., S. Koekebakker and F. Ollmar (2007). Extracting and Applying Smooth Forward Curves from Average-based Commodity Contracts with Seasonal Variation. *Journal of Derivatives*, Fall 2007, 52–66.

Blanco, C., D. Soronow and Stefiszyn, P. (2002). Multi-Factor Models for Forward Curve Analysis: An Introduction to Principal Component Analysis. *Commodities Now*, June.

Borovkova, S. (2004). The Forward Curve Dynamic and Market Transition Forecasts. In D.W. Bunn (Ed.) *Modelling Prices in Competitive Electricity Markets*. John Wiley & Sons Ltd., p. 24.

Borovkova, S. (2006). Detecting Market Transitions and Energy Futures Risk Management using Principal Components. *The European Journal of Finance* **12** (6–7), 495–512.

Borovkova, S. and H. Geman (2006). Seasonal and Stochastic Effects in Commodity Forward Curves. *Reviews of Derivatives Research* **9**, 167–186.

Brennan, M.J. and E.S. Schwartz (1985). Evaluating Natural Resource Investments. *Journal of Business* **58** (2), 135–157.

Clewlow, L. and C. Strickland (2000). *Energy Derivatives: Pricing and Risk Management*. Lacima Publications: London, UK.

Cortazar, G. and E.S. Schwartz (1994). The Valuation of Commodity-Contigent Claims. *The Journal of Derivatives* **1**, 27–39.

Cox, J.C., J.E. Ingersoll and S.A. Ross (1985). A Theory of the Term Structure of Interest Rates. *Econometrica*, **53**, 385–407.

Eydeland, A. and H. Geman (1998). Pricing Power Derivatives. *RISK*, September 1998.

Gabillon, J. (1995). Analyzing the Forward Curve. In: *Managing Energy Price Risk*, Risk Publications, Financial Engineering Ltd: London.

Geman, H. (2005). Energy Commodity Prices: Is Mean-Reversion Dead? *Journal of Alternative Investments*, Fall.

Geman, H. and O. Vasicek (2001). Forward and Futures Contracts on Non-Storable Commodities: The Case of Electricity. *Risk*, August.

Gibson, R. and E.S. Schwartz (1990). Stochastic Convenience Yield and the Pricing of Oil Contingent Claims. *Journal of Finance* **45** (3), 959–976.

Golub, B.W. and L.M. Tilman (1997). Measuring Yield Curve Risk using Principal Component Analysis, Value at Risk and Key Rate Duration. *Journal of Portfolio Management* **23**:4, 72–84.

Heath, D., R. Jarrow and A. Morton (1992). Bond Pricing and the Term Structure of Interest Rates: A New Methodology for Contingent Claims Evaluation. *Econometrica* **60** (1), 77–105.

Kaldor, N. (1939). Speculation and Economic Stability. *Review of Economic Studies* **7**, 1–27.

Koekebakker, S. and F. Ollmar (2001). Forward Curve Dynamics in the Nordic Electricity Market. *NHH Working paper* no. 2101.

Litterman, R. and J. Scheinkman (1991). Common Factors Affecting Bond Returns. *Journal of Fixed Income* **1**, 54–61.

Litzenberger, R.H. and N. Rabinowitz (1995). Backwardation in Oil Futures Markets: Theory and Empirical Evidence. *Journal of Finance* **50** (5), 1517–1545.

Lucia, J. and E.S. Schwartz (2002). Electricity Prices and Power Derivatives: Evidence from the Nordic Power Exchange. *Review of Derivatives Research* **5** (1), 5–50.

Miltersen, K.R. and E.S. Schwartz (1998). Pricing of Options on Commodity Futures with Stochastic Term Structures of Convenience Yields and Interest Rates. *Journal of Financial and Quantitative Analysis* **33**(1) 33–59.

Routledge, B.R., D.J. Seppi and C.S. Spatt (2000). Equilibrium Forward Curves for Commodities. *Journal of Finance* **55** (3), 1297–1338.

Schwartz, E.S. (1997). The Stochastic Behaviour of Commodity Prices: Implications for Valuation and Hedging. *Journal of Finance* **53** (3), 923–973.

Singh, M.K. (1997). Value-at-Risk using Principal Component Analysis. *Journal of Portfolio Management* **23**:4, 101–111.

Sorensen, C. (2002). Modeling Seasonality in Agricultural Commodity Futures. *Journal of Futures Markets* **22** (5), 393–426.

Tolmasky, C. and D. Hindanov (2002). Principal Components Analysis for Correlated Curves and Seasonal Commodities: The Case of the Petroleum Market. *Journal of Futures Markets* **22** (11), 1019–1035.

Weron, R. (2006). *Modeling and Forecasting Electricity Loads and Prices: A Statistical Approach*. John Wiley & Sons Ltd.: Chichester.

Working, H. (1948). The Theory of Price of Storage. *Journal of Farm Economics* **30**, 1–28.

3

Integrating Physical and Financial Risk Management in Supply Management

Paul R. Kleindorfer

3.1 INTRODUCTION

This chapter provides a brief survey of recent contributions to the use of options and other derivative contract forms in support of commodity hedging and supply management in B2B markets. Such derivatives play an important role in integrating long-term and short-term contracting between multiple buyers and sellers in commodity markets. A primary question of interest in this context is hedging commodity risk exposure associated with commodity procurement decisions. In the usual context, Sellers compete to supply Buyers in a market in which, in the short run, capacities and technologies are fixed. Buyers can reserve capacity through contracts for physical delivery obtained from any Seller, and Buyers can also hedge these contracts through financial contracts on the same underlying indices from financial intermediaries. Output on the day can be either obtained through executing such contracts or in the associated spot market. Such contract-spot markets have become prominent under e-commerce (e.g. Geman, 2005), and include commodity chemicals, electric power, natural gas, metals, plastics, agricultural products, and basic foodstuffs.

Prior to the emergence of B2B exchanges and the contracting innovations of interest here, the focus in procurement and supply management was on bilateral negotiation, which gave rise to an extensive literature on various idiosyncratic aspects of contracting (see Cachon (2003) for a review). The point of departure in this chapter is that contracting, screening, and supplier management will remain essential elements of supply chain management, and especially for non-codifiable goods and transactions.[1] However, the existence of exchanges has introduced a fine-tuning mechanism that improves operational performance and simultaneously helps to value longer-term contractual, capacity and technology decisions. The vortex or center point of this new perspective is the integration of traditional forms of contracting with shorter term market-driven transactions and associated derivative instruments.

Paul Kleindorfer is Anheuser-Busch Professor of Management Science (Emeritus), University of Pennsylvania and Distinguished Research Professor, INSEAD.
[1] See Kogut and Zander (1992) for a discussion of codifiability of transactions. The essential ingredient for tradable contracts is that these be standardized, both in terms of terminology and financial terms as well as for the underlying product or service that is the focus of these contracts. Off-grade or customized products may still be codifiable, but they may cease to be suitable for broad market-based transactions if they are only used by a few companies. In this case, however, these customized products may have prices sufficiently correlated with basic tradable products of the same family to allow financial hedging. More on this subject below.

Risk Management in Commodity Markets: From Shipping to Agriculturals and Energy   Edited by Hélyette Geman
© 2008 John Wiley & Sons, Ltd

Before embarking on our review of previous results in this area, it is important to understand the typical organizational context surrounding contracting and spot market purchases. A common feature of markets supporting commodity procurement for major buyers is the following. Any particular buyer has a limited set of sellers who compete for the buyer's business in the contract market, while still having access to a larger set (often a much larger set) who compete in the shorter-term market (the spot market) and whose actions determine a competitive spot market price. Contract sellers for a particular buyer are restricted to a pre-qualified set that is able to satisfy credit and settlement requirements, assurance of supply, access to supporting logistics, and other traditional supplier management issues. These features give rise to a setting in which buyers have restricted seller bases (of perhaps 1–5 pre-qualified contract sellers) in their contract markets, while using spot markets as a second source of supply as well as a means of hedging their physical procurement and evaluating the price levels they receive in their contract purchases. The interaction between contracting, spot market purchases, and hedging is thus of interest in the optimal portfolio of contracts and sellers for a buyer, as well as providing an interdependent valuation and hedging process.

Consider the beverage industry. Aluminum is an important element of the cost structure. For major buyers like Anheuser Busch, a restricted set of sellers is used, even though the aluminum spot market price is a key benchmark for sourcing and hedging and is determined by the actions of scores of global players. Here, sourcing arrangements with main sellers are typically set according to the spot price plus processing costs, and contracts are marked to market on a daily basis. Second, there may be value-added services undertaken by these contractors to take aluminum ingots and prepare them in a more suitable fashion for can production, and again here this would be done only with specifications for these services worked out with a few sellers. Thus, the typical setup in metals is for a restricted set of contract sellers, with spot purchases and hedging used to "top up" contract purchases or hedge overall cash flows associated with aluminum procurement.

As a second example, consider the restructured electricity market, where producing Sellers (Generators) and Buyers (Load Serving Entities and Distribution Companies) can sign bilateral contracts to cover the demands of their retail and wholesale customers. These bilateral contracts may cover purchases for up to a year in advance. Alternatively, Sellers and Buyers can interact "on the day" in a spot market. How much of their respective capacity and demand Sellers and Buyers should or will contract for in the bilateral contracting market, and how much they will leave open for spot transactions, is a fundamental question examined in a growing literature on energy trading (e.g., Clewlow and Strickland, 2000; Kleindorfer and Li, 2005). The same general market structure obtains in many other markets, from cocoa and sugar, to natural gas, to logistics, to plastics and to the commodity end of semiconductor devices (see Kleindorfer and Wu (2003), Geman (2005), and other chapters in this volume for a review of applications). It is the purpose of this chapter to provide some perspective on the theory and practice that is now maturing in companies with major commodity exposures to integrate physical and financial risk management in improving both their buying performance of major inputs (through better price discovery) and the quality of their earnings (through better risk management).

The chapter proceeds as follows. The next section briefly reviews some of the background literature on optimal contracting and options theory. Section 3.3 presents a simple modeling framework and an example of short-term and long-term contracting to introduce the subject. Section 3.4 follows with a survey of recent contributions in the literature, focusing primarily on the management science and operations research literature (which has been the primary outlet for work on supply management). In the process, we review recent innovative methodological applications (from real options theory and financial engineering) in this domain to provide an integrative perspective on these methodologies. Section 3.5 points to some important open research questions that surround this area of e-Business.

3.2   A PRIMER ON PREVIOUS SUPPLY MANAGEMENT CONTRACTING LITERATURE

The literature on contracting in economics has been driven by the transactions cost framework developed by Coase (1937), Klein *et al.* (1978), and Williamson (1985), and subsequently formalized in the Principal-Agent literature (Laffont and Tirole, 1998). The basic hypothesis of this approach is that transactions with one or more Buyers will be structured so as to minimize the total production and transactions cost of these transactions, including contracting, incentive, and monitoring costs. One of the key elements of B2B markets is arguably the reduction in transactions cost associated with automating transactions and providing appropriate IT platforms to support these (Kaplan and Sawhney, 2000). These problems are usually modeled in a context in which relationship-specific investments are required for efficient contracting, and such investments become the subject of hold-up behavior (what Williamson terms "ex post opportunism") after they are made. Clearly, a well-specified ex ante contract with verifiable information, as suggested by Williamson (1985), can be an important element in reducing these incentives.

A key question addressed in the economics literature has been the efficiency of various contracting structures. A well-known result in the economics contracting literature is Allaz and Vila (1993), which examines the efficiency of pure forward contracts in an oligopoly setting but with a deterministic spot market (which is fixed and common knowledge). Assuming homogeneous Sellers and instantaneous scalability (with no capacity limitations), they provide an important benchmark on the factors that can influence the efficiency of forward markets. Allaz and Villa show that forward markets can yield inefficient outcomes because of strategic use of these markets by Sellers with market power. These results have been extended and generalized in Kamat and Oren (2002), and recently for optimal trading policies by Martínez-de-Albeniz and Simón (2007).

Of course, the basic results from financial economics provide the underlying analytical framework for derivative instruments in the contracting markets of interest. The classic papers in this area are Bachelier (1900) and Black and Scholes (1973) (see Geman 2005 for a survey of more recent advances). The essential characteristics of the financial engineering modeling in the literature on derivative instruments include: continuous time stochastic dynamics for the underlying spot price; and on-going trading opportunities among market participants for the derivatives based on standard contracts. Option instruments and valuation models allow for different degrees of flexibility with regard to execution, including fixed expiration dates (European options), flexible expiration dates (American options), and various exotic options, such as Asian options that have payoffs based on average spot performance over a given period (Merton 1990). Each of these options forms, either in markets or in contracts, has found important applications in supply risk management.

In the context of supply chain contracting, an additional distinction is required in the types of options involved, between purely financial options and those connected to physical delivery of a particular good at a particular time and place. The early discussion and literature was focused on physical delivery options to fulfill a Buyer's sourcing needs. These options would entail delivery at a particular time and place (e.g. FOB Pittsburgh). In these markets, options backed by physical delivery are central to the Buyer's problem of arranging for sufficient supply to meet the Buyer's demand. However, once a functioning spot market exists, this market can be used to define financial options on the basis of the spot price. Major Buyers would then find it in their interest not only to arrange optimal sourcing from the contract and spot markets, for physical delivery of goods, but also to use the financial options defined in the market as risk hedge instruments. Thus, in livestock or grain markets, options serve both the purpose of fulfilling sourcing requirements for Buyers, but the same markets allow price discovery through active parallel trading of options for purely financial hedging purposes. It is this mix of physical and financial instruments that characterizes well functioning and liquid spot markets. Normally, the mix of options in such markets going to physical delivery is low, perhaps on the order of 1 % of total transactions, the remaining trading being purely financial to hedge residual risk.

A key factor influencing the incentives of Sellers and the Buyer to sign contracts is the existence of imperfect market access on the day, capturing possible access inefficiencies of the spot market, including cost and quality differences between contract markets and the spot market. In addition, in supply management for commodities, different grades and specifications for commodities often require prior contracting and procurement relations. These alternative situations give rise to various forms of commodity risk management, as shown in Table 3.1.

The standard problem of commodity sourcing and hedging (CSH) for a Buyer can be stated as follows:

$$Maximize \quad E\{\Pi(Q, \tilde{D}, \tilde{P}_s)\} \qquad \text{(CSH)}$$

Table 3.1 Alternative contexts for commodity risk management of supply

Description of context	Instruments used in optimal portfolio	Examples
Cost and access differences small and only standard commodities are sourced	Bilateral contracting and financial hedge instruments are defined on a common spot market and optimized jointly	Energy Commodity metals
Cost and access differences are large and only standard commodities are sourced	Bilateral contracting used for most physical procurement, with spot market used for topping up supply, and for financial hedge instruments	Logistics services (standard air and maritime cargo) Fed-cattle (beef), hogs and lamb markets
Non-standard commodities are sourced, but their prices are highly correlated with those of standard commodities	Bilateral contracting used for all physical procurement, with financial hedge instruments, defined on correlated standard products, used as an overlay	Plastic resins and commodity chemicals

subject to:

$$G(Q, F_D, F_{P_s}) \geqslant 0 \quad \text{Physical Delivery Constraints}$$
$$H(Q, F_D, F_{P_s}) \geqslant 0 \quad \text{Value-at-Risk Constraints}$$
$$Q \in X \qquad\qquad\quad \text{Other Constraints on Available Instruments}$$

where the maximization in (CSH) is over the vector of available financial and physical instruments Q at the time of contracting, where "demand" uncertainties are represented by $\tilde{D}$ and where spot price uncertainty is represented by the random variable $\tilde{P}_s$, with respective cdf's of F_D and F_{P_s}. On the day, of course, once D and P_s are observed, instruments are executed to fulfill the physical delivery constraints and to optimize profits by executing all options that are "in the money" or needed for physical fulfillment. This problem "on the day" can sometimes be interesting, but in theory it is straightforward. The problem of setting up and solving the overall portfolio problem integrating financial and physical instruments is less straightforward and typically sufficiently complicated that simulation vehicles must be used for valuation and optimization. Various forms of the (CSH) problem have been developed for various types of markets, and the details for these differ considerably across these markets.

The VaR constraint in (CSH) is usually represented as:

$$\Pr\{\Pi(Q, \tilde{D}, \tilde{P}_s) - F \geqslant -\text{VaR}\} \geqslant \gamma$$

where $\Pi(Q, \tilde{D}, \tilde{P}_s)$ are the cash flows resulting from the vector of contracts Q, where F represents fixed capital payment obligations, and VaR is the maximal Value-at-Risk allowed for the period in question, with confidence level γ (see and Marshall and Siegel (1997) and Crouhy *et al.* (2000) for a discussion of VaR). In the case where the normality assumption is reasonable for $\Pi(Q, \tilde{D}, \tilde{P}_s)$, this standard VaR constraint translates into a simple function of the mean and standard deviation of $\Pi(Q, \tilde{D}, \tilde{P}_s)$. Finding the efficient frontier (in $E\{\Pi\}$-VaR space) is then easily solved in the standard fashion via mathematical programming or simulation optimization techniques. Multi-period VaR constraints are also discussed in Kleindorfer and Li (2005) and Geman and Ohana (2008). For more complex problems, including sophisticated models of the evolution of the spot price and various exotic options, simulation can be used to tackle a wide variety of problems that arise in practice.

3.3 A MODELING FRAMEWORK AND A SIMPLE ILLUSTRATIVE CASE[2]

To gain some intuition, let us first consider the simplest case in which a Buyer can satisfy demand D in a particular period by purchasing input using either forward contracts (from pre-qualified Sellers) at a cost of r/unit or on a spot market at a cost of P/unit. It is easiest to think of the input in the simplest Non-storable Uniform Product Model (e.g. hotel rooms of a particular type for a particular day of the year). We imagine the Buyer's decision problem at the time the choice is made on the appropriate mix of these alternative procurement arrangements (which is to say at the time the Buyer is deciding on how much

---

[2] This is a simplified example based on Wu and Kleindorfer (2005) to motivate the review to follow while still highlighting the critical determinants of the SCM contracting literature.

input to purchase under forward contracts). At this point in time, we assume that the Buyer's demand D and spot price P are both random variables with known distributions, whose actual realizations will be known at the time when spot purchases are made. We assume that product sold under forward contract is slightly better in the sense that to achieve the same yield from a spot purchase requires an additional cost of a/unit, $a > 0$, of input processed. Let us also suppose that the Buyer can sell back to the spot market at the spot price P any of the input it purchases under a forward contract that is not needed. Finally, suppose the Buyer expects production costs per unit of input processed to be b/unit and the Buyer expects to sell output produced at a wholesale price w, where we assume that $w > r$ $\geqslant \mu = E\{P\}$, so that profits can be made at the expected spot price $E\{P\}$, and the expected value of this price is no less than the current going rate for forwards. The Buyer purchases $Q \geqslant 0$ units under the forward contract and produces D units on the day, purchasing X^+ $= Max\ [D - Q, 0]$ units on the spot market and selling $X^- = Max\ [Q - D, 0]$ units purchased under the forward contract to the spot market. The Buyer's profits under this arrangement would be calculated as follows:

$$\Pi_B(Q) = (w - b)D - rQ - (P + a)(D - Q)^+ + P(Q - D)^+ \tag{3.1}$$

where $z^+ = Max\ [z, 0]$. The first term is just the gross margin per units sold in the wholesale market; the second term is the cost of the forward purchases; the third term is the cost of spot purchases (computed at the full price of $P + a$); and the final term is the revenue from excess forwards sold in the spot market. This simplifies to:

$$\Pi_B(Q) = (w - b)D - rQ - P(D - Q) - a(D - Q)^+ \tag{3.2}$$

Denoting the cdf of demand D (as estimated at the time of contracting) as $F_D(x)$ and denoting mean spot price as $\mu = E\{P\}$, a little calculus shows that this standard Newsvendor problem (see Cachon (2003)) reduces to the following rule for the optimal portfolio of marketing arrangements (i.e., the optimal mix of forward and spot purchases):

$$I: \quad Q = 0,\ X^+ = D,\ X^- = 0 \qquad if\ r \geqslant \mu + a$$

$$II: \quad Q^* > 0,\ X^+ = (D - Q^*)^+,\ X^- = (Q^* - D)^+ \qquad if\ r < \mu + a \tag{3.3}$$

$$where\ Q^*\ is\ given\ as\ F_D(Q^*) = \Pr\{D \leqslant Q^*\} = \frac{a - (r - \mu)}{a}.$$

Thus, regime I entails purchases only in the spot market, while regime II entails non-zero purchases in both the spot and forward markets. Focussing on regime II, where the expected full price of spot purchases exceeds the unit cost of the forward ($\mu + a > r$), it is easily seen that the intensity of use of spots versus forwards depends on all the cost and demand parameters, as well as on the volatility of demand (the latter through the Newsvendor rule determining Q^* as a function of the cost parameters and the cdf of the demand distribution). In this simple case of a risk-neutral Buyer, only the mean of the spot price distribution enters into the decision rule. We will see that the volatility of the spot price is also an important element of the optimal portfolio choice problem when a few additional complexities are introduced.

The above simple problem can be extended in various ways: by adding risk aversion or risk constraints (e.g. of the Value-at-Risk or VaR type, as explained in Crouhy *et al.*

(2000)); by allowing production decisions to be different than demand decisions; by modeling price sensitivity of the Buyer's demand; by incorporating economies of scale in the Buyer's production function; by introducing capacity constraints and economies of scale for potential Sellers of forward contracts; by introducing competition into both the contracting and spot markets; and by considering more complex marketing arrangements. These complexities give rise to changes in the rules for determining the optimal mix of contracting arrangements, but the basic intuition remains similar to that of the above simple problem, namely purchasing forwards allows the Buyer and Seller to avoid the risks of price and demand volatility, but entails risks of its own in terms of opportunity costs of more favorable prices in the spot market and the ability to fine tune purchases or sales at the last minute.

To introduce some of these complexities, let us now consider a slightly more general version of the above problem, which will allow us then to motivate and summarize the literature on optimal contracting for commodities. We first describe a three-period timeline for trading in the B2B exchange, either using contracts or using the spot market (see Fig. 3.1). The reader can think of this as setting up the physical and financial contracting to solve the problem (CSH) for next month's or next quarter's procurement of a particular Buyer's production needs for some specific commodity input (e.g. aluminum or electric power).

Period 0: Before the fact, at Period 0, capacity and technology choices are made by Buyers and Sellers. As we will see, these choices will be different when rational managers know that they can fine-tune demand and supply through the spot market than when such a possibility does not exist.

Period 1: At Period 1, with updated information on the distribution of spot prices, Sellers and Buyers contract with one another, using options and forwards, for delivery of some good (either storable or non-storable) at Period 2.

Period 2: Finally, at Period 2, after possibly additional information updating, options are called, forwards are executed, deliveries are made and additional sales and purchases are made in the short-term spot (or cash) market.

Between Period 1 and Period 2, there may be additional trading of options and additional, possibly continuous, updating of information on spot prices. In this brief review, to keep matters simple, we will assume a discrete-time framework with no secondary trading. Thus, we will only be concerned with the indicated decision instants Period 0, 1, and 2.

We characterize the technology of each Seller by the triple (b, β, K), where b is the Seller's short-run marginal cost of providing a unit of output, β is the per unit/per period capacity cost (assumed pre-committed prior to contracting at t_1) and K is the Seller's total

Figure 3.1   Decision timeline for Seller(s) and Buyer(s)

available capacity, assumed fixed in the short-run (i.e. at the time contracting decisions are made).[3]

There may also be differences in the cost of finishing and transporting a unit of product to market depending on whether a forward contract is used, providing ample time for the Seller to plan for the fulfillment requirements, or whether the spot is used. In addition to these "production cost" differences, there may also be additional costs for the Buyer (these are referred to as "adaptation costs", denoted by "a" in the model (1)–(3) above) if purchasing product in the spot market rather than under planned contracts. The reader might think of these as off-spec quality or yield costs that are typically higher under spot purchases than under pre-planned contract and alliance purchases.

Contracts between Sellers and Buyers can take many forms in this model, depending on the amount of quantity flexibility involved and who has decision rights over it. It is useful to begin the analysis by assuming only a single aggregate Buyer.[4] We will also consider only forwards and call options, with the call option execution being in the hands of Buyers, in order to keep matters simple. The decision variables for Sellers are the optimal contracts of the form $[r, e, L]$ to offer to the Buyer, where L is the number of units offered, r is the reservation or contract cost per unit of capacity, and e is the execution cost per unit of output. Thus, if $e = 0$, then the contract is a pure forward as units ordered will have been paid for in advance with a fixed price r; if $e>0$, the contract is an options contract. One can also think of r as the pre-paid part of a fixed forward and e as the additional part of the unit forward price paid on the day of delivery (e.g. for transportation and processing costs). We will take both r and e to be fixed, though they could themselves be state-dependent or random (for example, the execution price might be defined as the additional cost of delivery on the day, and these might not be known except stochastically until the day of delivery).

The decision variables for the Buyer are how much to contract Q at Period 1 with each Seller, and at Period 2, how much to execute from the contract (denoted q) and how much to procure from the spot market (with spot market purchases denoted by x). The (distribution of) Buyer's total demand D on the day (at Period 2) is assumed to be common knowledge. Whatever its demand D is (which may depend on price in its own final markets and on other variables), the Buyer will attempt to fill this demand from its contract(s) and from the spot market at minimum cost. For example, if the Buyer only has one contract $[r, e, Q]$, and is choosing how much of this to execute versus filling demand from the spot market, it is easy to see that the cost-minimizing fulfillment strategy is to order the following quantity from his contract:

$$q(P_s, D, Q, e) = MIN[D, Q]\psi(P_s - e) \leqslant Q \qquad (3.4)$$

---

[3] See Martinez-de-Albeniz and Simchi-Levi (2005) for an analysis of the case in which capacity decisions are made at the same time as contracting decisions, as might be the case for some leasing decisions. The results for this case are quite similar to those derived by Crew and Kleindorfer (1976) for the diverse technology pricing and capacity problem in public enterprise pricing. Intuitively, the optimal capacity/contracting choices embody tradeoffs between the volatility of future demand and the capacity and variable costs that must be committed at the time of contracting to meet this demand. The results imply that high capacity costs and low variable cost capacity should be used to meet the first slice of contract demand, that the next highest capacity costs and next lower variable cost capacity should be used to meet the next slice of contract demand, and so forth. This is similar to the outcome in terms of the optimal amounts of generating plants of different types to be installed in electric power planning to meet an uncertain demand over the long run.

[4] The assumption of a single Buyer is without loss of generality in understanding equilibrium prices and contracts, provided there is no market power by Buyers. This is so since Buyers can simply be ranked according to their Willingness-to-Pay and awarded capacity accordingly, as would happen for example under an auction mechanism or other efficient market design.

where P_s is the spot price on the day and where $\psi(z)$ is the indicator function which takes the value of 1 if its argument z is positive and 0 otherwise. This means that if $e = 0$, then $q = Min [D, Q]$ will be taken under (what is then effectively) a forward contract.

The spot market price P_s is uncertain before it is revealed in Period 2. The spot market price is assumed here to be exogenous (open, competitive) and not subject to the influence of any of the contract market participants. The distribution function of the spot price is denoted $f(p)$ with mean $\mu = E\{P_s\}$; $f(p)$ also assumed to be common knowledge.

The objective of the Buyer is to maximize expected profit by choosing among the available forward and spot contracts. The objective of the Seller is to maximize expected profit, jointly obtained from sales in both the contract market and the spot market and subject to the Seller's capacity constraint. Either Buyer or Sellers may have additional risk-based constraints on their transactions, such as those derived from a Value-at-Risk framework. We will consider these risk-related issues further below.

A key factor influencing the incentives of Sellers and the Buyer to sign contracts is the existence of imperfect market access on the day, capturing possible access inefficiencies of the spot market via a function $m(P_s)$, which is defined as the probability that the Seller can find a last-minute Buyer on the spot market when the realized spot price is P_s. This market access probability can also be thought of as the proportion of the Seller's capacity that can be typically sold at the last minute. This function will be determined by different factors in different market settings but generally may be thought of as a measure of the liquidity of the market. When quality issues are present (which we will not formally analyze here) then $m(P_s)$ might also reflect the quality risk associated with spot purchases. We will use another approach, discussed below, to represent such quality risks.

As an instance of the above framework, consider the simplest case of a single risk-neutral Seller and a single risk-neutral Buyer,[5] and we assume no adaptation cost and no contract/spot production cost differences.

The Buyer's problem at Period 1 is to determine the optimal number of options, Q to contract for with the Seller, taking into consideration the Buyer's demand at Period 2. To find Q, the Buyer solves the problem using backward induction. At Period 2, the Buyer derives its optimal demand. If only the spot or cash market were available, then the Buyer's demand function at Period 2 would be given by the normal downward sloping demand curve,[6]

$$D_s(P_s) = arg\ max\ [U(D_s) - P_s D_s] = (U')^{-1}(P_s) \tag{3.5}$$

where $U(D_s)$ represents the profit to the Buyer from producing and selling D_s units, with first derivative U' and with inverse function $(U')^{-1}$, with U assumed to be strictly concave and increasing (this basically says that the normal demand curve $D_s(p)$ at Period 2 is downward sloping). In the presence of contract procurement Q, the Buyer's actual optimal demand curve on the day is seen to be kinked, accounting for the presence of the contract

---

[5] The consequences of risk aversion are intuitive. While the equilibrium results for integrated contracting and options markets have, to my knowledge, not been worked out at this point, as the reader can anticipate, risk aversion would tend to increase reliance by the respective party on the contract market rather than being exposed to the price volatility and access risk of the spot market.

[6] We are assuming here that the Buyer's demand curve is only a function of the prevailing price. More generally, the Buyer's WTP/Profit function U would depend on the state of the world, namely on external factors such as economic conditions, the weather, etc. For details on this more general case, see Spinler et al. (2003).

fulfillment, with the solution:

$$D = MAX[D_s(P_s), Q] = MAX[(U')^{-1}(P_s), Q] \qquad (3.6)$$

At Period 1, the Buyer's problem is to contract a reservation level Q so as to maximize its expected profits from contracts and spot procurement, given spot purchase opportunities that will be available on the day. This gives rise to the following problem:

$$Maximize_{Q \geqslant 0}\ E\{U(D) - rQ - rq - P_s x\} \qquad (3.7)$$

with q as specified in (3.4) above, $x = D - q$ = spot purchases, and D given by Eq. (3.6) above.

In Eq. (3.7), the first term is Willingness-To-Pay (WTP) (or profits) at P_s, evaluated at the realized demand D; the second and the third term together are the payment for the goods delivered under the long-term contract, and the fourth term is the payment for goods x purchased in the spot market. One sees in Eq. (3.7) the nature of the general problem facing a Buyer with choices in several markets (in this case in the contract market and in the spot or cash market). The Buyer is interested in maximizing profits from sales in its own market. The Buyer can utilize a long-term marketing arrangement (in this case represented by Q) as well as a shorter-term marketing arrangement (in this case represented by x). The Buyer executes his rights to buy q units under the contract Q at some "call date" and buys on the spot or cash market remaining units needed to cover profit-maximizing demand. The Buyer must anticipate the required demand and the dynamics of this process at the time he signs contracts. In the process, the Buyer will be comparing the cost of signing a contract with the (as yet unknown) price of spot purchases. The distribution of P_s and all of the underlying cost and technology conditions determining profits $U(D)$ are assumed known to the Buyer as a part of solving the above problem (3.7).

It can be shown (e.g. Wu and Kleindorfer (2005)) that the Buyer's optimal procurement strategy is to reserve the following number of units Q under contract:

$$Q(r, e) = D_s(G^{-1}(r + G(e)) = (U')^{-1}(r + G(e)) \qquad (3.8)$$

at Period 1, where $G(p)$, called the "effective price function", is defined as

$$G(p) = E\{MIN[P_s, p]\} \qquad (3.9)$$

and where $G^{-1}(g)$ is the inverse function of $G(p)$. It is easily shown, and intuitive, that $Q(r, e)$ is decreasing in both of its arguments. We note in passing that the effective price function $G(e)$ captures the notion of the expected price that the Buyer will have to pay for an additional unit of supply if they have the option of purchasing under contract the additional unit at an execution price of e. If $e = 0$, as in the case of a pure forward contract, then $G(0) = E\{P_s\}$, the mean spot price.

At Period 2, the optimal strategy for the Buyer is rather simple: If $P_s \geqslant e$, the Buyer will exercise all its options/contracts and procure any additional needs from the spot market. Otherwise if $P_s < e$, the Buyer will forgo its contracts but procure its entire needs from the spot market. If $e = 0$, the case of a pure forward, the Buyer will always "accept" the full forward contract. [Note: Many other cases are possible, with salvage values, penalties for not accepting deliveries of forwards, buy-back arrangements, minimum take quantities, etc. Most of these turn out to be special cases of the above general framework.]

One can invert Eq. (3.9) to obtain the price the Buyer is willing to pay per unit for a contract with reservation price r and execution price e, namely:

$$r = G(U'(Q)) - G(e) \qquad (3.10)$$

Note that the conventional wisdom of $r = E\{P_s\} - e = \mu - e$ does not hold here, as the Seller can only sell a percentage of his capacity if he only wants to sell at the last minute (Period 2). If he wants to sell in the contract market in advance at Period 1, he has to sell at a price less than $\mu - e$ in order for the Buyer to be interested.

Taking the Buyer's optimal response into consideration, the Seller's problem is to maximize his expected profit (neglecting fixed capacity investment, which is assumed fixed in this model) at Period 1 by bidding a contract in the form of $[r, e]$, i.e.

$$Maximize_{(r,e) \geqslant 0} E\{r Q(r, e) + (e - b)q + (P_s - b)^+ m(P_s)(K - q))\} \qquad (3.11)$$

Subject to: $q(P_s, D, Q, e)$ as in (3.4); $Q(r, e)$ as in (3.8).

where it is assumed that non-performance penalties are sufficiently high that the Seller does not sell under contract any more output than he has (i.e. (r, e) are set so that $Q(r, e) \leqslant K$ is assumed).[7] In the Seller's profit function, the first two terms represent the Seller's revenue from the contract, the third term is the Seller's cost of supplying q units to the Buyer, and the fourth term is the Seller's profit from the spot market.

Under weak regularity assumptions, it is straightforward to show that the Seller's optimal strategy is to bid its unit production cost ($e = b$), and then setting r by maximizing its expected profit (3.11) given $e = b$. The actual solution for the optimal reservation price r depends on whether the Buyer exhausts the Seller's capacity or not. The explicit solution is as follows (assuming that there is no competition in the Seller market, i.e. only one Seller): if $Q(r, e) < K$, then $r*$ is proportional to the Seller's opportunity cost $E\{m(P_s)(P_s - b)^+\}$ of selling a unit in the spot market and inversely proportional to the Buyer's demand elasticity at the optimal reservation demand formula $Q(r, e)$ given by Eq. (3.5), i.e. if $Q(r, e) = Q(r, b) < K$, then

$$r = \frac{E\{m(P_s)(P_s - b)^+\}}{1 - 1/\eta_r(Q(r, b))}; \quad Q < K \qquad (3.12)$$

where $\eta_r(Q)$ is the elasticity of $Q(r, e)$ with respect to r (i.e., $\eta_r(Q) = [\partial Q(r, e)/\partial r][r/Q(r, e)]$). If the solution to Eq. (3.12) yields a value of r such that at $e = b$, $Q(r, e) > K$, then r should be set to take additional rents from the Buyer by charging a reservation price r just high enough to equate Q and K. From Eq. (3.9), this occurs at:

$$r = G(U'(K)) - G(b); Q = K \qquad (3.13)$$

Why do the Seller and Buyer have the incentive to use the contract market even when they are both risk neutral? Consider first the Buyer. At Period 1, the Buyer is paying an

---

[7] Models assuming that the Seller may "overbook" are also common in the literature, e.g., where a penalty is paid by the Seller for each unfulfilled but contracted unit demanded on the day.

overall price less than the average spot market price, since (it can be shown) $r + G(b)$ $= G(U'(Q)) \leqslant G(U'(0)) \leqslant \mu$. The Seller is also willing to sell this option, since he is making more profit in the contract market than in the spot market per unit of capacity as long as $r > E\{m(P_s)(P_s - b)^+\}$, which also can be shown to be his minimum requirement to participate in the options market. The Buyer is willing to buy this option as long as the combined price $r + G(b)$ is less than mean spot price μ. Thus, for risk neutral traders, the active contract market trading spread lies between $E\{m(P_s)(P_s - b)^+\} \leqslant r \leqslant G(U'(0))$ $- G(b) \leqslant \mu - G(b)$. An increase in $m(P_s)$, which may be thought of as increased spot market liquidity, effectively shrinks the trade spread, even to the extent of suppressing the contract market entirely. Indeed, in this simple model, with no adaptation or production cost differences between spot and contract market production, when $m(P_s) = 1$, the contract market disappears.

We may extend the base model to allow contract production to be cheaper than spot production, reflecting the benefits of advanced planning. Thus, assume that contract production has variable cost b_c and spot production has variable cost b_s with $b_c < b < b_s$. Then the above options trade spread stretches in both ways,

$$E\{m(P_s)(P_s - b_s)^+\} < E\{m(P_s)(P_s - b)^+\} \leqslant G(U'(0)) - G(b) \leqslant \mu - G(b) < \mu - G(b_c)$$
$$(3.14)$$

indicating a stronger incentive for both parties to contract. In particular, even when the Seller has a perfect market access with $m = 1$, he still engages in long-term contracting, as well as spot purchases, trading as long as $b_s > b_c$.

We have focussed in the above discussion only on production cost differences, but similar results would obtain if the Buyer had to pay additional adaptation costs (i.e. with an eye on (1)-(2), when $a > 0$) when procuring at the last minute from the spot market relative to contract purchases. These effects might derive from better quality control, better yield management, better planning of capacity, any other advantages deriving from the longer-term planning and partnering inherent in contract versus spot procurement. On the other side of the coin, there may be additional costs to set up and negotiate contract procurement and these would obviously work to the advantage of spot procurement.

3.4   RECENT CONTRIBUTIONS TO THE OPTIMAL CONTRACTING LITERATURE

This section summarizes research on supply chain contracting and financial hedging related to the modeling of options trading and integrating contracting via B2B exchanges.

Araman *et al.* (2001) consider a Buyer who can procure from a Seller either via a contract, an internet exchange (spot market), or a combination of both. Their contract is a pure forward (execution price $= 0$) with a penalty if the Buyer does not call the fully reserved capacity with the Seller on the day. Thus, the spot market (the exchange) is only used to fulfill the residual demand after the reserved capacity has been used fully. They show that the spot market is beneficial from the Buyer's perspective, that both contracting and the spot market are sustainable, and that a mix between these two is optimal.

Spinler *et al.* (2003) generalize the single-Seller results of Wu *et al.* (2002) to the state-dependent case, whereby the WTP functions characterizing demand for Buyers could themselves depend on the state of the world (e.g., both demand and spot price might depend on temperature). They show the optimal Wu *et al.* (2002) structure basically goes through, but the results are more complicated, where the demand for options by the Buyer depends on the correlation between Buyer demand and spot price.

Mendelson and Tunca (2007) provide an important generalization of Wu *et al.* (2002) to the case of a closed spot market, where spot market price is determined endogenously (in a single Seller context). That is, the more capacity is withheld from the contracting market for sale in the spot market, the lower the resulting spot price distribution. Within this closed spot market framework, they focus on the impact of establishing the spot market (B2B exchange), where the Seller plays the role of Stackelberg leader. They derive necessary and sufficient conditions for the existence of the exchange. They analyze the impact of the exchange on the participants as a function of information quality. A surprising result is that the introduction of the exchange ($m > 0$) does not necessarily benefit the participants. This is because the exchange contributes to price volatility and quantity uncertainty. As a result, the Seller and the Buyers can all be worse off with the exchange than without, driving participants away from the exchange (spot market) to contracting. On the other hand, when the exchange is highly liquid, volatility will not be amplified by the exchange and Buyers and the Seller will rely completely on the exchange, even to the extent of forgoing contracting altogether. The corresponding conditions in the framework of Section 3.2 are when the Seller has perfect spot market access and/or when the cost of assuring codifiability is low (i.e. m is close to *1*).

Lee and Whang (2002) consider the impact of the internet-based secondary market, where Buyers can resell and trade their excess inventory in Period 2. Under the assumption of zero transaction costs, they show that the introduction of a secondary market always improves allocative efficiency but the welfare of the supplier may or may not increase.

Peleg *et al.* (2002) consider a "roll-out" spot market, with demands and purchases occurring at both time periods and unmet demand at Period 1 carried over to Period 2. The Buyer makes purchases from his current Seller in Period 1 and inventories any excess input if Period 1 demand does not exhaust the amount ordered. If demand exceeds the amount ordered, then excess demand is backlogged going into Period 2. At the beginning of Period 2, and prior to observing Period 2 demand, the Buyer may make additional purchases for delivery "on the day" under one of three arrangements: continued sourcing from the same Seller as in Period 1 (i.e. use long-term relationship-based strategic partner); an auction on the spot market (i.e. use a short-term strategy based solely on the use of procurement auctions); and some combination of both. They show that any of these three strategies can be optimal depending on the market characteristics (e.g., price distribution of the auction good) the Buyer is facing as well as the Seller's technologies. They show, in general, that internet-based reverse auctions can be beneficial for the Buyer.

Wu and Kleindorfer (2005) capture the interaction of competing technologies with alternative market structures, which accommodate both the extent of competition (in terms of the number of Sellers) as well as the relative cost and access advantages of alternative Sellers. The essential results in Wu and Kleindorfer (2005) are the following. First, it is shown that greedy contracting is optimal for the Buyer, i.e., it follows a merit order based on the index $r_i + G(b_i)$, where (r_i, b_i) is the bid of Seller i, with r_i being Seller i's reservation price and b_i is the execution price of i's contract, where b_i is (optimally set at) Seller i's marginal cost of supply (per the results of Section 3.2 above). Second, the necessary and sufficient conditions for market equilibrium are characterized. One key condition is the "law of one price", i.e. each Seller who participates in the options market must sell the option at the same "effective price" (i.e. the same $r_i + G(b_i)$). Third, in the absence of cost advantages of contract production over spot production, the two-part tariff structure of equilibrium contracts is efficient, while (per Allaz and Vila, 1993) a pure forward contract is not. Note, however, that the lower-indexed execution-cost contracts in the Buyer's optimal contract portfolio (those with the lowest $e_i = b_i$ will almost always be executed). Indeed, if spot price P_s exceeds b_i with probability one for some Seller, then the options contract $[s_i, b_i]$ is equivalent to a pure forward with parameters $[s_i + b_i, 0]$.

It is interesting to note that options markets, if competitive, assure efficiency. Complex flexibility provisions and penalty costs (as in Li and Kouvelis, 1999; Araman *et al.*, 2001) are not required; the standard options structure with competition achieves efficiency. This contrasts starkly with the inefficiency of pure forward markets in the well-known result of Allaz and Vila (1993). The difference here is in contract design; remove the restriction that contracts must all be pure forwards ($e = 0$), and the Allaz–Vila forward-market inefficiency disappears under competition (Wu and Kleindorfer, 2005).

The Wu and Kleindorfer (2005) results have also been generalized to integrate long-term capacity decisions at Period 0 (see Wu *et al.*, 2005) with contracting and spot market decisions, where the long-term decisions are modeled in a game theoretic framework with payoff functions based on the anticipated short-run game among Sellers that will materialize via the exchange given their capacity decisions. This long-term game illustrates the nature of efficient technology mixes likely to survive in long-run equilibrium when firms with heterogeneous cost structures compete, and follows the early work of Crew and Kleindorfer (1976) on the question of efficient diverse technology choices. The model results show that, in the long run, Sellers are segmented into four disjoint groups: participation in the options market only; participation in both the options market and the spot market; participation in the spot market only; and participation in neither market (those forced out of business). Note that these results assume the standard proportional bid-tie capacity allocation rule in case of a Seller bid-tie, namely when several Sellers have the same winning bid price, their capacity is allocated to Buyers in proportion to the amount of capacity these Sellers have bid into the market. Different allocation rules can affect the existence and structure of equilibrium outcomes, as discussed in Wu and Kleindorfer (2005).

Motivated by Williamson's transactions cost framework, Levi *et al.* (2003) provide an explicit modeling of codifiability and relationship-specific investment. Their model introduces fixed (relationship-specific) costs into contracting following Kleindorfer and Knieps (1982) and brings the following insights into the literature: (1) Underlying technology cost differences drive higher relationship-based investment; (2) Lower codifiability (in the form of higher adaptation costs for non-contract procurement) results in overall demand decreases at market equilibrium, and there is a shift to more intensive use of contracts, but with fewer Suppliers in the contract market.

3.5   SOME OPEN RESEARCH QUESTIONS AND IMPLICATIONS FOR PRACTICE

Let me begin by noting some of the practical challenges facing companies and supply managers who wish to profit from the innovations in risk management described in this chapter.

Developing the requisite internal capabilities in a company for B2B operations has been the focus of thousands of papers in trade magazines and the popular press, and more recently have been the subject of deeper research. The issues include whether and under what conditions enterprise resource planning (ERP) systems have paid off (Hitt *et al.*, 2002), and the requirements to achieve fully linked or networked organizations for interacting with close supply chain partners and arm's-length market participants. Accomplishing the needed changes in IT infrastructure to support B2B contracting presents one of the significant challenges of the past decade, both in terms of innovations in corporate strategy as well as in changes and improvements in internal processes and their links to the value chain.

In addition to the general challenges of taking advantage of new B2B opportunities via the web, there are special challenges associated with integrating long-term and short-term contracting along the lines of this chapter. First and foremost, it is foreign territory for most organizations to integrate finance and supply management/operations, and this is precisely what is required in order to have the full benefit of the options approach described here. Companies wishing to do so must radically expand the traditional focus of procurement on cost, quality and dependability to include tracking of spot market conditions, valuing options in operational and hedging terms, and linking these activities to an appropriate risk management structure. Companies that have done this well have recognized the need to develop capabilities in trading, data management, and financial reporting and management. These include new skills in pricing and valuation of contracts, new approaches to managing the portfolio of sourcing options for key manufacturing inputs, and a very different approach to supplier and customer segment valuation and management. We consider two examples, electric power and the fed-cattle (beef) industry, to illustrate these points.

Electric Power An important area of application of these concepts is energy. Kleindorfer and Li (2005) present a detailed roadmap to implementation of these concepts in electric power, which we briefly summarize here. They consider the problem facing an electric power utility, the "Buyer", that may own or lease generation, and that has a trading division that can sign contracts for Power Purchase Agreements (PPAs), as well as puts, calls and forwards based on an underlying wholesale spot market. The Buyer has some retail customers that are supplied by its wholly owned distribution subsidiary, called the Disco. Retail prices are regulated, and assumed fixed over the planning horizon of the problem. The Buyer's problem is to determine an optimal set of purchasing contracts to fulfill its retail demand obligations as well as, perhaps, to engage in additional speculative trading for profit. One requirement arising from regulation is that retail customers must be served by the Disco, either from the Buyer's portfolio of owned generation, PPAs and options/forwards, or from the spot market at the prevailing wholesale price at the time the retail customers make their demand. It is generally recognized that this feature of customer demand at regulated prices, together with the weather-driven level of spot prices and the non-storability of electric power, makes electricity supply a risky business.

This type of problem gives rise to what is known as the optimal portfolio problem for electric power sourcing. The portfolio in question is characterized by different levels of time-indexed instruments (puts, calls, forwards, etc.) that might be called upon either to fulfill retail demand or simply as part of profit-oriented trading/hedging activities by the Buyer's trading division. In this framework, owned generation and certain PPAs that have been pre-committed have a fixed execution price (e.g. the marginal running cost of own generation), but may be thought of as available at a reservation price of zero. Purchased forwards, which are prepaid, fixed obligations to deliver power may be viewed as call options having a zero execution price that therefore will always be executed by the Buyer on the day. Forwards sold by the Buyer have the same characteristic, i.e. they may be viewed as options contracts with a zero execution price (that therefore will be executed on the day). With these understandings, the options framework developed here envelops all of the essential contract forms/sources of power that are typically traded or used in existing electric power markets. Details of recent advances in this area for optimal VaR-constrained portfolio design are provided in Kleindorfer and Li (2005).

The Beef (Fed-Cattle) Industry Traditional (B2B) contracting models consider a single homogenous product model where a single unit of input is processed to produce a single unit of output. In fed-cattle supply chains, where there are spot markets for beef and beef products, one unit of input (beef) is processed to produce proportional amounts of multiple-outputs (hamburger, steak, etc.). The proportional product model can be applied in several other important markets as well (pork-hog, petroleum). In Boyabatli *et al.* (2008), initial results are provided for the proportional product model on the optimal mix of long-term and short-term (spot) contracting decisions in the context of fed-cattle supply chains. The paper analyzes the effects of product market volatility, correlation and the proportion of products on the optimal decisions and performance measures of packers in their choice of the optimal portfolio of contracts (or marketing arrangements). This research points to interesting additional resources of risk, and additional roles for commodity derivatives, in proportional output product structures.

These two examples point to the open questions associated with B2B exchanges and contracting can be described under two general headings. First, are the needed model-based developments to capture the essence of the supply–demand coordination problem and the necessary options-based instruments to achieve efficiency. Second, is the continuing development of theory to understand the necessary guidelines for the structure and governance of sustainable business models for the exchanges.

Concerning model-based developments, only a few results to date have considered multiperiod (dynamic) models, which would allow consideration of inventory and trading of options in a secondary market between the time they are first signed and their maturation date. Active trading in such secondary markets is commonplace in well-developed exchanges and assures such important features as non-arbitrage conditions. Some analytic insights on dynamic models are available in the work of Goel and Gutierrez (2006) and Milner and Kouvelis (2007), but evaluation of realistic portfolios remains almost solely in the domain of simulation.

Open spot markets are markets for which the price is assumed to be independent of the actions of individual market participants, while the price in closed spot markets may depend on actions of participants. Open markets are most appropriate where large numbers of Buyers and Sellers are active. Closed markets are most appropriate where, by reasons of market power or the thinness of trading partners, only a few pre-qualified participants can appropriately trade with one another on the exchange. To date, except for the papers by Mendelson and Tunca (2007) and Martínez-de-Albeniz and Simón (2007), there has been little work on closed markets. Also, state-dependent demand analysis is represented only by a few papers (Spinler *et al.*, 2003) and Hellermann (2006), although state-dependent demand can be expected to be central to markets (like energy) in which weather plays a significant role.

The second needed area of research concerns the structure of sustainable B2B exchanges. Two factors that seem to find emerging agreement among researchers and practitioners are liquidity and codifiability of transactions. Liquidity is often discussed in terms of the scale of operations of the exchange and the ability to satisfy the demands of a sufficiently large group of Buyers and Sellers to attract continuing use. But liquidity itself is obviously driven by the value-added character of a commodities exchange. Some seem to flourish and others not, but there is not yet a good understanding of what determines when a particular type of exchange may have a long-run economic value-adding role to play.

Perhaps the most important research challenge for B2B markets is the continuing development of the integration of economics, finance and operations, just as noted by Birge (2000) and Milner and Kouvelis (2007) for risk management in general. In my view, the emerging framework presented in this chapter on the use of B2B exchanges and supporting options instruments is likely to be a central feature underlying this integration. As always, empirical validation and testing in specific sectors is the foundation of harvesting the benefits of these innovations.

3.6 REFERENCES

Allaz, B. and J.-L. Vila (1993). Cournot Competition, Forward Markets and Efficiency. *Journal of Economic Theory* **59**, 1–16.

Araman, V., J. Kleinknecht and R. Akella (2001). Seller and Procurement Risk Management in E-business: Optimal Long-term and Spot Market Mix. Working Paper, Department of Management Science and Engineering, Stanford University, Stanford, CA 94305-4026, June.

Bachelier, L. (1900). Théorie de la Spéculation. *Annales Scientifiques de l'Ecole Normale Supérieure*, 3e Serie, **17**, 21–86.

Birge, J. (2000). Option Methods for Incorporating Risk into Linear Capacity Planning Models. *Manufacturing & Service Operations Management*, **2**(1).

Black, F. and M. Scholes (1973). The Pricing of Options and Corporate Liabilities. *Journal of Political Economics* **81**, 637–654.

Boyabatli, O., P. Kleindorfer and S. Koontz (2008). Integrating Long-term and Short-term Contracting in Fed-Cattle Supply Chains. Working Paper, Singapore Management University, December.

Cachon, G. (2003). Supply Chain Coordination with Contracts. In: Graves, S. and T. de Kok (Eds), *Handbooks in Operations Research and Management Science: Supply Chain Management*. North-Holland.

Clewlow, L. and C. Strickland (2000). *Energy Derivatives: Pricing and Risk Management*. Lacima Publications, London.

Coase, R. (1937). The Nature of Firm. *Economica N.S.* **4**, 386–405.

Crew, M.A. and P.R. Kleindorfer (1976). Peak Load Pricing with a Diverse Technology. *The Bell Journal*, Spring, 207–231.

Crouhy, M., R. Mark and D. Galai (2000). *Risk Management*. McGraw-Hill Trade.

Geman, H. (2005). *Commodities and Commodity Derivatives*. John Wiley & Sons Ltd.

Geman, H. and S. Ohana (2008). Time Consistency in Managing Commodity Portfolios: A Dynamic Risk Measure Approach. Forthcoming in *Journal of Banking and Finance*.

Goel, A. and G.J. Gutierrez (2006). Integrating Commodity Markets in the Optimal Procurement Policies of a Stochastic Inventory System. Working Paper, Case Western Reserve University.

Hellermann, R. (2006). *Capacity Options for Revenue Management: Theory and Applications in the Air Cargo Industry*. Springer Verlag: Heidelberg.

Hitt, L., D.J. Wu and X. Zhou (2002). Investment in Enterprise Resource Planning: Business Impact and Productivity Measures. *Journal of Management Information Systems* **19**(1), 71–98.

Kamat, R. and S. Oren (2002). Exotic Options for Interruptible Electricity Supply Contracts. *Operations Research* **50** (5) (September–October), 835–850.

Kaplan, S. and M. Sawhney (2000). E-Hubs: The New B2B Marketplaces. *Harvard Business Review* **78**(3), May–June.

Klein, B., R.A. Crawford and A.A. Alchian (1978). Vertical Integration, Appropriable Rents, and the Competitive Contracting Process. *Journal of Law and Economics* **21** (October), 297–326.

Kleindorfer, P.R. and G. Knieps (1982). Vertical Integration and Transaction-Specific Sunk Costs. *European Economic Review* **19**, 71–87.

Kleindorfer, P.R. and L. Li (2005). Multi-Period, VaR-Constrained Portfolio Optimization in Electric Power. *The Energy Journal*, January, 1–26.

Kleindorfer, P.R. and D.J. Wu (2003). Integrating Long-term and Short-term Contracting via Business-to-Business Exchanges for Capital-Intensive Industries. *Management Science* **49**(11), 1597–1615.

Kogut, B. and U. Zander (1992). Knowledge of the Firm, Combinative Capabilities, and the Replication of Technology. *Organization Science* **3**(3), August, 383–397.

Laffont, J.J. and J. Tirole (1998) (Third printing). *A Theory of Incentives in Procurement and Regulation*. Cambridge, MA: The MIT Press.

Lee, H. and S. Whang (2002). The Impact of the Secondary Market on the Supply Chain. *Management Science* **48**(6), 719–731.

Levi, M., P.R. Kleindorfer and D.J. Wu. (2003). Codifiability, Relationship-specific Information Technology Investment, and Optimal Contracting. *J. Management Information Systems* **20**(2), 79–100.

Li, C. and P. Kouvelis (1999). Flexible and Risk-sharing Supply Contracts under Price Uncertainty. *Management Science* **45**(10), 1378–1398.

Marshall, C. and Siegel, M. (1997). Value at Risk: Implementing a Risk Measurement Standard. *The Journal of Derivatives* **4** (Spring), 91–110.

Martínez-de-Albeniz, V. and D. Simchi-Levi (2005). A Portfolio Approach to Procurement Contracts. *Production and Operations Management* **14**(1), 90–114.

Martínez-de-Albeniz, V. and J.M.V. Simón (2007). A Capacitated Commodity Trading Model with Market Power. Working Paper, IESE Business School, University of Navarra, Barcelona.

Mendelson, H. and T. Tunca (2007). Strategic Spot Trading in Supply Chains. *Management Science* **53**, 742–759.

Merton, R. (1990). *Continuous Time Finance*. Basil Blackwell.

Milner, J.M. and P. Kouvelis (2007). Inventory, Speculation and Sourcing Strategies in the Presence of Online Exchanges. *Manufacturing & Service Operations Management* **9**:3, Summer. 312–331.

Peleg, B., H. Lee and W. Hausman (2002). Short-term E-procurement Strategies vs. Long-term Contracts. *Production and Operations Management* **11**(4).

Spinler, S., A. Huchzermeier and P.R. Kleindorfer (2003). Risk Hedging via Options Contracts for Physical Delivery. *OR Spectrum* **25**(3): 379–395.

Williamson, O.E. (1985). *The Economic Institutions of Capitalism*. New York: The Free Press.

Wu, D.J., P. Kleindorfer and J.E. Zhang (2002). Optimal Bidding and Contracting Strategies for Capital-intensive Goods. *European Journal of Operational Research* **137**(3) (March), 657–676.

Wu, D.J. and P.R. Kleindorfer (2005). Competitive Options, Supply Contracting and Electronic Markets. *Management Science* **15**:3, 452–466.

Wu, D.J., P.R. Kleindorfer, Y. Sun and J. Zhang (2005). Optimal Capacity Expansion in the Presence of Capacity Options. Special issue on Electric Power Applications, *Decision Support Systems*, October.

4

The Design of New Derivative Markets

4.1 INTRODUCTION

Commodity markets are rapidly changing. The emergence of new financial centers, the deregulation of older markets, financial and technological innovations all combine to change the market landscape. Older markets apply a variety of strategies to adapt to new realities, ranging from consolidation to development of new technologies and new lines of business. This chapter illustrates the main trends in this process, their motivations and the considerations that rule the implementation of these strategies.

The economic environment spanned by financial globalization enhances opportunities for trading derivatives on commodities and financial assets. Liberalization of the economy implies market deregulation and often leads to the privatization of industries previously considered to be natural monopolies. The aim of this process is to improve economic performance. However these steps are not sufficient if competition is not ensured. Therefore market design plays a crucial role for economic growth.

The price information and the better allocation of risk allowed by commodity markets may contribute to reduce uncertainty firms face, but these benefits may be negated by uncompetitive market structures. Atomistic markets with full information disclosure are the most competitive. Perfect competition, however, destroys profitability, threatening the long term survival of the market. Therefore market design must strike a balance between competitiveness and profitability, with the aim of maximizing long term value.

If new markets achieve competitiveness with existing markets, investors develop a keen interest in contracts matching their needs. New markets may arise to exploit these opportunities, though often economies of scale or scope may funnel growth towards existing markets. Growing markets, however, may attain an excessive concentration of risk, leading them to crises and loss of reputation or to very onerous capital requirements. Therefore the choice of venue for new markets implies also a tradeoff between profitability and risk.

Until recently it appeared that the future belonged to over-the-counter (OTC) markets, where large institutions trade among themselves with no intermediaries. However, the lack of transparency of OTC markets has been a major determinant of the 2007 crisis of credit markets (Pulliam and Ng, 2008). Open outcry exchanges may recover some of their appeal as a result of this crisis. They may be more expensive, but they offer better opportunities for

The Swiss Finance Institute and The University of Lugano
Author contact details: baroneg@lu.unisi.ch

Risk Management in Commodity Markets: From Shipping to Agriculturals and Energy   Edited by Hélyette Geman
© 2008 John Wiley & Sons, Ltd

price discovery and contract enforcement. However, as the ineffective warnings of Eurex to Société Générale in November 2007 show, exchanges' advantages over OTC markets may be diluted if exchanges process only part of the trading volume and members do not have an accurate picture of their global positions (Gauthier-Villars and Mollenkamp, 2008).

4.2   DETERMINANTS OF SUCCESS OF NEW DERIVATIVE MARKETS

Derivative markets augment trading opportunities offered by spot markets. The interest they generate depends on investors' perception that their welfare is enhanced by them. A necessary condition for that to occur is the perception that prices convey useful information, not subject to manipulation. This condition is hard to meet in markets dominated by one large player, as is often the case in the utility sector, or in markets dealing with non-standardized goods, such as artworks.

To limit opportunities for manipulation, occasionally restrictions on short sales are mandated. Restrictions on short sales curb interest not only because of the reduction in trading opportunities they imply, but also because the adjustment of price to new information becomes less efficient. Rather than leading to a better allocation of risk, derivative markets may then become sources of additional risk. Of course, allowing short sales requires appropriate regulation in order to preserve market integrity.

If the basic conditions outlined above are met, success depends on the market's ability to offer competitive pricing to its users. To illustrate this, assume for simplicity a derivative exchange with n potential users of equal size. Transactions among users are uniformly distributed. Then revenues typically are a quadratic function of the fraction of potential users who are active in the exchange, n, because transactions with counterparties who are not members take place outside the exchange. Therefore, as an example, a participation rate of 30 % translates into a probability of 9 % (30 % $\times$ 30 %) that a transaction can be completed through our exchange. Therefore we may write revenue R as a function of potential revenue a

$$R = an^2 \tag{4.1}$$

Exchange costs include processing costs and the expected cost of default, which is possibly insured at a fair premium. Processing cost, P, may be modeled as an affine function of volume, because it is partially fixed:

$$P(V) = p + bn^2 \tag{4.2}$$

The cost of default insurance is the present value of expected loss because of defaults. That includes also the exchange's charter value, F, if loss severity forces termination. Default cost, DC, minimization is reached at the capital level C^* such that the following function is minimized:

$$DC = E(L)[1 - g(C^*)] + Fg(C^*) \tag{4.3}$$

where $E(L)$ and $g(C^*)$ are respectively the expected loss due to members' insolvency and the exchange's probability of default per unit of time given the capital level C^*. The three equations above describe the economics of market operations. Operating profits, OP, are given by

$$OP = R - P - DC \tag{4.4}$$

Assuming a constant initial investment, maximizing value requires choosing the pricing policy a, in equation (4.1), that maximizes operating value over time.

4.3   PRICE DISCOVERY

Processing transactions through exchanges allows for price information to be made available to investors. Transparency in price dissemination allows investors to make correct market valuations of their positions. As a result of transparency, large surprises become less frequent and margining systems work more smoothly. However, transparency may impede the trading of very large positions, especially by informed traders. This problem in commodity markets is more acute than in the stock market, because physical constraints make the price of many commodities very sensitive to quantity. Therefore it is necessary to limit disclosure of traders' positions.

A recent empirical study by Simaan and Wu (2007) suggests that the International Securities Exchange system of competitive market makers, providing consolidated anonymous quotes, offers better price discovery than the more traditional systems of other option markets, based on modified open outcry or a single market maker. The increasing market share of ISE supports the success of its system. Other multiple dealer markets, such as the International Commodity Exchange, do not consolidate quotes and offer cleared as well as OTC contracts.

Liquidity can be measured directly by bid-ask spreads if trades occur at those prices. If trades occur at prices different from the posted quotes, it is possible to infer liquidity from the decomposition of the variance of transaction prices (Easly and O'Hara, 2003, Hasbrouk, 1995, 2003).

More liquid markets attract most trades, reinforcing their dominance. In any case liquidity varies over time, posing a potential threat to market viability. Liquidity risk becomes a major concern if the market is dominated by a few large traders, especially if sensitive inventory information leaks out. This was the case of the tin cartel (Hillman, 1988, Mitchell, 2005), where attempts to regulate market supply ran into unmanageable inventory financing cost.

Some exchanges attempt to limit liquidity risk by keeping the right to liquidate existing positions at a price set by the exchange. However, this is a device that may be employed only exceptionally without harming the credibility of the exchange. Lumpy trading underscores the existence of liquidity problems, with individual traders being able to affect prices. Violent price changes may then occur whenever traders are forced to change strategy. Lack of independence of subsequent transaction price changes indicates that liquidity is being drained (Khandani and Lo, 2007). Sudden regime switching then becomes more likely.

A traditional way to control this problem was to have different position limits for hedgers, who were likely to hold their position to maturity, and other traders. The widespread use of

OTC contracts with financial intermediaries by many traders has made this remedy obsolete. In fact financial intermediaries trade as hedgers independently of the original motivation of their clients. The increased riskiness stemming from insufficient price discovery limits liquidity and investment. In some electricity markets curbs on short sales are also seen as a mitigating device. That excludes some bearish investors from the price formation process. As a consequence, the resulting price is upward biased.

4.4   TRADING, CLEARING, AND MARGINING

To allow for trading to proceed speedily it is necessary to disentangle information about counterparty risk from the commodity market. This target is usually achieved by setting a clearing corporation to act as central counterparty to all the members. This legal device ensures that traders are not concerned with the default risk of the other side. Also settlement is then simpler, because the gains or losses for each clearing member can be consolidated in one account. Often, however, each clearing member is required to keep its proprietary account separate from its customers' consolidated account. This way the risks of clearing and non-clearing members are more transparent, improving market integrity.

Clearing corporations can be exchanged-owned or independent. The former solution is more common in derivative markets. It is increasingly coming under attack, because OTC networks find it difficult to shift liquidity from exchange-owned clearing platforms. Independent clearing houses that offer equal access would be ideal from the perspective of new networks. Such platforms are common in the equity industry. Their limited diffusion in derivative markets may be due to the protracted commitments that clearing contracts marked to market implies. Nevertheless, competition authorities are encouraging the separation of trading and clearing.

To cover usual daily changes in portfolio values, members are required to post margins with the clearing corporation. If the posted margin is not sufficient, the clearing house assumes the residual counterparty risk. In fact, although intraday margin calls are possible, the time lag of payment systems blunts their effectiveness. An often unnoticed shortcoming of the separation of proprietary and customer trades in only two accounts is that all the customers of one clearing member are mingled from the perspective of the clearing corporation. In case some of them and the clearing member default at the same time, the portfolios of the other non-clearing members are subject to unprotected losses. To mitigate this risk, margin calculations often are not only on net positions, but include also the total of long plus short positions.

At first glance the technology of margin computations appears obsolete. Typically, margin is computed for each contract separately, on the basis of recent daily price variations. For complex securities, such as options, conventional shocks to market variables are considered. This is the approach of the Chicago Board of Trade's SPAN. A drawback of this approach is that only limited margin offsets are available for related positions, such as a spread or a futures and a put. No attention is paid to aggregate portfolio risk.

The apparent neglect of margining systems for modern portfolio theory cannot be explained just with tradition. Perhaps it is explainable by the notion that allowing for risk reductions due to diversification in portfolio margining would benefit the largest clearing members most. Their large positions, however, are the most subject to liquidity risk. Therefore traditional margining may be seen as a heuristic method to deal with this risk.

The fact that margining is not a cost, except for the spread on interest rates members face, may explain the limited appeal of portfolio margining to date. A description of recent developments can be found in Hintze (2007). In spite of its slow start, competitive pressures between exchanges, which are also subject to increasing competition from OTC networks, suggests that portfolio margining will become more common among clearing members. Of course, in the light of the considerations above, it could be applied to non-clearing members only if their portfolios were not mingled.

4.5 MARKET INTEGRITY

Margins are designed to cover daily fluctuations. They are generally inadequate to cover extreme events. Therefore there is a residual risk, to be absorbed by counterparties in OTC trading or by the clearing corporation in organized exchanges. The clearing corporation needs additional capital resources to absorb this risk, from members or third parties. The low probability usually associated with extreme events discourages the permanent allocation of costly risk capital to cover them. Therefore insurance may become an attractive option. However insurance contracts may lack transparency. Moreover, risk may be difficult to insure if its nature is systemic. Though a wider net of capital providers can reduce the likelihood of failure, only public authorities can then fully ensure market integrity, especially if the timely provision of liquidity is crucial. Some exchanges, such as Euronext, address the need for immediacy in the provision of liquidity by having a bank subsidiary.

The recourse to third party capital, whether public or private, engenders moral hazard problems. In the allocation of losses between members and other parties it is necessary to balance the need to control moral hazard with the ability of the exchange to operate effectively after extreme events. That ability is compromised if the exchange's capital is severely impaired. A viable solution rests on loss sharing rules between members and outside investors.

Moral hazard also plays a role in clearing across markets. New memberships and risk allocation in cross-clearing become exceedingly cumbersome. For these reasons cross-clearing is not becoming more popular. Outright exchange mergers, as in the case of CBOT-CME, or joint exchange ownership, as in the case of the London Stock Exchange with Borsa Italiana, are often preferred.

Market integrity requires that sufficient capital resources be available. Scenario analysis allows for the quantification of capital requirements. As a consequence the quality of scenario analysis impacts directly on market survival. The design of scenarios can be based on historical experience, possibly augmented by statistical models through bootstrapping or expert knowledge. Barone-Adesi et al. (1999, 2002) propose to improve the reliability of bootstrapping through a statistical filter reflecting changing market conditions.

Expert knowledge is the only approach available for new products for which no data are available. The usefulness of expert knowledge, however, becomes questionable when dealing with complex payoffs, because the identification of the most critical scenarios is then non-trivial. That is a serious problem also in the approach based on extreme value theory (Embrechts and Kluppelberg, 1997), because it does not have immediate multivariate generalizations. In any case, there is no way to validate the correspondence of the modeling of the extreme tails of joint distributions of relevant random variables with future market outcomes. Even backtesting is then not applicable, because very few events occur in the relevant range.

Generally, statistical scenario generation, supplemented by stress testing on the basis of expert knowledge, is then preferable. Although this approach cannot provide accurate estimates of loss probability at extreme levels, it allows for the complete modeling of loss distribution and for validation at lower levels. At extreme levels, the fact that major players have incurred large losses may itself become a source of market uncertainty, drying up liquidity and preventing market recovery.

4.6 MARKET RECOVERY

Disaster recovery plans need to be in place to support market integrity after extreme events. Seizure and neutralization of defaulted portfolios need to be quickly feasible to prevent loss increase. Necessary operational and legal arrangements include the designation of members who will be assigned to liquidate defaulted portfolios and the legal framework that makes operational arrangements possible. If market liquidity does not allow immediate liquidation, hedging may buy the necessary time. In either case it is important to monitor portfolio risk during the liquidation process and follow trading strategies that keep risk under control.

Often it is assumed erroneously that it is sufficient to withhold information from the marketplace to liquidate unwanted positions. If these positions are very large, the trading pattern of a hasty liquidation is sufficient to drain market liquidity and multiply losses. Société Générale experienced this effect while liquidating its positions on 21 January 2008. It is reported that its loss of 2 billion Euro on European equities mushroomed to 5 billion Euro in one day.

A requirement for a correct liquidation is not to cause a panic by dumping a large amount of securities. If the position cannot be held and cannot be hedged elsewhere, it is preferable to negotiate its sale privately, as Amaranth did. However, that is also very costly. Amaranth's several attempts to unload its position were harmed by constraints on its assets, held as collateral by a creditor. A secondary distribution with several days of forewarning is certainly a better choice if the timing of liquidation is not binding.

A further issue concerns the legal enforcement of claims on margin or collateral. Other creditors may have claims on the same assets. Different jurisdictions may apply different priority rules or question the validity of existing contracts. If the market value of collateral changes, it may become insufficient. This risk is greater if collateral seizure requires more time. Haircuts on collateral value should reflect collateral risk.

4.7 MARKET OVERSIGHT

Trading rules need to provide a clear and equitable trading field to ensure continuing investor interest. Reliable and timely enforcement is necessary to discourage market manipulation. Judicial systems typically do not reach final results with the necessary speed. Therefore market oversight is the realm of special public or exchange authorities. Although the power balance rests with public authorities in civil law countries, common law privileges self-regulation. This solution allows for more specialized knowledge and more supple reactions to unexpected events. However, the discretional power that self-regulation implies should be applied with moderation. Otherwise market authorities risk appearing capricious or corrupt. Not surprisingly, historical heritage plays a major role in the choice of different jurisdictions' regulatory systems. While more experienced jurisdictions prefer to rely on a less rigid framework, to be able to adjust to unexpected events, newcomers attempt to codify behavior extensively, often with unwanted consequences and mixed results.

An interesting recent case of regulatory uncertainty concerns the market for credit default swaps (CDS). CDS are not recognized as securities. Therefore they are exempt from security regulation. Although they provide a type of protection that may be regarded as insurance, they are not subject to insurance regulation either. From a legal perspective they are simply private contracts, wagers between private parties. The usual private contract law applies. Perhaps some jurisdiction may even decide to apply antigambling rules and void CDS.

It is paradoxical that a market trading notional contracts for over 10 trillion dollars is so largely unregulated. On one side its mere existence calls into question the need for regulation. Bank regulation was in fact originally motivated by the need to protect deposits from liquidity and credit risk, that are very much at the heart of the CDS market. On the other side, recent solvency problems at a number of bond insurers highlights the danger of writing financial contracts with opaque counterparties. It is remarkable that the most regulated institutions in the world, international banks, are significantly exposed to unregulated counterparties they cannot monitor effectively. In some cases, banks have managed this risk by buying CDS on their CDS counterparties, to protect themselves from the risk of defaulting counterparties. This layered protection, however, has increased the uncertainty about the allocation of the overall exposure. The collapse of liquidity in the interbank market has been largely due to this uncertainty.

4.8   CASE STUDIES

Contract design plays a major role in ensuring success of new markets. A complete review of these markets is beyond the scope of our survey. In this section we will just review briefly some characteristics of contractual design that have experienced different degrees of market success.

Many countries have developed successful electricity markets, usually by ensuring that producers have equal access to the distribution grid. Markets that have linked grid fees to distance, as in Germany, or to the purchase of transmission rights, as in California, have experienced higher prices or more turbulence. In fact timely grid access rights are fundamental for electricity, because it cannot be efficiently stored.

Weather derivatives are also written on a commodity that cannot be stored. Though temperature derivatives enjoy some success, because of their direct link to energy costs, rainfall contracts have been unsuccessful, because the economic effects of rainfall depend mostly on its distribution. Moreover they are not linear at the extremes. Recently derivatives on the level of the water table have been proposed as alternative to rainfall contracts (I am in debt to A. Agarwal for this information), because they convey more useful information about floods or droughts. Their success cannot be assessed yet.

A market that quickly collapsed, in spite of careful planning, is bandwidth. Technological requirements for data transmission in fact have rapidly changed, to the point where bandwidth is no longer a scarce resource for many applications. Contract prices have therefore dropped close to zero.

Pollution permits in Europe have so far experienced a similar pattern. Governments' desire not to drive out heavy polluters has led to a system under which free allowances are given to firms on the basis of past pollution records. In theory, these allowances are set to generous levels initially, later reduced to give an economic incentive to pollution reduction. In fact, shortfalls should be bought at market price from other firms, or compensated by "green" investments. In reality, industry lobbying and shifting industry patterns have kept pollution permits as "free goods" to date.

Derivatives on property and casualty insurance contracts have also found little interest in the marketplace. The main reason is that it is not only hard for investors to assess heterogeneous risks, but also claims are often settled long after the maturity of traded derivatives. Derivatives on life insurance have more success, because events are more easily defined and their occurrence is easily timed.

Another market that suffers because of the heterogeneity of underlying contracts is real estate. Though price indices that overcome heterogeneity are becoming more available, the limited liquidity of the underlying contracts is still a challenge.

The volatility of financial markets is at the base of several derivatives traded in exchanges and OTC. Though volatility and other parameters of financial securities expand the set of available investments, liquidity in their markets is slow to develop. Most investors still prefer to monitor their portfolio's exposure to volatility rather than engage into volatility trading. Uncertainty about the behavior of basis risk and high market premiums are probably the reasons for their choice.

4.9 CONCLUSION

The numerous changes in market organization witnessed recently point to a continuing search for viable compromises between the numerous features influencing market success. The review of the main economic, legal and technological issues underpinning market design points to an evolution of older markets in search of economies of scale and scope to compete with newcomers. Consolidation and new business development are the two trends of this evolutionary process.

The competitive forces that fuel exchange growth may lead to excessive concentration of risk. That may make exchanges vulnerable to systemic events. Excessive regulatory rigidity may limit the ability of members to react to unusual market conditions, increasing danger. Although discretional market oversight is preferable, it carries its own risks of arbitrary and corrupt practices.

The rise of global financial institutions, able to trade with each other without exchange intermediation, appeared until recently destined to doom traditional organized exchanges. The current credit crisis underlines the advantages of traditional exchanges in terms of price discovery, transparency and market oversight. These benefits may be worth the additional cost of intermediation.

4.10 REFERENCES

Barone-Adesi, G., K. Giannopoulos and L. Vosper (1999). VaR without Correlations for Portfolios of Derivative Securities. *Journal of Futures Markets* 583–602.
Barone-Adesi, G., K. Giannopoulos and L. Vosper (2002). Backtesting Derivative Portfolios with Filtered Historical Simulation (FHS). *European Financial Management,* 31–58.
Easly, D. and M. O'Hara (2003). Time and the Process of Security Price Adjustment. *Journal of Finance* **58**, 577–605.

Embrechts, P. and C. Kluppelberg (1997). *Modelling Extreme Events for Insurance and Finance*. Springer.

Gauthier-Villars, D. and C. Mollenkamp (2008). How to Lose 7.2 Billion: A Trader's Tale. *The Wall Street Journal*, February 4, 2008.

Hasbrouck, J. (1995). One Security, Many Markets: Determining Contributions to Price Discovery, *Journal of Finance* **50**, 1175–1199.

Hasbrouck, J. (2003). Intraday Price Formation in US Equity Index Markets. *Journal of Finance* **58**, 2375–2399.

Hillman, J. (1988). Malaya and the International Tin Cartel. *Modern Asian Studies* **22**, 237–261.

Hintze, J. (2007). Portfolio Margining Approval Issued. *Securities Industry News*, 4 May 2007.

Khandani, A.E. and A.W. Lo (2007). *What Happened to Quants in August 2007?* Manuscript, MIT.

Mitchell, W.J. (2005). The Crushed Tin Cartel. *Time*, 18 April 2005.

Pulliam, Susan and Serena Ng, (2008). Wall Street Next Hole. *The Wall Street Journal*, 18 January 2008.

Simaan Y.E. and L. Wu (2007). Price Discovery in the US Stock Option Market. *The Journal of Derivatives* **15**:2, 20–38.

5

Risk Premia of Electricity Futures: A Dynamic Equilibrium Model

Wolfgang Bühler and Jens Müller-Merbach

5.1 INTRODUCTION

Electricity futures prices generally contain risk premia or discounts on the expected spot price. As electricity is not storable, those premia do not indicate market inefficiencies due to lacking arbitrage activity, but rather reflect rational behavior of risk averse investors.

Accordingly, the explanation of electricity futures prices can be split into two problems. The first one is to determine the expected spot price for the delivery period of an electricity forward. This problem is mainly an econometric challenge. The second is to model the term structure of the risk premium which is more interesting from an economic point of view for three reasons.

First, electricity is a homogenous, exchange-traded commodity that is virtually not substitutable at short notice. Premia in futures prices are therefore not diluted by market frictions or interdependencies to related markets, but primarily reflect the market members' taste for risk. Second, knowledge of the term structure of risk premia helps an individual firm to find the optimal timing of hedging. Third, exploiting the term structure of risk premia is an interesting area for speculative traders as specialized hedge funds, which are increasingly active in electricity and other energy markets.

The literature on spot and futures markets for electricity can be classified into three groups, econometric models, reduced-form models, and equilibrium models. They strongly differ in their ability to derive theoretical predictions on the sign and the term structure properties of risk premia in futures prices.

Econometric models identify major factors that explain the observed behavior of spot prices, especially mean reversion, high volatility, right skewness, price spikes, and seasonality (Fleten and Lemming (2003), de Jong (2005), Johnsen (2001), Salerian *et al.* (2000), Huisman and Mahieu (2001)). These approaches are useful to determine one part of the risk premia, the expected spot prices.

Reduced-form models have to specify exogenously the market price of electricity risk as electricity is not storable. By a no-arbitrage argument they derive the term structure of futures prices and risk premia as a function of the state variables, their dynamics, and

Wolfgang Bühler: Chair of Finance, University of Mannheim, D-68131 Mannheim, Germany, w.buehler@uni-mannheim.de.
Jens Müller-Merbach: BHF-Bank Aktiengesellschaft, D-60311 Frankfurt, J.Mueller-Merbach@gmx.de.

Risk Management in Commodity Markets: From Shipping to Agriculturals and Energy   Edited by Hélyette Geman

the market price of risk (Pilipović (1997), Kellerhals (2001), Geman and Vasicek (2001), Koekebakker and Ollmar (2005), Audet *et al.* (2004), Lucia and Schwartz (2002), Villaplana (2003), Geman and Roncoroni (2006), Hinz and Weber (2005)). The risk premia are derived by assumptions on the exogenous market price of risk. Geman and Vasicek find in their empirical investigation that risk premia will in general be positive at the short end and explain this finding by the excess demand for hedging against price spikes in the spot market.

Our model belongs to the third class that focusses on the production and demand structure of electricity. Spot prices, futures prices, and risk premia are derived endogenously. A fundamental dynamic model of this type was published by Routledge *et al.* (2001), which is, however, difficult to test empirically. Bessembinder and Lemmon (2002) developed a mean-variance based one-factor model with risk-averse electricity producers and retailers which trade futures to reduce their risk exposure. They verify the predictions of their model empirically. By the static design of their approach these tests are restricted to one-period risk premia. Benth *et al.* (2007) propose a continuous-time equilibrium for risk-averse producers and retailers who incorporate time-dependent market power. They argue that producers are committed to long-term investments and are thus willing to grant discounts for longer maturities in order to reduce variability in their profits, but for shorter maturities consumers have a larger incentive to hedge and are thus willing to pay a positive premium on the expected spot price.

Our contribution to the literature is twofold. On the theoretical side we extend the model by Bessembinder and Lemmon (2002) to a dynamic equilibrium model. This generalization allows us to derive an endogenous term structure of electricity futures prices and the incorporated risk premia. From an extensive comparative static analysis we derive predictions on the sign of risk premia and the shape of their term structure.

On the empirical side we test some of the predictions. Following Longstaff and Wang (2004) we estimate the unobservable risk premia as differences between futures prices at a certain date before maturity and the average of the observed spot prices during the delivery period. In our empirical analysis we use data from the Scandinavian exchange Nord Pool, which is one of the oldest electricity exchanges in Europe. Our sample comprises almost eight years of prices and includes periods of rather calm markets as well as the winter of 2002–03 when extreme weather conditions resulted in high volatilities at Nord Pool.

Our main findings are that our one-factor equilibrium model is flexible enough to generate monotonically increasing, decreasing, and all kinds of hump-shaped term structures of risk premia. It predicts that the term structure becomes flat for long maturities of futures contracts. The empirical study shows that the predictions of our model are fulfilled to a large extent: If the current demand for electricity is equal to the average demand the risk premia are on average positive, monotonously increasing for maturities up to eight weeks and becoming flat for longer maturities.

Our paper is organized as follows. In Section 5.2, we shortly review the applied dynamic equilibrium model. Section 5.3 presents the comparative statics. The empirical analysis based on Nord Pool data is given in Section 5.4. Section 5.5 concludes.

5.2 THE DYNAMIC EQUILIBRIUM MODEL

In this section we develop a multi-period extension of the static model by Bessembinder and Lemmon (2002). It has several degrees of freedom that we specify in Section 5.3 when providing comparative statics.

The market structure is characterized by competitive, risk-averse producers G and retailers R of electricity. Both groups are aggregated to representative agents. We model their preference function by a mean-variance approach on terminal wealth $\tilde{W}_\Theta$ at some future date Θ. At date t, they maximize the objective function

$$E_t\{\tilde{W}_\Theta^A\} - \tfrac{1}{2}\lambda^A \text{Var}_t\{\tilde{W}_\Theta^A\}, \quad A \in \{G, R\}, \tag{5.1}$$

where λ^G and λ^R are related to the risk aversion of the producers and the retailers, respectively. The terminal wealth is determined by the cash flows that the representative agents receive from either producing or retailing electricity, as well as from their trading activities. Both agents must trade in the spot market to satisfy the exogenous total end-user demand $\tilde{D}_t$ at each date t. As electricity is not storable we assume that the production volume is equal to the demand. Both agents may trade electricity futures with different maturities to increase their risk-adjusted terminal wealth (Eq. (5.1)).

If the producer does not use futures contracts he receives the cash flow

$$C_t'(\tilde{D}_t)\tilde{D}_t - C_t(\tilde{D}_t) \tag{5.2}$$

at the end of the interval t, $t = 1, \ldots, \Theta$. $C_t(D)$ denotes the variable production cost as a (possibly time-varying) function of the produced volume of electricity, D, and $C_t'(D)$ denotes the marginal cost function. In a competitive equilibrium marginal costs equal the spot price. We assume that C_t' is continuous and strictly increasing in the production volume.

The retailer receives the cash flow

$$p\tilde{D}_t - C_t'(\tilde{D}_t)\tilde{D}_t. \tag{5.3}$$

p represents the fixed end-user price per unit of electricity which is assumed to be independent of the consumed quantity of electricity.

By trading futures, both representative agents can reduce their risks by adding compounded cash flows to their final wealth from the marking-to-market. Solving Eq. (5.1) determines the futures prices in equilibrium. As discussed in Basak and Chabakauri (2007), two solution concepts are available. The global solution is not time-consistent and its implementation needs a commitment device. We consider the time-consistent solution based on the dynamic programming approach. In equilibrium we obtain the following futures prices at time t with maturity date T:

$$F_{t,T} = E_t\{\tilde{F}_{t+1,T}\} - \xi \sum_{\theta=t+1}^{\Theta} e^{r(\Theta-\theta)}\text{Cov}_t\{p\tilde{D}_\theta - C_\theta(\tilde{D}_\theta); \tilde{F}_{t+1,T}\}, \quad t < T \le \Theta. \tag{5.4}$$

In Eq. (5.4) $\xi = \frac{\lambda^R\lambda^G}{\lambda^R+\lambda^G}$ denotes the combined risk aversion factor and r the constant interest rate. In the last period before maturity, Eq. (5.4) can be written as

$$F_{T-1,T} = E_{T-1}\{\tilde{F}_{T,T}\} - \xi \sum_{\theta=T-1}^{\Theta} e^{r(\Theta-\theta)}\text{Cov}_{T-1}\{p\tilde{D}_\theta - C_\theta(\tilde{D}_\theta); C_T'(\tilde{D}_T)\}, \quad t < T \le \Theta$$

$$\tag{5.5}$$

where $F_{T,T} = C_T'(D_T)$ is the final settlement price and equal to the spot price P_T.

The equilibrium futures price in Eq. (5.4) is equal to the expected next period's futures price or spot price, respectively, minus a risk premium. This risk premium is the sum of the covariances between future cash flows and the next period's futures or spot price. The term $p\tilde{D}(\theta) - C_\theta(\tilde{D}_\theta)$ denotes the aggregate net cash flow that the whole electricity sector receives in the economy. The representative retailer receives $p\tilde{D}_t$ and the producer has to pay $C_t(\tilde{D}_t)$ for producing during the time interval $[t, t + 1)$. The spot and the futures market allocate the aggregate cash flow and the cash flow risk between the producer and the retailer.

5.3 COMPARATIVE STATICS

Two factors in the equilibrium model are yet to be specified: The process of the state variable, i.e. the end-user demand D_t, and the cost structure.

We assume that the stochastic demand process $\tilde{D}_t$ is the sum of a deterministic component $\overline{D}_t$ and a stochastic component $\tilde{S}_t$. $\overline{D}_t$ reflects the characteristic seasonal patterns:

$$\tilde{D}_t = \overline{D}_t + \tilde{S}_t. \tag{5.6}$$

The stochastic component $\tilde{S}_t$ is modeled as a first-order autoregressive process:

$$\tilde{S}_t = \rho\tilde{S}_{t-1} + \sigma\tilde{\varepsilon}_t, \quad \tilde{\varepsilon}_t \sim \mathcal{N}(0, 1) \text{ i. i. d.} \tag{5.7}$$

This choice is motivated by two reasons: First, our objective is to use a rather simple process in order to not dilute the effects of the equilibrium model by those from a (principally admissible) more sophisticated demand process. Second, the AR(1) model in Eq. (5.7) corresponds to one-factor mean-reversion models as, e.g., in Lucia and Schwartz (2002) and therefore allows a direct comparison with a one-factor reduced form model. As we want to avoid negative demands we cut off the normal distribution appropriately.[1]

To avoid time dependencies that are a result of the seasonal structure of $\overline{D}_t$ we assume for the comparative static analysis that $\overline{D}_t$ is time-invariant. The value of $\overline{D}_t = \overline{D} = 40$ GWh corresponds to the average Scandinavian electricity demand during our sample period.

In our basic setup, we set $\rho = 0.6$, $\sigma = 4$ GWh, and the retailer's rate p to 30 Euro/MWh. The marginal cost function is given by

$$C'(D) = dD^3/\overline{D}^3 \tag{5.8}$$

with $d = 30$. This parameter setting induces a spot price of 30 Euro/MWh for the average demand $\overline{D}$. The third order ensures that spot prices exhibit a strong volatility and is also chosen by Bessembinder and Lemmon (2002) in their analysis. This price level approximately corresponds to mean prices at Nord Pool during the two-year period from 2002 until 2003. Figure 5.1 shows the right-skewed distribution of the spot price $C'(\tilde{D}_t)$ for the symmetrically distributed demand.

Figure 5.2 presents the one-period cash-flows depending on the demand for the producer and the retailer. They exhibit asymmetric risk exposures. The producer's loss is almost

---

[1] Note that the cut-off of the lower tail introduces an intertemporal dependency between $\tilde{\varepsilon}_t$ and $\tilde{\varepsilon}_{t+1}$. However, with appropriate values of ρ and σ, this dependency is negligibly small in comparison to the autocorrelation introduced by ρ.

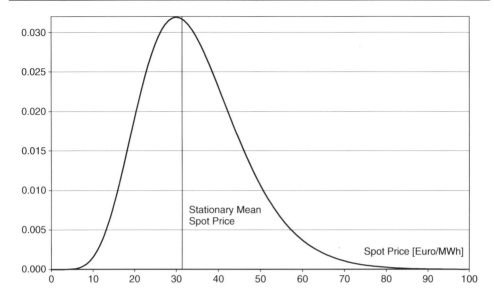

Figure 5.1 The stationary right-skewed probability density of the spot price at a current demand of $\overline{D} = 40$ GWh. The median is 30.00 Euro/MWh, the mean is 31.41 Euro/MWh with a standard deviation of 11.60 Euro/MWh

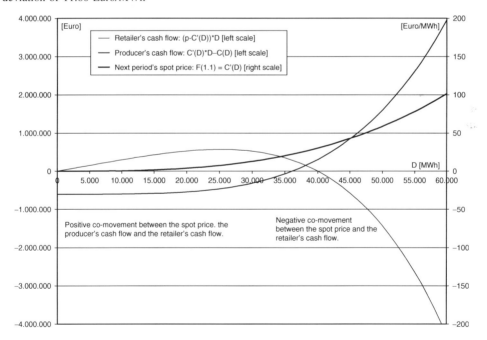

Figure 5.2 Example of the producer's and the retailer's unhedged cash flows depending on the exogenous aggregate demand. The marginal cost function is given by $C'(D) = 30 \cdot D^3/\overline{D}^3$, where $\overline{D} = 40$ GWh is the unconditionally expected demand. The retailer's rate p is set to 30 Euro/MWh. The retailer breaks even when the realized demand hits the unconditional expected demand $\overline{D}$. For demand levels below 25 GWh, the retailer's cash flow shows slightly positive co-movement with the spot price

constant and bounded for low demand levels, whereas his profit is unbounded in D. The retailer can achieve a maximum profit at a demand level below about 25,200 MWh and is exposed to severe losses for high demand levels.

As the level of the interest rate on commodity futures prices is of minor concern, we assume $r = 0$. Finally, we set the parameters of risk aversion: $\lambda^G = \lambda^R = 2 \cdot 10^{-7}$, i.e. $\xi = 10^{-7}$.

The following analysis is structured as follows: First, we discuss the term structure of futures prices and risk premia. In the second part we examine how the premia react if we change the allocation of risk and market power between the producer and the retailer. Third, we vary the parameters of the demand process.

We usually consider three to five different values for the demand D_0 in the first period. This demand characterizes the initial value of the state variable $\tilde{D}_t$. The time interval between two maturities of futures contracts as well as the step size between hedging decisions of the agents is one week. The planning horizon covers $\Theta = 26$ weeks and we determine expected spot and futures prices up to 20 weeks.

5.3.1 Forward curve and risk premia

First we consider the futures prices as a function of the contract's maturity. Figure 5.3 shows these prices at time $t = 0$ for five different values of the initial total demand.

For long maturities, the current value of the state variable D has only little impact on the futures prices. This result is a consequence of our AR(1) specification of the demand process $\tilde{D}_t$. The futures prices converge towards the current spot price $C'(D_0)$ for decreasing time to maturity.

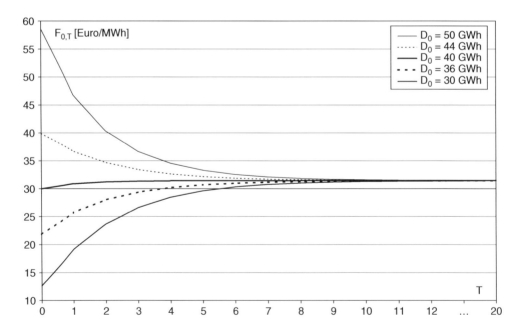

Figure 5.3 The forward curve at time $t = 0$ for maturities of 1 to 20 periods in five constant states, i.e., levels of demand. $F_{0,0}$ denotes the spot price

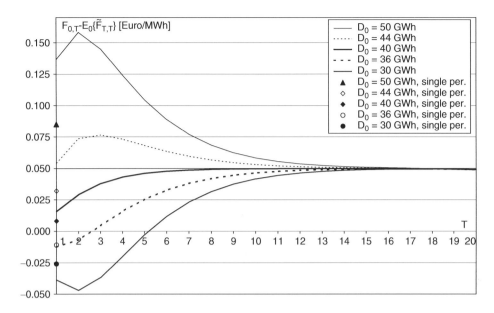

Figure 5.4 The risk premia $F_{0,T} - E_0\{\tilde{F}_{T,T}\}$ for different states and maturities. For comparison, we present the premia for the single-period model (Bessembinder and Lemmon (2002))

We observe that for the reference case of $D_0 = \overline{D} = 40$ GWh the futures prices lie above the spot price of 30 Euro/MWh for two reasons: First, due to the convexity of the marginal cost function the expected spot price is always greater than the spot price of expected demand. This effect also holds in the case of risk neutral agents. Second, the futures price premium $F_{0,T} - E_0\{\tilde{F}_{T,T}\}$ is positive for $D_0 = \overline{D}$. To discriminate the two effects, Figure 5.4 shows the premium for the five different values of the initial total demand as in Fig. 5.3. For comparison, we also present the premia for the single-period model by Bessembinder and Lemmon (2002).

We can draw several conclusions. First, as in the static model by Bessembinder and Lemmon (2002), the premium increases in the state variable, and thus in the expected demand. However, in the multi-period model the premia of the futures with one period to maturity are larger in absolute terms than in the single-period model. This result is caused by cross-hedging effects. The agents use a certain contract not only to hedge their exposure to the corresponding maturity, but also other maturities. Second, the premia and discounts converge to a positive value. The reason for this observation is that for values of D_0 about 40 GWh the retailer has a worse risk position compared to the producer as the gap between the retailer's cash inflow pD and his outflow $C'(D)D$ increasingly widens (cf. Fig. 5.2). This enables the producer, who typically enters short positions in futures, to enforce a premium. As we will show in Section 5.3.2 a discount is also possible, e.g., if we assume a higher rate p (see Fig. 5.8).

Third, the premium can have a contango- or backwardation-like shape, or it can be hump-shaped with either a local maximum or a local minimum. Fourth, for a low expected total demand, the retailer can have an advantage compared to the producer. This is the case if the current demand is low and T is also small. Then, the retailer is able to achieve a discount.

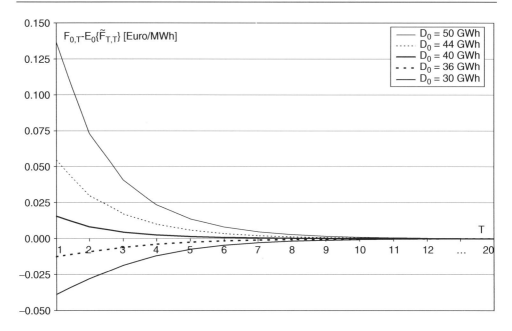

Figure 5.5   The term structure of the one-period premia $F_{0,T} - E_0\{\tilde{F}_{1,T}\}$ for different values of the current demand D_0

As the agents may trade futures at each time, we are also interested in the one-period premia and discounts. Figure 5.5 shows that futures with a long time to maturity have virtually no premium or discount on their expected next period's price. The reason for this fading effect in one-period premia can be traced back to the assumption that the demand follows an AR(1)-process. If the state variable changes, futures prices with a long time to maturity will virtually not be affected, and their variance will be low. This last property is shown in Fig. 5.6. This figure shows the term structure of the standard deviation of the one-period futures price changes, $\sqrt{\mathrm{Var}_0\{\tilde{F}_{1,T}\}}$, conditional on the current demand D_0. As expected, the standard deviation strongly decreases with maturity. Furthermore, it increases with the current demand D_0. This is caused by the right-skewness of the spot prices.

Finally, we take a look at the relative premia or discounts defined as the conditional one-period futures price premium divided by the conditional standard deviation:

$$\Lambda_{0,T} = \frac{E_0\left\{\frac{F_{0,T}-\tilde{F}_{1,T}}{F_{0,T}}\right\}}{\sqrt{\mathrm{Var}_0\left\{\frac{F_{0,T}-\tilde{F}_{1,T}}{F_{0,T}}\right\}}} = \frac{F_{0,T} - E_0\{\tilde{F}_{1,T}\}}{\sqrt{\mathrm{Var}_0\{\tilde{F}_{1,T}\}}} \tag{5.9}$$

As shown in Fig. 5.7, the relative one-period risk premia depend only weakly on the futures' maturity, i.e., the absolute premia and its standard deviation depend in about the same way on the time to maturity of the futures. However, the current value of the demand has a strong effect on the relative premia. This result is a strong contrast to the behavior of the premium $F_{0,T} - E_0\{\tilde{F}_{T,T}\}$ that shows a dependence on the current demand only for short maturities. This effect is due to the producer's and retailer's focus on their cash flow risk

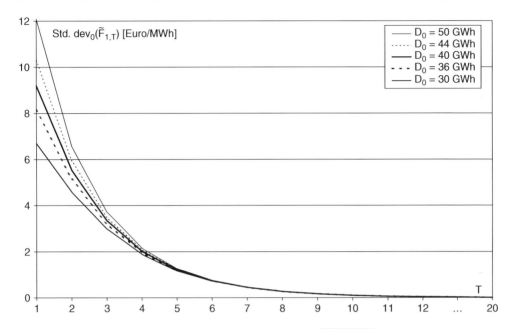

Figure 5.6 The conditional one-period standard deviation $\sqrt{\mathrm{Var}_0\{\tilde{F}_{1,T}\}}$ of the one-period futures price changes conditioned on the current demand level D_0

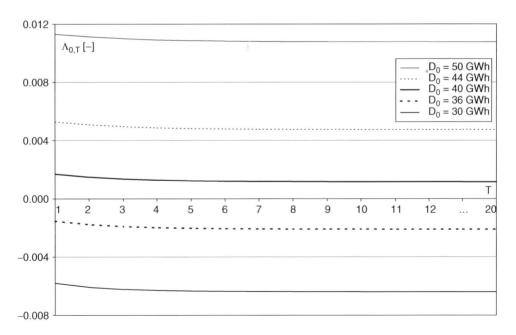

Figure 5.7 The conditional relative premia, $\Lambda_{0,T}$, as defined in (5.9) for different levels of the current demand D_0

instead on the price risk only. Values of the demand variable D_0 around 30 GWh result in a lower cash-flow risk for the retailer relative to the producer. In order to accept the producer's selling orders the retailer requires compensation.

Surprisingly, the relative premia slightly increase for all values of D_0 when maturity comes close. We also observe this effect in a setting that is in favor of the retailer, i.e., for a larger rate p (not shown). It compensates for the skewness of next-period prices. The spot prices exhibit the largest skewness, meaning that futures with one period to maturity incorporate the largest one-period relative risk premium. With increasing time to maturity the skewness decreases. In our setting, futures prices with more than 10 periods to maturity are almost symmetrically distributed. Without the skewness, i.e., when applying a linear function of marginal cost instead of Eq. (5.8), the relative premia are equal for all maturities.

5.3.2   Parameters of risk allocation

The size of the risky market cash flows is determined by the rate p that the representative retailer receives and the production costs that the producer has to pay. Since $p\tilde{D}$ and $C(\tilde{D})$ show asymmetric risk, the two parameters p and d and the order of the polynomial cost function also determine how the risk is allocated among the two agents. In the following we analyze the premium $F_{0,T} - E_0\{\tilde{F}_{T,T}\}$ for variations of p and of the marginal cost function's parameters.

Figure 5.8 shows the premia and discounts $F_{0,T} - E_0\{\tilde{F}_{T,T}\}$ for various values of p. Not surprisingly, the futures price premia are almost linear in p. Without showing we state that the value of p that minimizes the retailer's cash flow variance is much larger than 30. Thus, for the range presented here, higher values of p reduce the retailer's risk and his

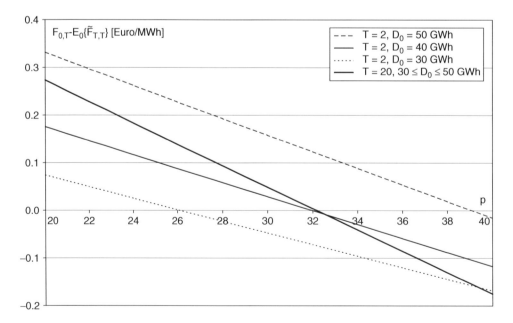

Figure 5.8   The price premia $F_{0,T} - E_0\{\tilde{F}_{T,T}\}$ of futures contracts with two and twenty periods to maturity as a function of p. The premia of the three long-term futures are virtually equal (bold line)

need to hedge with futures. Furthermore, Fig. 5.8 shows that the sensitivity of the premia with respect to p increases with time to maturity. Note that for the futures contracts with longer maturity the graphs coincide, i.e., these premia are almost independent of the state variable D_0.

To study the effect of different marginal cost functions

$$C'(D) = d_n D^n / \overline{D}^3 \tag{5.10}$$

we vary simultaneously the exponent n and d_n with $d_n = 30 \cdot \overline{D}^{(3-n)}$ in order to ensure that the spot price is equal to 30 Euro/MWh for a current demand of $D_0 = \overline{D}$ in all cases.

Figure 5.9 shows the results. For a current demand of 40 and 50 GWh the futures price premium evolves in favor of the producer if n increases. This indicates that a steeper cost function allocates a higher portion of risk towards the retailer. The reason is that the sales $C'(D)D$ of the producer increase more strongly than his costs $C(D)$. Simultaneously the net cash flow of the retailer decreases. This finding is consistent with a result by Bessembinder and Lemmon (2002) who state that the premium increases with the skewness of spot prices.

For the case $T = 2$ and $D_0 = 30$ GWh the risk premium is negative and increases in absolute terms with n for $2 \leqslant n \leqslant 5$. Figure 5.2 explains this effect. For demand levels around 25 GWh, the retailer faces a low risk whereas the producer's risk increases with the polynomial degree of the cost function.

Finally, we discuss the impact if the composite risk aversion factor ξ is varied. It follows from Eq. (5.4) that the one-period futures price bias is linear in ξ. This property does not hold for the premium $F_{0,T} - E_0\{\tilde{F}_{T,T}\}$, $T \geqslant 2$. As this premium is the result of a recursive

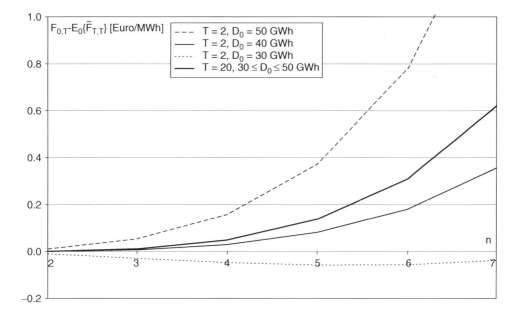

Figure 5.9   The risk premia $F_{0,T} - E_0\{\tilde{F}_{T,T}\}$ of futures contracts with two and twenty periods to maturity, depending on the order n of the cost function. The premia of the three long-term futures are virtually equal (bold line)

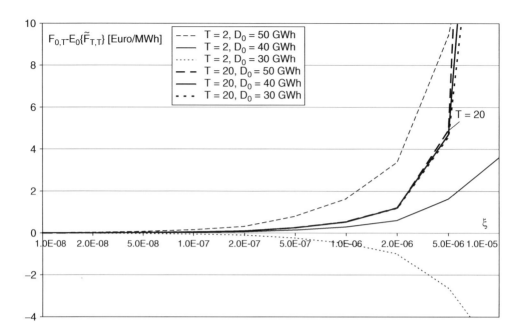

Figure 5.10   The risk premia $F_{0,T} - E_0\{\tilde{F}_{T,T}\}$ of futures contracts with two and twenty periods to maturity with the composite risk aversion factor ξ varied. Note that ξ is not linearly aligned

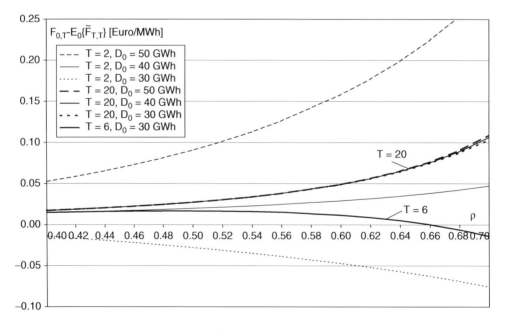

Figure 5.11   The risk premia $F_{0,T} - E_0\{\tilde{F}_{T,T}\}$ of futures contracts with two and twenty periods to maturity as a function of the autocorrelation factor ρ. In addition, the risk premium for a futures contract with six periods until maturity is shown

application of Eq. (5.4), ξ does have an influence of higher order. Figure 5.10 shows this non-linear behavior. Note that the abscissa is scaled logarithmically.

5.3.3 Parameters of the demand process

In our setting, the two parameters ρ and σ determine the conditional variance of the total demand. Since they both influence the stochastic behavior of $\tilde{D}$ in a similar way, we only analyze ρ.

For most parameter constellations an increase in ρ also increases the absolute values of the premia and discounts. However, the futures price premium can also change its sign. In Fig. 5.11 the futures contract with six months to maturity shows this behavior for an initial demand of 30 GWh. Again, the allocation of risk between producer and retailer explains this behavior: For small values of the state variable, the retailer experiences a low cash flow risk in comparison to the producer. If ρ increases, larger future values of D become less probable. The retailer's risk decreases faster than the producer's risk, and the positive premium decreases and changes its sign.

5.4 EMPIRICAL STUDY

In our empirical study we check whether our model's predictions on the term structure of risk premia hold for the Scandinavian electricity market. This market is one of the earliest liberalized electricity markets in Europe. Trading at the Scandinavian electricity exchange Nord Pool began in 1992.

For our purposes, we need to observe two market segments at Nord Pool: The spot market (day ahead market) and the so-called financial market. Futures, forwards, and options are traded at the latter. All prices are given in NOK/MWh.[2] In the spot market electricity is traded for physical delivery during each single hour of the subsequent day (or days, if weekends or exchange holidays follow).

In the financial market futures and forwards are traded continuously. The underlying of all contracts is the 24-hour-delivery of electricity per day at a constant rate during a specified delivery period. All contracts are cash settled. The delivery periods of the listed contracts range from one day to one year. Futures are used for shorter delivery periods, forward contracts are listed for delivery periods of one month and longer. The time-to-maturity of the listed contracts, i.e., the time until the delivery period begins, ranges from two days up to three years. For our empirical study we use only week and block contracts as those were the most liquid ones during our observation period. They are characterized by the following features.

- *Week futures* have a delivery period from Monday through Sunday. They may have a time-to-maturity up to eight weeks. They are the most actively traded contracts at Nord Pool, however, liquidity decreases with increasing time-to-maturity.
- *Block futures* cover a delivery period of four weeks. The listed maturities comprise the time interval from eight up to 48 weeks. Block futures were actively traded but were successively replaced by month forwards in 2003–2004. Block futures have a special

---

[2] Beginning 2003, Nord Pool successively switched to Euro/MWh for some forward contracts.

cascade structure as it becomes common in electricity and gas markets. Eight weeks before maturity they are split into a volume-equivalent bundle of the corresponding four-week futures contracts. This cascade structure allows the market participants to hedge their exposures more precisely for closer maturities.

Nord Pool does not provide intra-day prices for the financial market but only so-called closing prices that are applied for the daily settlement of futures. The closing price is the last registered trading price at a randomly chosen point in time within the last ten minutes before trading ends.[3] If there were no trades on a certain exchange day, Nord Pool uses several procedures to estimate a settlement price. Nord Pool also provides the daily trading volumes for each contract so that we can identify closing prices that are based on trading.

5.4.1 Spot Prices

Daily spot prices have been available since 1992. We do not use spot prices before 1 November 1996 when Finnish electricity firms gained access to Nord Pool.[4] Figure 5.12 plots the level of the daily spot price until 10 August 2004, and its first difference. Table 5.1 shows some descriptive statistics for several 12-month periods as well as for the whole period. It is well known that electricity spot prices exhibit significant daily, weekly, and yearly seasonal patterns. However, this seasonality is superimposed by strong changes in the mean level

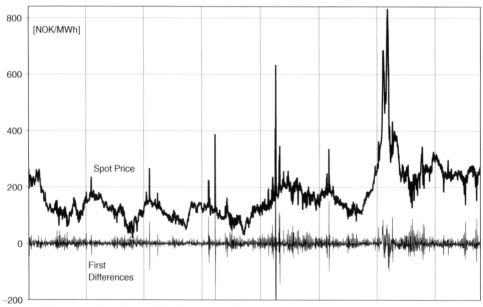

Figure 5.12 The daily spot price and its first difference at Nord Pool from 1 November 1996, until 10 August 2004

---

[3] See Nord Pool (2004) for details.
[4] Nord Pool (1998), p. 9.

Table 5.1 Descriptive statistics for the daily spot price P_t and its first differences at Nord Pool in the period between 1 November 1996 and 10 August 2004 (whole sample) and for subperiods of 12 months each. Instead of calendar years we select subperiods between April and March in order to clearly separate the winter periods

	04/01/97– 03/31/98	04/01/98– 03/31/99	04/01/99– 03/31/00	04/01/00– 03/31/01	04/01/01– 03/31/02	04/01/02– 03/31/03	04/01/03– 03/31/04	whole sample
	Daily spot price, P_t [NOK/MWh]							
Obs.	365	365	366	365	365	365	366	2841
Mean	130.27	110.52	108.98	125.33	178.08	258.84	252.70	171.39
Std. dev.	29.14	31.69	30.37	60.11	27.15	162.99	33.23	90.45
Skewness	−0.018	−0.202	2.381	2.511	0.710	1.399	−0.388	2.378
Kurtosis	−0.29	1.24	19.12	15.22	2.40	1.65	1.20	10.47
Minimum	58.21	21.27	50.43	31.85	119.07	80.65	128.91	21.27
Maximum	234.25	266.47	387.78	633.36	335.80	831.41	343.25	831.41
	Daily spot price differences, $P_t − P_{t-1}$ [NOK/MWh]							
Obs.	365	365	366	365	365	365	366	2840
Mean	0.04	−0.07	0.03	0.26	−0.22	0.33	0.02	0.00
Std. dev.	10.09	11.23	20.02	37.50	17.40	19.66	16.42	20.09
Skewness	0.750	−0.599	3.920	3.156	1.722	−0.223	0.964	3.358
Kurtosis	3.54	21.12	111.60	66.41	18.82	6.71	4.77	121.88
Minimum	−42.02	−96.44	−197.32	−264.29	−98.79	−95.92	−55.65	−264.29
Maximum	45.58	76.81	265.49	440.59	151.74	94.00	89.03	440.59

of the spot price. Table 5.1 shows that in the last two years the mean spot price as well as its median were about twice as high as in earlier periods. Remarkable are the unusually high spot prices during the two-month period from December 2002 to January 2003. This behavior contrasts strongly with the other price peaks that last only for one, sometimes two days.

5.4.2 Estimation of Risk Premia

Futures prices also exhibit seasonal patterns as well as an increasing trend during the observation period. Figure 5.13 shows exemplarily the term structures on the first Wednesdays of the years 2000 to 2003. We abstain from presenting detailed descriptive statistics on futures prices, but focus on the differences between futures and spot prices.

Following Longstaff and Wang (2004), we estimate the unobservable risk premium of a futures contract by the ex-post difference between the futures prices $F_{t,T}$ observed at time

$$F_{t,T} - \frac{1}{N_D} \sum_\tau P_{T+\tau} \tag{5.11}$$

t and the average realized spot price $1/N_D \sum P_{T+\tau}$ during the delivery period of the particular futures contract. N_D denotes the number of days (seven or 28 days for week or block futures, respectively) of the delivery period. These differences provide a first empirical insight into

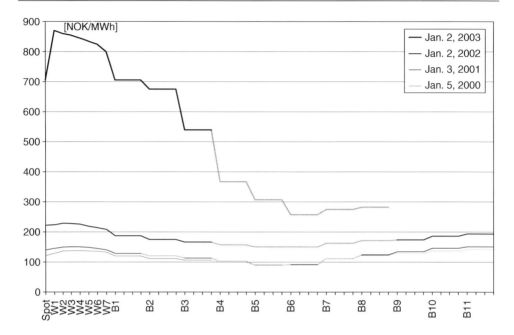

Figure 5.13 The term structures of observed week and block futures at Nord Pool. The first Wednesday in each year between 2000 and 2003 was selected (first Thursday in 2003). Grey colored lines indicate settlement prices of futures that have not been traded on the particular observation day.

the term structure of the risk premia. As the number of transaction prices for futures vary we use weekly averages of traded futures prices in the above defined difference, and omit settlement prices of futures that have not been traded on a certain day. As a consequence, we obtain one estimate for the risk premium in each week for each futures contract, if there was at least one transaction in the futures contract in a particular week.

Table 5.2 presents the estimates of the average risk premium for maturities from one week to one year. Wx denotes week futures with x weeks until maturity, Bx denotes block futures with x 4-week periods until decomposition in four equivalent week futures.

For the whole sample we find a positive estimate for the risk premium of 3.70 NOK/MWh or 2.16 % of the average spot price. This result is in line with the prediction of our model, as presented in Fig. 5.4 for the case that the demand D_0 in the first period equals the average demand $\overline{D}$. Given the positive trend of the spot prices in the sample period, this result is remarkable. If this trend was not – at least partially – reflected in the futures prices, one would expect negative ex-post differences between futures prices and average spot prices in the delivery period.

The predictions of the model hold also for week futures. Up to a maturity of eight weeks the estimated risk premium is strictly monotonously increasing in maturity. The huge risk premium for the week futures W8 does not represent a reliable estimate as it is based on a relatively small sample of only 20 observations. For block futures, the estimated average risk premium decreases in maturity and becomes negative for maturities of 20 weeks and more. We suspect that this behavior of long-term contracts is driven by the unusual dry summer of 2002 and the resulting peak of spot prices in December 2002 and January 2003. Therefore, we re-estimated the average risk premia without those week and block futures whose delivery period fully or partly covers this two-week period. The results are presented in Table 5.3.

Comparing Tables 5.2 and 5.3 we find a number of remarkable differences. First, the mean risk premium for all contracts increases from 3.70 to 8.51 NOK/MWh. This increase is exclusively caused by an increase of the long-term block futures' risk premium from −0.36 to 9.86 NOK/MWh. We attribute this increase to the not-fully-anticipated high spot prices in the December/January period for long-term contracts.

Second, the risk premia in week futures are still increasing in their maturity but on a lower level. We interpret this surprising result as an overestimate of the future risk related to the increase of the spot prices in October and November 2002.

Third, the average risk premia of all block futures are now positive and, as predicted by our model, no longer exhibit a trend.

Fourth, the standard deviation of the risk premia increases in Table 5.2 for week and block futures in their maturities. In Table 5.3 this monotonicity holds only for week futures and the standard deviations are lower for both types of futures contracts. As a consequence, the risk premia of all futures contracts in Table 5.3 are – contrary to those of Table 5.2 – significant on the 5 % level using the t-test with the correction by Newey/West.

5.5 CONCLUSION

As electricity futures cannot be hedged by holding the underlying, electricity futures prices may contain implicit risk premia additional to the expected spot price during the delivery period. By extending Bessembinder and Lemmon (2002) we develop a dynamic one-factor equilibrium model that is based on risk-averse producers and retailers of electricity. From this model we derive a recursive structure for the endogenous futures prices and their risk premia. The comparative static analysis based on a specific demand process shows that our one-factor model is flexible enough to produce upward, downward, and all kinds of hump-shaped term structures of risk premia. The shape and the sign of the risk premia depend on the expected demand conditioned on the demand in the first period. The risk premia are positive when the current demand level is high and negative for low demand levels.

We furthermore show that the relative one-period risk premium, defined as the ratio of the one-period risk premium and the conditional standard deviation of the futures price, increases with decreasing time to maturity. This effect represents the hedging demand of the retailer who faces a risk profile that is asymmetric to the producer's profile.

In our empirical study we used a sample of almost eight years of spot and futures prices from the Scandinavian exchange Nord Pool. We find evidence that electricity futures prices contain the largest positive risk premia several weeks before maturity. They decrease if the maturity shortens, but they remain positive on average.

We conclude that the term structure of the risk premium in electricity futures prices can be explained basically by the risk-averse behavior of producers and retailers in combination with asymmetric risk profiles of these two groups as they are common in energy markets. This result distinguishes our equilibrium approach from reduced-form models that depend on an exogenously specified market price of risk.

To our knowledge quite a few electricity retailers and consumers follow a rolling strategy to hedge the risk of spot prices in that they increase their hedge ratio with decreasing time to

Table 5.2 The ex-post calculated differences between observed futures prices before maturity and realized spot prices during the delivery period. Weekly average futures prices during the period between 1 November 1996 and 10 August 2004 were used

	all futures	week futures	block futures	W1	W2	W3	W4	W5	W6	W7	W8
Obs.	5121	2258	2863	406	406	405	399	300	208	114	20
Mean	3.70	8.84	−0.36	4.26	7.04	8.50	9.06	10.61	13.10	14.87	36.05
Std. dev.	67.38	48.47	78.95	24.21	39.98	47.20	53.86	59.20	60.93	64.02	51.96
Skewness	−1.416	3.462	−2.111	5.168	4.333	4.114	3.610	2.260	2.704	2.186	0.450
Kurtosis	15.27	35.44	9.43	54.61	45.27	42.30	36.09	24.92	19.64	16.16	−1.52
Min.	−380.52	−341.33	−380.52	−87.51	−219.63	−239.68	−287.98	−341.33	−220.17	−235.73	−28.31
Median	7.90	5.16	11.96	2.56	4.12	5.75	6.53	7.78	6.29	7.22	13.33
Max.	530.09	530.09	406.29	279.79	412.78	479.53	530.09	498.65	462.47	417.39	116.18

	B1	B2	B3	B4	B5	B6	B7	B8	B9	B10	B11
Obs.	352	348	340	327	318	301	271	238	191	120	57
Mean	6.55	5.26	2.27	0.27	−1.03	−3.62	−5.28	−4.55	−2.37	−5.67	−16.62
Std. dev.	65.19	74.88	78.06	79.87	76.22	76.89	83.63	86.44	82.86	91.54	104.91
Skewness	−0.084	−0.996	−1.857	−2.299	−2.744	−2.757	−2.610	−2.409	−2.162	−2.147	−2.324
Kurtosis	11.48	11.73	10.20	9.38	10.56	9.98	8.54	7.55	6.99	6.28	5.27
Min.	−302.03	−352.58	−365.73	−373.68	−377.52	−376.90	−372.77	−380.52	−376.40	−372.85	−353.69
Median	7.39	6.66	8.99	12.93	17.17	19.36	15.11	12.00	8.17	14.32	18.98
Max.	388.16	406.29	292.56	200.36	174.42	95.00	102.14	124.97	122.72	148.72	76.70

Table 5.3 The ex-post calculated differences between observed futures prices before maturity and realized spot prices during the delivery period. The sample comprises the period between 1 November 1996 and 10 August 2004, but omits futures contracts with a delivery period that partly or fully lies between 1 December 2002 and 31 January 2003

	all futures	week futures	block futures	W1	W2	W3	W4	W5	W6	W7	W8
Obs.	4950	2192	2758	394	394	393	387	291	202	111	20
Mean	8.51	6.81	9.86	2.62	5.10	6.60	7.40	8.61	9.60	11.42	36.05
Std. dev.	44.14	29.15	53.09	13.92	21.91	27.44	31.69	35.63	37.41	40.83	51.96
Skewness	0.239	0.685	0.103	−0.274	0.216	0.320	0.462	0.490	0.648	0.499	0.450
Kurtosis	7.55	3.96	5.55	2.76	1.96	2.33	2.93	2.71	1.98	2.43	−1.52
Min.	−174.68	−126.29	−174.68	−66.66	−80.28	−105.11	−117.21	−124.74	−103.39	−126.29	−28.31
Median	8.39	5.00	13.29	2.27	4.10	5.75	6.84	7.74	6.24	7.12	13.33
Max.	406.29	149.73	406.29	58.26	94.31	132.45	147.99	149.73	139.85	137.87	116.18

	B1	B2	B3	B4	B5	B6	B7	B8	B9	B10	B11
Obs.	340	336	328	315	307	292	260	227	184	116	53
Mean.	9.98	13.37	12.29	11.43	9.44	6.21	7.77	9.52	8.41	6.79	8.68
Std. dev.	47.04	55.50	54.03	52.89	49.50	51.16	52.29	55.15	59.44	62.97	50.55
Skewness	2.389	2.197	0.989	−0.035	−0.954	−1.216	−1.087	−0.939	−0.848	−0.736	−0.814
Kurtosis	18.65	14.65	6.51	2.76	2.07	1.59	1.61	1.43	0.94	0.65	−0.16
Min.	−137.06	−157.31	−169.22	−168.01	−157.88	−165.76	−173.59	−174.68	−173.34	−172.84	−103.40
Median	7.88	8.21	10.45	14.61	19.72	20.65	17.06	14.27	8.86	14.88	21.61
Max.	388.16	406.29	292.56	200.36	174.42	95.00	102.14	124.97	122.72	148.72	76.70

maturity. Our results are useful for the timing of hedging activities and they are interesting for speculators who want to exploit the spreads between risk premia of different maturities.

5.6 REFERENCES

Audet, N., P. Heiskanen, J. Keppo, and I. Vehviläinen (2004). Modelling Electricity Forward Curve Dynamics in the Nordic Market. In: D.W. Bunn (Ed.). *Modelling Prices in Competitive Electricity Markets* Chapter 12, 251–266. John Wiley & Sons Ltd.: Chichester.

Basak, S. and G. Chabakauri (2007). Dynamic Mean-Variance Asset Allocation. Working Paper, London Business School.

Benth, F.E., A. Cartea and R. Kiesel (2007). Pricing Forward Contracts in Power Markets by the Certainty Equivalence Principle: Explaining the Sign of the Market Risk Premium. Working Paper, to appear in the *Journal of Banking and Finance*.

Bessembinder, H. and M. Lemmon (2002). Equilibrium Pricing and Optimal Hedging in Electricity Forward Markets. *The Journal of Finance* **57**(3): 1347–1382.

de Jong, C. (2005). The Nature of Power Spikes: A Regime-switch Approach. Working Paper ERS-2005-052-F&A, Erasmus-Universiteit Rotterdam.

Fleten, S.-E. and J. Lemming (2003). Constructing Forward Price Curves in Electricity Markets. *Energy Economics* **25**(5): 409–424.

Geman, H. and A. Roncoroni (2006). Understanding the Fine Structure of Electricity Prices. *Journal of Business* **79**(3): 7–14.

Geman, H. and O. Vasicek (2001). Plugging into Electricity. *Risk* 93–97.

Hinz, J. and M. Weber (2005). Währungswechsel, Zinsstrukturtheorie und Bewertung von Strom-Derivaten In: I. Zenke and R. Schäfer (Eds). *Energiehandel in Europa*. Chapter 13, 235–246. Beck: München.

Huisman, R. and R. Mahieu (2001). Regime Jumps in Electricity Prices. Working Paper, University of Rotterdam.

Johnsen, T.A. (2001). Demand, Generation and Price in the Norwegian Market for Electric Power. *Energy Economics* **23**(3): 227–251.

Kellerhals, P. (2001). Pricing Electricity Forwards under Stochastic Volatility. Working Paper, Universität Tübingen.

Koekebakker, S. and F. Ollmar (2005). Forward Curve Dynamics in the Nordic Electricity Market. *Managerial Finance* **31**(6): 73–94.

Longstaff, F.A. and A.W. Wang (2004). Electricity Forward Prices: A High-Frequency Empirical Analysis. *The Journal of Finance* **59**(4): 1877–1900.

Lucia, J.J. and E.S. Schwartz (2002). Electricity Prices and Power Derivatives: Evidence from the Nordic Power Exchange. *Review of Derivatives Research* **5**(1): 5–50.

Nord Pool (Ed.) (1998). *The Nordic Power Exchange's 5th anniversary issue*. Elbørsen Nr. 1/98.

Nord Pool (Ed.) (2004). *Trading Rules for Financial Electricity Contracts and Certificate Contracts*.

Pilipović, D. (1997). *Energy Risk*. McGraw-Hill: New York.

Routledge, B.R., D.J. Seppi and C.S. Spatt (2001). The Spark Spread: An Equilibrium Model of Cross-Commodity Relationships in Electricity. Working Paper, Carnegie Mellon University, USA.

Salerian, J., T. Gregan and A. Stevens (2000). Pricing in Electricity Markets. *Journal of Policy Modeling* **22**(7): 859–893.

Villaplana, P. (2003). Pricing Power Derivatives: A Two-factor Jump-diffusion Approach. Working Paper, Universitat Pompeu Fabra.

6

Measuring Correlation Risk for Energy Derivatives

Roza Galeeva, Jiri Hoogland, and Alexander Eydeland

6.1 INTRODUCTION

The importance of correlation as a measure of dependence has been often emphasized in the context of pricing derivatives whose payoffs depend on the joint distribution of underlying prices, indices, or rates. There is no doubt that at present these derivatives are getting noticeably more popular and numerous. For example, they include a vast class of basket options, i.e. options on linear combinations of various price indices from different markets. Another example can be found in commodity markets, where spread options, both standard and, increasingly, "multi-legged", are omnipresent.

Obviously, there are limitations to the use of the correlation, especially in the case of complex joint distributions. However, even under these circumstances practical considerations often force one to use correlations as measure of dependence.

Once the correlation is used for pricing, an immediate question arises: namely, the question of estimating the sensitivity of derivative prices to the correlation parameters, and with it the question of corresponding correlation risk measure. In this chapter we discuss various ways to define and compute one such measure, the correlation VaR.

We start with a brief recap of the correlation and its properties. We discuss various approaches to parametrization of the correlation matrix. We then introduce different methods to generate distributions of correlations matrices. Finally, we apply these methods to determine the correlation VaR of a typical energy derivative. We conclude with a discussion.

6.2 CORRELATION

Linear correlation is the most widely used measure of dependence between random variable X and Y with finite variances. It is defined as:

$$\rho(X, Y) = \frac{\text{Cov}[X, Y]}{\sqrt{\sigma^2[X]\sigma^2[Y]}}$$

MG, Morgan Stanley
The authors are employees of Morgan Stanley. Roza Galeeva works in the Finance Division and can be contacted at Roza.Galeeva@MorganStanley.com. Jiri Hoogland and Alex Eydeland work in the Fixed Income Division, a sales and trading division of Morgan Stanley, and can be contacted at Jiri.Hoogland@MorganStanley.com and Alex.Eydeland@MorganStanley.com. Please see additional information at the end of this chapter.

Risk Management in Commodity Markets: From Shipping to Agriculturals and Energy   Edited by Hélyette Geman
© 2008 John Wiley & Sons, Ltd

where $\text{Cov}[X, Y]$ is the covariance between X and Y, $\text{Cov}[X, Y] \equiv E[XY] - E[X]E[Y]$ and $\sigma^2[X] \equiv \text{Cov}[X, X]$, $\sigma^2[Y]$ denote the variances of X and Y. The linear correlation is a measure of linear dependence. For the *elliptical* family of joint distributions, which include joint normal, lognormal and others, the linear correlation together with the variances is sufficient to describe the dependency structure. The pitfalls and limitations of the concept of a linear correlation are investigated in detail in the excellent paper by Embrechts, McNeil and Straumann (1999).

If we are dealing with n random variables $X_1, X_2, \ldots X_n$ (for example returns of financial variables), then correlations ρ_{ij} between different pairs i, j of returns are expressed in terms of matrices. Correlation matrices must satisfy the following properties $(i, j = 1, \ldots, n)$:

- All entries have to be in the interval $[-1, 1]$: $-1 \leqslant \rho_{ij} \leqslant 1$
- The diagonal terms of a correlation matrix are equal to one: $\rho_{ii} = 1$
- The matrix has to be symmetric: $\rho_{ij} = \rho_{ji}$
- The matrix has to be positive *semidefinite*, i.e., the variance of any portfolio with correlation matrix ρ, is non-negative: $\forall W$, $V\sigma_P^2 = (Z)^T \rho(Z) Z \geqslant 0$, where $W = w_1, \ldots, w_n$ is the array of weights of the portfolio, $V = v_1, \ldots, v_n$ is the array of standard deviations of the returns, $Z = w_1 v_1, \ldots, w_n v_n$ and T denotes transpose of a matrix.

In financial applications, correlation matrices are most commonly estimated from the historical data. Another way is to get *implied* correlations, i.e. to calibrate a model using market prices of correlation-dependent derivatives in the same way implied volatilities are obtained from options quotes. The advantage of the first approach is that typically more data is available for its implementation. The drawback–it is backward looking. The second approach has less data, but it is forward looking.

6.3 PERTURBING THE CORRELATION MATRIX

In order to estimate correlation risk we need an ability to generate a random sample of correlation matrices, so that we can analyze the corresponding distribution of portfolio values, i.e. calculate the *correlation VaR*. This task is not easy, since a correlation matrix is a fairly rigid object, especially with respect to the requirement of positive definiteness.

In this section we will discuss four different approaches to perturbing the correlation matrix: bootstrapping, element-wise perturbation, perturbation with the help of angle parametrization of the Cholesky matrix, and perturbation of the eigen-values.

6.3.1 Bootstrap method

The bootstrap methodology is a Monte Carlo *resampling* method. It was introduced by Efron (1979). Suppose that we want to estimate the density of the correlation ρ between two random variables X and Y based on historical observations $\{X_i, Y_i\}_{i=1}^N$. The basic bootstrapping algorithm to create a distribution for ρ is as follows.

1. Generate N uniform i.i.d. random integers $n_1, n_2, \ldots, n_N$ in the interval $[1, N]$.
2. Create a sample $\hat{X} \equiv \{X_{n_i}, Y_{n_i}\}_{i=1}^N$ using the $n_1, \ldots, n_N$.
3. Calculate $\hat{\rho}$ using the sample $\hat{X}$.
4. Repeat the previous steps M times with M being a large number.

Instead of drawing single values from observations, one can use *block* bootstrap. This means that the data is split into blocks of length m and the above procedure is applied. Engler and Schwendner (2003) used blocks of length $m = 3$. They quantify the error in the correlation estimates from historical data by approximating the asymptotic distribution of the correlation via block bootstrapping. The bootstrapped correlation distributions are then mapped on prices of three standard types of multi-asset options: a basket option, minimum option and maximum option. Bid-ask spreads of the prices are computed at statistical quantiles of the resulting price distributions.

6.3.2 Perturbing individual correlations

Turkay et al. (2003) propose perturbing the correlation matrix locally to a desired target matrix while ensuring that the irrelevant correlations remain the same, and the new correlation matrix remains positive semi-definite. They obtain an analytical solution for the bounds of a single correlation term of a positive semi-definite correlation matrix. The methodology is based on the elegant idea of re-ordering of the assets that define the matrix and applying the Cholesky decomposition to localize the perturbation to the last entries in the Cholesky matrix. They also present an iterative application of the single correlation stress test methodology in order to stress a number of correlations.

6.3.3 Perturbing angles in the angle representation of the correlation matrix

The *Triangular Angles Parametrization* (*TAP*) parametrization of the correlation matrix through a *unique* set of angles was put forward in Brigo et al. (2002). This is an extension of results proposed in Rebonato and Jäckel (2000), which were the first to apply the results of Pinheiro and Bates (1996) in a financial context. See also Geman and Souveton (1997).

The essential idea is that the correlation matrix can be parameterized through a unique lower-triangular matrix, where the entries are angles taking values in $[0, \pi]$. This angle-representation maps to a Cholesky matrix from which we can compute the correlation matrix. The good thing about this approach is that we automatically satisfy the correlation constraints specified in Section 6.2.

We start with the Cholesky decomposition of the correlation matrix (see Section 6.2). In this decomposition the correlation matrix ρ is represented as a product of a lower-triangular matrix L and its transpose:

$$\rho_{ij} = \sum_{k=1}^{N} l_{ik} l_{jk}$$

The elements of the lower-triangular matrix L are then parameterized in terms of cosines and sines of $N(N-1)/2$ angles θ_{ij} ($j < i$) between 0 and π.

$$l_{ij} = \begin{cases} \cos\theta_{ij} \prod_{k=1}^{j-1} \sin\theta_{ik} & j < i \\ \prod_{k=1}^{i-1} \sin\theta_{ik} & j = i \end{cases} \tag{6.1}$$

The angles are found via a robust and efficient procedure which makes the whole approach very attractive. Moreover, through these angles the space of *all* correlation matrices is covered.

One implication of having the angle representation of correlation matrices is that if we have an algorithm to sample the angles, then we also have an algorithm to sample the correlations with some width around the base correlations, thus providing an alternative way to generate the correlation VaR.

The simplest algorithm for generating distribution of correlation matrices is to generate random angles θ_{ij} around the base angles θ_{ij}^0 with some distribution $\pi(\theta_{ij}|\theta_{ij}^0)$, which is symmetric and centered around the base-correlation θ_{ij}^0 for every i, j. Random angles are simulated using the historical distribution. From our analysis we find that the angles tend to be distributed around the mean, with a standard deviation in the order of $\sigma = 5\%$. Based on this analysis we propose two perturbation methods. In the first approach we perturb all angles using one standard normal variate $z \sim N(0, 1)$,

$$\hat{\theta}_{ij} = \arctan(\tan(\theta_{ij} + \frac{\pi}{2})(1 + \sigma z)) + \frac{\pi}{2} \tag{6.2}$$

In the second approach all angles θ_{ij} are perturbed by i.i.d. standard normal variates $z_{ij} \sim N(0, 1)$,

$$\hat{\theta}_{ij} = \arctan(\tan(\theta_{ij} + \frac{\pi}{2})(1 + \sigma z_{ij})) + \frac{\pi}{2} \tag{6.3}$$

6.3.4 Perturbing eigenvalues

In this section we consider the generation of random correlation matrices around the base correlation matrix through the perturbation of eigenvalues. We can express the correlation matrix in terms of its eigen-system (Λ, V) via

$$\rho_{ij} = \sum_{k,l=1}^{n} V_{ik} \Lambda_{kl} V_{lj}$$

where $\Lambda_{kl} \equiv \lambda_k \delta_{kl}$ is the diagonal matrix with the eigenvalues λ_i on the diagonal. We assume that the eigenvalues by $\lambda_1 \geqslant \lambda_2 \geqslant \ldots \lambda_n \geqslant 0$. Furthermore the eigenvalues satisfy the constraint $\sum_{k=1}^{n} \lambda_i = n$.

We consider the following four algorithms to perturb the eigenvalues. The first algorithm is as follows.

1. Generate n i.i.d random standard normal variates $z_i \sim N(0, \sigma_i)$, $(i = 1, \ldots, n)$
2. Compute the perturbed eigenvalues

$$\hat{\lambda}_i = \lambda_i e^{\sigma_i z_i}$$

The other three algorithms are variations of the following algorithm.

1. Generate a random index $K \in [1, \ldots, n]$ according to some distribution $p_i \geqslant 0$ with $\sum_{i=1}^{n} p_i = 1$.
2. Generate an i.i.d. standard normal variable $z \sim N(0, 1)$.

. Compute the perturbed eigenvalue λ_K

$$\hat{\lambda}_K = \lambda_K e^{\sigma_K z}$$

The three cases we will consider are

. Perturb the largest eigenvalues more: $p_i = \frac{\lambda_i}{n}$
. Perturb the eigenvalues uniformly: $p_i = \frac{1}{n}$
. Pick one specific eigenvalue: $p_i = \delta_{iK}$

Having perturbed eigenvalues, we define the perturbed correlation matrix via

$$\hat{\rho}_{ij} = \sum_{k,l=1}^{n} V_{ik} \hat{\Lambda}_{kl} V_{lj}$$

where $\hat{\Lambda}_{kl} \equiv \hat{\lambda}_k \delta_{kl}$ is the diagonal matrix with the perturbed eigenvalues $\hat{\lambda}_i$. To ensure that $\sum_{i=1}^{n} \rho_{ii} = n$ we need to renormalize the random correlation matrix $\hat{\rho}$:

$$\tilde{\rho}_{ij} = \frac{\hat{\rho}_{ij}}{\sqrt{\hat{\rho}_{ii}\hat{\rho}_{jj}}}$$

6.4   CORRELATION VAR

The question we want to ask is the sensitivity of the value of a trade or portfolio to the correlation matrix. To this end we need an efficient and practical method to perturb the correlation matrix. We will use the methods discussed in the previous section to compute the sensitivity of a portfolio to correlation.

As we mentioned above, how we perturb the correlations, i.e. what probabilities we attach to a particular perturbation of the correlation matrix, is an important and difficult choice. We will take a practical point of view here and leave the more satisfying theoretical results for a future work.

In calculating the correlation VaR, we will perturb the correlation matrix according to some perturbation scheme, which effectively means that we have some distribution $\pi(\rho|\rho^0)$ and compute the density for the portfolio value as a function of the correlation as follows.

$$\pi(v) = \int \delta(v - V(\rho))\pi(\rho|\rho^0)d\rho \tag{6.4}$$

From this we can then determine the correlation VaR.

6.5   SOME EXAMPLES

In this section we apply the above methodology to the valuation of a typical energy derivative subject to correlation inputs. We value a hypothetical power plant with a switching capability between the gas and oil. The value of the power plant is modeled by the following strip of spread options:

$$V = Q \left\{ \sum_{m=1}^{m=N} H_m^{on} S_m^{on} + H_m^{off} S_m^{off} \right\} \tag{6.5}$$

where H_m^{on} and H_m^{off} are the numbers of on-peak and off-peak hours in month m and S_m^{on} and S_m^{off} are the spread options for month m, whose payoff for month m is given by

$$S^{on} = \max \left\{ P^{on} - HR_G G, P^{on} - HR_F F, 0 \right\} \tag{6.6}$$

$$S^{off} = \max \left\{ P^{off} - HR_G G, P^{off} - HR_F F, 0 \right\} \tag{6.7}$$

Here P^{on} and P^{off} are the on-peak and off-peak power prices, G is the gas price, F is the oil price and HR_G, HR_F are the heat rates for gas and oil respectively. For simplicity we ignore variable costs and assume zero interest rates.

We value the power plant on 1 January 2006, over the period of calendar year 2007. The inputs listed in Table 6.2 include forward on-peak and off-peak prices, gas and oil forward prices, volatilities for on-peak, off-peak power, gas and oil. For the current example we have $N = 12$ and the amount Q of MW is set to $Q = 100$.

For a given correlation matrix ρ we compute the value of the power plant using a Monte Carlo simulation. We repeat this for a sample of random correlation matrices using one of the methods described in the previous sections. Using Eq. (6.4), we then compute the density of the value V in Eq. (6.5). In order to get a distribution of the eigenvalues or the angles, we perform a bootstrap on historical prices. Based on this analysis, we make the assumption that the eigenvalues have a lognormal distribution and generate the random angles using Eq. (6.3).

The base correlation matrix ρ_{ij}^0 is calculated from historical returns of forward prices. We use three years of historical data. Given the base correlation matrix we can compute the corresponding Cholesky decomposition and the lower-triangular angle matrix θ_{ij}. In order to estimate the variations of the angles, we compute the angles using a sliding window. We calculated the correlation matrix and the corresponding angle matrix for every year using that year's data. In general we find that the standard deviation of the angles is in the order of 5 %. We will use this number to perturb the angles.

We apply the methods we discussed earlier to simulate correlation matrices and compute the density of the power plant values as a function of the correlation perturbations. In Table 6.1 we give the mean, standard deviation, and 95 % left VaR for the power plant value as a function of the different methods that we discussed in this chapter. We use 1000 simulations of correlation matrices, and 10 000 simulations in the underlying Monte Carlo to evaluate the V. The corresponding histograms are in Fig. 6.1. From these histograms it is clear that the distribution of the basket values depends on the method of perturbing the correlation matrix. If we choose a uniform density over the eigenvalues the smallest eigenvalues gets too much weight and the density is very narrow. As we put more weight on the larger eigenvalues the density will widen. The case where we only perturb the largest eigenvalue can be considered as the worst-case scenario. As for the perturbation through the angles we see that, as expected, the case with a *correlated* perturbation of the angles leads to a wider distribution of the value.

Table 6.1 Power plant with value 15.8 *MM*. Sample size is 1000

Method	Largest eigenvalue	Weighted eigenvalues	Uniform eigenvalues
Mean (MM)	15.81	15.80	15.81
Standard deviation (MM)	0.23	0.17	0.09
5 % CorVaR (MM)	15.41	15.53	15.66

Method	Parallel shift angles	Uncorrelated angles	Bootstrap
Mean (MM)	15.79	15.82	16.04
Standard deviation (MM)	0.67	0.22	0.65
5 % CorVaR (MM)	14.69	15.47	15.01

Table 6.2 Forward prices and volatilities inputs for the valuation of a power plant

Contracts	Power on-peak	Power off-peak	Gas	Oil	On peak vol	Off peak vol	Gas vol	Oil vol
1/1/2007	100	70	10.2	50.5	0.83	0.71	0.64	0.27
2/1/2007	90	65	9.4	48	0.69	0.59	0.67	0.27
3/1/2007	80	60	8.4	50	0.65	0.55	0.69	0.26
4/1/2007	80	56	8.2	50	0.50	0.43	0.42	0.26
5/1/2007	75	50	7.5	51	0.52	0.44	0.40	0.26
6/1/2007	85	54	6.8	50	0.54	0.45	0.40	0.26
7/1/2007	110	70	6.5	49	0.58	0.49	0.40	0.25
8/1/2007	105	70	6.4	50	0.58	0.49	0.40	0.25
9/1/2007	90	60	6.6	49	0.52	0.44	0.42	0.25
10/1/2007	85	61	7	49.2	0.51	0.43	0.44	0.24
11/1/2007	93	65	9	49	0.51	0.43	0.48	0.24
12/1/2007	102	78	10.8	49.5	0.51	0.43	0.47	0.24

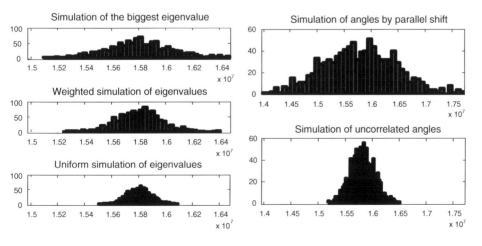

Figure 6.1 We plot the histograms for the value of the power plant with all different methods discussed in the article. The sample size is 1000

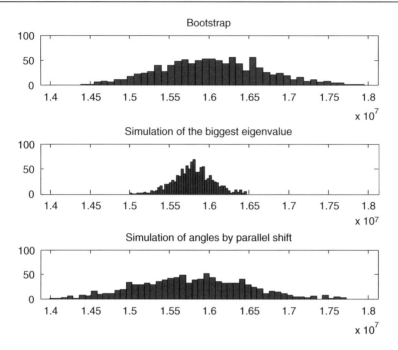

Figure 6.2 Comparison of the three different cases: bootstrap, largest eigenvalue, parallel shift angles. The graph shows the results for the power plant value

In Fig. 6.2 we compare the bootstrap method with the largest eigenvalue perturbation and the parallel shift of angles for the two examples we consider. It shows that the distribution of the bootstrap case is wider than the case of the other two methods.

6.6   DISCUSSION AND CONCLUSIONS

We have described various methods to perturb the correlation matrix and compute the correlation VaR. The simplest method is the bootstrap method, which is essentially a resampling of the historical timeseries. The second method involves the local perturbation of the correlation matrix elements. The third method uses a perturbation of the correlation matrix through perturbation of the angles in the TAP parametrization. Finally we propose a method to perturb the correlation matrix via the perturbation of the eigenvalues.

We provide some numerical results for these methods applied to the valuation of a power plant with two fuels. Different methods lead to different results for the correlation VaR. This is not surprising since there is clearly a lot of freedom in the choice of perturbations and underlying densities. Given this freedom, it would be natural to argue in favor of using the simplest method, the bootstrapping of the correlation matrix. However, there is a clear advantage in having a perturbation method with a readily available control parameter. Among other benefits, such a method is very useful for devising and carrying out stress testing. Needless to say, both the angle and eigenvalue perturbation methods do provide such control parameters.

To summarize, the present work shows that the use of some parameterized method, be it angles or eigenvalues, gives us a convenient tool to stress-test complicated portfolios of instruments and to do it in a well-defined manner. A consistent application of the correlation VaR measures described in this chapter improves our understanding of product sensitivity to correlation and provides us with a useful approach to product comparison.[1]

6.7 REFERENCES

Brigo, D., F. Mercurio and F. Rapisarda (2002). *Parametrizing Correlations: A Geometric Interpretation*. Working Paper: http://www.fabiomercurio.it.

Efron, B. (1979). Bootstrap Methods: Another Look at the Jackknife. *Annals of Statistics* **7**, 1–26.

Embrechts, P., A.J. McNeil and D. Straumann (1999). *Correlation: Pitfalls and Alternatives*. RISK, May.

Fengler, M.R. and P. Schwendner (2003). *Correlation Risk Premia for Multi-Asset Equity Options*. Working paper. Humboldt.

Geman, H. and Souveton, R, 1997. No Arbitrage between Economics and Correlation, Risk Management. *Journal of Computational Economics*, **10**(2).

Pinheiro, J.C. and D.M. Bates (1996). Unconstrained Parameterization for Variance-Covariance Matrices. *Statistics and Computing*, 289–296.

Rebonato R. and P. Jäckel (2000). The Most General Methodology for Creating a Valid Correlation Matrix for the Risk Management and Option Pricing Purposes: A Geometric Interpretation. *Journal of Risk* **2**(2), 17–27.

Turkay, S., E. Epperlein and N. Christofides (2003). Correlation Stress Testing for Value-at-Risk. *Journal of Risk* **5**(4), 75–90.

7

Precaution and a Dismal Theorem: Implications for Climate Policy and Climate Research

Gary W. Yohe and Richard S. J. Tol

7.1 INTRODUCTION

Economic efficiency has long been a gold standard for evaluating policies. In the context of climate change, the search for efficient solutions to the policy problem began in earnest with Nordhaus (1991), and it has evolved into using elaborate, regionally disaggregated integrated assessment models to judge the relative expected benefits and costs of various policy options across a wide range of possible futures. Cline (1992, 1997, 2004), Maddison (1995), Nordhaus (1991, 1993, 1994), Nordhaus and Yang (1996), Nordhaus and Boyer (2000), Roughgarden and Schneider (1999), Stern *et al.* (2006), Tol (2002) and Uzawa (2003) are all examples of this approach. These and many other studies are fundamentally optimization exercises, and many use Monte Carlo simulations to set the expected marginal benefits of emission reduction equal to its expected marginal cost. This is why calculations of the social cost of carbon (SCC) have become so popular.[1]

It is widely known that published estimates of the social cost of carbon vary widely. An early survey conducted by Tol (2005) reported that fully 12 % of then available published estimates were non-positive. Their median was $13 per tonne of carbon, and their mean was $85 per tonne. Tol (2007) offers an updated survey of more than 200 estimates. His new results show a median for peer-reviewed estimates with a 3 % pure rate of time preference and without equity weights of $20 per tonne of carbon with a mean of $23 per tonne of carbon. Moreover, he reports a 1 % probability that the social cost of carbon could be higher than $78 per tonne given the same assumptions, and he notes that the estimates increase rapidly as the assumed discount rate falls. Tol (2007) thereby suggests at least one reason why the range of estimates of the social cost of carbon is so large.

Gary W. Yohe: Woodhouse/Sysco Professor of Economics, Wesleyan University, Middletown, CT, USA. Contact: Department of Economics, 238 Church Street, Middletown, CT, USA 06459; gyohe@wesleyan.edu.
Richard S. J. Tol: Economic and Social Research Institute, Dublin, Ireland; Institute for Environmental Studies, Vrije Universiteit, Amsterdam, The Netherlands; Department of Spatial Economics, Vrije Universiteit, Amsterdam, The Netherlands; Department of Engineering and Public Policy, Carnegie Mellon University, Pittsburgh, PA, USA. Contact: ESRI, Whitaker Square, Sir John Rogerson's Quay, Dublin 2, Ireland; richard.tol@esri.ie.
The social cost of carbon is defined as the (expected) discounted marginal damage of carbon emissions at any point in time. Estimates of the SCC can, therefore, be interpreted as estimates of the (expected) marginal benefit of mitigation.

Risk Management in Commodity Markets: From Shipping to Agriculturals and Energy   Edited by Hélyette Geman
© 2008 John Wiley & Sons, Ltd

Hope (2006) provided some additional insight derived from exercising his PAGE2002 model. He reported that the choice of discount rate and the incorporation of equity weights are extremely important, and both lie within the purview of decision-makers. High discount rates sustain low estimates because future damages become insignificant. Conversely, low discount rates produce high estimates because future damages are important. Meanwhile, strong equity weighting across the globe support high estimates because poor developing countries are most vulnerable. Alternatively, weak or no equity weighting can produce low estimates because poor developing countries do not factor heavily in the overall calculation. Hope (2006) concluded, however, that the climate sensitivity (i.e. the increase in global mean temperature that would result from a doubling of greenhouse gas concentrations from pre-industrial levels) is the largest source of variation. It is possible to derive high estimates for the social cost of carbon even if with low discount rates and/or almost no equity weighting. All that is required is the assumption that the climate sensitivity lies at the high range of the latest range of estimates.[2]

For present purposes, it is enough to recognize that the range of estimates of the SCC of carbon is enormous for a variety of reasons – some related to decisions that human beings make in their decision process, and some related to decisions over which "Mother Nature" has purview. As a result, the cost-benefit approach to climate policy has long been vulnerable to concerns about its ability to handle adequately the scope of the underlying uncertainties and diversities of opinion.

Results drawn from the optimization approach have also been suspect because many of the potential impacts of climate change (particularly non-market impacts and low-probability but high consequence ramifications of abrupt climate change) cannot easily be quantified in economic terms. The basis of this critique of incomplete and perhaps infeasible coverage is best visualized in a matrix presented by Downing and Watkiss (2003) that tracks the degree to which the complication of climate change science is captured by benefit analysis. Three rows catalog coverage of scientific uncertainty from relatively well-established (although still uncertain) trends in climate change (e.g., average temperature, sea level rise) through considerations of the bounded risks of extreme events (including precipitation events on both sides of the distribution) and other manifestations of climate variability, and finally into representations of possible abrupt change and/or abrupt impacts. Three columns catalog coverage of economic uncertainty from relatively well-established coverage of market impacts through less robust economic assessments of non-market impacts, and into socially contingent impacts (e.g. abrupt social, political or economic changes driven by famine, migration across national borders, etc.) across multiple metrics that cannot always be quantified in economic terms. Yohe and Tirpak (2008) report that the economic analyses required to inform fully the cost-benefit approach to global climate policy has adequately covered very few of the nine combinations and permutations in the matrix.

It must be emphasized, however, that neither of these sources of concern about the applicability of the cost-benefit apparatus to climate policy is really new. Indeed, both have long histories in the literature. Early on, authors like Alcamo and Kreileman (1996), Toth et al. (1997) and Swart et al. (1998) responded to them by arguing in favor of taking a precautionary approach to climate policy – i.e., defining the boundaries of "tolerable" climate impacts calibrated in terms of temperature targets (both absolute levels and sometimes

---

[2] One might, for example, take climate sensitivity to be greater than 5°C and only be at the 80th percentile of the distribution reported in Andronova and Schlesinger (2001).

rates of change) and working from there. In this context, policy designers ask economists simply to calculate emissions (reduction) paths that would avoid the proscribed boundaries of climate change at minimum expected cost.[3] Wigley *et al.* (1996) and Manne and Richels (1997) are perfect examples of this type of analysis.

Many of the remaining issues for the precautionary approach pertain to defining the boundaries of tolerable climate change (or, in the parlance of the United Nations Framework Convention on Climate Change, the boundaries of "dangerous anthropogenic interference with the climate system") and coping with adaptation; see, for example, Yohe and Toth (2000). It must be noted as well, however, that the precautionary approach is not immune from its own vulnerability to enormous uncertainty. Both Stern *et al.* (2006) and the Fourth Assessment Report of the Intergovernmental Panel on Climate Change in Yohe *et al.* (2007) and elsewhere in and (IPCC 2007a, 2007b) make it clear that limiting atmospheric concentrations of greenhouse gases to any specific level cannot guarantee that increases in global mean temperature will be held below any target identified as the boundary of "dangerous" climate change regardless of how it is identified.

7.2   A NEW SOURCE OF CONCERN: WEITZMAN'S DISMAL THEOREM

This debate between the cost-benefit approach and the precautionary approach has recently been informed by a "Dismal Theorem" offered by Weitzman (2007). It shows that profound uncertainty about fundamental parameters like climate sensitivity cannot be overcome for any positive rate of risk aversion and any positive rate of pure time preference for any distribution of events (outcomes) whose moment generating function is infinite and includes the potential for catastrophic climate impacts (here defined as a prolonged period of falling welfare per capita). To be more specific, trouble arises for power-law or lognormal distributions or any distribution with "thick tails" where the probability falls only with a power of the size of the event. In these cases, the impact or consequence of an event can grow exponentially while the probability falls with a power law so that the expected impact becomes unbounded. In practice, the theorem draws its significance from our inability to observe the events in the tails with enough frequency to learn anything useful about relative likelihoods of associated catastrophic consequences. It follows that uncertainty will dominate any calculation of expected climate damage because Bayesian learning about the critical variables (even with very strong time discounting) is never strong enough to keep expected marginal damages finite.

Weitzman's "Dismal Theorem" clearly casts doubt on results derived from a cost-benefit approach to climate policy, at least for studies in which the equity implications of declining marginal utility are recognized. Indeed, Weitzman has suggested that a warning label be attached to integrated assessment models that rely on the cost-benefit approach – something like "Warning: To be applied only to non-extreme climate change possibilities". The Dismal Theorem marginalizes the debate over the social cost of carbon and the associated discussions about what makes estimates high or low because it means that all of the existing

---

[3] Because tolerable boundaries are typically defined in terms of temperature limits and because temperature change depends, to a first approximation, on cumulative emissions over long periods of time, the appropriate economic response can be visualized by solving for an initial shadow price for carbon (and other warming gases) with the expectation that it would increase over time at an endogenously determined rate of interest.

estimates are infinitely too small. It similarly renders obsolete the current obsession of some of the scientific community for reaching model-based consensus on central tendencies about climate change.[4] The action is, quite simply, in the dismal tails.

On the positive side, the result indicates that the value of some types of information is far greater (and perhaps infinitely greater) than the value of other information. It can therefore offer some guidance on where to devote scarce research resources in climate and policy science. Moreover, it seems to offer sound theoretic footing for a generalized precautionary approach designed explicitly to examine and clarify the definition of tolerable climate change. More careful examination of these implications suggests that another warning label needs to be written, but more on that later.

Before proceeding to make that point, it is important to focus on one important condition of the Dismal Theorem – that decision-makers view the world with some aversion to risk (and thus some aversion to inequality).[5] We could therefore find our way around the Dismal Theorem by simply asserting that policymakers should always proceed as if they were completely risk-neutral. Doing so would, however, mean rewriting much of current economic policy; and doing so only in the climate arena would mean that the United Nations Framework Convention on Climate Change would have to be completely overhauled.

Since neither of these responses will be accepted by the policy community, there is no easy way to dismiss the implications of the Dismal Theorem for climate policy and climate science. To explore these implications a little more fully, it is appropriate to contemplate its applicability in a few different cases. Tol (2003), for example, worked within a cost-benefit framework that recognized multiple regions with and without equity weighting. Even without recognizing the consequences of thick tails in the distribution of climate sensitivity, his Monte Carlo simulations noted the small but non-zero probability that marginal utility could grow infinitely large in one or more regions where even "routine" climate change, particularly when it materializes in the form of declining precipitation, can drive economic activity to subsistence levels. As long as these regions were given non-zero weight in the expected utility calculation, their plight would dominate the policy calculus because expected marginal damages would approach infinity. This was, perhaps, a precursor of the Dismal Theorem.

7.3   IMPLICATIONS OF THE "DISMAL THEOREM"

Yohe (2003) suggested that the problem highlighted in Tol (2003) could be overcome by implementing a second policy instrument designed to maintain economic activity above subsistence levels everywhere – a foreign aid program designed simply to prevent economic collapse anywhere in real time. Tol and Yohe (2007) examined this suggestion within the original modeling framework and found that, with sufficient aid, the issue of infinite marginal damage could be avoided. While this work did not envision events characterized in the fat tails of climate sensitivity, it nonetheless suggests that timely social or

---

[4] Evidence of this obsession is seen in IPCC (2007a) where the potential contributions of Greenland Ice Sheet melting and collapse of the West Antarctic Ice Sheet from sea level rise estimates were deleted (even though they had been included in IPCC (2001) because there was no model based scientific consensus that could explain what is going on (IPCC, 2007a). In the logic of the Dismal Theorem, this makes the ice sheets more policy relevant, not less.

[5] This assumption is captured simply by allowing the marginal utility of consumption to rise indefinitely as consumption falls to a subsistence level (and to fall as consumption rises beyond the range currently experienced by developed economies).

economic interventions that effectively "lop off the thick tails" of regional climate impacts could undercut the power of the Dismal Theorem. If, however, the impacts of the profound uncertainty were felt globally so that no country or region would have the wherewithal to underwrite the subsistence of another, then the Dismal Theorem could still persist. It is here, therefore, that a generalized precautionary principle – the logical implication of the Dismal Theorem – comes into play.

Can the Dismal Theorem inform the boundaries of precaution? To answer this question, it is important to recognize that these boundaries can be defined in many different ways. Put another way, policymakers are not confined to Bayesian learning about the climate sensitivity and other critical parameters in climate models, and this is a good thing. Roe and Baker (2007) show, for example, that "the probability of large temperature increases" is "relatively insensitive to decreases in uncertainties associated with the underlying climate processes". Allen and Frame (2007) responded by arguing that it was pointless for policy makers to count on narrowing this fundamental uncertainty. Rather than tilting at this (and other similar) windmill(s) like Don Quixote, perhaps the policy community should ask the research community to develop greater understandings of the fundamental processes in other areas – processes that produce catastrophic *impacts* from whatever climate change happens to materialize, for example. Even if they cannot rely on the scientific community to reduce the range of "not implausible" scenarios in the temperature domain, they could ask it to (1) explore the triggers of more regional catastrophe, (2) identify the parameters of fundamental change that define those triggers, (3) contribute to the design of monitoring mechanisms that can track the pace of change relative to these triggers, and (4) conduct small- and large-scale experiments in models, laboratories and perhaps the real world to learn more about the relevant processes. Assuming that the rate of change of these manifestations of climate change could be calibrated to something like the pace of change in global mean temperature, it might then be possible to calibrate some of the fuzzy and politically determined boundaries of "dangerous anthropogenic interference".

Three possibilities emerge for this effort. In the first, regional catastrophic impacts are reversible, but doing so could involve draconian global intervention into the economic sectors from which greenhouse gas emissions were being released. Given the great inertia of the climate and political systems, however, affected societies would probably have to cope with catastrophic impacts for a certain and potentially long period of time. In these cases, the precautionary principle would tell us to restrict emissions along a least cost path for a concentration target as a hedge against both the cost of draconian interventions required to retreat back across the lowest thresholds and the transient costs of enduring "temporary" catastrophes. Nothing would be certain in the calculation of how vigorously to restrict emissions, of course, so the expense involved in their reduction would be have to be seen as an investment in reducing risk – specifically reducing the probability factor in the "probability times consequence" definition of pecuniary risk. Political decisions about exactly how much risk might be considered tolerable would have to be taken, and they would have to evolve as more information about the regional processes became available.

In the second case, one or more of the catastrophic processes is irreversible. Here, the precautionary principle tells us to hedge more strongly against "falling off a cliff". The hedging strategy would presumably impose more stringent emissions reductions much earlier than contemplated in the first instance, and calls for a geo-engineering solution could be expected – a strategy with its own risks, to be sure. In the third case, one or more of the catastrophes is irreversible and unavoidable. In this extreme possibility, preparing for the worst in the affected regions would be the only option, and global mitigation policy might still operate as if one of the other two cases were in force ubiquitously.

To put these three storylines into a "not-implausible" context, consider the collapse of the Atlantic thermohaline circulation (the THC) as an example of a potentially catastrophic event across many parts of the globe. The higher the climate sensitivity, the more likely it becomes and the sooner it might occur. The implications of such a collapse are unknown, particularly in the socio-economic context, but the planet has experienced another climate equilibrium in which it does not exist. Three different explanations of the process by which it might collapse (Keller *et al.*, forthcoming) have been advanced, but each would point to its own critical parameter for monitoring. Because we do not know the precise process, we cannot identify the triggering threshold and so we cannot calibrate global policy in terms of an increase in global mean temperature. Schlesinger *et al.* (2005) and Yin *et al.* (2006) have told us, however, that the THC can collapse in a matter of decades once the trigger is pulled and that reversal, if possible, would take as long as a century to achieve.

Clearly, fundamental research into process understanding of circulation dynamics makes more sense in this example than work designed to make marginal changes in the distribution of climate sensitivity. Anticipating progress there, other research could investigate the sensitivity of least cost approaches to hedging strategies to alternative socio-economic futures and the evolution of new scientific knowledge. To be clear, the policy community would find value in this work *only if* the scientific community could clarify (1) the triggering mechanisms, (2) estimate the lag time between the triggers and climatological commitments to crossing the associated thresholds, (3) devise mechanisms for monitoring circulation intensity and other factors with enough precision to inform the likelihood of commitment, and (4) allow statisticians to calculate probabilities of type 1 and type 2 errors along a range of transient futures based on those monitoring exercises. None of these tasks involves Bayesian learning about climate sensitivity. That is reassuring, but none of them is simple either. Faced with an impossibility theorem and persistent uncertainty about climate sensitivity, however, tackling these difficult problems is the lesser of two evils.

7.4   SOME CONCLUDING REMARKS

We have argued that integrated assessment models that rely on a cost-benefit approach to conduce their policy analyses cannot always accommodate profound uncertainties, particularly in the context of persistent thick tails in the distributions of critical parameters like climate sensitivity. It should now be clear why the scientific community must move beyond trying to nail down consensus about the central baseline tendencies of climate change and embrace (though not exclusively) an organized effort designed to examine the "dark tails" of our possible futures across the range of possible impacts and associated key vulnerabilities. Only then can we begin to define the boundaries of tolerable change to support rigorous analyses of decision-making criteria that account, explicitly, for the enormous uncertainties that characterize our understanding of the climate system.

What does all of this mean for the social cost of carbon? Cast in the context of an informed and rigorously defined precautionary approach to policy design, the social cost of carbon can be viewed as the marginal cost of mitigation at any point in time – i.e., the shadow price of the precautionary constraints that reduce the likelihood of catastrophic impacts to tolerable levels. In other words, the calculation of the social cost of carbon would be tied directly to the scarcity rent that minimizes the expected cost of politically palatable hedging. This is not necessarily an easy calculation, but there is some good news. Climate sensitivity would not be an issue because the social cost of carbon would be tied to the marginal cost of meeting a concentration target (though the distribution of climate sensitivity would be involved in the discussions that try to translate temperature targets into concentration limits). The discount rate would not be an issue either, because the rate applied to other public investments and not the one that ponders the ethical complications of intergenerational equity would now apply. Indeed, this calculation would exclude some of the sources of uncertainty that explain the enormous range of social cost of carbon estimates noted above. However, issues like valuation and equity weighting do not go away, as they are essential ingredients to the definition of what constitutes a catastrophic impact.

We hope to have shed some preliminary light on the "So what?" implications of the Dismal Theorem on the design of climate policy and climate research. We now turn to the warning label that we promised. The Dismal Theorem is derived from taking limits, so it is tempting to take its conclusion to its logical extremes. One might, for example, read the Dismal Theorem as saying that the value of some improved information about what might be going on in the thick tail of the climate sensitivity distribution is infinite. If that is so, then we need to do as much as we can to sharpen the climate signal by, for example, burning as much coal as quickly as we can. One might also apply the generalized precautionary principle to all social issues for which there are unfortunate consequences in the fat tails of the distributions of critical variables because expected marginal damages are infinite for all of them. But then, how should we set priorities for distributing the planet's finite resources in the social interest? The economic tradeoffs would simply be undefined. Because neither of these implications is particularly attractive, we offer a concluding warning label on the Dismal Theorem: "Warning: Not to be taken to its logical extreme in application to real world problems."

Acknowledgements

The authors gratefully acknowledge the contributions of Martin Weitzman in the preparation of this chapter, as well as the comments offered by participants in the Climate Change Impacts workshop in Snowmass, Colorado in the summer of 2007. All remaining errors reside with the authors.

7.5   REFERENCES

Alcamo, J. and E. Kreileman (1996). Emissions Scenarios and Global Climate Protection. *Global Environmental Change* **6**, 305–344.

Allen, M. and D. Frame (2007). Abandon the Quest. *Science* **328**, 582–583.

Andronova, N.G. and M.E. Schlesinger (2001). Objective Estimation of the Probability Density Function for Climate Sensitivity. *Journal of Geophysical Research* **106**, 605–622.

Cline, W.R. (1992). *The Economics of Global Warming*. Institute for International Economics: Washington, D.C.

Cline, W.R. (1997). Modelling Economically Efficient Abatement of Greenhouse Gases, in Y. Kaya and K. Yokobori (Eds): *Environment, Energy, and Economy*. United Nations University Press: Tokyo, 99–122.

Cline, W. R. (2004). *Meeting the Challenge of Global Warming*. National Environmental Assessment Institute: Copenhagen.

Downing, T. and P. Watkiss (2003). The Marginal Social Costs of Carbon in Policy Making: Applications, Uncertainty and a Possible Risk Based Approach. Paper presented at the DEFRA International Seminar on the Social Costs of Carbon, July 2003.

Hope, C. (2006). The Marginal Impact of CO2 from PAGE2002: An Integrated Assessment Model Incorporating the IPCC's Five Reasons for Concern. *Integrated Assessment* **6**, 1–16.

Intergovernmental Panel on Climate Change (IPCC) (2007a). *Climate Change 2007: The Science. Contribution of Working Group I to the Fourth Assessment Report*, Cambridge University Press: Cambridge, UK.

Intergovernmental Panel on Climate Change (IPCC) (2007b). *Climate Change 2007: Impacts, Adaptation and Vulnerability. Contribution of Working Group II to the Fourth Assessment Report*, Cambridge University Press: Cambridge, UK.

Keller, K., G.W. Yohe and M.E. Schlesinger (forthcoming). Managing the Risk of Climate Thresholds: Uncertainties and Information Needs. *Climatic Change*.

Maddison, D.J. (1995). A Cost-Benefit Analysis of Slowing Climate Change. *Energy Policy* **23**, (4/5), 337–346.

Manne, A. and R. Richels (1997). On Stabilizing CO_2 Concentrations – Cost-effective Emission Reduction Strategies. *Environmental Modeling and Assessment* **2**, 251–266.

Nordhaus, W. (1991). To Slow or Not to Slow: The Economics of the Greenhouse Effect. *Economic Journal* **101**, 920–937.

Nordhaus, W.D. (1993). Rolling the "DICE": An Optimal Transition Path for Controlling Greenhouse Gases. *Resource and Energy Economics* **15**, 27–50.

Nordhaus, W.D. (1994). *Managing the Global Commons: The Economics of Climate Change*. The MIT Press: Cambridge, MA.

Nordhaus, W.D. (2007). Critical Assumptions in the Stern Review on Climate Change. *Science* **317**, 201–202.

Nordhaus, W.D. and Z. Yang (1996). RICE: A Regional Dynamic General Equilibrium Model of Optimal Climate-Change Policy. *American Economic Review* **86**: 4, 741–765.

Nordhaus, W.D. and J.G. Boyer (2000). *Warming the World: Economic Models of Global Warming*. The MIT Press: Cambridge, MA.

Roe, G. and M. Baker (2007). Why is Climate Sensitivity so Unpredictable? *Science* **328**, 629–632.

Roughgarden, T. and S.H. Schneider (1999). Climate Change Policy: Quantifying Uncertainties for Damages and Optimal Carbon Taxes. *Energy Policy* **27**, 415–429.

Schlesinger, M.E., J. Yin, G. Yohe, N.G. Andronova, S. Malyshev and B. Li (2005). Assessing the Risk of Collapse of the Atlantic Thermohaline Circulation, in J. Schellnhuber, W. Cramer, N. Nakicenovic, T. Wigley, and G. Yohe (Eds) *Avoiding Dangerous Climate Change: A Scientific Symposium on Stabilisation of Greenhouse Gases.* Cambridge University Press: U.K. Meteorological Office, Exeter, U.K., 37–47.

Stern, N.H., S. Peters, V. Bakhshi, A. Bowen, C. Cameron, S. Catovsky, D. Crane, S. Cruickshank, S. Dietz, N. Edmonson, S.-L. Garbett, L. Hamid, G. Hoffman, D. Ingram, B. Jones, N. Patmore, H. Radcliffe, R. Sathiyarajah, M. Stock, C. Taylor, T. Vernon, H. Wanjie and D. Zenghelis (2006). *The Economics of Climate Change: The Stern Review.* Cambridge University Press, Cambridge, UK.

Swart, R., M. Berk, M. Janssen, E. Kreileman, and R. Leemans (1998). The Safe Landing Approach: Risks and Tradeoffs in Climate Change, in J. Alcamo, R. Leemans, and E. Kreileman (Eds): *Global Change Scenarios of the 21st Century – Results from the IMAGE 2.1 Model*. Pergamon/Elsevier Science: Oxford: 193–218.

Tol, R.S.J. (2002). Welfare Specifications and Optimal Control of Climate Change: An Application of FUND. *Energy Economics* **24**, 367–376.

Tol, R.S.J. (2003). Is the Uncertainty about Climate Change Too Large for Expected Cost-benefit Analysis?. *Climatic Change* **56**, 265–289.

Tol, R.S.J. (2005). The Marginal Damage Costs of Carbon Dioxide Emissions: An Assessment of the Uncertainties. *Energy Policy* **33**, 2064–2074.

Tol, R.S.J. (2007). The Social Cost of Carbon: Trends, Outliers and Catastrophes. Economics Discussion Papers, http://www.economics-ejournal.org/economics/discussionpapers/2007–44.

Tol, R.S.J. and G.W. Yohe (2007). Infinite Uncertainty, Forgotten Feedbacks, and Cost-Benefit Analysis of Climate Change. *Climatic Change* **83**, 429–442.

Toth, F.L., H.-M. Fussel, M. Leimbach, G. Petschel-Held and H.-J. Schellnhuber (1997). The Tolerable Windows Approach to Integrated Assessment, O. K. Cameron, K. Fukuwatari and T. Morita (Eds), *Climate Change and Integrated Assessment Models (IAMs) – Bridging the Gaps*. *Center for Global Environmental Research*, National Institute for Environmental Studies: Tsukuba, Japan, 401–403.

Uzawa, H. (2003). *Economic Theory and Global Warming*. Cambridge University Press: Cambridge, UK.

Weitzman, M.L. (2007). The Role of Uncertainty in the Economics of Catastrophic Climate Change. http://www.economics.harvard.edu/faculty/Weitzman/papers/Catastrophe.pdf.

Wigley, T., R. Richels and J.A. Edmonds (1996). Economic and Environmental Choices in the Stabilization of Atmospheric CO_2 Concentrations. *Nature* **379**, 240–243.

Yin, J., M.E. Schlesinger, N.G. Andronova, S. Malyshev and B. Li (2006). Is a Shutdown of the Thermohaline Circulation Irreversible? *Journal of Geophysical Research*.

Yohe, G.W. (2003). More Trouble for Cost-benefit Analysis. *Climatic Change* **56**, 235–244.

Yohe, G. and Toth, F. (2000). Adaptation and the Guardrail Approach to Tolerable Climate Change. *Climatic Change* **45**, 103–128.

Yohe, G.W., R.D. Lasco, Q.K. Ahmad, N. Arnell, S.J. Cohen, C. Hope, A.C. Janetos and R.T. Perez (2007). Perspectives on Climate Change and Sustainability. M.L. Parry, O.F. Canziani, J.P. Palutikof, C.E. Hanson and P.J. van der Linden (Eds): *Climate Change 2007: Impacts, Adaptation and Vulnerability. Contribution of Working Group II to the Fourth Assessment Report of the Intergovernmental Panel on Climate Change*. Cambridge University Press: Cambridge.

Yohe, G. and D. Tirpak (2008). A Research Agenda to Improve Economic Estimates of the Benefits of Climate Change Policies. *Integrated Assessment Journal* **8**, 1–17.

8

Incentives for Investing in Renewables

Paolo Falbo, Daniele Felleti and Silvana Stefani

8.1 INTRODUCTION AND BACKGROUND

Electricity markets, once strongly characterized by direct government intervention and frequently implemented by vertically integrated public enterprises, have been subjected to radical transformation throughout the world. Reforms have introduced a new institutional framework intended to ease competitive entry, to provide incentives to efficiency in the generation, transmission, distribution and retailing of output, and also to reduce tariffs and allow direct access to producers to the market. Within this new industrial framework and as a result of the relevant pressure originating from social, economic and political issues, an efficient electricity generation portfolio mix is becoming a strategic issue for all power producers (probably, *the* strategic issue). The matter is particularly important for Italy, where the demand for energy continues to rise ahead of the European average, and undercapacity has driven prices higher than those seen in other major European countries. This motivates research into the impact of Renewable Energy Sources (RES) on current portfolio mix, which at present is based, at least in Italy, mainly on fossil fuels. From an economic perspective, RES offer an important diversification opportunity as their marginal costs are negligible. This leads us to consider wind as a key renewable source to be analyzed next to more traditional fuels (coal, gas and oil), and to frame the analysis of profit functions in expected return/risk terms as long as risk is evaluated in an integrated approach. Under an integrated risk analysis, not only the degree of dependence of prices on alternative energy sources is relevant, but equally relevant are the optimal allocation of electricity quantity to sell spot, the cost of input for conventional energy, and as well as the estimates of the wind distribution volumes to be used for electricity generation and the evaluation of the spark spread option embedded in the producer profit function to generate conventional energy.

However, when comparing the profitability of renewable and conventional plants, investment costs play a critical role, since a renewable plant is significantly more expensive than a conventional one. Moreover, the effective production of a renewable plant is just a fraction of the nominal installed capacity (i.e. the maximum producible capacity) since its profit

Paolo Falbo: University of Brescia, falbo@eco.unibs.it
Daniele Felletti: University of Milano Bicocca, daniele.felletti@unimib.it
Silvana Stefani: University of Milano Bicocca, silvana.stefani@unimib.it

stream is largely driven by weather conditions.[1] On the other hand, if there is a rise of fuel price, necessary to generate conventional energy, the earnings from renewable can become competitive. In fact, deployment of renewable energy technologies can reduce natural gas demand and thus put downward pressure on natural gas prices, since they need not rely on volatile supplies of fuel (Sovacool and Cooper, 2006). In 2004 wind production generated a spare in fuel in Europe of about five billion euros (EWEA, 2005).

In any case, at least so far, renewable power must be subsidized to be competitive. There is a debate about whether fixed price incentives (like capital subsidies) can support renewables better than market-based incentives (like Green Certificates) (EWEA, 2005; Rickerson and Grace, 2007; Shirkey, 2005; Sovacool and Cooper, 2006). We do not take position, but our results show that choosing one or another support to renewables is not indifferent and can have different effects on the integrated risk management producer policy.

In this chapter we identify levels for incentives sufficient to make wind electricity production an efficient choice. In other words, we study the conditions under which an investment in green energy (wind in particular) is profitable, or reaches the expected profitability of an investment in conventional energy. First, in a risk neutral framework, we compare the profitability of two plants (a wind plant and a gas plant) and estimate the incentive which makes the two plants equally (expectedly) profitable. Among the many possible interventions, we consider capital subsidies which reduce the investment cost, feed-in tariffs and tradeable green certificates (GC), with the duty for producers to produce by renewables a fraction of their total production. We further assume that the producer, a price taker, can sell energy in the spot market in a uniform price auction (as in Germany and Italy) and he can take advantage of the spark spread option embedded in selling conventional energy in the spot market, i.e. he can shut the plant off if the unit cost of fuel is higher than the spot price. The prices we determine are a benchmark to define when producers should invest in green energies. We do not treat here other additional (dis)incentives like CO_2 emission certificates or white certificates.

Next, having made renewable and conventional energy equally profitable, we analyze in an integrated risk setting (Doherty, 2000; Henney and Keers, 1998) the energetic portfolio mix using VaR (Gaivoronski and Pflug, 2005) as a risk measure.

Statistical estimations are carried on the IPEX (Italy) and EEX (Germany) markets.

Previous research of the authors has focused on several closely related problems. In Falbo et al. (2008) the optimal portfolio selling mix in conventional production is analyzed. A price taker producer must decide the quantity of his production capacity to commit to bilateral contracts (at fixed sale price), offering the remainder to the spot market. Such a problem evidences the role of the spark spread option that a producer owns, as he can observe spot prices and can therefore decide to halt production when marginal costs are higher. The maturity effect of forward contracts to hedge against fuel price volatility is also considered.

In Falbo et al. (2007) a continuous time bivariate model of two correlated mean reverting processes is proposed to describe important issues in integrated energy risk management: hedging in conventional energy production and optimal timing of technical investments. Since in both problems the decision-maker faces uncertainty both in the price of input

---

[1] Only plants with storage, e.g. hydro plants with basin, can hold a desired production, at least in the short run, under regular weather conditions. New techniques are currently developed to this aim (e.g. compressed-air energy storage, CAES). Nevertheless any additional energy conversion implies a loss which is usually significant and/or economically expensive.

(typically oil, gas or other commodities necessary for production) and in the price of output (electricity), we show that the positive correlation between input and output prices can be exploited to help reduce the production risk.

The chapter is organized as follows: the subsidies are illustrated in Section 8.2, the theoretical results are in Section 8.3, the empirical application is in Section 8.4, risk is introduced in Section 8.5, conclusions are in Section 8.6.

8.2   SUBSIDIES FOR ENERGY

At least 64 countries have some type of policy to promote renewable power generation (REN21, 2007).

There are many other forms of policy support for renewable power generation, including green certificates, direct capital investment subsidies and rebates, tax incentives and credits, sales tax and value-added tax (VAT) exemptions, direct production payments or tax credits, net metering and direct public investment or financing (REN21, 2007). In this chapter we will focus on three forms of promotion policies, namely capital subsidies, green certificates and feed-in tariffs.

Renewable energy certificates, also known as "green certificates" (GCs), "green tags" or "tradeable renewable certificates", represent the environmental attributes of the power produced from renewable energy projects and are sold separately from commodity electricity. Renewable energy plants are entitled to receive GCs, related to the energy produced. GCs are issued by the national governments with reference to the previous year's effective production or in accordance with the foreseeable quantity of energy that will be produced the following year by the requesting operator. Each GC represents a certain quantity of energy for a given year of production (e.g., in Italy, one Green Certificate corresponds to 1 MWh).[2] The GC system involves also non-green producers, which actually play a central role. They are enforced to guarantee an annual target of green energy production which can be fulfilled by installing renewable energy plants or buying GCs for the corresponding energy. GCs therefore play a double role: they represent an incentive for green energy producers, but they mean additional costs for producers lacking the minimal green target (for example in Italy the annual target for 2006 has been fixed to 3.05 % of the energy produced during the previous year).

Capital subsidies are the second most common incentive policy applied worldwide. Only quite recently feed-in tariffs have started to replace them in some countries. Capital subsidies, through competitive grant application mechanisms, are still available in the UK through the Low Carbon Buildings Programme and in local and regional schemes in Austria, Germany, France and the Netherlands. They are a simple form of incentive consisting of a one-time payment by the national government or a utility to cover a percentage of the capital cost of a renewable plant investment.

Feed-in tariffs are the most common promotion policy, available in 37 countries and nine states or provinces worldwide (see REN21, 2007). Feed-in tariffs have noticeably enhanced innovation and sustained renewable energy investment in many countries. These policies have received much attention from wind power operators, but have also influenced solar PV, biomass and small hydro development. Many changes and additions were made during 2006/2007, particularly in Europe. Citing the REN21 (2007) report: "... Portugal

---

[2] During 2006 the minimum size of GCs in Italy was 50 MWh.

modified its feed-in tariff to account for technology differences, environmental impacts, and inflation. Austria amended its renewable electricity law to permit a new feed-in tariff system. Spain modified feed-in tariff premiums (which are added to base power prices) to de-couple premiums from electricity prices and avoid windfall profits when electricity prices rose significantly. And Germany proposed modifications to its "EEG" feed-in law. Elsewhere, Indonesia revised its feed-in tariff to cover plants up to 10 MW in size, from a previous limit of 1 MW. Thailand adopted a new feed-in policy for wind, solar, biomass, and micro-hydro." This incentive plan has also been made available to individuals. The above mentioned German Act (EEG) assures a fixed feed-in-tariff for grid-connected solar electricity over a time span of 20 years (currently about 460 €/MWh, depending on the kind of system). Despite such differences the common feature of feed-in tariffs remains the incentive linked to effective energy production in favor of the green operator. Feed-in tariffs set a fixed guaranteed price at which power producers can sell renewable power into the electric power network. Some policies provide a fixed tariff while others provide fixed premiums added to market- or cost-related tariffs. This form of subsidy is easy to implement, and is administratively is the most cost efficient. In contrast to GCs, feed-in tariffs do not imply any detriment for non-green producers.

From a product cycle perspective, stimulus of early deployment, following the research and development phase may probably best be supported by targeted measures such as capital subsidies, while the green certificates markets will probably provide a more adequate enhancement to further commercialization before full competitiveness is achieved (Midttun and Gautesen, 2007).

8.3 THE MODEL

8.3.1 Capital subsidies

Let C_G and C_W be the cost per installed MW for a gas and a wind plant respectively. Let I_{CS} be the capital subsidies per installed MW for the wind plant. For ease of comparison, we consider two plants with the same investment cost, so 1MW of a gas plant will be compared to $\frac{C_G}{C_W - I_{CS}}$ MW of a wind plant.

As in Falbo *et al.* (2008) we assume that a producer can produce only when it is profitable,[3] so he can take advantage of the spark spread option embedded in his profit function. Thus the hourly profit from the gas plant is

$$G_G = \max(p - c, 0) - C_{OMG} \tag{8.1}$$

where

- G_G is the profit per hour

- p is the hourly spot price for energy

- c is the price of fuel required to produce 1MWh of energy

---

[3] We showed that offering in a uniform auction at a bid price equal to marginal cost (i.e. fuel cost c) is optimal for a price taker producer. For a producer with market power this is not true, so that G_G is a lower bound for his profits.

- C_{OMG} are fixed costs and are essentially O&M (operations and maintenance) costs per hour and per installed MW.

The hourly profit from the wind plant is

$$G_W = \frac{C_G}{C_W - I_{CS}} (\gamma_W\, p - C_{OMW}) \tag{8.2}$$

where

- G_W is the profit per hour

- p is the hourly spot price for power

- γ_W is the effective performance of the turbine and depends on the wind flow. $\gamma_W = 0$ when there is no wind (or the wind is so strong that the turbine must be stopped), $\gamma_W = 1$ when the wind power is adequate

- C_{OMW} are fixed costs, i.e. O&M costs per hour and per installed megawatt.

The incentive I_{CS} that equates the expected profits of the plants is:

$$I_{CS} : E[G_G] = E[G_W]$$

$$\Leftrightarrow E[\max\,(p - c, 0)] - C_{OMG} = \frac{C_G}{C_W - I_{CS}} (E[\gamma_W\, p] - C_{OMW}) \tag{8.3}$$

$$\Leftrightarrow I_{CS} = C_W - \frac{E[\gamma_W\, p] - C_{OMW}}{E[\max\,(p - c, 0)] - C_{OMG}} C_G$$

8.3.2   Feed-in tariffs

Feed-in tariffs have been introduced to reward real production since capital subsidies reward the installation of the plant (i.e. its "nominal capacity"), not its efficiency.

One megawatt of a gas plant must be compared to $\frac{C_G}{C_W}$ MW of a wind plant to ensure the same investment.

The profit from the gas plant remains as in Eq. (8.1), while the profit from the wind plant is

$$G_W = \frac{C_G}{C_W} (\gamma_W\, (p + p_{FI}) - C_{OMW}) \tag{8.4}$$

where p_{FI} is the fixed tariff determined by the government.

The same expected profit is reached when

$$E[G_G] = E[G_W]$$

$$\Leftrightarrow E[\max\,(p - c, 0)] - C_{OMG} = \frac{C_G}{C_W} (E[\gamma_W\, p] - E[\gamma_W]\, p_{FI} - C_{OMW})$$

$$\Leftrightarrow p_{FI} = \frac{1}{E[\gamma_W]} \left[\frac{C_W}{C_G} (E[\max\,(p - c, 0)] - C_{OMG}) - (E[\gamma_W\, p] - C_{OMW}) \right]$$

$$\tag{8.5}$$

Capital subsidies and feed-in tariffs look very similar (we will show they are not); hence a simple formula relates p_{FI} to I_{CS}:

$$\frac{I_{CS}}{C_W} = \frac{E[\gamma_W] \, p_{FI}}{E[\gamma_W \, p] + E[\gamma_W] \, p_{FI} - C_{OMW}} \tag{8.6}$$

8.3.3 Green certificates

Whenever 1 MWh is produced by the gas plant, k MWh of wind power must be produced or the same amount of green certificates must be bought. Green certificates for the remaining (when positive) wind production can be sold. This is the same as selling GCs for the total wind production and buying GCs for a fraction k of the gas production. If p_{GC} is the GC price for 1MW, the marginal cost of gas production is now $c + k \, p_{GC}$. So the optimal bid price in the spot market for a price taker producer is now $c + k \, p_{GC}$. In the meantime, every wind produced MW is now remunerated $p + p_{GC}$. Without capital subsidies, 1MW gas plant must be compared to $\frac{C_G}{C_W}$ MW wind plant. The profits of the plants are respectively equal to:

$$G_G = \max \left(p - c - k \, p_{GC}, 0 \right) - C_{OMG} \tag{8.7}$$

and

$$G_W = \frac{C_G}{C_W} \left(\gamma_W \, (p + p_{GC}) - C_{OMW} \right) \tag{8.8}$$

The price for the GC that equates the expected profits is defined below:

$$p_{GC} : E[G_G] = E[G_W]$$

$$\Leftrightarrow \quad E[\max \left(p - c - k \, p_{GC}, 0 \right)] - C_{OMG} \tag{8.9}$$

$$= \frac{C_G}{C_W} \left(E[\gamma_W \, p] + E[\gamma_W] p_{GC} - C_{OMW} \right) \quad \Leftrightarrow$$

$$\Leftrightarrow \quad E[\max \left(p - c - k \, p_{GC}, 0 \right)]$$

$$= \frac{C_G}{C_W} E[\gamma_W] \, p_{GC} + \frac{C_G}{C_W} \left(E[\gamma_W \, p] - C_{OMW} \right) + C_{OMG} \tag{8.10}$$

With respect to p_{GC}, the first term in Eq. (8.10) is a decreasing function, while the second term is linear and increasing: thus there is just a unique p_{GC} solution of the equation. This value is positive if

$$\frac{C_G}{C_W} \left(E[\gamma_W \, p] - C_{OMW} \right) < E[\max \left(p - c - k \, p_{GC}, 0 \right)] - C_{OMG} \tag{8.11}$$

i.e. if, without incentives, gas plants are more profitable than wind plants.

8.4   STATISTICAL ESTIMATIONS

We apply the model to German and Italian power markets during year 2006 to compare different market scenarios. Italian power prices are higher on average, both during base and peak hours, but in EEX spikes occur more frequently and are much stronger (see Figs 8.1 and 8.2). Figure 8.3 shows gas prices[4] during 2006.[5]

To evaluate the wind production, we considered whole EON wind production (7800MW installed all over Germany) for Germany, and a small wind park (22MW installed by Fortore Energia s.p.a. in Val Fortore, Puglia) for Italy. The average wind production was almost the

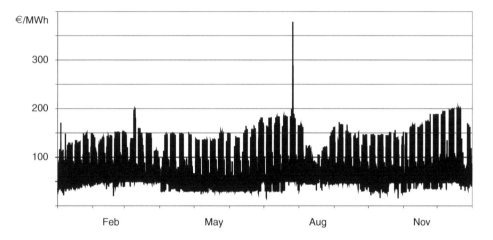

Figure 8.1   2006 power prices. Italian market

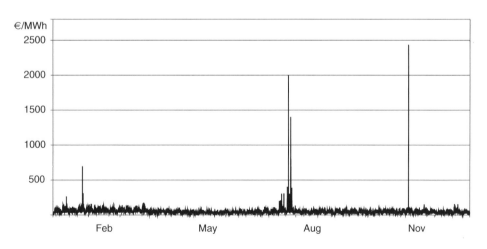

Figure 8.2   2006 power prices. German market

---

[4] Source: Datastream. UK natural gas, 1 day forward.
[5] Prices have been converted into €/MWh assuming conventionally that the gas plant has an efficiency of 39 % (i.e. 39 % of thermal energy produced by combustion of fuel is converted into electricity).

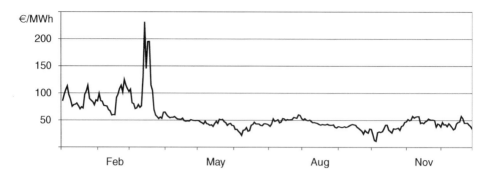

Figure 8.3   2006 gas prices in Europe

same in both cases: $E[\gamma_W] = 19.01\,\%$ of the installed capacity for EON, $E[\gamma_W] = 19.76\,\%$ for Fortore.

Table 8.1 reports investment and O&M costs for standard wind and gas plants. Table 8.2 reports some estimations and results.[6]

As far as capital subsidies are concerned, incentives of 77.95 % and 69.11 % over the wind plant investment cost are required for Italy and Germany respectively.

Table 8.1   Investment and O&M costs for standard gas and wind plants

	Gas plant		Wind plant	
Investment costs (€/kW)	C_G	750	C_W	1500
O&M costs (€/MWh)	C_{OMG}	3.5	C_{OMW}	5

Table 8.2   Market statistics

	Italian market	German market
$E[p]$	74.75 €/MWh	50.79 €/MWh
$E[c]$	55.76 €/MWh	
$E[\gamma_W]$	19.76 %	19.01 %
$E[\gamma_W\, p]$	15.16 €/MWh	8.64 €/MWh
$E[\max(p - c, 0)]$	26.54 €/MWh	9.34 €/MWh
I_{CS}/C_W	77.95 %	69.11 %
p_{FI}	181.81 €/MWh	42.82 €/MWh
p_{GC}	150.06 €/MWh	(38.05 €/MWh)

For the year 2006 in Italy, GSE issued GCs at a price equal to 125.28€/MWh, but GME reports a weighted average price for GCs exchanged in the market during 2006 equal to 144.23€/MWh. This means that the market priced GCs somehow correctly, very close to our computed benchmark 150.06€/MWh.

Feed-in tariffs were decreed by law from the year 2008 for wind power equal to 300 €/MWh.[7]

---

[6] p_{GC} for the German case (in brackets) is an "as if" price since there is not a market for GC in Germany.
[7] Italian producers must decide whether to accept the feed-in tariff for 15 years or to receive the corresponding GC for the same term (l. 244, Dec. 24, 2007). Note that with respect to 2006 prices, our benchmark was $p_{FI} + \frac{E[\gamma_W\, p]}{E[\gamma_W]} \simeq$

8.5   RISK ANALYSIS

Even if a proper incentive makes gas and wind plants indifferent with respect to expected profits, the distributions of the profits differ significantly.

Now we consider a "balanced" production under the incentive that makes power generation indifferent both to investment costs and expected profits: we consider a producer who owns gas plants for $(1 - \lambda)$ MW and wind plants for $\lambda \frac{C_G}{C_W - I_{CS}}$ MW (when considering capital subsidies) or $\lambda \frac{C_G}{C_W}$ MW (when considering feed-in tariffs and GCs), with $\lambda \in [0, 1]$. Clearly $\lambda = 0$ is a purely gas production, while $\lambda = 1$ is a purely wind production.

As mentioned, the weights $\frac{C_G}{C_W - I_{CS}}$ or $\frac{C_G}{C_W}$ ensure that the investment cost is the same for every λ. Besides we consider I_{CS} (or p_{FI} or p_{GC}) such that $E[G_G] = E[G_W]$. Since

$$G(\lambda) = (1 - \lambda) G_G + \lambda G_W \tag{8.12}$$

the previous conditions ensure the same investment cost (C_G €/MW) and the same average profit ($E[G(\lambda)] = E[G_G] = E[G_W]$) for every λ.

To better illustrate how risk changes with respect to λ, we make use of the following risk measure:

$$R_\varepsilon = VaR_\varepsilon[-G] \tag{8.13}$$

The minus sign accounts for risk-aversion: smaller R_ε is preferable.

A plant allocation (λ) is assigned a risk R_ε if it suffered an hourly loss greater than R_ε with a probability not greater than $1 - \varepsilon$. Equivalently: it ensured a profit greater than $-R_\varepsilon$ with a probability greater than ε.

8.5.1   Capital subsidies

8.5.1.1   Italian case

If the Italian wind plant had been subsidized for $I_{CS}/C_W = 77.95\%$ of its initial cost, the investment for 1 MW gas plant and $\frac{C_G}{C_W - I_{CS}} = 2.27$ MW wind plant would have been the same. Both plants yielded the same average profit during 2006: 23.04 €/h.

Table 8.3 shows that different risk profiles are associated with the same profit. The gas plant is off for about 29% of the time because $p < c$, in which case the associated loss coincides with O&M costs (see Table 8.1). The wind plant works more than 90% of the time (5.3% of time wind was scanty). The wind plant is riskier than the gas plant. For high VaR levels (e.g. $\varepsilon = 99\%$ and $\varepsilon = 95\%$) the wind plant suffered losses equal to $\frac{C_G}{C_W - I_{CS}} C_{OMW} = 11.34$ €/h, while the gas plant suffered losses equal to $C_{OMG} = 3.5$ €/h (indeed, for different reasons, both plants have been off-duty more than 5% of time).

181.81 + $\frac{15.16}{0.1976}$ = 258.53 €/MWh. Italian feed-in tariff is a "fixed price" tariff, which differs from the "premium" tariff we are analyzing here because in the former case the profit is

$$G_W = \frac{C_G}{C_W} (\gamma_W P_{FI*} - C_{OMW}).$$

Nevertheless when $P^*_{FI} = p_{FI} + \frac{E[\gamma_W p]}{E[\gamma_W]}$ the expected profit is the same.

Table 8.3 Italian case. Risk (for different percentiles) for gas and wind plants if renewables were subsidized with $I_{CS}/C_W = 77.95\,\%$. R in €/h

	99 %	95 %	90 %	80 %	70 %	60 %	50 %
Gas plant ($\lambda = 0$)			3.5		2.27	−5.12	−13.09
Wind plant ($\lambda = 1$)	11.34		11.10	9.37	6.94	3.47	−1.33

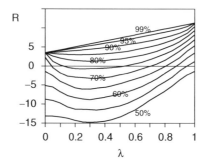

Figure 8.4 Italian case. Risk (for different percentiles) vs percentage (λ) of renewables if renewables were subsidized with $I_{CS}/C_W = 77.95\,\%$. R in €/h

Besides, even for low VaR levels ($\varepsilon = 50\,\%$) the gas plant yielded a profit greater than 13.09 €/h, while the wind plant yielded a profit greater than only 1.33 €/h.

Figure 8.4 shows that a balanced production can reduce risk. Consider for example $R_{75\%}$. The gas plant ($\lambda = 0$) suffers a loss equal to 3.5 €/h. The wind plant ($\lambda = 1$) suffers a loss equal to 8.27 €/h. However mixing wind with thermal generation would have ensured even positive profits for the same probability: setting $\lambda = 0.25$ would have generated profits greater than 0.72 €/h more than 75 % of time.

Figure 8.4 suggests that in these conditions $\lambda \simeq 0.3$ (i.e. a wind capacity corresponding to the 30 % of the capital invested) would reduce the frequency of losses.

8.5.1.2 German case

For $\frac{C_G}{C_W - I_{CS}} = 1.62$ MW wind plant yielded the same profit of 1 MW gas plants (5.89 €/h). They would require also the same investment if wind plant were subsidized for the 69.11 % of the initial cost (see Table 8.2).

Table 8.4 shows that until 50 % the risk of gas plants does not change. This happened because $c > p$ for 60 % of time during 2006, so that we observed losses given by O&M costs. On the other hand, wind generation never dropped to zero because EON plants are

Table 8.4 German case. Risk (for different percentiles) for gas and wind plants when renewables are subsidized with $I_{CS}/C_W = 69.11\,\%$. R in €/h

	99 %	95 %	90 %	80 %	70 %	60 %	50 %
Gas plant ($\lambda = 0$)				3.5			
Wind plant ($\lambda = 1$)	7.74	7.23	6.67	5.33	3.68	1.74	−0.75

scattered all over Germany. In spite of this, wind plants are still riskier when considering high levels of VaR (e.g. $\varepsilon > 70\%$). The reason is that German prices are often low (during base hours), and particularly much lower than Italian prices. So wind power can suffer greater losses because of the higher incidence of maintenance costs:

$$C_{OMG} = 3.5 \, \text{€}/\text{h} < 8.09 \, \text{€}/\text{h} = \frac{C_G}{C_W - I_{CS}} C_{OMW} \tag{8.14}$$

Figure 8.5 shows that, as in Italian case, a balanced production can reduce risk. However a greater λ is required in this case: $\lambda \simeq 70\%$ (i.e., 70% of investment should be wind).

8.5.2   Feed-in tariffs

Here we analyze a "Premium" tariff. Nevertheless the results of risk analysis do not differ significantly when considering a "fixed price" tariff. Therefore we can state that the volatility of spot prices is a very weak source of risk for the wind plant and risk is actually due to wind variability.

8.5.2.1   Italian case

A mix of 1 MW gas plant and $\frac{C_G}{C_W} = 0.5$ MW wind plant incentivized with a tariff $p_{FI} = 181.81 \, \text{€}/\text{MWh}$ is now considered. Any balanced plant gave an average profit equal to 23.04 €/h.

With respect to capital subsidies, feed-in tariffs reduce the risk of the wind plant because of smaller O&M costs (the wind capacity now is 0.5 MW, while it was 2.27 MW with capital subsidies).

The gas plant is riskier than the wind plant with feed-in tariffs (see Table 8.5). It was not with capital incentives.

Figure 8.6 shows that "optimal" λ are between 40% and 75%.

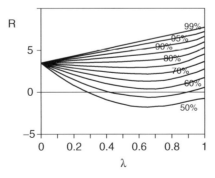

Figure 8.5   German case. Risk (for different percentiles) vs percentage (λ) of renewables when renewables are subsidized with $I_{CS}/C_W = 69.11\%$. R in €/h

Table 8.5 Italian case. Risk (for different percentiles) for gas and wind plants when $p_{FI} = 181.81 \, €/MWh$. R in $€/h$

	99 %	95 %	90 %	80 %	70 %	60 %	50 %
Gas plant ($\lambda = 0$)			3.5		2.27	−5.12	−13.09
Wind plant ($\lambda = 1$)	2.5		2.30	0.75	−1.36	−4.21	−8.37

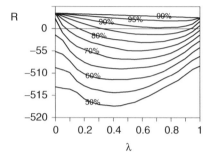

Figure 8.6 Italian case. Risk (for different percentiles) vs percentage (λ) of renewables when $p_{FI} = 181.81 \, €/MWh$. R in $€/h$

8.5.2.2 German case

We have already shown that in German market wind generation needs lower incentives than in Italian market. The price for the tariff that makes the wind plant as profitable as the gas plant is only $42.82 \, €/MWh$.

Table 8.6 shows that the wind plant is not as risky as the gas plant. The comparison between Figure 8.7 and Figure 8.5 confirms that, even though the average profit would have been still $5.89 \, €/h$, feed-in tariffs reduce the risk of wind generation. Therefore "optimal" λ are now in the range $80 \% - 90 \%$.

Table 8.6 German case. Risk (for different percentiles) for gas and wind plants when $p_{FI} = 42.82 \, €/MWh$. R in $€/h$

	99 %	95 %	90 %	80 %	70 %	60 %	50 %
Gas plant ($\lambda = 0$)				3.5			
Wind plant ($\lambda = 1$)	2.24	1.93	1.53	0.63	−0.44	−1.73	−3.30

8.5.3 Green certificates

8.5.3.1 Italian case

Here we consider the Italian case with GCs priced $p_{GC} = 150.06 \, €/MWh$.

Such a price would give both plants (1 MW gas plant and $\frac{C_G}{C_W} = 0.5 \, MW$ wind plant) an average profit equal to $19.90 \, €/h$: compared to capital subsidies and feed-in tariffs, GCs reduce the profitability of traditional generators. Even if the "spark-spread" protection offered by sales on the spot market partially offsets GC cost ($k \, p_{GC}$), it increases the

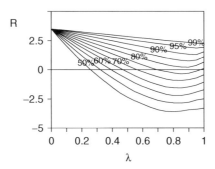

Figure 8.7 German case. Risk (for different percentiles) vs percentage (λ) of renewables when $p_{FI} = 42.82 \, €/MWh$. R in $€/h$

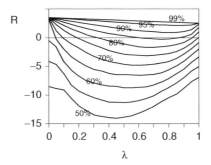

Figure 8.8 Italian case. Risk (for different percentiles) vs percentage (λ) of renewables when $p_{GC} = 150.06 \, €/MWh$. R in $€/h$

probability of the gas plant to be off-duty, which is an event that occurred about 34 % of the time in 2006. So, with respect to feed-in tariffs, GCs reduce the profit and increase the risk of the traditional plant (see Figure 8.8 and Figure 8.6).

Gas plants are riskier than wind plants in this case because the "equivalent" wind O&M costs are smaller:

$$C_{OMG} = 3.5 \, €/h > 2.5 \, €/h = \frac{C_G}{C_W} C_{OMW} \tag{8.15}$$

With GC the wind plant yields positive profits 75 % of the times, while the gas plant does it only 65 % of times (see Table 8.7). Nevertheless a balanced production can still perform better. This time the "optimal" allocation is not unique: $\lambda \simeq 0.45$ ensured a profit greater

Table 8.7 Italian case. Risk (for different percentiles) for gas and wind plants when $p_{GC} = 150.06 \, €/MWh$. R in $€/h$

	99 %	95 %	90 %	80 %	70 %	60 %	50 %
Gas plant ($\lambda = 0$)			3.5			−0.54	−8.52
Wind plant ($\lambda = 1$)		2.5	2.32	0.97	−0.88	3.37	−6.96

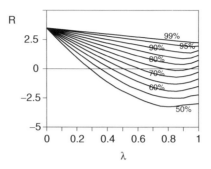

Figure 8.9   German case. Risk (for different percentiles) vs percentage (λ) of renewables if GC were introduced (with an obligation $k = 0.0305$) and $p_{GC} = 38.06$ €/MWh. R in €/h

than 14.07 €/h for 50 % of time (which is clearly a better performance than both 8.52 €/h and 6.96 €/h ensured by the gas and the wind plant respectively). However with $\lambda \simeq 80\%$ the maximum probability to avoid losses is ensured (positive profits for 85 % of times).

8.5.4   German case

For completeness and comparison purposes, we apply the model to German GC case, which we assume similar to Italy. We assume that Germany introduced a compulsory renewable production of $k = 3.05\%$ of the whole generation. Still comparing 1 MW gas plant to $\frac{C_G}{C_W} = 0.5$ MW wind plant, we have already estimated the price for the GC that brings gas production equivalent to wind: 38.06 €/MWh, which is much lower than Italian p_{GC}. Such a GC would reduce the average profit to 5.44 €/h.

Table 8.8   German case. Risk (for different percentiles) for gas and wind plants if GC were introduced and $p_{GC} = 38.06$ €/MWh. R in €/h

	99 %	95 %	90 %	80 %	70 %	60 %	50 %
Gas plant ($\lambda = 0$)				3.5			
Wind plant ($\lambda = 1$)	2.25	1.96	1.58	0.74	−0.27	−1.49	−2.97

Even though p_{GC} is not high enough to change significantly the risk of gas plants (instead of 60 %, the gas plants would have been off 61.5 % of time), with GC the wind plant is not as risky as the gas plant, while it was with capital subsidies. "Optimal" λ is now about 85 % which ensures positive profits in 75 % of the time. Figure 8.9 and Figure 8.7 show that feed-in tariffs and GC cases are very similar for what risk is concerned, but, as mentioned, GCs reduced the profits of about 0.45€/h.

8.6   CONCLUSIONS

This chapter offers several insights on the recent problem introduced by the introduction of incentives and other ways to subsidize renewable electricity sources (RES). While arguments can be given in favor or not for capital subsidies, feed-in tariffs rather than green certificates, there is no doubt that subsidies can encourage investments in renewables. While this is a rather obvious result, nevertheless we showed here that some form of subsidies are a necessary condition to make renewable plants economically viable, given current market prices. We stated the conditions on the three incentive forms to make wind and gas plants equivalent with respect to their hourly expected profit.

We also analyzed some risk management issues. Based on Italian and German data (prices and generation) of wind and gas plants, we estimate different VaR levels at different generation capacity mix.

We observe that capital subsidies, feed-in tariffs and GC are non equivalent in term of generation portfolio management. It turns out that under capital subsidies wind plants show higher values of VaR, i.e. are riskier than conventional plants. The opposite happens for feed-in tariffs and GC: wind plants result clearly less risky than conventional ones with GC showing a slightly stronger improvement of VaR measure. In all cases however the "optimal" VaR levels are achieved through a generation mix. Such results are therefore in favor of a progressive introduction of RES in the generation portfolio rather than a radical lump conversion. Further we find that the larger the uncertainty about fuel costs is, the more economically attractive investing in green energy is, with negligible marginal costs. Our results can help establish benchmark prices for subsidies and Green Certificates and address policy guidelines for a more effective institutional intervention.

An interesting aspect to be addressed for future research is that of the unique EU market for GC. Given the results of our chapter, a unique price for GC would be a huge opportunity for some countries but also a dangerous obstacle for others. In particular a GC price lower than what is required to make renewable production economically attractive, can result in RES stopping in those countries where traditional fuel has a comparative advantage. This in turn implies the risk of transferring all the burden of conversion to renewable energy resources on the shoulders of those countries already suffering for higher traditional fuel generation costs.

8.7   REFERENCES

Doherty, N.A. (2000). *Integrated Risk Management*. McGraw Hill.

EWEA – European Wind Energy Association (2005). Support Schemes for Renewable Energy. A Comparative Analysis of Payment Mechanisms in the EU. http://www.ewea.org.

Falbo, P., Felletti, D. and S. Stefani (2007). A Continuous Time Model for Correlated Energy Price Processes. Working Papers 119 Dept. Quantitative Methods, Univ. Milano-Bicocca.

Falbo, P., Felletti, D. and S. Stefani (2008). Integrated Risk Management for an Electricity Producer. Working Papers 144 Dept. Quantitative Methods, Univ. Milano-Bicocca.

Gaivoronski, A.A. and G. Pflug (2005). Value-at-Risk in Portfolio Optimization: Properties and Computational Approach. *Journal of Risk*, vol. **7**(2), 1–31.

Henney, A. and G. Keers (1998). Managing Total Corporate Electricity/Energy Market Risks. *The Electricity Journal*, vol. **11**(8), 36–46.

Meola, A. and F. Polidoro (2004). Caratteristiche di Costo e di Esercizio degli Impianti di Generazione Alimentati da Fonti Fossili, Rinnovabili, Assimilate, di Cogenerazione e di Generazione Distribuita. Ricerca di Sistema CESI.

Midttun, A. and K. Gautesen (2007). Feed In or Certificates, Competiton or Complementarity? Combining a Static Efficiency and a Dynamic Innovation Perspective on the Greening of the Energy Industry. *Energy Policy*, **35**, 1419–1422.

REN21 (2008). *Renewables 2007, Global Status Report*. (Paris: REN21 Secretariat and Washington, DC: Worldwatch Institute). Copyright ©2008 Deutsche Gesellschaft für Technische Zusammenarbeit (GTZ) GmbH, (http://www.ren21.net/).

Rickerson, W. and R.C. Grace (2007). *The Debate over Fixed Price Incentives for Renewable Electricity in Europe and the United States: Fallout and Future Directions*. The Heinrich Böll Foundation mimeo February.

Shirkey, R. (2005). *Incentives for Renewable Energy*. University of Victoria mimeo.

Sovacool, B.K. and C. Cooper (2006). Green Means Go? A Colorful Approach to a US National Renewable Portfolio Standard. *The Electricity Journal*, Vol. **19**(7), 19–32.

— 9 —

Hedging the Risk of an Energy Futures Portfolio[§]

Carol Alexander

This chapter considers a hedging problem for a trader in futures on crude oil, heating oil and unleaded gasoline and on the crack spreads based on these energy commodities. We first explain how the trader can map his current position to use constant maturity futures as risk factors. This has many advantages over using spot price or prompt futures prices plus discount rates as risk factors. Then we show how the trader can quantify his key risk factors, assess the risk of his portfolio and determine the most cost-effective hedging strategies.

The outline of this chapter is as follows. Section 9.1 explains the risk factor mapping process, and the advantages of using constant maturity futures as risk factors; Section 9.2 describes the portfolio to be hedged and Section 9.3 explains how principal component analysis is applied to reduce the dimension of the risk factor space and to isolate the key sources of risk; Section 9.4 assesses the risk of the portfolio and describes how best to hedge this risk; and Section 9.5 concludes.

9.1 MAPPING PORTFOLIOS TO CONSTANT MATURITY FUTURES

Constant maturity futures are not traded instruments. However, a time series of constant maturity commodity futures can be obtained by *concatenation* of adjacent futures prices. For instance, a time series for a constant maturity 1-month futures price can be obtained by taking the prompt futures with expiry less than or equal to 1 month and the next futures with expiry greater than 1 month and linearly interpolating between the two prices. So if the prompt futures contract with price P_1 has maturity $T_1 \leqslant 1$ month and the futures contract with price P_2 is the next to expire with maturity $T_2 > 1$ month, and T_1 and T_2 are measured in years, then the 1-month futures price is

$$P = \frac{\left(T_2 - \frac{1}{12}\right) P_1 + \left(\frac{1}{12} - T_1\right) P_2}{(T_2 - T_1)}.$$

ICMA Centre, University of Reading.
[§] Abstracted from C. Alexander (2008). *Pricing, Hedging and Trading Financial Instruments*, Volume III of C. Alexander, *Market Risk Analysis*, John Wiley and Sons (2008).
Carol Alexander, Professor of Financial Risk Management and Director of Research, ICMA Centre, University of Reading, UK; c.alexander@icmacentre.rdg.ac.uk.

Risk Management in Commodity Markets: From Shipping to Agriculturals and Energy   Edited by Hélyette Geman
© 2008 John Wiley & Sons, Ltd

For instance, suppose we wish to construct a 3-month futures series when the maturity dates are 16 March, 16 June, 16 September and 16 December. On 1 September we use the September and the December contracts, with prices P_1 and P_2 respectively. The number of days between the September contract expiry date and our 3-month expiry date (which is 1 December on 1 September) is 76 and the time interval between the December contract expiry date and our expiry date is 15 days. Hence, the concatenated price is

$$\frac{15 \times P_1 + 76 \times P_2}{91}.$$

We can continue to use the September and December contract prices in the construction of the 1-month futures price. For instance, on 12 September, our 3-month expiry date is 12 December, so the concatenated price would be

$$\frac{4 \times P_1 + 87 \times P_2}{91},$$

where P_1 and P_2 are now the prices of the September and December futures contracts on 12 September.

Since prices can behave oddly a few days before expiry, we should drop the September contract from our calculations after 12 September, and instead take the 3-month maturity contract price to be equal to the December contract price for a few days. However, on 17 September we can start using linear interpolation between the December and March futures prices as above, but now with the December contract being the shorter one. As time moves on we decrease the weight of the December price in our calculation of the concatenated futures price and increase the weight on the March futures price.

The main advantage of using constant maturity futures as risk factors for commodity portfolios is that the use of spot prices plus discount rates as risk factors assumes futures are always at their fair price, and thus ignores the basis risk due to fluctuations in carry costs and convenience yields, as well as the variation of the market price of the futures within its no arbitrage range. All these sources of uncertainty in the basis are considerable: carry costs due to storage, insurance and transportation are difficult to measure precisely; convenience yields are intangible and even more difficult to assess; and since the spot cannot be shorted the no arbitrage range has no lower bound, whence substantial decoupling of spot and futures prices is often evident when demand surges or supply drops for reasons beyond the control of the market participants.

Constant maturity futures provide a long time series of futures prices that can be used to assess the market characteristics. These characteristics vary considerably from market to market. Prices are determined by unpredictable demand and supply factors such as the weather and the economic climate. For instance, the weather affects the supply of corn and the demand for gas and the outbreak of war affects the price of oil. But prices may also be affected by speculative trading, and the "herding" behaviour of speculative investors can lead to prolonged price trends in futures prices that have nothing to do with demand and supply of the actual commodity.

The process of mapping a portfolio to constant maturity futures is very similar to the process of mapping a cash flow to fixed maturity interest rates. This can be done in a present value and volatility invariant manner as the examples below will demonstrate. The methodology is a simple adaptation of the cash flow mapping methods that are described for interest rate sensitive portfolios in Alexander (2008c) on pp. 332–337.

Example 1   Mapping commodity forward positions to constant maturity futures

Suppose we have just two forward positions on crude oil: a long position with present value $2 million in 1 month and 10 days and a short position with present value −$1 million in 1 month and 20 days. How should we map these to equivalent positions on constant maturity crude oil futures at the 1-month and 2-month maturity?

Solution

Suppose there are 30 days in a month. We could simply use linear interpolation and map 2/3 × 2 − 1/3 × 1 = $1m to the 1-month vertex and 1/3 × 2 − 2/3 × 1 = 0 to the 2-month vertex. But this will change the volatility of the portfolio. Instead we can use a present value and volatility invariant map, depicted in Fig 9.1. For this we need to know the volatilities of the 1-month and 2-month futures and their correlation − suppose the volatilities are 30 % and 27 % as shown and the correlation is 0.95. Using linear interpolation on the variances we infer the volatilities of 29.03 % for the 1 month 10 day position and 28.04 % for the 1 month 20 day position.

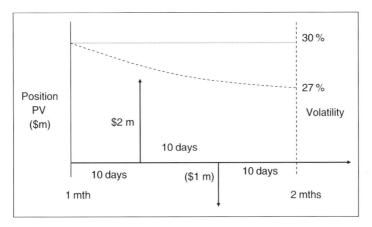

Figure 9.1   A volatility invariant commodity futures or forwards mapping

For the mapped position to have the same volatility as the original position, the proportion x of the long position of $2 million at 1 month 10 days that is mapped to the 1-month future must satisfy

$$29.03^2 = 30^2 \times x^2 + 27^2 \times (1 - x)^2 + 2 \times 0.95 \times 30 \times 27 \times x \times (1 - x).$$

This quadratic equation has one solution between 0 and 1, i.e. $x = 0.762092$. Similarly, the proportion y of the short position of $1 million at 1 month 20 days that is mapped to the 1-month future must satisfy

$$28.04^2 = 30^2 \times y^2 + 27^2 \times (1 - y)^2 + 2 \times 0.95 \times 30 \times 27 \times y \times (1 - y),$$

and solving this gives $y = 0.464239$. Thus in total we must map

$$0.762092 \times \$2\,000\,000 - 0.464239 \times \$1\,000\,000 = \$1\,059\,945$$

to the 1-month future, and

$$0.237908 \times \$2\,000\,000 - 0.535761 \times \$1\,000\,000 = -\$59\,945$$

to the 2-month future. This way the present value and the volatility of the mapped position is the same as the volatility of the unmapped position.

Example 2   Determining the number of contracts

Suppose the mapping in Example 1 was performed on a day when the prices of the crude oil forwards and futures were as shown in Table 9.1. Each forward contract is for 100 barrels and each futures contract is for 1000 barrels of crude oil. How many contracts are in the mapped position?

Table 9.1   Prices of crude oil forwards and futures ($ per barrel)

30 days	40 days	50 days	60 days
98.35	99.01	100	100.57

Solution

The solution is summarized in Table 9.2. The second row of the table shows the unmapped and mapped value of the positions, the number of barrels is this position value divided by the price per barrel and the number of contracts is the number of barrels divided by the number of barrels in each contract (1000 for the futures and 100 for the forwards).

Table 9.2   Positions on crude oil forwards and futures

Maturity	30 days	40 days	50 days	60 days
Price	98.35	99.01	100	100.57
Position Value	1 059 945	2 000 000	−1 000 000	−59,945
Number of Barrels	10 777.28	20 200	−10 000	−596.05
Number of Contracts	10.777	202	−100	−0.5961

Of course, there is no need to round the resulting number of futures contracts to the nearest integer, since we are only mapping the portfolio to these non-traded risk factors.

9.2   THE PORTFOLIO AND ITS KEY RISK FACTORS

Suppose that on 1 August 2006 a trader in energy futures holds long and short positions that have been mapped to constant maturity futures as shown in Table 9.3. Each futures contract is for 1000 barrels and the minus sign indicates a short position. Note that these positions could result from both straight futures trades and from positions on the two crack spread futures, i.e. unleaded gasoline–crude oil and heating oil–crude oil.

Figures 9.2–9.4 show how the daily prices of the constant maturity futures on all three products have evolved over a very long period. All prices spiked before the outbreak of

Table 9.3   Number of futures contracts in an energy futures trading book

Maturity (months)	Crude oil	Heating oil	Unleaded gasoline
1	−100	70	20
2	180	−60	−60
3	−300	150	100
4	−400	200	250
5	250	−180	−100
6	−100	100	30

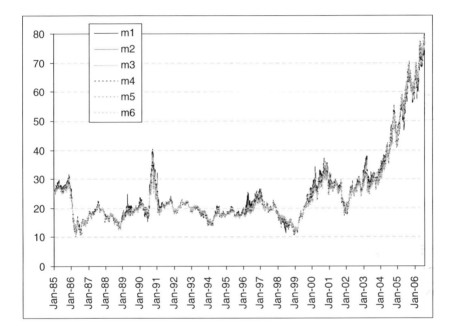

Figure 9.2   NYMEX WTI crude oil constant maturity futures prices

the Gulf war in 1991, and since the war in Iraq in 2003 prices have risen tremendously. For instance, the crude oil futures prices rose from around $20 per barrel to nearly $80 per barrel in August 2006 and the prices of the futures on the refined products rose even more. The daily price fluctuations of futures of different maturities on each product are always very highly correlated, as are those on futures of different products.

We do not need to use 30 years of data for the portfolio risk analysis; in fact looking back into the 1990s and beyond may give misleading results since energy markets have become much more volatile during the last few years. But we do need fairly high frequency data, because the trader needs to understand his short term risks. So we shall use daily data between 2 January 1999 and August 2006. In the spreadsheet for this case study we first calculate the average correlation of daily returns on each of the futures over the sample period. The correlation matrix is too large to be reported in the text, but Table 9.4 shows some of these correlations.

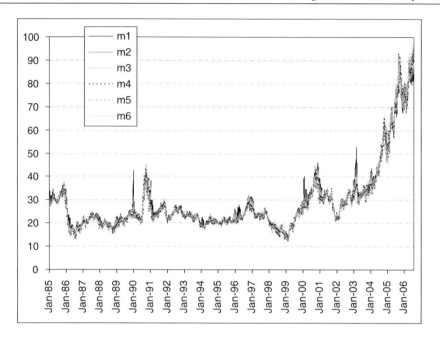

Figure 9.3   NYMEX heating oil constant maturity futures prices

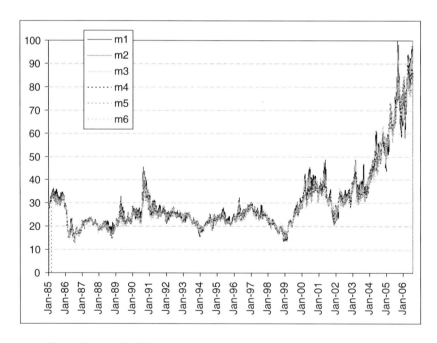

Figure 9.4   NYMEX unleaded gasoline constant maturity futures prices

Table 9.4 Daily correlations of futures prices at selected maturities

Correlations	m1–m2	m2–m3	m3–m4	m4–m5	m5–m6
Crude oil (CO)	0.972	0.994	0.997	0.998	0.998
Heating oil (HO)	0.946	0.986	0.986	0.991	0.991
Unleaded gasoline (UL)	0.918	0.951	0.951	0.947	0.949
Cross-correlations	m1	m2	m3	m4	m6
HO–CO	0.776	0.878	0.888	0.895	0.894
UL–CO	0.728	0.839	0.857	0.849	0.852
HO–UL	0.695	0.804	0.815	0.812	0.811

The crude oil futures behave like a typical term structure, with the correlation being higher at the long end and decreasing as the maturity gap between the futures increases. All correlations are very high indeed. The same comments apply to heating oil and unleaded gasoline futures, and although their term structures are a little less highly correlated than crude oil there is still a very high degree of correlation. The lower part of Table 9.4 shows that the cross-correlations between futures on different products are lower than the correlations of futures on one of the products, but they are still very high. Note that the 1-month futures tend to have slightly lower correlations than futures of 2 months' maturity and longer.

9.3 IDENTIFYING THE KEY RISK FACTORS

We have a total of 18 risk factors. But since they are so highly correlated we should perform a principal component analysis (PCA) to reduce the dimension of the risk factor space.[1] In the spreadsheet we apply PCA to the entire system of 18 risk factors. This way the principal component risk factors capture correlated movements across futures on different commodities, as well as within futures on the same commodity. The PCA may be applied to either the correlation or the covariance matrix of returns, with the latter accounting for any difference between the risk factor volatilities. In each commodity the 1-month futures have noticeably higher volatilities than the other futures, so we shall perform the PCA on the covariance matrix.

The results for the first four components from the PCA on the covariance matrix are displayed in Table 9.5. The entries in Table 9.5 are the eigenvectors corresponding to the first, second, third and fourth largest eigenvalues. The percentage of the total variation that is explained by each eigenvalue is shown in the first row of the table. Examining the eigenvalues and eigenvectors we deduce that, between January 1999 and August 2006:

- 86 % of the historical variations were a similar and simultaneous shift and tilt in all three term structures;
- 5 % of the historical variations were when the crude oil and unleaded gasoline futures shift and tilt in opposite directions and the heating oil futures term structure tilts changes convexity;

---

[1] See Alexander (2008) Section I.2.6 and Chapter II.2 for further details of principal component analysis.

Table 9.5   Results of PCA on the futures returns covariance matrix

	86%	5%	3%	2%
WTI m1	0.2594	0.1326	0.3522	0.0562
WTI m2	0.2448	0.1183	0.3055	0.0387
WTI m3	0.2284	0.1159	0.2908	0.0303
WTI m4	0.2157	0.1133	0.2802	0.0255
WTI m5	0.2053	0.1112	0.2697	0.0225
WTI m6	0.1965	0.1086	0.2587	0.0183
HO m1	0.2750	0.2245	−0.5156	−0.2024
HO m2	0.2629	0.2342	−0.3045	−0.0457
HO m3	0.2449	0.2242	−0.2283	0.0654
HO m4	0.2316	0.1979	−0.1618	0.1777
HO m5	0.2210	0.1611	−0.1158	0.2479
HO m6	0.2126	0.1120	−0.0772	0.2676
UL m1	0.2835	−0.6028	−0.1512	0.5121
UL m2	0.2630	−0.3950	−0.0172	0.0412
UL m3	0.2390	−0.2952	0.0183	−0.2175
UL m4	0.2210	−0.2249	0.0066	−0.3559
UL m5	0.2094	−0.1452	0.0018	−0.4224
UL m6	0.2039	−0.0810	−0.0041	−0.4057

- 3 % of the historical variations were when the crude oil and heating oil futures term structures shift and tilt in opposite directions and the unleaded gasoline futures remain static except at the very short end;
- 2 % of the historical variations were when the crude oil futures remain almost static, and the heating oil futures and unleaded gasoline futures tilt in opposite directions.

The first four principal components are time series that represent the four key risk factors for any portfolio on these oil futures. The common trend principal component risk factor is much the most important, since 86 % of the historical variation in these futures was due to movements of this type. Taking the first four components together captures 96 % of the historical variations in these energy futures since January 1999.

9.4   HEDGING THE PORTFOLIO RISK

Figure 9.5 shows a reconstructed price series for the portfolio, holding the positions constant at the values shown in Table 9.3 and revaluing the portfolio using the historical prices of the constant maturity futures. Since the portfolio has short positions its value could become negative, hence we base our analysis on the portfolio P&L and not on portfolio returns.

The current value of the portfolio is $10.025 million and its historical P&L volatility based on the reconstructed price series is extremely high, at over $3.5 million per annum. The 1 % 1-day historical Values at Risk (VaR) is $656 509 (measured as minus the 1 % percentile of the daily P&L distribution).[2] Assuming the returns are independent and identically distributed, we apply the square root of time rule to estimate the 1 % 10-day historical VaR as $656 509 × $\sqrt{10}$ = $2 076 065.

---

[2] See Alexander (2008d) Chapter IV.3 for further details on historical VaR. Note that we have not used filtered historical simulation here, hence the square root of time rule was applied to scale the 1-day VaR.

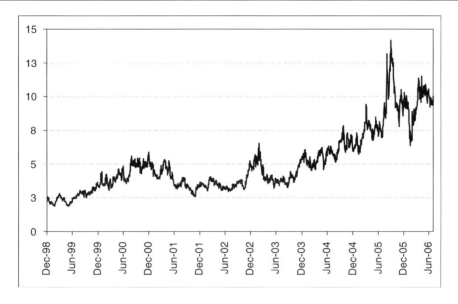

Figure 9.5   Reconstructed price series for the portfolio ($ million)

Concerned about the high probability of large losses on the portfolio, the trader decides to reduce the volatility of the portfolio returns by hedging. Our question is, which futures should he trade, and how many contracts should he buy or sell?

The principal component representation allows a close approximation of the portfolio in terms of its sensitivities to the four major risk factors. We first express the return on each constant maturity futures using its principal component representation. For instance,

$$R_{m1}^{WTI} \approx 0.2594 P_1 + 0.1326 P_2 + 0.3522 P_3 + 0.0562 P_4,$$

where R_{m1}^{WTI} is the daily return on the 1-month crude oil futures and P_1, P_2, P_3 and P_4 are the first four principal components. Then we map the portfolio return to the principal component risk factors using the portfolio representation shown in Table 9.5. We obtain:

$$P\&L = 2.7914 P_1 - 4.2858 P_2 - 17.0186 P_3 - 5.56101 P_4$$

where the coefficients are measured in millions of US dollars.

This representation tells that if the first principal component shifts up by 1 % leaving the other components fixed then the portfolio will gain about 1 % of $2.791 million, i.e. about $27 910. The first component is where all futures of the same maturities move by approximately the same amount.[3] The largest sensitivity of the portfolio is to the third principal component. Thus a rise in price on the short term heating oil contract is the largest risk exposure of this portfolio. It is not easy to see this from the portfolio composition. Nevertheless, we shall now confirm this by showing that selling the 1-month heating oil

---

[3] From Table 9.5 we know that a 1 % upward shift in the first component implies that the 1-month crude oil futures price increases by 0.2594 %, the 1-month heating oil futures price increases by 0.275 %, the 1-month gasoline futures price increases by 0.2835 %; and so on for the 2-month futures.

contract is indeed the best hedge for the portfolio amongst all single contract futures hedges, according to the reduction in P&L volatility that it achieves.

We now consider a partial hedge using a single futures contract and targeting a reduction on P&L volatility from over $3.5 million to less than $2.5 million per annum. For each of the futures contracts in turn, we calculate how many futures contracts of this type we need to sell to minimize the variance of the hedge portfolio P&L.

The results are summarized in Table 9.6. For each commodity we first report the risk factor P&L volatility, and the correlation between this risk factor P&L and the portfolio P&L. Below this we show the number of contracts on the futures that should be sold to minimize the variance of the hedged portfolio's P&L. The futures having the highest correlation with the reconstructed portfolio P&L are the 1-month heating oil futures (P&L correlation = 0.746) and the corresponding minimum variance hedge ratio implies that 145.45 contracts on the 1-month heating oil futures should be sold, and this trade effects the largest possible reduction in volatility compared with any other trade on a single futures contract.

Table 9.6 Minimum variance hedges to reduce to volatility of the futures portfolio

Risk factor	WTI m1	WTI m2	WTI m3	WTI m4	WTI m5	WTI m6
Risk factor P&L Volatility ($)	13.23	12.26	11.52	10.97	10.55	10.20
Correlation	0.411	0.441	0.440	0.440	0.440	0.441
No. contracts	111.44	128.88	137.10	143.72	149.56	155.17
Hedged portfolio P&L volatility ($)	$3 269 509	$3 219 570	$3 219 902	$3 221 064	$3 221 055	$3 218 688
1% 10-day historical VaR ($)	$1 939 370	$1 948 219	$1 976 805	$1 976 222	$1 974 615	$1 975 345
Risk factor	**HO m1**	**HO m2**	**HO m3**	**HO m4**	**HO m5**	**HO m6**
Risk factor P&L volatility ($)	18.39	16.79	15.70	14.86	14.22	13.67
Correlation	0.746	0.739	0.722	0.699	0.682	0.673
No. contracts	145.45	157.80	164.84	168.64	172.02	176.52
Hedged portfolio P&L volatility ($)	$2 389 086	$2 416 350	$2 483 014	$2 565 397	$2 622 976	$2 653 691
1% 10-day historical VaR ($)	$1 472 834	$1 509 869	$1 588 319	$1 725 051	$1 791 145	$1 852 938
Risk factor	**UL m1**	**UL m2**	**UL m3**	**UL m4**	**UL m5**	**UL m6**
Risk factor P&L volatility ($)	22.20	18.21	15.98	14.81	14.09	13.71
Correlation	0.661	0.679	0.703	0.740	0.682	0.682
No. contracts	106.82	133.81	157.67	179.24	173.56	178.55
Hedged portfolio P&L volatility ($)	$2 690 058	$2 631 691	$2 552 091	$2 411 291	$2 622 860	$2 621 616
1% 10-day historical VaR ($)	$1 501 297	$1 479 477	$1 458 825	$1 366 632	$1 642 830	$1 599 100

The hedge is effected using exchange traded heating oil futures that are equivalent, under the mapping described in Section 9.1, to 145.45 contracts on the 1-month heating oil futures. The result will be a portfolio with a historical P&L volatility of $2.389 million, compared with over $3.5 million without this hedge. Similarly, the hedge reduces the 1% 10-day historical VaR from $2.076 million to $1.473 million.

Other single contract hedges can also reduce the risk considerably. For instance, taking a position equivalent to selling 179.24 of the 4-month futures contract on unleaded gasoline would reduce the P&L volatility to $2.411 million and the 1% 10-day VaR to $1.367

million. Clearly, hedging with more than one futures contract would effect an even greater reduction in portfolio risk. For instance, using both the 1-month heating oil and 4-month gasoline futures in a single hedge, we determine the minimum variance hedge ratios using multiple regression.[4] The ordinary least squares estimated model, with t-statistics below the coefficients in parentheses is:

$$P\&L = -2.603_{(-0.809)} + 83.840_{(18.923)}P\&L^{HO}_{m1} + 97.928_{(17.802)}\ P\&L^{UL}_{m4}$$

Taking positions equivalent to 83.84 contracts on the 1-month heating oil futures and 97.928 contracts on the 4-month unleaded gasoline futures reduces the portfolio P&L volatility to 2.217 million and the 1% 10-day VaR to $1.274 million.

9.5   CONCLUSIONS

This chapter has used a practical and realistic example to demonstrate how to identify the key risk factors of energy futures portfolios. These are the principal components of a set of constant maturity futures on related energy products – in this case, crude oil, heating oil and unleaded gasoline. Due to the very high correlation of these futures, PCA is a statistical tool that serves to reduce the dimensions of the risk factor space considerably. In our case we reduced dimensions from 18 constant maturity futures to just four principal components. Moreover, using PCA we can identify the key risk factors of the portfolio. For instance, we showed that the most common types of movement in energy futures term structures is a similar and simultaneous shift and tilt in crude oil, heating oil and unleaded gasoline futures.

Then we considered a particular portfolio, and used PCA to demonstrate that the greatest risk exposure was to short term heating oil futures, a fact that is not evident from a direct examination of the portfolio composition. We demonstrated empirically that hedging with a position that is equivalent to 145.45 contracts on the 1-month heating oil futures reduces the portfolio P&L volatility from over $3.5 million to $2.389 million, and reduces the 1% 10-day historical VaR from $2.076 million to $1.473 million. Composite hedging with more than one futures contract reduces the P&L volatility and VaR even further.

9.6   REFERENCES

Alexander, C. (2008a) *Market Risk Analysis,* Volume I: *Quantitative Methods in Finance.* John Wiley & Sons Ltd.: Chichester.

Alexander, C. (2008b) *Market Risk Analysis,* Volume II: *Practical Financial Econometrics.* John Wiley & Sons Ltd.: Chichester.

Alexander, C. (2008c) *Market Risk Analysis,* Volume III: *Pricing, Hedging and Trading Financial Instruments.* John Wiley & Sons Ltd.: Chichester.

Alexander, C. (2008d) *Market Risk Analysis,* Volume IV: *Value-at-Risk Models.* John Wiley & Sons Ltd.: Chichester.

---

[4] See Alexander (2008), pp. 111–113.

10

Spark Spread Options when Commodity Prices are Represented as Time Changed Processes

Elisa Luciano

Spark spread options are defined on the difference between the price of electricity and the price of the fuel used to generate it, usually natural gas. Being output-minus-input spread options, they approximate the cost of converting gas into electricity. They are not only used as hedging tools, but also play a key role in power plant valuation: they represent by far the most important correlation product in the energy context. Their pricing relies on the ability to model not only the single underlying processes, but also their dependence, and therefore their joint dynamics.

At the marginal level, it is well known that commodities, energy in particular, have trajectorial and statistical properties much more complex – or with greater deviations from normal returns – than some other assets. Return models able to describe skewness, kurtosis, and other deviations from normality have been proposed during the last decade, not only for commodities, but also – or, *a fortiori* – for energy. Lévy models, which include diffusive Brownian motion on the one hand, pure jump processes on the other, by now seem to be the general environment in which commodity processes for the 21st century can be studied. However, not all Lévy models seem to be able to capture the observed features of market prices and returns. The interest of the research community has been attracted by non diffusive, pure jump Lévy models for at least two reasons: they can easily accommodate for observed deviations of asset returns from normality; they can be represented, studied and in some cases simulated as time-changed Brownian motions. Time change in turn represents information and trade, and as such is economically well grounded.

At the joint level, the literature on time changed or pure jump Lévy processes is scarce, if one wants different time changes – or different trade patterns – to apply to different assets. Even scarcer is their application to correlation products in the commodity domain. In order to price spark spread options, Benth and Benth (2006) have modelled directly the spread as a single Lévy process, while Benth and Kettler (2006) have coupled two marginal processes through a static copula. To our knowledge however, there exists no application to correlation

University of Turin and ICER and Collegio Carlo Alberto, Turin.
The author is extremely grateful to Hélyette Geman for having made her discover the commodities domain. She wishes to thank Roberto Marfé for extremely valuable research assistance and Patrizia Semeraro for computational assistance. The usual disclaimers apply.

Risk Management in Commodity Markets: From Shipping to Agriculturals and Energy Edited by Hélyette Geman
© 2008 John Wiley & Sons, Ltd

products such as spark spread options of a well defined multivariate Lévy process, consistent with the dynamics of both its margins.

In this chapter we will briefly review some features of time changing, and then concentrate on the challenges it poses for energy pricing. We study the feasibility and advantages of time changed processes in the commodity domain, when it comes to modeling several commodities without superimposing a copula structure and allow for different time changes or trade behaviors. In order to do so, we will provide a full marginal calibration to PJM and NYMEX Natural Gas data, and discuss the spark spread option pricing issue in a calibrated model, able to incorporate different dependence levels.

The paper is structured as follows. Section 10.1 introduces the spark spread option. Section 10.2 recalls the basic properties of time changed Lévy processes. Section 10.3 reviews their application to energy. Section 10.4 calibrates a number of time-change specifications to natural gas and electricity prices and proceeds to spark spread pricing. Section 10.5 concludes and outlines further research.

10.1 SPARK SPREAD OPTIONS

A spark spread option is a European call written on the difference between the price of electricity and that of fuel – often natural gas – needed to produce it. The final payoff of the spark spread option with maturity T can be written as

$$\max \left(S_e(T) - H_{eff} S_g(T) - K, 0 \right)$$

where $S_e(T)$ and $S_g(T)$ are the values at time T of two future contracts with maturity $t \geqslant T$, respectively on electricity and gas, K is the strike, while H_{eff} is the heat rate, or efficiency factor, of a power plant, which summarizes the conversion capability of the plant from input (gas) to output (electricity). As a consequence, spark spread options are typically in \$/MWh, with gas price in \$/MBtu, and the heat rate in Btu/KWh.

Spark spread options are of paramount importance for two reasons. First, they are powerful risk mitigation vehicles in energy markets, for hedging exposure to gas and electricity price fluctuations, especially by power plant operators. Their use as a hedging tool has been fostered since the liberalization of the electricity industry (see for instance Hsu (1998)), while liquidity has been provided by gas and electricity producers, traders and other market participants. Second, spark spread options are of particular importance as real options, in order to evaluate the convenience of new plants for electricity production. Their payoff is – in a nutshell – the one of a plant able to transform gas into electricity. As such, spark spread options are also named paper plants. A detailed example of such a use is in Geman (2005a), where the valuation of new plants as spread options is compared with a more traditional net present value (NPV) one. Essentially, as in every cost-benefit analysis through NPV as opposed to the real option one, the advantage of the second methodology consists in a proper appraisal of the volatility of the underlying input and output prices.

The importance of spark – as well as other – spread options is in contrast with the lack of a closed form pricing formula for them, even in the simplest Black–Scholes case, in which both underlyings are geometric Brownian motions. In the Black–Scholes framework, an analytical pricing formula exists for the case $K = 0$: with a null strike, spark spread options become options to exchange gas for electricity, and can be evaluated using the Margrabe formula. When $K \neq 0$, closed pricing formulas cease to exist and Monte Carlo approaches or analytical approximations are usually adopted. The former approach, which is adopted for instance in Geman (2005a), consists of sampling from the final distribution of gas and electricity, taking into consideration the possible correlation between the diffusive components of their dynamics. The second approach can consist of using the good fit that normal random variates provide for the difference between two lognormal random variables (gas and electricity prices at T in the Black–Scholes world). This approach is named after Bachelier and its properties are surveyed in Carmona and Durrleman (2003). Alternatively, one can exploit a family of upper and lower bounds, provided by Carmona and Durrleman (2003), which allows easy computation of the Greeks. Last but not least, Kirk's (1995) approximating formula is available. Similarly to the supremum of Carmona and Durrleman's lower bounds, it provides excellent hedges and outperforms Bachelier's approach.

The extension of the spread option pricing problem to geometric Brownian motions with jumps is quite straightforward: once more, we refer the reader to the excellent survey of Carmona and Durrleman. A more delicate issue is mixed jump-diffusion pricing outside the geometric Brownian motion case: Fusai and Roncoroni (2005, chapter 19) provide a fully calibrated spark pricing methodology when gas presents mean reversion and electricity is represented as in Geman and Roncoroni (2006).

The treatment of the case in which both underlying assets are pure jump processes instead is far from easy. To this end, one can adopt the methodology of Dempster and Hong (2000), who extend the Fast Fourier Transform (FFT) methodology of Carr and Madan (1999): their method can be applied any time the joint characteristic function of the underlying prices is known in closed form. It is based on breaking the region where the option is in the money into a series of rectangles, and was originally designed to efficiently deal with stochastic volatility and correlation. Very recently, Jackson *et al.* (2007) provided an alternative methodology, which extends to the bivariate case their Fourier Space time-stepping (FST) for option pricing with Lévy models. The basic idea consists of treating symmetrically the diffusive and integral terms in the partial integro-differential equation (PIDE) which formalizes the pricing problem in the Lévy case. The Fourier transform is applied to the PIDE, so as to obtain a linear system of ordinary differential equations. By so doing, they reap the computational efficiency of FFT and are able to deal with path dependent options. As in the Dempster and Hong case, the application of their pricing approach to spark spread options relies on the knowledge of the joint characteristic function. For pure jump processes of the type we intend to use in this chapter, namely the ones in which each margin results from a different trade behavior and time change, such a knowledge is far from elementary. Indeed, the joint characteristic function readily follows from the univariate one, as soon as the bivariate process is assumed to be generated by a unique time change of different, independent Brownian motions. This is the case, for instance, for the multivariate Variance Gamma (VG) of Madan and Seneta (1990). A unique time change however, as we will argue in Section 10.3 below, does not provide enough flexibility in dependence and marginal description of Lévy processes. For this reason, the spark spread literature existing so far, at least to our knowledge, does not rely either on Dempster and Hong or on Jackson *et al.*, which is in addition a very recent contribution.

In order to extend the valuation of spark spread options to non diffusive cases, Benth and Benth (2006) directly modelled the difference between the two underlying prices with a jump-diffusion process. This approach simplifies the bivariate pricing problem into a univariate one, but does not ensure consistency with the dynamics of each single underlying. To ensure consistency, Benth and Kettler (2006) assumed instead a non Gaussian

Ornstein-Uhlenbeck couple of processes for gas and electricity, and fitted an externally spec-ified, approximating copula to their (detrended and de-seasonalized) time series. They then computed the spark spread price by Monte Carlo simulation of the final payoff. However, such an approach has two main drawbacks. First, the whole calibration is performed on time series data, and therefore an assumption of invariance of the marginal price processes and their dependence when switching from the historical to the risk neutral measure is needed: in other words, no risk premium for skewness, kurtosis, or dependence must exist. Second, their copula approach does not ensure dynamic consistency, since the copula, as defined by Sklar's theorem, should be derived by inverting the bivariate process at each single point in time. In the pure jump Lévy case as opposed to the BS framework, it is well known (see Kallsen and Tankov (2006)) that one cannot define the marginal processes, assume a (time independent) copula for them and preserve the Lévy property for the bivariate process. Benth and Kettler use a time independent copula, which therefore must be understood as an approximation to the actual one.

Our approach to the spark spread option pricing problem is as follows: we rely on a well defined time changed bivariate process, outlined in Section 10.3 and detailed – for the VG case – in Appendix A, for which the time change is not unique over different commodities and the bivariate characteristic function is still known in closed form. Then we price the spread option by FST. The FST approach can be adopted without superimposing an approximating copula: the characteristic function of the multivariate time changed process already encapsulates dependence and guarantees dynamic consistency.

As an application of such a modelling approach, we consider its calibration to PJM and NYMEX Natural Gas. First we calibrate the two marginal processes and provide a best fit analysis of competing time changed descriptions. After the marginal calibration, we will be able to appreciate the accuracy of the multivariate time change in capturing the statistical properties of the underlying data.[1] Then we proceed to spark spread option pricing. In order to provide an economic foundation to our use of marginal time changed processes and to provide the analytical set up for its multivariate extension with more than one time change, in the next two sections we will review the motivations for time changed processes and their univariate – as well as multivariate but single-subordinator – applications to energy markets. Last but not least, we will provide foundations for a multivariate time-change extension.

10.2   TIME CHANGE IN A NUTSHELL

Time change basically consists in recognizing that asset prices must be described differently whether they are in the calendar-time scale or in the business or trading-time one. As Clark (1973) says, "the different evolution of price series on different days is due to the fact that information is available to traders at a varying rate. On days when no new information is available, trading is slow, and the price process evolves slowly. On days when new information violates old expectations, trading is brisk, and the price process evolves much faster." Business time, then, is supposed to run according to market activity, and to depend on the dynamics of demand and supply order arrival. It is inherently stochastic, since it is driven by information flow and by the unpredictable matching of supply and demand orders: features such as number and magnitude of orders are its determinants. The idea of a

---

[1] We will not consider trajectorial properties since we calibrate on a single day cross section of univariate option prices (under the risk-neutral measure) and do not work on time series or historical prices.

stochastic, order or market activity driven business time dates back to Clark (1973). In the last decade, it has been extensively advocated as a way to explain volatility, both from the econometric and theoretical point of view.

As a consequence of the discrepancy between calendar and business time, a natural question arises. Even if in business time we are willing to accept the traditional view that asset prices are diffusions, what do they look like in calendar time, which is used for modelling purposes? And what do they become if we want them to be diffusions as simple as Brownian motions in business time?

As Geman (2005b) vividly reports, the theoretical answer was very promising right from the early developments of the time change technique: Monroe's (1978) theorem indeed guarantees that any semimartingale is a time changed Brownian motion. And semimartingales correspond to the absence of arbitrage in financial markets, since they generate martingales. Given the relationship between semimartingales, martingales, and no arbitrage, the class of time changed Brownian motions was immediately perceived by the financial community as being large enough for any practical modelling purpose. At the same time, influential microstructure papers such as Easley and O'Hara (1992) provided a link between the existence of information, the timing of trades and the stochastic process of prices, which was consistent with time change.

The answer proved to be empirically sound too: Geman and Ané (1996) and Ané and Geman (2000) studied first the S&P and FTSE 100 futures over the time period 1993–97, then two high frequency dataset for technology stocks in 1997. In the second paper they investigated whether stock returns had the Brownian motion features in a time scale represented by either the number of orders (trades) or their value (volume). They indeed found empirical evidence of their claim, especially when business time was (non parametrically) approximated by the number of orders. Their evidence was consistent with earlier unrelated contributions on the superior explanatory power of the number of trades for volatility, as opposed to volume (Jones et al. (1994)). Some other papers, including and following Clark's seminal contribution, insist on the unobservability of business time, and on the fact that trading activity – be it measured by the number of orders, their value or other measures, such as turnover – is but one proxy of business time or market activity.

However, the answer was challenging too: Geman et al. (2001) indeed observe that if the time change were continuous, it would produce a continuous price process, but it would also be locally deterministic.[2] Since the whole purpose of modelling business time is to incorporate the intuition of order and information-driven trading clock in the world of stochastic processes for asset pricing, ending up with a locally deterministic trading time does not seem to be appropriate. Let us forget about continuous price or log-price processes then, and consider jump ones. Geman et al. (2001) observe that, "as time changes are increasing random processes, they are for practical purposes purely discontinuous, if they are not locally deterministic". And pure jump time changes generate pure jump price processes.

Pure jump Lévy models then reconcile the willingness of representing business time with the one of excluding "naive" representations of it. And if this seems useful for general asset prices, it seems even more helpful in the commodity domain. From now on we will therefore focus on pure jump time changes and price processes.

---

[2] Provided some fairly general technical conditions are met.

10.3   TIME CHANGE AND COMMODITY PRICES

10.3.1   Univariate models

It is not by chance that Clark (1973) started the study of time changed Brownian motions while analyzing cotton futures data. It is not so since the importance of demand and supply, as well as related notions such as quantity in stock and delivery needs, are more important in the commodity domain than for traditional financial assets. Temporary imbalances between demand and supply, but above all frictions such as time or costs of delivery, seem to be at odds with the smoothness of prices. This is why Lévy time changed prices have been introduced in order to describe commodity prices. In such a framework, if $S(t)$ is a commodity price at calendar time t, the general representation of its log return, $Y(t) = \ln(S(t)/S(0))$, will be

$$Y(t) = \mu G(t) + \sigma B(G(t))$$

where μ and σ are constant, $B(G(t))$ is a standard Brownian motion, evaluated at time $G(t)$; $G(t)$ is a pure jump time changing process (a subordinator, most of the times[3]).

Even without explicit reference to the change-of-time issue, pure jump Lévy processes have been successfully applied to energy pricing. Eberlein and Stahl (2003) advocate the use of generalized hyperbolic (GH) distributions to model electricity prices and compute the corresponding risk measures. They show that the GH parametrization monitors volatility more accurately than the classical empirical variance estimator. Risk measures based on GH calibrated models perform very well in backtests. Benth and Saltyte-Benth (2004) separately fit a Normal Inverse Gaussian (NIG) dynamics to gas and oil prices. Benth et al. (2007) use a non Gaussian, pure jump Ornstein-Uhlenbeck process for electricity spot modelling and derivatives pricing; even though their model is additive instead of exponential, in order to facilitate the passage from spot to forward dynamics, it has in common with the time changed representation studied here both the pure jump feature and the fact of being simple enough to ensure tractability. Geman and Roncoroni (2006), in order to reproduce both the trajectorial and statistical properties peculiar to electricity prices, introduce a jump-reversion model and calibrate it to a database of US different markets: they obtain excellent fits for the first four moments, with a partial exception for skewness.

10.3.2   Multivariate models

When one moves from the univariate model just presented to the need of representing – say – two assets, one question immediately arises. Do we need to consider the same time change, or different ones? And in the second case, should the time changes be dependent or independent?

The traditional answer consists in adopting a unique time change: a review of the theoretical results is in Sato (1999). Madan and Seneta (1990) for instance, when introducing their (symmetric) multivariate Variance Gamma (VG) process, a pioneering example of pure jump dynamics, assume that a unique gamma subordinator drives all assets. The resulting prices have a common parameter driving kurtosis, fixed dependence and cannot be independent. Even outside the VG case, the presence of a unique subordinator limits the generality of the

---

[3] Subordinators are a subclass of time changes, with independent and stationary increments.

model, the common kurtosis behavior and lack of independence being but two reasons. Such reasons limit the practical flexibility of multivariate time changed processes with one subordinator. Indeed Börger *et al.* (2007) applied such a common subordinator model, namely its GH specification, to commodity prices in order to provide risk measures: according to their same opinion, their statistical analysis should support further theoretical extensions, since the restrictions on parameters imposed by a unique subordinator – which in the GH case too affect kurtosis – are extremely important in the commodity domain. They show on their data set how tails can differ from one commodity to the other.

A contrasting view with respect to the unique time change solution would be to assume different time changes, or multivariate subordinators. Such multivariate time changes model the fact that trade and information arrival are not the same for different assets or commodities: every market has its own business time. Barndorff-Nielsen *et al.* (2001) first characterized multivariate subordinators and the corresponding time changed or subordinated processes. They studied the mathematical properties of subordination of independent Lévy processes, even outside the Brownian motion case. Based on their arguments, for n assets one can then suggest a multivariate time change of the following type:

$$Y_j(t) = \mu_j G_j(t) + \sigma_j B_j(G_j(t)) \qquad j = 1, 2, \ldots n \qquad (10.1)$$

where the Brownian motions are independent one from the other and with respect to the time changes, while the subordinators $G_j(t)$, $G_i(t)$, $i \neq j$ need not be independent.

In order to keep the model analytically tractable, but above all in order to maintain calibration by avoiding the introduction of an excessively large number of parameters, Geman *et al.* (2008) suggest the adoption of a multivariate time change obtained as the sum of a common and an idiosyncratic component, proper of each asset. By so doing, they model the idea that trade in different commodities has a common component, on top of the commodity-specific ones, and provide empirical ground for such an idea (see Geman *et al.* (2008)). As an application of the general multivariate change with a common component, Semeraro (2007) introduced a VG with such a subordinator – named $\alpha-$VG – which is parametrized, for each couple of assets, by one parameter in addition to the marginal ones. We summarize the mathematical properties of such multivariate $\alpha-$VG in Appendix A.

In the VG case, the unique subordinator version of Madan and Seneta entails restrictions on the marginal parameters, in particular on the one driving kurtosis, which is the same for every margin. It also restricts correlation, which depends on the marginal parameters only. This means that, for fixed margins, the modeler cannot describe different correlation levels or, in other words, that marginal calibrations can turn out to be inconsistent with empirical estimates of correlation.

In the $\alpha-$VG multivariate case of Geman *et al.* (2008), the marginal (kurtosis, in particular) parameter restrictions which are required in the unique subordinator case do not exist any more, and a whole range of linear dependence can be captured, even for fixed margins. Indeed, time changes $G_j(t)$ are distributed according to a gamma of parameters $(t/\alpha_j, 1/\alpha_j)$, where the parameters α_j form the vector α. As a result, every margin is characterized by three different parameters, σ_j, μ_j, α_j. Linear correlation of the $Y_j(t)$, $Y_i(t)$ returns is given in Appendix A, and is independent of time. It depends on an additional parameter a, which determines the weight of the common component in each time change with respect to the idiosyncratic one. Luciano and Semeraro (2008) studied the dependence properties of such a process by comparing its implied copula – i.e. the copula which results from the inversion of the actual bivariate process distribution at each point in time – with the Gaussian one, in order to understand how much the process departs from Gaussianity not only at the marginal, but also at the joint level. In order to do this, they calibrated the process to a number of stock indices and measured the distance of the implied copula in respect to the Gaussian copula which has the same correlation coefficient.

The VG specification will indeed prove to be among the best fitting ones in the calibration of time changed processes to PJM and Natural Gas which follows: its $\alpha-$VG multivariate version will therefore be used to price the spread option.

We will enrich the study with a discussion of the PJM-NYMEX actual dependence, or implied copula, which is inherently time dependent. We will also compare it with the Gaussian copula, which is independent of time. Indeed, we advocate the use of a consistently dynamic bivariate process, instead of forcing a pre-specified, or external copula $C(v, z)$, onto two marginally well defined processes, on theoretical rigorousness grounds. However, since for practical reasons one can be interested in approximating the true process behavior by forcing an external copula, we compare the actual, implied copula of the process with an external, canonical and very well known one, namely the Gaussian. The implied copula of the process at time t, C_t, is obtained from the (empirical version) of the distribution function of the joint process at time t, F_t, by inverting Sklar's theorem:

$$C_t(v, z) = F_t \left(F_{et}^{-1}(v), F_{gt}^{-1}(z) \right)$$

where F_{et}^{-1} and F_{gt}^{-1} are the (generalized) inverses of the marginal distribution functions of electricity and gas, at time t.

The Gaussian copula C_{Ga} instead is given by:

$$C_{Ga}(v, z) := \int_{-\infty}^{\Phi^{-1}(v)} \int_{-\infty}^{\Phi^{-1}(z)} \frac{1}{2\pi\sqrt{1-\rho^2}} \exp\left(\frac{2\rho sw - s^2 - w^2}{2\left(1-\rho^2\right)} \right) ds dw$$

where ρ is the linear correlation coefficient between the underlying processes $S_e(t)$ and $S_g(t)$, which is constant over time, and Φ is the standard normal distribution function. In order to make the comparison sensible, such a parameter must be chosen so as to match the linear correlation of the bivariate process, which in the $\alpha-$VG case is given by (10.9) in Appendix A.

In order to appreciate the difference, for any specific tenor t, between the actual and approximating copula, C_t and C_{Ga}, one can compute a distance between the corresponding level curves. In the sequel we will adopt the normalized L^1 distance, namely

$$d(t) = 6 \times \int_0^1 \int_0^1 | C_{Ga}(v, z) - C_t(v, z) | dv dz$$

since such a distance respects the concordance order. Normalization is obtained by multiplying the integral times the constant 6, since the maximum value of the un-normalized distance, which obtains between the minimum and maximum copulas, is 1/6 (while, evidently, the minimum value is zero). The properties of such a distance are illustrated in Luciano and Semeraro (2008).

Obviously, any other distance could be used, and other comparison copulas could be chosen. Our selection is motivated by the desire of knowing how far dependence of the actual gas and electricity processes is from the Gaussian, linear one.

10.4   AN APPLICATION TO PJM ELECTRICITY AND NYMEX NATURAL GAS

The marginal gas and electricity prices involved in the spark payoff are those of future contracts. The principal ways of coping with the presence of futures instead of spot prices consist in either identifying spot and futures, considering that the latter have a short expiry, or in building an HJM model for forward prices. We follow the first route, since the contracts on which we calibrate the model are written on futures with a one-month expiry maximum. The spark spread option will be written on futures with the same expiry.

The PJM electricity and NYMEX Natural Gas processes are calibrated on univariate call and put option data for different strikes and maturities, as provided by Bloomberg. We restrict our attention to the most liquid contracts, by excluding far in and out of the money options. Actually, the moneyness of the selected contracts is between 0.9 and 1.1 for both commodities. We include only maturities between 5 and 13 months. We could have used subsets of such maturities, in order to take into account possible seasonalities. The calibrations which follow have been checked for robustness in respect to seasonality, by performing them on subsamples of maturities: 5 to 7, 8 to 10 and 11 to 13 months. The short maturity subsample has indeed parameter and moment features apparently different from the others, while both the medium and long horizon subsamples provide very similar results. Since in this chapter we are interested in the bivariate properties of the calibrations, and in pricing spread options for maturities close to one year, we maintain the marginal calibration results for the overall sample. However, we recommend using marginal calibrations performed on specific maturities in case one wants to account for seasonality appropriately.

For the purpose of our illustrative example we used 79 contracts on the PJM and 49 on natural gas. We considered the Bloomberg quotes of PJM electricity and NYMEX Natural Gas on a single day (5 November 2007). However, we performed a robustness check of the calibration results also in terms of reference day, and verified that the results were robust in respect to the extension of the dataset to close days.[4]

We used as interest rate the one-year spot one on the US market, at the time of the calibration, namely 4.01 %.

The convenience yield is the implied one: it is obtained as the average, for each single option maturity, of the yields which ensure put call parity between the quoted options, over different strikes.[5]

10.4.1   Marginal calibration and marginal fit

The following processes are calibrated for each commodity: Black Scholes (BS), Variance Gamma (VG), Normal Inverse Gaussian (NIG), Meixner, Carr Geman Madan Yor (CGMY), Generalized Hyperbolic (GH). The probabilistic features of such processes are described in Appendix B. The calibration is performed, as usual, by minimizing the pricing errors between the observed and theoretical prices, obtained with the univariate Fourier space-time stepping technique of Jackson *et al.* (2007). The robustness of the numerical search for the minimum

---

[4] A complete analysis of the dataset, under the risk-neutral measure, is in the Master's dissertation of Roberto Marfé (Marfé 2008); it has been presented at the II FIMA Conference, January 2008, under the title "Pure Jump Models for Natural Gas and Electricity Pricing". A copy is available from the author upon request.

[5] For each single maturity, the yields which guarantee the parity over different strikes are very close to each other, so that taking their average does not introduce a distortion in the calibration.

in respect to the choice of the initial guesses has been checked throughout the VG case: in the other cases, the starting point has been selected so that the moments matched the optimized VG ones. Table 10.1 presents the resulting errors for the two energy prices at hand.

Table 10.1 Pricing errors of different time changed processes for PJM electricity and natural gas prices, measured as relative root mean square error (RRMSE), root mean square error (RMSE), absolute relative average absolute error (ARPE), and average absolute error (AAE)

PJM	RRMSE	RMSE	ARPE	AAE
BS	20.375 %	53.771 %	6.141 %	46.635 %
VG	8.282 %	23.662 %	2.099 %	16.892 %
NIG	9.391 %	26.433 %	2.533 %	19.892 %
MEIXNER	8.910 %	25.226 %	2.421 %	19.138 %
CGMY	8.217 %	23.675 %	2.105 %	17.054 %
GH	8.186 %	23.703 %	2.102 %	17.090 %
NAT GAS	RRMSE	RMSE	ARPE	AAE
BS	5.415 %	5.718 %	4.542 %	4.864 %
VG	4.115 %	3.984 %	3.333 %	3.236 %
NIG	4.240 %	4.289 %	3.714 %	3.716 %
MEIXNER	4.120 %	4.111 %	3.546 %	3.506 %
CGMY	4.081 %	3.971 %	3.335 %	3.242 %
GH	4.070 %	3.957 %	3.326 %	3.229 %

RMSE is the root mean square error, which is calculated as the root of the squared errors between market and model prices, divided by the number of options in the sample. AAE is the average of the absolute error, in which the discrepancies between model and actual prices are taken in absolute value instead of being squared. They broadly correspond to L^2 and L^1 distances between actual and model valuations. RRMSE and ARPE are the relative versions of the previous measures, in which the errors are computed as percentages of the market price, so as to eliminate the influence of more valuable options in respect to cheap ones.

It is important to notice three features of Table 10.1. First, independently of the measure selected, the BS model severely underperforms the pure jump models, usually with errors twice as big as those of the competing models. Second, for any fixed measure, the other models produce errors quite close in magnitude one to the other. Third, the ranking in minimizing the pricing error is almost preserved, when one moves from one measure to the other. However, we feel that, given the presence in the sample of options with quite different prices, relative measures are more appropriate. We therefore concentrate our attention on the RRMSE and ARPE measures. Based on these, the models GH and VG seem to be the most appropriate for describing electricity and gas, on the chosen sample.

The optimal values of the parameters are reported in Table 10.2.

The parameters, whose meaning and whose relationship with the moments of the processes are listed in Appendix B, are as follows: σ for Black Scholes, σ, μ, α for the VG, α, β, δ for NIG and Meixner, C, G, M, and Y for CGMY, α, β, δ, and ν for GH. From the above parameters, Table 10.3 shows how moments of the underlying distributions can be calculated using the formulas in Appendix B.

Table 10.2   Fitted parameters of PJM and Natural Gas, under various assumptions on the underlying distribution

Model	PJM parameters			
	σ			
BS	0.34572			
	σ	μ	α	
VG	0.435241	−0.04037	2.019923	
	α	β	δ	
NIG	1.169762	−0.13568	0.206466	
MEIXNER	2.058221	−0.41856	0.089707	
	C	G	M	Y
CGMY	0.279627	1.497869	1.97856	0.257689
	α	β	δ	ν
GH	1.842239	−0.24571	0.043524	0.245334
Model	Nat Gas parameters			
	σ			
BS	0.4042			
	σ	μ	α	
VG	0.5048	−0.1254	1.3668	
	α	β	δ	
NIG	1.5981	−0.4571	0.3571	
MEIXNER	1.6567	−0.8631	0.1740	
	C	G	M	Y
CGMY	0.3979	1.3655	2.3911	0.3047
	α	β	δ	ν
GH	1.9749	−0.5190	0.0990	0.3596

Table 10.3   Moments of the PJM and Nat Gas, under various assumptions on the underlying distribution

PJM	variance	skewness	kurtosis
BS	0.12	−	−
VG	0.19	−0.30	3.38
NIG	0.19	−0.55	9.26
Meixner	0.18	−0.71	16.18
CGMY	0.20	−0.98	15.11
GH	0.20	−0.85	11.70
NAT GAS	variance	skewness	kurtosis
BS	0.16	−	−
VG	0.28	−0.95	7.71
NIG	0.26	−1.21	10.45
Meixner	0.29	−1.42	10.76
CGMY	0.30	−1.28	9.74
GH	0.30	−1.34	9.91

Such moments confirm the non-Gaussianity of the underlying, risk-neutral distributions and show that they present negative skewness, as expected, and pronounced kurtosis. We cannot directly compare such moments with the ones obtained from the time series of PJM or NYMEX Natural Gas, since we are working under the risk-neutral measure. However, let us remark that negative skewness and pronounced kurtosis were also characteristics of the daily return time series in the whole year preceding our analysis, which we do not report here.

10.4.2   Behavior of the bivariate gas-electricity process and of the spark spread

Simulation of a single time changed Brownian motion, as well as of the n-tuples in (10.1), is quite an easy task once the distribution of the multivariate time change is known in closed form. This is the case for the $\alpha - \mathrm{VG}$ multivariate process above. Keeping in mind that the pricing errors of the pure jump models are such that none strongly outperforms the others, we therefore restrict the gas and electricity joint study, as well as the spark spread option price, to the VG case. The only parameter which we did not obtain from the marginal option calibration is the one driving dependence, namely a, which is in one-to-one relationship with linear correlation via (10.9) in Appendix A. We present below both the independence ($a = 0$) and the maximal linear dependence case ($a = \max(1/\alpha_1, 1/\alpha_2) = 0.49$). We do not attempt a calibration of correlation since we would need the risk neutral one, and we do not have liquidly traded spark options for inferring it. We do not use the historical correlation between gas and electricity, since we do not want to impose invariancy of dependence from the historical to the risk neutral measure.

Figure 10.1 presents two paths of the return processes on PJM and NYMEX Natural Gas, named respectively $Y_1(t)$, $Y_2(t)$, obtained by simulating 10 000 joint realizations over a unit (one year) interval, and the corresponding scatter plot at time one, when linear dependence is null.

Figure 10.2 presents the corresponding paths and scatter, when the dependence is maximal, and the corresponding parameter is $a = 0.49$.

The spark spread dynamic behavior corresponding to the decorrelated case, when the initial values of the gas and electricity prices are as on our dataset, and assuming a heat rate equal to 7.5, is given in Fig. 10.3.

In Fig. 10.4 we concentrate on the time evolution of dependence, by comparing the copula level curves respectively at time 1 and 10 with the ones of the Gaussian copula which has the same correlation coefficient. Evidently, we perform the comparison for the case with dependence, since under independence both copulas collapse into the product one. You find on the left hand the copula comparison at time one, on the right hand the time at ten one. Dependence resembles more and can be better approximated by the Gaussian one when the horizon increases.

In order to fully understand such dependence behavior, let us now compute the distance between the implied copula of the VG process and the corresponding Gaussian one, for different time horizons (Table 10.4). Such a distance decreases, without tending to zero. Dependence therefore can be better approximated by the Gaussian copula as time elapses, but does not collapse into Gaussian dependence.

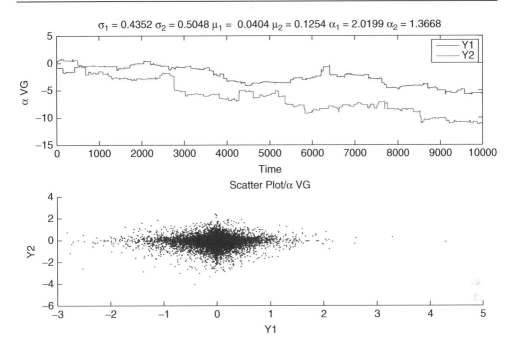

Figure 10.1 An example of path and a scatter plot at time 1 of the electricity (Y1) and gas returns (Y2), decorrelated case. The path has been obtained with 10 000 time steps: the number of time steps appears on the horizontal axis

10.4.3 Multivariate FST prices of the spark spread

In the $\alpha-$VG case the spark spread option price, for a fixed heat rate and for fixed marginal and joint parameters, can be obtained both by Monte Carlo simulation of the time-T values of the processes, or using the double FFT approach. We present here the FFT results, obtained via the enhanced Fourier-time stepping (FST) of Jackson *et al.* (2007): the Monte Carlo ones are almost identical, for an appropriate number of simulations.

The maturity has been fixed to one year in the first part of the table, ten years in the second; the strike is zero, while the riskless rate is the same as for the calibration; the efficiency rate is equal to 7.5. For the sake of comparison we present also the Black–Scholes price, which has been obtained using the corresponding calibrated parameters for the margins (namely, the BS volatility reported in Table 10.2) and the linear correlation corresponding to the two selected values of a.[6]

Please remember that no approximating copula has been superimposed on the bivariate VG process. As the reader can notice, all others equal, the α-VG call price is always greater than the BS price, since the former accounts for fat tails, while the latter does not. Both decrease with correlation, as expected, but the sensitivity of the α-VG price is higher, since it includes also non linear dependence. If we change the time to expiry of the option, the

---

[6] Please notice that, differently from what happens under a unique subordinator, the spark spread option can be obtained under various hypotheses on linear correlation.

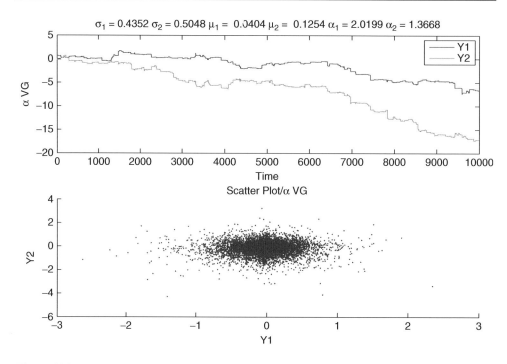

Figure 10.2 An example of path and a scatter plot at time 1 of the electricity (Y1) and gas returns (Y2), correlated case. The path has been obtained with 10 000 time steps: the number of time steps appears on the horizontal axis

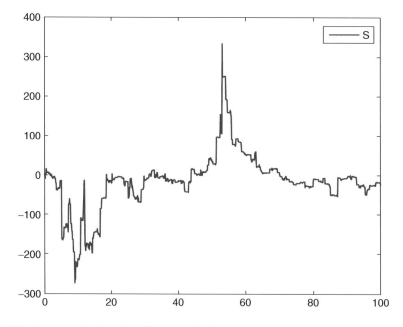

Figure 10.3 An example of path until time 1 of the spark spread, decorrelated case, when the heat rate is 7.5. The number of time steps shows up on the horizontal axis

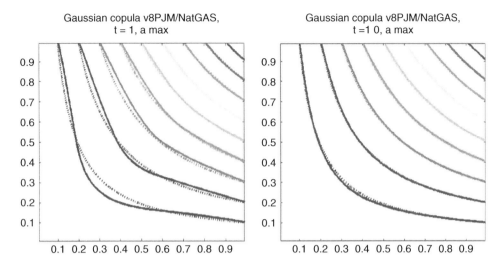

Figure 10.4 Comparison between the implied copula PJM/NatGas and the corresponding Gaussian copula, at time 1 (left hand side) and 10 (right hand side). The implied copula level curves (from 0.1 to 0.9) are solid lines, the corresponding Gaussian are dotted

Table 10.4 Distances between the implied and corresponding Gaussian copula, for different time horizons, correlated case

$a \neq 0$	t			
	1/2	1	10	100
$d(t)$		8.2578 %	3.2839 %	3.2691 %

Table 10.5 Spark spread prices with expiry one year (T = 1) and 10 years (T = 10), K = 0, for the decorrelated (a = 0) and correlated case (a = 0.49), in the Black–Scholes (BS) calibrated model and in the corresponding α−VG one. The left hand side presents call option prices (the spark spread ones), while the right hand side presents the corresponding put prices

	call option price		put option price	
	BS	α-VG-Fourier-time stepping	BS	α-VG-Fourier-time stepping
$T = 1$				
$a = 0$	18.1594	20.0222	11.2644	13.1272
$a = 0.49$	17.9646	19.0772	11.0696	12.1822
$T = 10$				
$a = 0$	35.8644	45.1430	28.9694	38.2480
$a = 0.49$	35.5606	44.8865	28.6656	37.9915

difference between the BS and VG call prices changes because of the difference in the margins over time (BS wrt VG)[7] and because the VG dependence evolves over time, while the BS does not. As a whole, the call difference increases with time. Symmetric comments hold for the put prices.

Table 10.6 presents the behavior of the spark spread prices in respect to moneyness, when $T = 1$. Call prices decrease and put prices increase with K, as expected.

Table 10.6 Spark spread prices with expiry one year, for different non null strikes K, for the decorrelated (a = 0) and correlated case (a = 0.49), in the Black–Scholes (BS) calibrated model and in the corresponding $\alpha-$VG one

	call option price		put option price	
	BS	α-VG-Fourier-time stepping	BS	α-VG-Fourier-time stepping
$K = 5$				
$a = 0$	15.3846	17.2782	13.2883	15.1819
$a = 0.49$	15.1843	16.2802	13.0880	14.1839
$K = 10$				
$a = 0$	12.9007	14.8758	15.6030	17.5781
$a = 0.49$	10.7170	13.9810	13.4193	16.6833
$K = -5$				
$a = 0$	21.2125	23.0752	9.5188	11.3815
$a = 0.49$	21.0272	22.2675	9.3335	10.5738
$K = -10$				
$a = 0$	24.5252	26.4045	8.0329	9.9122
$a = 0.49$	24.3527	25.7602	7.8604	9.2679

10.5 CONCLUSIONS AND FURTHER RESEARCH

This chapter priced the spark spread option, a correlation product of paramount importance in hedging and real option valuation in energy markets. It used subordination to model joint commodity behavior and – for a case in which subordination gave explicitly the joint characteristic function – exploited the recent FST numerical approach to spread pricing.

Marginally, we have been able to provide an excellent fit. Jointly, we have adopted a multivariate subordinator, i.e. we have assumed that the change of time – or trade, or information arrival – is not the same over different commodities. Apart from intuitive sense, such a multivariate change of time has the main advantage, compared to a univariate subordinator representation, of imposing no constraints on the marginal parameters and allowing a study of prices as function of dependence, as is evident from Tables 10.2 and 10.6 above. With a unique subordinator, such possibilities are precluded. In the VG case in particular the adoption of a univariate subordinator would have led to equating the kurtosis parameter – and therefore the heavy-tailedness – of each margin. It would have also produced a unique correlation coefficient, since with a unique subordinator marginal parameters by themselves

---

[7] Please notice that we left seasonality out of the picture on purpose. However, seasonality could be added for practical applications, by adjusting appropriately the marginal risk neutral calibration as specified in Section 10.4.1.

determine dependence. On the contrary, from the approach of this chapter we are able to capture different correlation levels to adapt to real world dependence and its higher level during crises.

In spite of multivariate change of time, spark spread option prices can be easily obtained by FST transforms without superimposing a copula.

The progressive disclosure of spark spread quotes will allow us to calibrate dependence to observed deals or to monitor their consistency with stress tested correlations. Hedging ratios too are in the agenda for future research.

10.6   APPENDIX A: MODELLING SPECIFICATION IN THE MULTIVARIATE CASE

The multivariate subordinator applied here for spread option pricing is studied in Geman *et al.* (2008). It can be defined starting from an infinitely divisible law, as follows: let the random variables X_j, $j = 1, \ldots , n$ and Z be non negative, independent and infinitely divisible. Define the components of the random vector W as the weighted sums of the common component Z and the idiosyncratic ones, X_j:

$$W = (W_1, W_2, \ldots , W_n)^T = (X_1 + \alpha_1 Z, X_2 + \alpha_2 Z, \ldots , X_n + \alpha_n Z)^T, \tag{10.2}$$

where α_j, $j = 1, \ldots , n$ are non negative parameters. Define $G = \{G(t), t \geqslant 0\}$ as the Lévy process which has the law $\mathcal{L}$ of W at time one:

$$\mathcal{L}(G(1)) = \mathcal{L}(W). \tag{10.3}$$

Given that G is a subordinator, assume that it has zero drift.

Let $B_j = \{B_j(t), t \geqslant 0\}$ $j = 1, \ldots , n$ be independent standard Brownian motions, independent of G too, which we will time-change. Consider the process $B = \{B(t), t \geqslant 0\}$

$$B(t) = (\mu_1 t + \sigma_1 B_1(t), \ldots , \mu_n t + \sigma_n B_n(t))^T, \tag{10.4}$$

the Lévy triplet of which is obviously $(\mu, \Sigma, 0)$, where $\mu = (\mu_1 .. \mu_n)^T$ and $\Sigma = diag(\sigma_1, \ldots , \sigma_n)$.

The time changed processes at time t will be collected in the vector $Y(t)$ and interpreted as log returns. The multiparameter log return process $Y = \{Y(t), t > 0\}$ is indeed obtained by time changing B via the subordinator G:

$$Y(t) = \begin{pmatrix} Y_1(t) \\ \ldots \\ Y_n(t) \end{pmatrix} = \begin{pmatrix} \mu_1 G_1(t) + \sigma_1 B_1(G_1(t)) \\ \ldots \\ \mu_n G_n(t) + \sigma_n B_n(G_n(t)) \end{pmatrix}. \tag{10.5}$$

The process Y, as given by (10.5), is a Lévy process with characteristic function

$$E[e^{i\langle z, Y(t)\rangle}] = \exp(t\Psi_G(\log \psi_B(z))), \ z \in \mathbb{R}^n_+, \tag{10.6}$$

where ψ_B is the characteristic function of the Brownian motion B and for any $w = (w_1, \ldots, w_n)^T \in \mathbb{C}^n$ with $Re(w_j) \leqslant 0$, $j = 1, \ldots, n$,

$$\Psi_G(w) = \int_{\mathbb{R}^n} (e^{\langle w, x \rangle} - 1)v(dx)$$

is the characteristic exponent of G.

The characteristic triplet $(\gamma_Y, \Sigma_Y, \nu_Y)$ of Y is as follows

$$\gamma_Y = \int_{\mathbb{R}^n_+} \nu_G(ds) \int_{|x| \leqslant 1} x \rho_s(dx),$$

$$\Sigma_Y = 0, \tag{10.7}$$

$$\nu_Y(B) = \int_{\mathbb{R}^n_+} \rho_s(B)\nu_G(ds),$$

where $\rho_s = \mathcal{L}(B(s))$, $s \in \mathbb{R}^n_+$, $x = (x_1, \ldots, x_n)^T$ and $B \in \mathbb{R}^n \setminus \{0\}$.

Let us now consider the particular case in which the random variables defining the subordinator are gamma ones, namely

$$\mathcal{L}(X_j) = \Gamma(\frac{b}{\alpha_j} - a, \frac{b}{\alpha_j})$$

$$\mathcal{L}(Z) = \Gamma(a, b)$$

and $0 < \alpha_j < \frac{b}{a}$. Under independency of Z from all the X_j, this entails

$$\mathcal{L}(W_j) = \Gamma(\frac{b}{\alpha_j}, \frac{b}{\alpha_j})$$

$$\mathcal{L}(G_j(t)) = \Gamma(\frac{tb}{\alpha_j}, \frac{b}{\alpha_j})$$

and the subordinated process, named $\alpha-$VG and first introduced in Semeraro (2007), is an extension of the multivariate VG in Madan and Seneta (1990). For normalization purposes, in financial applications b is taken to be one: at each point in time the common component is therefore a gamma random variable, the "magnitude" of which is measured by the a parameter. Such a parameter obviously appears in the characteristic function of the ultimate process, Y. The characteristic function (10.6) of Y is indeed

$$\psi_{Y(t)}(u) = \prod_{j=1}^{n}(1 - \sum_{j=1}^{n}\alpha_n(i\mu_j u_j - \frac{1}{2}\sigma_j^2 u_j^2))^{-t(\frac{1}{\alpha_j} - a)}(1 - \sum_{j=1}^{n}\alpha_n(i\mu_j u_j - \frac{1}{2}\sigma_j^2 u_j^2))^{-ta}$$

$$\tag{10.8}$$

and it comes down to the multivariate VG one when only the common time change exists.

The linear correlation of the subordinated process Y in the $\alpha-$VG case is

$$\rho_{Y(t)}(l, j) = \frac{\mu_l \mu_j \alpha_l \alpha_j a}{\sqrt{(\sigma_l^2 + \mu_l^2 \alpha_l)(\sigma_j^2 + \mu_j^2 \alpha_j)}}. \tag{10.9}$$

10.7   APPENDIX B: ALTERNATIVE MODELLING SPECIFICATIONS IN THE UNIVARIATE CASE

Appendix B collects the definitions of the univariate processes tested in section 10.4.1 above.

10.7.1   Variance gamma

A *variance gamma* VG process with parameters $\sigma > 0$, μ, $\alpha > 0$, is a real Lévy process $X_{VG} = \{X_{VG}(t),\ t \geqslant 0\}$ with characteristic function

$$\psi_{VG}(u) = (1 - iu\mu\alpha + \frac{1}{2}\sigma^2\alpha u^2)^{-\frac{t}{v}}.$$

It can be obtained as a Brownian motion with drift time changed by a gamma process. In turn, a gamma process $\{G(t),\ t \geqslant 0\}$ with parameters (a, b) is a Lévy process such that the defining distribution of $X(1)$ is gamma with parameters (a, b) (shortly $\mathcal{L}(X(1)) = \Gamma(a, b)$). Its characteristic function is

$$\psi_G(u) = (1 - iu/b)^{-a}.$$

VG processes have been introduced by Madan and Seneta (1987, 1990).

A VG process has no Gaussian component. The paths of the VG process are of infinite activity and finite variation. Its moments at time 1, namely the mean m, the variance v, the skewness s and the kurtosis k, are as follows:

$$m = \mu \tag{10.10}$$

$$v = \sigma^2 + \alpha\mu^2 \tag{10.11}$$

$$s = \frac{\mu\alpha(3\sigma^2 + 2\alpha\mu^2)}{(\sigma^2 + \alpha\mu^2)^{3/2}} \tag{10.12}$$

$$k = 3(1 + 2\alpha - \alpha\sigma^4(\sigma^2 + \alpha\mu^2)^{-2}) \tag{10.13}$$

10.7.2   Normal inverse Gaussian

A *normal inverse Gaussian* (NIG) process with parameters $\alpha > 0$, $-\alpha < \beta < \alpha$, $\delta > 0$ is a real Lévy process $X_{NIG} = \{X_{NIG}(t),\ t \geqslant 0\}$ with characteristic function

$$\psi_{NIG}(z) = \exp t(-\delta(\sqrt{\alpha^2 - (\beta + iu)^2} - \sqrt{\alpha^2 - \beta^2}), \tag{10.14}$$

and Lévy measure given by

$$\nu_{NIG}(dx) = \frac{\alpha\delta}{\pi}\exp(\beta x)K_1(\alpha\,|\,x\,|)/\,|\,x\,|\,dx$$

where K_1 is the Bessel function of the first kind.

It can be obtained as a time changed Brownian motion when the time change is IG. In turn, an *inverse Gaussian* (IG) process with parameters (a, b) is a Lévy process for which the defining distribution of $X(1)$ is IG with parameters (a, b) (shortly $\mathcal{L}(X(1)) = IG(a, b)$). The IG process has the following characteristic function:

$$\psi_{IG}(z) = \exp t(-a(\sqrt{-2iu + b^2} - b). \tag{10.15}$$

NIG processes have been introduced by Barndorff-Nielsen (1995).

A NIG process has no Gaussian component. It has infinite activity and infinite variation. Its moments at time 1, namely the mean m, the variance v, the skewness s and the kurtosis k, are as follows:

$$m = \frac{\delta\beta}{\sqrt{\alpha^2 - \beta^2}} \tag{10.16}$$

$$v = \alpha^2\delta(\alpha^2 - \beta^2)^{-\frac{3}{2}} \tag{10.17}$$

$$s = 3\beta\alpha^{-1}\delta^{-\frac{1}{2}}(\alpha^2 - \beta^2)^{-\frac{1}{4}} \tag{10.18}$$

$$k = 3(1 + \frac{\alpha^2 + 4\beta^2}{\delta\alpha^2\sqrt{\alpha^2 - \beta^2}}) \tag{10.19}$$

10.7.3 Meixner

A *Meixner* (M) process, with parameters α, β, δ, is a Lévy process $X_M = \{X_M(t), t \geqslant 0\}$ with characteristic function

$$\psi_M(u) = \left(\frac{\cos(\beta/2)}{\cosh((\alpha u - i\beta)/2)}\right)^{2\delta} \tag{10.20}$$

The Meixner process can be obtained as a time changed Brownian motion when the time change is Meixner with parameters $(2, 0, t)$.

The Meixner process has been introduced by Schoutens and Teugel (1998). It has no Gaussian part. The paths have infinite variation. The moments at time 1, namely the mean m, the variance v, the skewness s and the kurtosis k, are as follows:

$$m = \alpha\delta \tan(\beta/2) \tag{10.21}$$

$$v = \frac{1}{2}\alpha^2\delta/\cos^2(\beta/2) \tag{10.22}$$

$$s = \sqrt{2/\delta} \sin(\beta/2) \tag{10.23}$$

$$k = 3 + \frac{2 - \cos\beta}{\delta} \tag{10.24}$$

10.7.4 CGMY

A *Carr Geman Madan Yor* (CGMY) process, with parameters C, G, $M > 0$ and $Y < 2$, is a Lévy process $X_{CGMY} = \{X_{CGMY}(t), t \geqslant 0\}$ in which the characteristic function is

$$\psi_{CGMY}(u) = \exp(Ct\Gamma(-Y)((M - iu)^Y - M^Y + (G + iu)^Y - G^Y)), \qquad (10.25)$$

The CGMY process can be obtained as a time changed Brownian motion when the time change is characterized as in Madan and Yor (2005).

CGMY processes have been introduced by Carr *et al.* (2002). If $Y < 0$ the paths have finite activity; if $Y \in [0, 1)$ they have infinite activity and finite variation; if $Y \in [1, 2)$ they have infinite activity and variation. The CGMY moments at time 1, namely the mean m, the variance v, the skewness s and the kurtosis k, are as follows:

$$m = C(M^{Y-1} - G^{Y-1})\Gamma(1 - Y) \qquad (10.26)$$

$$v = C(M^{Y-2} - G^{Y-2})\Gamma(2 - Y) \qquad (10.27)$$

$$s = \frac{C(M^{Y-3} - G^{Y-3})\Gamma(3 - Y)}{\left[C(M^{Y-2} - G^{Y-2})\Gamma(2 - Y)\right]^{3/2}} \qquad (10.28)$$

$$k = 3 + \frac{C(M^{Y-4} - G^{Y-4})\Gamma(4 - Y)}{\left[C(M^{Y-2} - G^{Y-2})\Gamma(2 - Y)\right]^2} \qquad (10.29)$$

10.7.5 GH

The *Generalized Hyperbolic (GH)* process, with parameters α, β, δ and v, is a Lévy process $X_{GH} = \{X_{GH}(t), t \geqslant 0\}$ with characteristic function

$$\psi_{GH}(u) = \left(\frac{\alpha^2 - \beta^2}{\alpha^2 - (\beta + iu)^2}\right)^{v/2} \frac{K_v\left(\delta\sqrt{\alpha^2 - (\beta + iu)^2}\right)}{K_v\left(\delta\sqrt{\alpha^2 - \beta^2}\right)}, \qquad (10.30)$$

The GH process can be obtained as a time changed Brownian motion when the time change is Generalized Inverse Gamma.

GH processes have been introduced by Barndorff-Nielsen (1997) The paths have finite activity and infinite variation. The GH first moment at time 1, namely the mean m, is:

$$m = \beta\delta\frac{K_{v+1}\left(\delta\sqrt{\alpha^2 - \beta^2}\right)}{\left(\alpha^2 - \beta^2\right)K_v\left(\delta\sqrt{\alpha^2 - \beta^2}\right)}$$

10.8 REFERENCES

Ané, T. and H. Geman (2000). Order Flow, Transaction Clock and Normality of Asset Returns. *The Journal of Finance* **55**, 2259–2284.

Barndorff-Nielsen, O.E. (1995). Normal Inverse Gaussian Distributions and the Modeling of Stock Returns. Research report no. 300, Department of Theoretical Statistics, Aarhus University.

Barndorff-Nielsen, O.E. (1997) Normal Inverse Gaussian Distributions and Stochastic Volatility Models. *Scandinavian Journal of Statistics* **24**, 1–13.

Barndorff-Nielsen, O.E., J. Pedersen and K.I. Sato (2001). Multivariate Subordination, Self Decomposability and Stability. *Advances in Applied Probability* **33**, 160–187.

Benth, F.E. and J. Saltyte-Benth (2004). The NIG Distribution and Spot Price Modelling in Energy Markets. *International Journal of Theoretical and Applied Finance* **7**, 177–192.

Benth, F.E. and J. Saltyte-Benth (2006). Analytical Appproximation for the Price Dynamics of Spark Spread Options. *Studies in Nonlinear Dynamics & Econometrics* **10**.

Benth, F.E., Kettler, P.C., (2006) Dynamic Copula Model for the Spark Spread, E-print no. 14, Department of Mathematics, University of Oslo.

Benth, F.E., J. Kallsen and T. Meyer-Brandis (2007). A Non-Gaussian Ornstein-Uhlenbech Process for Electricity Spot Prices Modeling and Derivatives Prices. *Applied Mathematical Finance* **14**, 153–169.

Börger, R.H., A. Cartea, R. Kiesel, and G. Schindlmayr (2007). A Multivariate Commodity Analysis and Application to Risk Management. Available at: http://ssrn.com/abstrac=981127.

Carmona, R. and V. Durrleman (2003). Pricing and Hedging Spread Options. *SIAM Review* **45**, 627–685.

Carr, P., H., Geman, D. Madan and M. Yor (2002). The Fine Structure of Asset Returns: An Empirical Investigation. *Journal of Business* **75**, 305–332.

Carr, P. and D. Madan (1999). Option Valuation using the FFT. *Journal of Computational Finance* **2**, 61–73.

Clark, P.K. (1973). A Subordinated Stochastic Process with Finite Variance for Speculative Prices. *Econometrica* **41**, 135–155.

Dempster, M.A.H. and S.S.G. Hong (2000). Spread Option Valuation and the FFT. Centre for Financial Research, Judge Institute wp 26/2000.

Easley, D. and M. O'Hara (1992). Time and the Process of Security Prices Adjustment. *Journal of Finance* **47**, 577–605.

Eberlein, E. and G. Stahl (2003). Both Sides of a Fence: A Statistical and Regulatory View of Electricity Risk. *Risk* **8**, 34–38.

Fusai, G. and A. Roncoroni (2005). *Implementing Models in Quantitative Finance: Methods and Cases*. Springer-Verlag.

Geman, H. (2005a). *Commodities and Commodity Derivatives*. John Wiley & Sons Ltd.: Chichester.

Geman, H. (2005b). From Measure Changes to Time Changes in Asset Prices. *Journal of Banking and Finance* **29**, 2701–2722.

Geman, H. and T. Ané (1996). Stochastic Subordination. *Risk* **9**, 145–149.

Geman, H., E. Luciano and P. Semeraro (2008). Multivariate Time Changes and Evidence of Factor Structure in Financial Trade. Work in progress.

Geman, H., D. Madan and M. Yor (2001). Time Changes for Lévy Processes. *Mathematical Finance* **11**, 79–96.

Geman, H. and A. Roncoroni (2006). Understanding the Fine Structure of Electricity Prices. *Journal of Business* **79**.

Hsu, M. (1998). Spark spread options are hot. *The Electricity Journal* **11**, 28–39.

Jackson, K.R., S. Jaimungal and V. Surkov (2007). Fourier Space-time Stepping for Option Pricing with Lévy Models. University of Toronto wp.

Jones, C., L. Kaul, and M. Lipson (1994). Transaction, Volume and Volatility. *Review of Financial Studies* **7**, 631–65.

Kallsen, J. and P. Tankov (2006). Characterization of Dependence of Multidimensional Lévy Processes using Lévy Copulas. *Journal of Multivariate Analysis* **97**, 1551–1572.

Kirk, E. (1995). *Correlation in the Energy Markets, In Managing Energy Price Risk*. Risk Publications and Enron.

Luciano, E. and P. Semeraro (2008). Dynamic Dependence Modelling and Copulas: The Variance Gamma case. MAF 2008 – Mathematical and Statistical Methods for Actuarial Sciences and Finance, Venice, March 2008.

Madan, D.B. and E. Seneta (1987). Chebyshev Polynomial Approximations and Characteristic Function Estimation. *Journal of the Royal Statistical Society Series B* **49**: 2, 163–169.

Madan, D.B. and E. Seneta (1990). The Variance-Gamma Model for Share Market Returns. *Journal of Business* **63**, 511–24.

Madan, D.B. and M. Yor (2005). CGMY and Meixner Subordinates are Absolutely Continuous with Respect to One Sided Stable Subordinators. Unpublished manuscript.

Marfé, R. (2008). Pure Jump Models for Natural Gas and Electricity Pricing. II FIMA Conference, http://www.fimaonline.it/conference/abstracts.php.

Monroe, I. (1978). Processes that can be Embedded in Brownian Motion. *Annals of Probability* **6**, 4–56.

Sato, K. (1999). *Lévy Processes and Infinitely Divisible Distributions*. Cambridge University Press.

Schoutens, W. and J.L. Teugel (1998). Lévy Processes, Polynomials and Martingales. *Communication in Statistics: Stochastic Models* **14**, 335–49.

Semeraro, P. (2007). A Multivariate Variance-Gamma Model for Financial Application. *International Journal of Theoretical and Applied Finance* **11**, 1–18.

11

Freight Derivatives and Risk Management: A Review

Manolis G. Kavussanos and Ilias D. Visvikis

11.1 INTRODUCTION

During the last two decades there has been a significant growth in financial instruments that can be used to address the need of "protection" in the volatile economic environment in which business operate. While financial derivatives products such as futures, forwards, options, and swaps, have a long history in the management of risk for various commodities, these instruments have started to be used consistently by the shipping industry only during the last decade.

Shipping markets can be characterized as being capital intensive, cyclical, volatile, and seasonal, while shipping companies are exposed to the international business environment. Shipping freight derivatives have the potential to offset (hedge) freight rate risk of the dry-bulk and wet-bulk (tanker) sectors of the shipping industry.[1] The volatility observed in freight rates constitutes a major source of business risk for both the shipowner and the charterer. For the charterer wishing to hire-in vessels for transportation requirements, increasing freight rates leads to higher costs. For the shipowner, lower freight rates involves less income from hiring out the vessels. For a detailed analysis of the business risks prevalent in the shipping industry, and the traditional and derivative strategies that may be used to tackle them see Kavussanos and Visvikis (2006a, 2007).

Freight derivatives can provide real gains for market participants in shipping, as their existence has made risk management cheaper, more flexible and readily available to parties exposed to adverse movements in freight rates. Freight derivatives contracts, compared to time-chartering a vessel (a traditional risk management method), are more effective instruments for managing freight market risks. This is because shipowners retain operational

Manolis G. Kavussanos, Ph.D., Professor of Finance, Athens University of Economics and Business, 76 Patission St., 10434, Athens Greece., Email: mkavus@aueb.gr.

Ilias D. Visvikis, Ph.D. Assistant Professor of Finance, ALBA Graduate Business School, Athinas Ave. & 2A Areos St., 16671, Vouliagmeni, Athens, Greece, Email: ivisviki@alba.edu.gr.

[1] In the dry-bulk sector, vessel markets are segmented as follows: Capesize vessels (100 000–180 000 dwt – deadweight) carrying iron ore and coal; Panamax vessels (50 000–79 000 dwt) carrying coal, grain, bauxite; Supramax vessels (52 000 dwt); Hanymax vessels (25 000–49 999 dwt); and Handysize vessels (10 000–24 999 dwt) carrying minor bulks and smaller parcels of major bulks such as grain, coal and bauxite. In the wet-bulk (tanker) sector, vessel markets are segmented as follows: Ultra-Large Crude Carriers (ULCCs, 320 000 + dwt); Very-Large Crude Carriers (VLCCs, 200 000–319 999 dwt); Suezmax vessels (120 000–199 999 dwt); Aframax vessels (75 000–119 999 dwt); Panamax vessels (50 000–74 999 dwt); and Small Product Tankers (Coasters, 10 000–49 999 dwt), all carrying crude oil and oil products.

Risk Management in Commodity Markets: From Shipping to Agriculturals and Energy   Edited by Hélyette Geman

control of their vessels and at the same time benefit from favourable spot market conditions. Also, charterers are free from any operational risks which are present in time-charter agreements. Freight derivatives contracts allow entrepreneurs in the sector to get on with the business they know best, and yet manage their freight rate risk through this separate "paper" market. Commissions payable to brokers are lower in freight derivatives compared to chartering agreements. The low commission structure and their simple nature imply that it is cheaper and easier to trade in and out of freight derivatives positions prior to the settlement month than trading in and out of physical positions, where the costs are higher. Also, there is no physical delivery involved with freight derivatives. They simply settle in cash upon conclusion of the agreed terms.

Besides the above benefits to principals (shipowners and charterers) freight derivatives are useful to: (i) energy and commodity traders, since they allow them the opportunity to participate in pure trading and/or to hedge their physical shipping exposure; (ii) financial institutions, which participate in this market for proprietary trading and to offer hedging services to their clients; (iii) oil/energy companies/refineries for the opportunity they offer to hedge against the physical shipping freight rate volatility and to create a positive cash-flow management; and (iv) institutional non-shipping investors (such as hedge funds, private individuals, etc.), as they provide the opportunity to invest in a commodity with different cycle patterns compared to other sectors, thus providing the opportunity for arbitrage between sectors and complement/diversify their shipping equities portfolio.

Market participants using the freight derivatives markets come from all sectors of the shipping industry. They include shipowners (20%), charterers and operators (fleet managers/freight traders, 30%), trading companies (grain, coal, electricity, oil traders, 40%), financial houses and banks (10%). Regional trading during 2006/2007 is estimated to be: 70% from Europe, 25% from Asia and approximately 5% from the US. The value of trading for speculation is more than twice that for hedging, being 70% and 30% respectively.

Currently, market participants utilize various derivatives products in order to hedge themselves against the adverse freight rate fluctuations; these products are Over-The-Counter (OTC) and cleared – through a clearing-house – freight forwards, exchange-based cleared freight futures and OTC and cleared freight options. This chapter aims to provide an outline of the characteristics and markets of these products and discuss the empirical work presented in the literature thus far. Section 11.2 discusses forward freight agreements, namely FFAs. Section 11.3 presents the freight futures contracts listed in the specialized maritime products exchange, namely the International Maritime Exchange (IMAREX), and lately at the New York Mercantile Exchange (NYMEX). Section 11.4 discusses the issue of credit risk in FFAs and how the London Clearing House (LCH.Clearnet) and the Singapore Exchange AsiaClear provide solutions to this problem. Freight options are presented in Section 11.5. Section 11.6 outlines the empirical research findings in these markets, while Section 11.7 concludes the chapter.

11.2 FORWARD FREIGHT AGREEMENTS

The first OTC freight derivatives product appeared in 1992 and is called the Forward Freight Agreement (FFA) contract. FFAs are private principal-to-principal Contracts for Difference (CFDs) between a seller and a buyer to settle a freight rate, for a specified quantity of cargo or type of vessel, for usually one, or a combination of the major trade routes of the dry-bulk or tanker sectors of the shipping industry. Since FFAs are "tailor-made" to suit the needs of their users, they have become very popular with market participants wishing to hedge freight rate fluctuations (Kavussanos and Visvikis, 2003a, b).

In OTC derivatives markets each party accepts credit-risk (or counter-party risk) from the other party. The institutions that facilitate this market are major shipbrokers, investment banks, and other financial intermediaries in the fund management industry. The primary advantage of an OTC market is that the terms and conditions of the contract are tailored to the specific needs of the two parties. This gives investors flexibility by letting them introduce their own contract specifications in order to cover their specific needs. The OTC market allows its participants to quickly respond to changing needs and circumstances by developing new variations of old contracts.

The dry-bulk trading routes, which serve as the underlying assets of the FFA contracts today, are either from the Baltic Panamax Index BPI (Table 11.1), the Baltic Capesize Index (BCI), the Baltic Supramax Index (BSI) or the Baltic Handysize Index (BHSI).[2] These indices comprise freight rates designed to reflect the daily movement in rates across dry-bulk spot voyage and time-charter rates.[3] Regarding wet-bulk trades, the underlying trading routes are from the Baltic Dirty Tanker Index (BDTI) and the Baltic Clean Tanker Index (BCTI). As can be seen in Table 11.1 for example, each (major) route included in these indices is given a number, which is recorded in the first column of the table. They refer to: vessel size (column 2); certain cargo (column 3); route description (column 4); while the weight assigned to each route is reported in the last column of the table. Each route is given an individual *weighting* to reflect its importance in the world-wide freight market at the time the index is constructed.

Table 11.1 Baltic Panamax Index (BPI) Composition, 2007

Routes	Vessel Size (dwt)	Cargo	Route Description	Weights
P1A_03	74 000	T/C	Transatlantic round voyage	25 %
P2A_03	74 000	T/C	Skaw–Gibraltar range to Far East	25 %
P3A_03	74 000	T/C	Japan–South Korea range to Pacific	25 %
P4_03	74 000	T/C	Far East to NOPAC South Korea pass	25 %
P1	55 000	Light Grain	US Gulf to Amsterdam, Rotterdam Antwerp (ARA) region	0 %
P2	54 000	HSS	US Gulf to Japan	0 %
P3	54 000	HSS	NOPAC to Japan	0 %

Notes:

- The vessel size is measured by its carrying capacity (dwt – deadweight tonnes) and includes the effective cargo, bunkers, lubricants, water, food rations, crew and any passengers.
- Routes P1A, P2A, and P3A and P4 refer to time-charter (T/C) contracts, while P1, P2, and P3 refer to voyage routes.
- HSS stands for Heavy Grain, Soya and Sorghum.

Source of data: Baltic Exchange.

[2] The detailed composition and description of the Baltic indices can be found at the website of the Baltic Exchange (www.balticexchange.com). The Baltic was formed in 1883 to bring together market participants wishing to buy and sell freight services. This physical pooling of participants in an organized market is equivalent, amongst other things, to pooling of information, which helps discover prices and contributes towards the efficient working of markets.

[3] Voyage charters are paid as freight in US$/ton to move goods from port A to port B and all costs paid by the shipowner. Time-charters are paid as freight in US$/day, under which the shipowner earns hire every 15 days or every month. He operates the vessel under instructions from the charterer who pays voyage costs.

Provision is made so that the composition of the Baltic indices is altered over time, in line with developments in the sub-sectors of the shipping industry, in order to continue to reflect changing trading patterns. Specifically, at all times, the routes in the indices are chosen carefully by analysis of the percentage revenue value of the main commodities on the physical (spot) market, the total number and frequency of voyage fixtures by each commodity, and the balance of geographic origin and ton-mile contribution.

Since their introduction, FFA deals have grown substantially in both volume and value terms. Figures 11.1 and 11.2 show, respectively, the volume (number of contracts) and market value (in US$ billion) of dry-bulk FFA transactions, from inception until the end of 2006. The volume/value of trading has followed an exponential rise. The current growth of the FFA trades is expected to continue, with FFAs covering increasingly larger proportions of the underlying market. The exponential rise in FFA trading and the increasing liquidity and transparency of the market create increasing benefits to both shippers and direct customers, as well as intermediaries, such as forwarders and brokers.

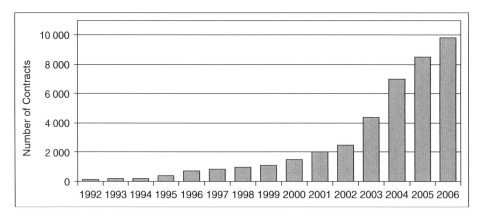

Figure 11.1   Yearly volumes of dry-bulk FFA contracts (Jan. 1992–Dec. 2006)
Source of data: Clarksons Securities Ltd.

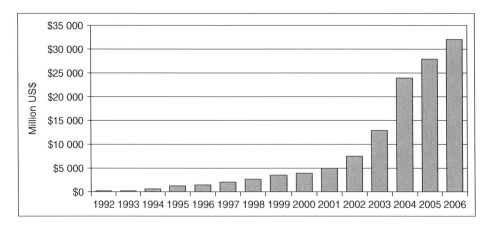

Figure 11.2   Yearly market values of dry-bulk FFA contracts (Jan. 1992–Dec. 2006)
Source of data: Clarksons Securities Ltd.

The following example illustrates their use. Assume that today is 25 September 2007 and that a charterer, which has to pay the cost of transporting his cargo of grain, believes that in one month (30 October 2007) freight rates in the trading route BPI, P2A (Skaw–Gibraltar range to Far East – 45 days) may increase from today's level of $78 000/day. In order to protect himself from a potentially more expensive market, he buys an FFA contract through his freight derivatives broker, in order to hedge his physical market exposure of $3 510 000 (= $78 000/day × 45 days). The broker will match this interest by finding another party, say a shipowner, which is the provider of the shipping service. The latter offers his Panamax vessel for hire, and anticipates that freight rates in the BPI P2A route may fall in one month from now. The shipowner will then sell an FFA, which expires in one month, at $78 000/day agreed today. Both parties, the shipowner and the charterer, would have locked their freight hire rate at $78 000/day.

To see this, assume that during 30 October 2007, the settlement price that is the average of the last seven business days prior to expiry is $91 000/day. As the freight market has increased, contrary to the expectations of the shipowner, the seller (shipowner) must pay $13 000/day (= $91 000–$78 000) to the buyer (charterer), which amounts to $585 000 (= $13 000/day × 45 days). Payment between the two parties is made by money transfer in US dollars within five business days following the settlement date. However, in the stronger physical (spot) market, the shipowner (charterer) gains (loses) $13 000/day, i.e., $585 000 more than he was expecting. Therefore, the net effect for both parties is that their cash-flows from the combined FFA–spot market portfolio were stabilized by locking in October's rates at $78 000/day.

In the dry-bulk market, voyage-based contracts are settled on the difference between the contracted price and the average prevailing value of the route selected in the index over the last seven working days of the settlement month. Time-charter-based contracts are settled on the difference between the contracted price and the average index value over the calendar settlement month. In the tanker market, a tanker FFA contract is an agreement between two parties to fix a freight rate in Worldscale units on a predetermined tanker route, over a voyage, at a mutually agreed price.[4] Settlement takes place at the end of each month, where the fixed forward price is compared against the monthly average of the spot price of the tanker route selected. If freight rates fall below the agreed rate, the charterer pays the difference between the agreed FFA price and the settlement spot price; if rates increase, then the charterer receives the difference.

11.3 FREIGHT FUTURES

The first freight derivatives product was the Baltic International Freight Futures Exchange (BIFFEX) contract, which was trading in the London International Financial Futures and Options Exchange (LIFFE) from May 1985 until April 2002. Its underlying asset was the index basket value of the Baltic Freight Index (BFI). However, the BIFFEX contracts did not produce overly effective hedges as discussed in Kavussanos (2002). The

---

[4] "Worldscale" was created in 1969 to assist the oil market have an independent unit of measurement of rates. Market levels of freight rates are expressed as a percentage of the scale rates instead of a plus or minus percentage. Worldscale rates are derived assuming that a "nominal" tanker functions on round voyages between designated ports. The calculated schedule rate (which equates to different US$/ton equivalents for each different route combination) is referred to as "Worldscale 100" or "Flat rate". Thus, Worldscale 100 means 100 points of 100 percent of the published rate or, in other words, the published rate itself.

unsatisfactory hedging effectiveness, the lack of liquidity towards the end of BIFFEX's life, coupled with the inception in 1992 of the OTC-traded FFA contracts, contributed to the decline in the volume of trading of BIFFEX contracts to levels which did not make it sustainable any more and during April 2002 LIFFE withdrew the contracts from its trading floor.

Since then, freight futures have been available in the organized exchanges of the International Maritime Exchange (IMAREX) in Oslo and the New York Mercantile Exchange (NYMEX) and are cleared in their associated clearing-houses. Clearing offers multilateral netting, removal of credit risk, standardized contracts, daily mark-to-market of positions, and increase in trading liquidity. According to market sources, contract clearing has reached 25 % of the total freight derivatives trades as of July 2007. Clearing allows not only new shipping entrants but attracts non-shipping related companies as well (for example, steel mills, coal mines, energy houses, and other companies in China, India, and Japan). Other new participants coming into the market are banks, hedge funds (e.g. Castalia Fund Management Ltd., Clarkson Fund Management Ltd., Global Maritime Investments (GMI), etc.) and other financial institutions, resulting in a more sophisticated and liquid market.

11.3.1 Freight futures at the International Maritime Exchange (IMAREX)

IMAREX launched a complete marketplace for freight derivatives on 2 November 2001. Its initial focus was to establish a market for trading and clearing tanker freight derivatives. In mid-2002, its operations extended to the dry-bulk cargo sector. In partnership with the Norwegian Options and Futures clearing-house (NOS), IMAREX has become a regulated marketplace for trading and clearing freight derivatives.[5]

Trading for market participants can be facilitated directly on the IMAREX trading screen or via an authorized third-party freight derivatives broker (e.g. Clarksons, Simpson Spence & Young, Freight Investors Services, etc.). A potential trader on IMAREX can obtain either a direct membership account or get access to the IMAREX marketplace through a financial intermediary, called a General Clearing Member (GCM), which can be a shipping derivatives broker or a shipping lending bank. In a direct membership structure, principals enter into membership agreements with both IMAREX and NOS. On 18 December 2006, NOS expanded its clearing facilities for freight market investors by opening for clearing via GCMs. Customer segments at IMAREX include international shipping companies, energy companies, refineries, commodity and financial trading houses.

Table 11.2 presents the "Dirty" and "Clean" tanker freight futures (listed), FFAs (non-listed) and options (non-listed) contracts offered by IMAREX at the time of writing. Freight derivatives on other freight routes are also offered upon demand by negotiation, but do not appear on the table. As can be observed, the IMAREX derivatives products have as the underlying commodity (that they use for settlement) the route freight indices constructed by either the Baltic Exchange or Platts.[6] Market agents can select either contracts that are listed at IMAREX or non-listed contracts. Both are cleared through NOS.

---

[5] More information about IMAREX can be obtained at: www.imarex.com.

[6] Platts is a provider of energy news, price benchmarks, energy intelligence, and decision-support services to the industry. It covers the petroleum, petrochemical, electricity, natural gas, coal, metals, nuclear power, bunker fuels, and freight rate markets. Its products range from real-time news and pricing services to newsletters and magazines, market reports and in-depth studies, databases, electronic directories, and research services. Its customers include producers, traders, market-makers, refiners, and analysts. More information about Platts can be obtained at: www.platts.com.

Table 11.2 IMAREX dirty and clean tanker derivatives, 2007

Routes	Sector	Route Description	Cargo Size (mt)	Cargo Size (barrels)	Type of Contract	Settlement Index
Panel A: Dirty Tanker Derivatives						
TD3	VLCC	AG – East	260 000	1 925 000	Listed – Futures, Asian Option	Baltic
TD4	VLCC	West Africa – USG	260 000	2 002 000	Listed – Futures	Baltic
TD5	Suezmax	West Africa – USAC	130 000	1 001 000	Listed – Futures, Asian Option	Baltic
TD7	Aframax	North Sea – UK/Cont	80 000	616 000	Listed – Futures, Asian Option	Baltic
TD9	Aframax	Caribs – USG	70 000	539 000	Listed – Futures	Baltic
TD8	Aframax	AG – Singapore (FO)	80 000	616 000	Non-Listed – FFA	Baltic
TD10	Panamax	Caribs – USAC	50 000	385 000	Non-Listed – FFA	Baltic
TD12	Panamax	ARA – USG	55 000	423 500	Listed – Futures Non-Listed – FFA	Baltic
Panel B: Clean Tanker Derivatives						
TC1	LR 2	AG – Japan	75 000	577 500	Listed – Futures	Platts
TC2	MR	Cont – USAC	37 000	254 100	Listed – Futures	Baltic
TC4	MR	Sing – Japan	30 000	231 000	Listed – Futures, Asian Option	Platts
TC5	LR 1	AG – Japan	55 000	423 500	Listed – Futures	Platts
TC6	MR	Algeria/Euromed	30 000	–	Listed – Futures	Baltic

Notes:
- LR 1 refers to Long Range Product Carriers between 55,000mt and 85,000mt.
- LR 2 refers to Long Range Product Carriers over 85,000mt.
- MR refers to Middle Range Product Carriers between 25,000mt and 55,000mt.
- The trading unit is Worldscale (WS) prices.

Source of data: IMAREX.

At the time of writing, there were four single-route freight futures contracts written on the dry-bulk routes produced by the Baltic Exchange. These are shown in Table 11.3, panel A. They involve the Capesize voyage routes C4 and C7 and the Panamax time-charter routes P2A and P3A, as these routes attract most of the dry-bulk freight derivatives trading, both at IMAREX and in OTC markets. Besides the futures contracts written on the Baltic single route indices, Table 11.3, panel B shows the three time-charter "basket" futures contracts, which are listed and traded at IMAREX. These "baskets" of time-charter rates are constructed from the Baltic dry-bulk route indices of Capesize, Panamax, and Supramax markets' routes. Thus, the four time-charter values of routes C8, C9, C10, and C11 of the BCI are used to calculate CS4 T/C, representing the average time-charter rate that could be earned in the Capesize sector. Similarly, the average of the four Panamax time-charter routes (P1A, P2A, P3A, and P4) of the BPI produces the PM4 T/C, while the SM6 T/C is the average of the six Supramax BSI routes (S1A, S1B, S2, S3, S4A, and S4B).

Table 11.3 IMAREX single route and T/C "basket" dry-bulk derivatives, 2007

Routes	Sector	Route Description	Cargo Size (mt)	Type of Contract
		Panel A: Single Route Dry-Bulk Derivatives		
C4	Capesize	Richards Bay – Rotterdam	150 000	Listed – Futures
C7	Capesize	Bolivar – Rotterdam	150 000	Listed – Futures
P2A	Panamax	T/C Skaw Gibraltar – Far East	74 000	Listed – Futures
P3A	Panamax	T/C S.Korea – Japan Pacific R/V	74 000	Listed – Futures
		Panel B: T/C Basket Dry-Bulk Derivatives		
CS4 T/C	Capesize	Capesize T/C routes Average	172 000	Listed – Futures
PM4 T/C	Panamax	Panamax T/C routes Average	74 000	Listed – Futures
SM6 T/C	Supramax	Supramax T/C routes Average	54 000	Listed – Futures

Source of data: IMAREX.

11.3.2 Freight futures at the New York Mercantile Exchange (NYMEX)

Since 16 May 2005, the New York Mercantile Exchange (NYMEX) has offered nine tanker freight derivatives in its electronic trading platform. NYMEX is the world's largest physical commodity futures exchange and the trading forum for energy and precious metals.[7] Transactions executed on the exchange avoid credit risk because its clearing-house, Clear-Port(sm), acts as the counterparty to every trade. They use as underlying commodities the Baltic Exchange or the Platts indices. Table 11.4 presents the specifications of the underlying indices; they are the five "dirty" tanker routes TD3, TD5, TD7, TD9, and TD10, shown in

Table 11.4 NYMEX listed dirty and clean tanker futures, 2007

Baltic Routes	NYMEX Coding	Sector	Route Description	Cargo Size (mt)	Type of Contract	Settlement Index
			Panel A: Dirty Tanker Futures			
TD3	TL	VLCC	Middle Eastern Gulf to Japan	260 000	Listed – Futures	Baltic
TD5	TI	Suezmax	West Africa – USAC	130 000	Listed – Futures	Baltic
TD7	TK	Aframax	North Sea – Europe	80 000	Listed – Futures	Baltic
TD9	TN	Panamax	Caribbean to US Gulf	70 000	Listed – Futures	Baltic
TD10	TO	Panamax	Caribbean to USAC	50 000	Listed – Futures	Baltic
			Panel B: Clean Tanker Futures			
TC1	TG	LR 2	Ras Tanura to Yokohama	75 000	Listed – Futures	Platts
TC2	TM	MR	Europe to USAC	37 000	Listed – Futures	Baltic
TC4	TJ	MR	Singapore to Japan	30 000	Listed – Futures	Platts
TC5	TH	LR 1	Ras Tanura to Yokohama	55 000	Listed – Futures	Platts

Source of data: NYMEX.

---

[7] More information about NYMEX can be obtained at: www.nymex.com.

panel A of the table, and the four "clean" tanker routes TC1, TC2, TC4, and TC5, presented in panel B of the same table.

11.4 "HYBRID" (CLEARED) FFAs

In response to demands from market participants to address the issue of credit risk present in OTC FFA contracts, a set of new derivatives contracts appeared. We call them "hybrid" FFAs, as they are OTC agreements, but cleared through a clearing house. Thus they maintain the flexibility of the FFAs and, for a fee, have credit risk eliminated through mark-to-market clearing, as in freight futures. These "hybrid" FFAs are cleared in the London Clearing House Clearnet (LCH.Clearnet) and in the Singapore Exchange AsiaClear (SGX AsiaClear).

11.4.1 Freight forwards at the London Clearing House Clearnet (LCH.Clearnet)

On 22 December 2003 the London Clearing House (LCH) Limited merged with Clearnet S.A. to form the "LCH.Clearnet" Group. On 13 September 2005, LCH.Clearnet launched a clearing and settlement platform for OTC FFAs. Potential members establish a relationship with a LCH.Clearnet clearing member for the management of margin and cash-flows, agreeing the commercial terms bilaterally, with the credit risk lying between the client and the clearing member. Alternatively, potential members can sign up to LCH.Clearnet as a clearing member.[8]

Table 11.5 presents the underlying indices upon which the freight forward contracts, which are cleared at LCH.Clearnet, are based. They include six tanker FFAs (crude and refined products), presented in panel A of the table; four dry-bulk voyage FFAs, presented in panel B; three "baskets" of dry-bulk time-charter FFAs, shown in panel C; and two dry trip time-charter FFAs, shown in panel D. In the tanker sector, forwards are written on the "dirty" TD3, TD5, TD7 routes and the "clean" TC2, TC4, TC5 routes. In the dry-bulk sector, FFAs are written on the Capesize voyage routes C3, C4, C5, and C7; on Capesize, Panamax, and Supramax time-charter "baskets"; and on the Panamax time-charter P2A and P3A routes. Moreover, LCH.Clearnet, during February 2008, launched three cleared freight options on the Capesize (CTCO), Panamax (PTCO), and Supramax (STCO) time-charter baskets.

11.4.2 Freight forwards at the Singapore Exchange AsiaClear (SGX AsiaClear)

In May 2006, Singapore Exchange Limited (SGX) launched SGX AsiaClear, its OTC clearing facility for energy and freight derivatives. In response to Asia's OTC market needs, SGX AsiaClear offers a network of Asia-based counterparties to facilitate OTC trading and clearing activities, to enhance credit and risk management, and to increase OTC operations and position-netting efficiencies. The SGX AsiaClear facility provides immediate 20-hour central counterparty clearing for OTC FFAs. OTC market participants can conveniently use their OTC Inter-Dealer Brokers (IDBs) to register trades electronically on the SGX Asia-Clear Trade Registration System for clearing and netting, under accounts maintained with SGX OTC Clearing Members. Clearing for the SGX AsiaClear facility is supported by the Singapore Exchange Derivatives Clearing Limited.[9]

---

[8] More information about LCH.Clearnet can be obtained at: www.lchclearnet.com.

[9] More information about SGX AsiaClear can be obtained at: www.asiaclear.com.sg.

Table 11.5   Listed forward contracts at LCH.Clearnet, 2007

Routes	Sector	Route Description	Cargo Size (mt)
Panel A: Tanker Forwards			
TD3	VLCC	Middle Eastern Gulf to Japan	260 000
TD5	Suezmax	West Africa – USAC	130 000
TD7	Aframax	North Sea – USAC	80 000
TC2	MR	Continent to USAC	37 000
TC4	MR	Singapore – Japan	30 000
TC5	LR 1	ME – Japan	55 000
Panel B: Dry Voyage Forwards			
C3	Capesize	Tubarao/Beilun and Baoshan	150 000
C4	Capesize	Richard Bay/Rotterdam	150 000
C5	Capesize	West Australia/Beilun-Baoshan	150 000
C7	Capesize	Bolivar/Rotterdam	150 000
Panel C: Dry Time-charter Basket Forwards			
CTC	Capesize	Capesize 4 T/C routes Average	–
PTC	Panamax	Panamax 4 T/C routes Average	–
STC	Supramax	Supramax 5 T/C routes Average	–
Panel D: Dry Trip Time-Charter Forwards			
P2A	Panamax	Skaw – Gibraltar/Far East	–
P3A	Panamax	Transpacific Round – Japan	–

Source of data: LCH.Clearnet.

Table 11.6 presents the underlying indices upon which the FFA contracts of SGX Asia-Clear are based. They include three tanker FFAs (crude and refined products), presented in panel A of the table; four dry voyage FFAs (dry-bulk commodities) presented in panel B; three "baskets" of dry time-charter FFAs, shown in panel C; and two dry trip time-charter FFAs, shown in panel D. In the tanker sector, FFAs are written on the "dirty" TD3 route and the "clean" TC4 and TC5 routes. In the dry-bulk sector, FFAs are written on the Capesize voyage routes C3, C4, C5, and C7; on Capesize, Panamax, and Supramax time-charter "baskets"; and on the Panamax time-charter P2A and P3A routes.

The development of allowing FFA contracts to be settled through a clearing-house in order to eliminate credit risk, is in response to calls from the industry. Potential market participants have always voiced their concern in relation to counterparty risk. These "hybrid" FFAs seem to combine the best of futures and forwards into one contract. That is, counterparty risk is removed and yet they retain their flexibility in terms of adjusting their terms according to the needs of the counterparties.

11.5   FREIGHT OPTIONS

Freight options contracts are available OTC on individual routes of the dry and tanker Baltic indices, as well as on baskets of time-charter routes, and are offered by the same derivatives brokers that trade FFA contracts and specialist investment banks (e.g. Macquarie Bank).

Table 11.6 Listed dirty and clean tanker forwards at SGX AsiaClear, 2007

Routes	Sector	Route Description	Cargo Size (mt)
Panel A: Tanker Forwards			
TD3	VLCC	Middle Eastern Gulf to Japan	260 000
TC4	MR	Singapore to Japan	30 000
TC5	LR 1	Middle Eastern Gulf to Japan	55 000
Panel B: Dry Voyage Forwards			
C3	Capesize	Tubarao/Beilun and Baoshan	150 000
C4	Capesize	Richard Bay/Rotterdam	150 000
C5	Capesize	West Australia/Beilun-Baoshan	150 000
C7	Capesize	Bolivar/Rotterdam	150 000
Panel C: Dry Time-charter Basket Forwards			
CTC	Capesize	Capesize 4 T/C routes Average	–
PTC	Panamax	Panamax 4 T/C routes Average	–
STC	Supramax	Supramax 5 T/C routes Average	–
Panel D: Dry Trip Time-Charter Forwards			
P2A	Panamax	Skaw – Gibraltar/Far East	–
P3A	Panamax	Transpacific Round - Japan	–

Source of data: SGX AsiaClear.

The Asian freight option contract is either a freight put option (floor) or a freight call option (cap). They settle the difference between the average spot rate over a defined period of time and an agreed strike price.[10] A shipowner anticipating falling freight rates will buy a put option, thus agreeing to sell his freight service in the future at a price agreed today. He would exercise the option to sell at the agreed price if the market freight rate falls below the agreed price, otherwise he will let the option expire worthless. On the other hand, a charterer would buy a call option, which he will exercise (to buy the freight service at the agreed price) if the market freight rate at expiry is higher than the agreed price. Both the charterer and the shipowner would pay a premium to purchase these options. In contrast to FFAs and freight futures, the downside cost is known in advance and is equal to the option's premium. The upside potential in a call option is unlimited, just as in the case of FFAs and freight futures. A detailed analysis of the various basic and advanced freight option strategies can be found in Kavussanos and Visvikis (2006a).

During 1 June 2005 the first cleared tanker IMAREX Freight Option (IFO) contract was launched, on route TD3 (AG – East, VLCC 260,000mt), cleared through NOS. The IFOs are available for trading and clearing for all IMAREX and NOS members and are structured as monthly call and put Asian style options, with monthly, quarterly and yearly maturities. During 2007, IMAREX announced IFO contracts on the following tanker routes: TD5 (West Africa – USAC), TD7 (North Sea – Continent), TC2 (Continent – USAC), TC4 (Singapore to Japan), and TC5 (AG – Japan) (see Panel A of Table 11.7). Moreover, dry-bulk

---

[10] An Asian option is an option that is exercised against an average over a period of time. Asian options are often used in thinly traded, volatile commodity markets to avoid problems with price manipulation of the underlying commodity near or at maturity. Freight markets fall into this category.

Table 11.7   IMAREX Asian Freight Options (IFO)

Routes	Sector	Route Description	Cargo Size (mt)
		Panel A: Tanker Asian IFOs	
TD3	VLCC	AG – East	260 000
TD5	Suezmax	West Africa – USAC	130 000
TD7	Aframax	North Sea – Continent	80 000
TC2	MR	Continent – USAC	33 000
TC4	MR	Singapore – Japan	30 000
TC5	LR 1	AG – Japan	55 000
		Panel B: Dry-Bulk Asian IFOs	
CS4TC	Capesize	T/C Average	–
PM4TC	Panamax	T/C Average	–
SM6TC	Supramax	T/C Average	–
C4 AVG	Capesize	Richards Bay – Rotterdam	150 000
C4	Capesize	Richards Bay – Rotterdam	150 000

Source of data: IMAREX.

IFOs have been launched on Capesize, Panamax, and Supramax time-charter basket averages and on Capesize route C4 (see Table 11.7, Panel B).

Tanker and dry-bulk IFOs are settled against the Baltic Exchange quotes (with the exception of routes TC4 and TC5, where Platts assessments are used). More specifically, settlement prices for the tanker routes (measured in Worldscale points and 1 Lot = 1000mt), and the dry-bulk time-charter routes (measured in US\$/day and 1 Lot = 1 Day) are calculated as the arithmetic average across all trading days in a calendar month and those for the dry-bulk voyage routes (measured in US\$/ton and 1 Lot = 1000mt) are calculated as the arithmetic average of the spot prices over the number of Index days in the Delivery Period.

11.6   EMPIRICAL RESEARCH ON FREIGHT DERIVATIVES

Relatively limited research has been conducted on freight derivatives, in comparison with derivatives on other "commodities".[11] Part of the reason for this situation has been the lack of availability of data which could be used to support empirical work in these markets. Until recently, research work had to rely on primary data collected from freight derivatives brokers' records, often meeting the reluctance of agents in the "secretive" shipping industry to provide data and information for research. Currently, there are several derivatives exchanges, which collect those data and, for a fee, can make them available to interested parties.[12]

---

[11] Several empirical studies have examined the economic functions of the now redundant BIFFEX contract: Cullinane (1991, 1992) investigates the predictive power of short-term forecasts of the BFI by the use of the BIFFEX contract; Chang and Chang (1996) examine the predictability of BIFFEX with respect to the dry-bulk shipping market; Thuong and Visscher (1990), Haralambides (1992), Haigh and Holt (2002), and Kavussanos (2002) present studies that have examined the risk management function, through hedging, of the BIFFEX contract; Tvedt (1998) derives a pricing formula for European futures options in the BIFFEX market; Kavussanos and Nomikos (1999) and Haigh (2000) examine the unbiasedness hypothesis in the BIFFEX market using cointegration techniques.

[12] For an analytical survey of the recent empirical evidence that has appeared in economic studies relevant to freight derivatives see Kavussanos and Visvikis (2006b).

The success or failure of a derivatives contract is determined by its ability to perform its economic functions efficiently and, therefore, to provide benefits to economic agents over and above the benefits they derive from the spot market. Those economic functions that have attracted much research interest are price discovery and risk management through hedging. If the derivatives market does not perform one or both of these functions satisfactorily, then market agents have no reason to trade in the derivatives market, which eventually leads to loss of trading interest. Together with these important economic functions, research work has appeared in the literature on issues which include: the impact of the introduction of the FFA: markets on the volatility of the freight rates; the predictive power of freight derivatives prices; the relationship between FFA bid-ask spreads and expected volatility; the forward freight rate dynamics; the pricing of freight options; and the application of Value-at-Risk (VaR) models for measuring freight market risk. These are presented in Section 11.6.1.

11.6.1 Price discovery in freight derivatives

Following Working (1960), price discovery refers to the use of one price series (e.g. derivatives returns) for determining (predicting) another price series (e.g. spot returns). The lead-lag relationship between the price movements of derivatives returns and the underlying spot market returns illustrates how fast one market reflects new information relative to the other, and how well the two markets are linked.

A special feature of the freight derivatives market is that the underlying commodity is a service, which cannot be stored. The theory governing the relationship between spot and derivatives prices of continuously storable commodities is developed in Working (1960) amongst others, while that of non-storable commodities is examined in studies such as Eydeland and Geman (1998), Geman and Vasicek (2001), and Bessembinder and Lemmon (2002) in the electricity derivatives markets. The non-storable nature of the FFA market implies that spot and FFA prices are not linked by a cost-of-carry (storage) relationship, as in financial and agricultural derivatives markets. Thus, futures/forward prices on freight rates are driven by the expectations of market agents regarding the spot prices that will prevail at the expiry of the contract.

For a storable commodity, it is argued that the price of a forward contract, written on the commodity, must be equal to the spot price of the commodity today plus the financial and other costs (e.g. storage and insurance) to carry it forward in time. If this is not the case and the forward price is overpriced (underpriced), arbitrageurs/investors can simultaneously sell (buy) the forward contract, buy (sell) the underlying commodity, and store it until the expiry of the contract. At expiry, reversing these positions will produce a risk-free profit. These movements by arbitrageurs ensure that correct prices always prevail in efficiently working markets, and they will be:

$$F_{t,T} = S_t + C_{T-t} \qquad (11.1)$$

where, $F_{t,T}$ = price of a forward contract at time t, maturing at time period T; S_t = spot price of the underlying commodity in period t; and C_{T-t} = costs of carrying the commodity forward in time between period t and T.

There are, however, a number of factors that may lead to a large deviation of spot prices from derivatives prices, thus resulting in the existence of arbitrage opportunities. For instance, arbitrage opportunities may arise due to the existence of regional supply and demand imbalances, regulatory changes, market distortions created by market participants with large positions, etc. Therefore, the aforementioned relationship can be used to identify the existence of arbitrage opportunities in the market.

Kavussanos (2002) and Kavussanos and Visvikis (2004, 2006b) point out that freight services, as the underlying commodity of freight derivatives, are not storable. This violates the usual arbitrage arguments, presented above, that lead to the pricing of futures and forward contracts in storable commodities. In fact, in the above studies and in Kavussanos and Visvikis (2006b) it is shown that in this case, pricing of FFA and freight futures contracts takes the following form:

$$F_{t,T} = E(S_T) + u_t \quad ; \quad u_t \sim iid(0, \sigma^2) \tag{11.2}$$

where $F_{t,T}$ is the FFA price formed at period t for settlement at period T, $E(S_T)$ denotes the expected value of the spot (underlying) freight asset at the settlement date, and u_t is an independent and identically distributed stochastic error-term with a mean value of zero and variance σ^2. Provided the relationship is verified with actual data, it can be argued that the freight forward/futures market satisfies its price discovery functions. This is because futures or forward prices today can help discover spot prices in a future time period, specifically at the expiry of the derivatives contract. Thus, the identification of risk-less arbitrage opportunities in non-storable commodities, and therefore market efficiency, becomes a research issue.

In the spot (physical) market, several studies have investigated if time-charter rates are formed through expected spot rates, following the Expectations Hypothesis of the Term Structure (EHTS). Kavussanos and Alizadeh (2002) test the EHTS in the formation of time-charter rates and report rejection of the relationship, arguing that this is due to the existence of time-varying risk premiums, which moreover vary with the duration of the time-charter contract and with the vessel size. Adland and Cullinane (2005) reinforce these findings and show that the risk premium also varies with the market conditions. Alizadeh *et al.* (2007) examine if the implied forward 6-month time-charter rates in the dry-bulk freight market, which are derived through the difference between time-charters with different maturities based in the term structure model, are efficient and unbiased predictors of actual future time-charter rates. They report that implied forward rates are indeed unbiased predictors of future time-charter rates. However, despite the finding of unbiasedness, on average, chartering strategies based on technical analysis are able to generate economic profits.

Kavussanos *et al.* (2004) and Kavussanos and Visvikis (2004) investigate two different aspects of the price discovery function of the FFA market, namely the relationship between current forward prices and expected spot prices – embodied in the unbiasedness hypothesis, and the lead-lag relationship in returns and volatility between spot and forward prices, respectively. They examine the following constituent routes of the BPI: (a) the Atlantic voyage route P1 (US Gulf/Antwerp–Rotterdam–Amsterdam); (b) the Atlantic time-charter route P1A (Transatlantic round to Skaw–Gibraltar range); (c) the Pacific voyage route P2 (US Gulf/Japan); and (d) the Pacific time-charter route P2A (Skaw Passero–Gibraltar/Taiwan–Japan).

11.6.1.1 The unbiasedness hypothesis

According to the unbiasedness hypothesis, derivatives (futures/forward) contract prices must be unbiased estimators of spot prices of the underlying asset that will be realized at the expiration date of the contract. The existence of derivatives markets therefore can help discover prices which are likely to prevail in the spot market. Theoretically, a forward price is equivalent to the expected spot price at maturity, under the joint hypothesis of no risk-premium and rational use of information. The relationship can be tested empirically through the following equation:

$$S_t = \beta_1 + \beta_2 \, F_{t,t-n} + u_t \quad ; \quad u_t \sim iid(0, \sigma^2) \tag{11.3}$$

where $F_{t,t-n}$ is the forward price at time $t-n$, for delivery at time t, S_t is the spot price at the maturity of the contract and u_t is a white noise error process. Unbiasedness holds when the following parameter restrictions $(\beta_1, \beta_2) = (0, 1)$ are valid.

Because most macroeconomic (time-series) variables are found to be non-stationary (they have a unit root) use of Ordinary Least Squares (OLS) to estimate Eq. (11.3), result in inconsistent coefficient estimates and t- and F-statistics which do not follow standard distributions. The following Vector Error-Correction Model (VECM) cointegration framework, developed by Johansen (1988), is used instead to resolve the problem and reliably test for unbiasedness:

$$\Delta X_t = \mu + \sum_{i=1}^{p-1} \Gamma_i \Delta X_{t-i} + \Pi X_{t-1} + u_t \quad ; \quad u_t \sim IN(0, \Sigma) \tag{11.4}$$

where X_t is the 2×1 vector $(S_t, F_{t,t-n})'$, μ is a 2×1 vector of deterministic components which may include a linear trend term, an intercept term, or both, Δ denotes the first difference operator, u_t is a 2×1 vector of residuals $(u_{S,t}, u_{F,t})'$ and Σ the variance/covariance matrix of the latter. The VECM specification contains information on both the short- and long-run adjustment to changes in X_t, via the estimates of Γ_i and Π, respectively.

In the FFA market, Kavussanos et al. (2004) report that parameter restriction tests on the cointegrating relationship between spot and FFA prices indicate that FFA prices one and two months prior to maturity are unbiased predictors of the realized spot prices in all investigated routes. However, the efficiency of the FFA prices three months prior to maturity gives mixed evidence, with routes P2 and P2A being unbiased estimators, and routes P1 and P1A being biased estimators of the realized spot prices. Thus, it is argued that unbiasedness depends on the market and type/length of contract under investigation. For the investigated routes and maturities for which unbiasedness holds, market agents can use the FFA prices as indicators of the future course of spot prices, in order to guide their physical market decisions.

Ishizaka et al. (2007) examine several factors determining equilibrium spot and futures/forward rates in shipping markets, assuming non-storability of freight rates. Based on the work of Tezuka and Ishizaka (2006), they extend the Bessembinder and Lemmon (2002) model to the freight market, which makes allowance for non-storability. In their study they take an equilibrium approach to derive futures/forward rates, rather than the cost-of-carry relationship. They construct a forward curve from wet-bulk sector (VLCC – AG/JP route) data, and examine the unbiasedness hypothesis. They use the futures curve in order to see if there are differences between the futures price and the expected value of the spot price at the maturity date (existence of risk-premiums) when market structures and conditions differ.

To specify the demand process, they use a Markov Regime Switching process model and assume a low demand situation and a high demand state. In their model it is assumed that the demand process can start either from a high or a low state and then change distribution at certain probability. Regarding the distribution of demand, the results show that when starting either from a high or a low state, it deviates from the state in which the process is at time 0. After observing the futures curve and risk-premium curve (biasness), which is the difference between the futures price and the expected value of the spot price at the maturity, the results indicate biasedness in all market conditions. Starting from a high demand state, futures curves tend to be upward sloping, but the risk-premium curves tend to be decreasing. On the other hand, starting from a low demand state the slopes of futures curves are downward, but the risk-premiums are upward. This may mean that in a high (low) demand period, market participants believe that the present (future) period is more important than future (present) periods and therefore, negative (positive) risk-premiums might exist for the future. Thus, it is suggested that the degree of biasedness depends on the initial demand conditions. Generally, in a high demand period, each participant values higher the present compared to any future period, and vice versa.

11.6.1.2 The lead-lag relationship

Kavussanos and Visvikis (2004) investigate the second dimension of the price discovery role of derivatives markets: that is, the lead-lag relationship between FFA and spot freight markets, both in terms of returns and volatilities. By using a VECM model (similar to that of Eq. (11.4)), to investigate the short-run dynamics and the price movements in the two markets, causality tests and impulse response analysis indicate that there is a bi-directional causal relationship between spot and FFA prices in all routes, implying that FFA prices can be equally as important sources of information as spot prices. However, the results from causality tests on the unrestricted VECM models suggest that causality from FFA (spot) to spot (FFA) returns is stronger than in the other direction on routes P1 and P2A (on routes P1A and P2).

The finding that FFA markets informationally lead the underlying spot markets may be due to the fact that FFA trades are cash-settled deals, which require no chartering of vessel or movement of cargo, and therefore have lower transactions costs than the underlying/physical spot market. Furthermore, an investor can have an FFA contract on one or more of the trading routes for several time intervals, providing him ease of shorting. In contrast to FFA transactions that can be implemented immediately with no up-front cash, spot fixtures require greater initial costs and take longer to be completed. Therefore, market agents react to new information faster through the FFA market, in comparison to spot transactions. As a consequence, spot prices will lag behind FFA prices.

In order to investigate for volatility spillovers between the spot and FFA markets, an augmented bivariate VECM – Generalised Autoregressive Conditional Heteroskedasticity (GARCH) model is utilized, with the following positive definite parameterization of the variance-covariance matrix:

$$H_t = A'A + B'H_{t-1}B + C'\varepsilon_{t-1}\varepsilon'_{t-1}C + S1'u_{1,t-1}u'_{1,t-1}S1$$
$$+ S2'u_{2,t-1}u'_{2,t-1}S2 + E'(z_{t-1})^2E \qquad (11.5)$$

where A is a 2×2 lower triangular matrix of coefficients, B and C are 2×2 diagonal coefficient matrices, with $\beta_{kk}^2 + \gamma_{kk}^2 < 1$, $k = 1,2$ for stationarity, S1 and S2 are matrices which contain parameters of spillover effects, $u_{1,t-1}$ and $u_{2,t-1}$ are matrices whose elements are lagged square error-terms ($u_{1,t-1}$ represents the volatility spillover effect from the spot to the derivatives market and $u_{2,t-1}$ represents the volatility spillover effect from the derivatives to the spot market), $(z_{t-1})^2$ is the lagged squared basis, and E is a 1×2 vector of coefficients of the lagged squared basis. In this diagonal representation, the conditional variances are a function of their own lagged values (old news), their own lagged error terms (new news), volatility spillover parameters, and a lagged squared basis parameter, while the conditional covariance is a function of lagged covariances and lagged cross products of the ε_t's.

The results indicate that the FFA market volatility spills information to the spot market volatility in route P1. In route P1A the results indicate no volatility spillovers in either market. In routes P2 and P2A there is a bi-directional relationship as each market transmits volatility to the other. The previous results, in routes P1 and P2A, indicate that informed participants are not indifferent between trading in the FFA or in the spot market, as new market information is disseminated in the FFA market before the spot market. Thus, it seems that FFA prices for those routes contain useful information about subsequent spot prices, beyond that already embedded in the current spot price, and therefore can be used as price discovery vehicles, since such information may be used in decision-making. More specifically, market participants who have collected and analyzed new information regarding the expected level of spot and FFA prices in routes P1 and P2A, will prefer to trade in the forward market than in the spot market. Furthermore, the FFA contracts for routes P1, P2, and P2A contribute to the volatility of the relevant spot rate, and therefore further support the notion of price discovery. By explicitly modelling conditional variance dynamics, practitioners can have a clearer understanding of the price interactions in the spot and FFA markets. This can lead to a better assessment of risk management, ship-chartering, and budget planning decisions.

11.6.2 Hedging effectiveness of freight derivatives

Derivatives markets exist in order to provide instruments for businesses to reduce or control the unwanted risk of price change by transferring it to others more willing to bear the risk. This function of derivatives markets is performed through hedging the spot position by holding an opposite position in the derivatives market. Kavussanos and Visvikis (2005) investigate the risk management function of the FFA market by examining the effectiveness of time-varying hedge ratios in reducing freight rate risk in the four aforementioned routes of the BPI. Comparison between the effectiveness of different hedge ratios is made by constructing portfolios implied by the computed ratios each week and then comparing the variance of the returns of these constructed (hedged) portfolios over the sample.

According to Johnson (1960) and Ederington (1979), the hedge ratio that minimizes the risk of the spot position is given by the ratio of the covariance (measuring co-movement) between spot and derivatives price changes over the variance (measuring volatility) of derivatives price changes. The ratio is known as the Minimum Variance Hedge Ratio (MVHR). The MVHR methodology postulates that the objective of hedging is to minimize the variance of the returns in the hedge portfolio held by the investor. Therefore, the hedge ratio that generates the minimum portfolio variance should be the optimal hedge ratio. This is equivalent to the slope coefficient, $h*$, in the following regression:

$$\Delta S_t = h_0 + h^* \Delta F_t + \varepsilon_t; \varepsilon_t \sim iid(0, \sigma^2) \tag{11.6}$$

where $\Delta S_t = S_t - S_{t-1}$ is the logarithmic change in the spot position between $t-1$ and t; $\Delta F_t = F_t - F_{t-1}$ is the logarithmic change in the FFA position between $t-1$ and t, and $h*$

is the optimal hedge ratio. The degree of variance reduction in the hedged portfolio achieved through hedging is given by the coefficient of determination (R^2) of the regression, since it represents the proportion of risk in the spot market that is eliminated through hedging; the higher the R^2 the greater the effectiveness of the minimum variance hedge.

To account for the simultaneous estimation of spot and FFA prices and to allow for the time variation in h^*, VECM-GARCH are used in in- and out-of-sample tests. They indicate that, in voyage routes P1 and P2, the relationship between spot and FFA prices is quite stable and market agents can use simple first-difference regression models in order to obtain optimum hedge ratios. In contrast, on time-charter routes P1A and P2A, it seems that the arrival of new information affects the relationship between spot and FFA prices, and therefore time-varying hedging models should be preferred. Also the hedging effectiveness varies from one freight market to the other. This is because freight prices, and consequently FFA quotes, are affected by different regional economic conditions. Market agents can benefit from this result by developing appropriate hedge ratios for each route, and thus controlling their freight rate risk more effectively.

11.6.3 The impact of freight derivatives trading on spot market price volatility

Derivatives markets can be seen to be enhancing economic welfare by allowing for new positions, expanding investment sets, providing instruments for reducing risks and enabling existing positions to be taken at lower costs. However, the issue of whether derivatives trading increases or reduces volatility in the spot market has been the subject of considerable empirical analysis and has received the attention of policymakers.

Kavussanos *et al.* (2004) investigate the impact of FFA trading on spot market price volatility of the four aforementioned routes of the BPI, by employing a GARCH model modified along the lines of the GJR-GARCH model of Glosten *et al.* (1993). This allows for the asymmetric impact of news (positive or negative) on volatility. Thus, the mean equation of the GJR-GARCH process is defined as follows:

$$\Delta S_t = \varphi_0 + \sum_{i=1}^{p-1} \varphi_i \Delta S_{t-i} + \varepsilon_t \quad ; \quad \varepsilon_t \sim IN(0, \mathrm{h}_t) \qquad (11.7)$$

where S_t is the natural logarithm of the daily spot price change, Δ is the first-difference operator and ε_t is the regression error-term, which follows a conditional normal distribution with mean zero and time-varying covariance, h_t. The conditional variance of the process is specified as follows:

$$\mathrm{h}_t = \mathrm{a}_0 + \mathrm{a}_1 \mathrm{h}_{t-1} + \beta_1 \varepsilon_{t-1}^2 + \gamma_1 \varepsilon_{t-1}^2 \mathrm{D}_{t-1}^- \qquad (11.8)$$

where D_{t-1}^- is a dummy variable that takes the value of unity if the error is negative ($\varepsilon_{t-1}^{<0}$) and zero otherwise. When the coefficient of D_{t-1}^- is zero (i.e. $\gamma_1 = 0$), the model of Eq. (11.8) is the symmetric GARCH model. A negative shock ($\mathrm{D}_{t-1}^- = 1$) can generate an asymmetric response on volatility, in comparison to a positive shock. When $\gamma_1 > 0$ ($\gamma_1 < 0$), the model produces a larger (smaller) response for a negative shock compared to a positive shock of equal magnitude. *A priori* one expects a positive sign for the γ_1

coefficient, as there is evidence in the literature which shows that bad news has a larger impact on price volatility than good news.

The impact of the onset of FFA trading is examined in two ways. First, the model of Eq. (11.8) is estimated for the period before and after the onset of FFA trading and the estimated coefficients in the two models are compared. Thus, the asymmetry of the relationship between information and volatility before and after the onset of FFA trading may be inferred through the value of the estimated coefficient γ_1 before and after FFAs. Secondly, in order to examine how the onset of FFA trading has affected volatility, a dummy variable (D_1) is introduced (with a coefficient γ_2) in the variance equation representing the time period before and after FFA trading. A significant positive γ_2 coefficient indicates increased unconditional spot price volatility in the post-FFA period, whereas a significant negative γ_2 coefficient indicates decreased unconditional spot price volatility in the post-FFA period.

The results suggest that the onset of FFA trading has (i) reduced the spot price volatility of all investigated routes; (ii) a decreasing impact on the asymmetry of volatility (market dynamics) in routes P2 and P2A; and (iii) substantially improved the quality and speed of information flow for routes P1, P1A, and P2. These findings have several implications for the way in which the FFA market is viewed. It appears that there has been an improvement in the way that news is transmitted into prices following the onset of FFA trading. It is argued that by attracting more, and possibly better informed, participants into the market, FFA trading has assisted the incorporation of information into spot prices more quickly. Thus, even those market agents who do not directly use the FFA market have benefited from the introduction of FFA trading.

11.6.4   The predictive power of freight derivatives

Batchelor *et al.* (2007) test the performance of several time-series models (multivariate Vector Autoregressive – VAR; VECM; Seemingly Unrelated Regressions Estimation – SURE-VECM; and univariate Autoregressive Integrated Moving Average – ARIMA) in predicting spot and FFA rates on P1, P1A, P2, and P2A freight routes of the BPI.

Univariate ARIMA (p, d, q) models of the following form are used to generate forecasts of spot and FFA prices:

$$\Delta S_t = \mu_{1,0} + \sum_{i=1}^{p} \mu_{1,i} \Delta S_{t-i} + \sum_{j=1}^{q} \gamma_{1,j} F_{t-j} + \varepsilon_{1,t} \quad ; \quad \varepsilon_{1,t} \sim iid(0, \sigma_1^2) \qquad (11.9a)$$

$$\Delta F_t = \mu_{2,0} + \sum_{i=1}^{p} \mu_{2,i} \Delta S_{t-i} + \sum_{j=1}^{q} \gamma_{2,j} F_{t-j} + \varepsilon_{2,t} \quad ; \quad \varepsilon_{2,t} \sim iid(0, \sigma_2^2) \qquad (11.9b)$$

where ΔF_t and ΔS_t are changes (first-differences) in log FFA and spot prices respectively, and $\varepsilon_{k,t}$; $k = 1,2$, is a white noise random error-term. For an ARIMA (p, d, q) model the terms p, d, q refer to the lagged values of the dependent variable, the order of integration and the lagged values of the error-term respectively, in the specification of the model.

The bivariate VAR(p) model of the following form is also used to produce forecasts of spot and FFA prices in a simultaneous spot-FFA framework:

$$\Delta S_t = \mu_{1,0} + \sum_{i=1}^{p} \mu_{1,i} \Delta S_{t-i} + \sum_{j=1}^{q} \gamma_{1,j} F_{t-j} + \varepsilon_{1,t} \tag{11.10}$$

$$\Delta F_t = \mu_{2,0} + \sum_{i=1}^{p} \mu_{2,i} \Delta S_{t-i} + \sum_{j=1}^{q} \gamma_{2,j} F_{t-j} + \varepsilon_{2,t} \quad ; \quad \varepsilon_{k,t} \sim iid(0, \sigma_k^2)$$

Finally, the unrestricted and restricted versions of the bivariate VECM(p) model of the following form is used to generate simultaneous out-of-sample forecasts for spot and FFA prices:

$$\Delta S_t = \mu_{10} + \sum_{i=1}^{p} \mu_{1,i} \Delta S_{t-i} + \sum_{j=1}^{q} \gamma_{1,j} F_{t-j} + \alpha_1 (S_{t-1} - \beta_1 F_{t-1} - \beta_0) + \varepsilon_{1,t} \tag{11.11}$$

$$\Delta F_t = \mu_{20} + \sum_{i=1}^{p} \mu_{2,i} \Delta S_{t-i} + \sum_{j=1}^{q} \gamma_{2,j} F_{t-j} + \alpha_2 (S_{t-1} - \beta_1 F_{t-1} - \beta_0) + \varepsilon_{2,t}$$

$$\varepsilon_{i,t} | \Omega_{t-1} \sim IN(0, \mathbf{H})$$

where the term in brackets represents the cointegrating (long-run) relationship between the spot and FFA prices. The error-terms follow a normal distribution with mean zero and covariance matrix, H.

Independent non-overlapping forecast sets are created by generating N-period ahead multiple forecasts, from recursively estimated model parameters. The results indicate that while conditioning spot returns on lagged FFA returns generates more accurate forecasts of spot prices for all forecast horizons (up to 20 days ahead), conditioning FFA returns on lagged spot returns enhances forecast accuracy only up to four days ahead. For longer forecast horizons, simple univariate ARIMA models seem to be the best models for forecasting FFA prices. Thus, FFA prices can enhance the forecasting performance of spot prices and, consequently, by selecting the appropriate time-series model for forecasting purposes, market participants can design more efficient investment and speculative trading strategies.

On the other hand, it seems that spot prices cannot help in enhancing the forecasting performance of FFA prices, which indicates that the forward rate does contain significantly more and different (and maybe better) information than is embodied in the current spot rate. The implication of this is that even if market participants do not use the FFA market for hedging reasons, by collecting and analyzing FFA prices they can obtain "free" information about the future direction of spot freight prices.

11.6.5 Microstructure effects in freight derivatives markets

Transactions costs are an important consideration in investors' investment decisions. One such significant cost is the Bid-Ask Spread (BAS). Brokers match buy and sell contracts and the price charged for this service is known as the BAS; that is, the difference between the buying (bid) and selling (asked) price per contract. This normally is regarded as compensation to brokers for providing liquidity services in a continuously traded market. There should be a positive relationship between the BAS and price volatility on the grounds that the greater the variability in price, the greater the risk associated with performance of the function of the brokers. Intuitively, unambiguous *good* or *bad* news regarding the fundamentals of the price of the asset should have no systematic effect on the spread. However, greater uncertainty regarding the future price of the asset, as associated with greater volatility of the price of the asset, is likely to result in a widening of the spread.

Batchelor *et al.* (2005) examine the relationship between expected volatility and bid-ask spreads in the FFA market using the four aforementioned routes of the BPI. In order to derive an estimate of the FFA volatility, the following AR(p)-GARCH(1,1) model is employed:

$$\Delta F_t = \varphi_0 + \sum_{i=1}^{p-1} \varphi_i \Delta F_{t-i} + \varepsilon_t \; ; \; \varepsilon_t \sim \text{iid}(0, h_t) \; ; \; h_t = a_0 + a_1 h_{t-1} + \beta_1 \varepsilon_{t-1}^2 \quad (11.12)$$

where F_t is the natural logarithm of FFA prices (average mid-point of the bid-ask quotes), Δ is the first-difference operator, and ε_t is a white noise error-term with mean zero and time-varying variance, h_t.

One-step ahead conditional volatility estimates (h_{t+1}), derived from the above model are used to analyze the relationship between expected volatility and current BAS$_t$. Specifically, the BASs are regressed against variables that represent risk, information and a lagged BAS, as in the following equation:

$$\text{BAS}_t = \beta_0 + \beta_1 h_{t+1} + \beta_2 \text{BAS}_{t-1} + \beta_3 \Delta F_t + u_t \; ; \; u_t \sim \text{iid}(0, h_t) \quad (11.13)$$

where risk is captured by the one-step ahead conditional volatility (h_{t+1}) from a GARCH(1,1) model, information effects are accounted for by the logarithmic first-difference of the FFA price series (ΔF_t) and BAS$_t$ is defined as the difference of the natural logarithm of the ask quote minus the natural logarithm of the bid quote [$\ln(\text{Ask}_t) - \ln(\text{Bid}_t)$]. The model is estimated via the Generalized Method of Moments (GMM), thus avoiding any simultaneity bias and yielding heteroskedasticity and autocorrelation consistent estimates.

The results indicate that there is a positive relationship between bid-ask spreads and expected price volatility for routes P1, P2, and P2A. In contrast, on route P1A there is no significant relationship between bid-ask spreads and expected volatility. This finding may be explained by the thin trading of FFA contracts for the latter route. The results can provide a better understanding of the movements of FFA prices, and the consequent effect on transactions costs. Market participants using information on the behaviour of bid-ask spreads have a better insight into the timing of their FFA transactions and the future direction of the FFA market, as a widening bid-ask spread corresponds to an anticipation of increased future volatility.

11.6.6 Market surveys on the use of freight derivatives

Dinwoodie and Morris (2003) survey the attitudes of tanker shipowners and charterers towards freight hedging and their risk perceptions of FFAs. The survey includes questionnaire replies from seven countries over 22 shipowners and eight charterers. They argue that although FFAs were widely viewed as an important development, some respondents were unaware of their function and the majority had not used them. Most of the participants in this survey were concerned about the risk of payment default on settlement. Many shipowners also feared that FFAs might expose their risk management policies to counterparties. The link between freight hedging activity and participants' risk aversion was not clear-cut, but they argue that improved "technical" education is essential for widespread acceptance.

Kavussanos *et al.* (2007) explore the importance of hedging through a questionnaire survey of 31 Greek shipping counterparties. The general attitudes and common perceptions of the use of shipping derivatives by Greek shipowners involved in both dry-bulk and tanker trades are investigated. The results indicate that: (i) risk management and shipping derivatives are at an early stage of development and understanding in the Greek shipping market, although participants in the sample seem to know about them; (ii) the traditional ways of thinking must be changed and replaced with modern risk management concepts, which should form part of the overall business strategy of the company; (iii) liquidity and credit (counterparty) risk are considered to be major obstacles in the use of shipping derivatives; (iv) in line with the findings of Dinwoodie and Morris (2003), they consider education to be of paramount importance for them; and finally, (v) there seems to be a positive view of the future of shipping derivatives in Greece, especially if the banks endorse them.

11.6.7 Forward freight rate dynamics

Koekebakker and Adland (2004) investigate the forward freight rate dynamics by modelling them under a term-structure model. They transform time-charter rates into average based forward freight rates. They then assume that there exists a continuous forward freight rate function that correctly prices the average based forward freight rate contracts. For their analysis, they use time-charter rates for a Panamax 65 000 dwt vessel under three different time-charter maturities: six months, one year, and three years. These data are then used to construct, each day, a forward rate function using a smoothing algorithm in order to investigate the factors governing the dynamics of the forward freight rate curve. Results indicate that the volatility of the forward curve is bumped, with volatility reaching a peak for freight rates with roughly one year to maturity. Moreover, correlations between different parts of the term-structure are in general low and even negative. They conclude that these results are not found in other markets. Such a forward freight rate model provides a tool to perform freight rate derivatives valuation and hedging.

Adland *et al.* (2007) investigate the volatility structure of the forward freight rate function in the route-specific tanker freight futures market using IMAREX quarterly and calendar year freight futures contracts. They argue that knowledge of the volatility structure is important when pricing freight options and when measuring the market risk inherent in the freight derivatives portfolio. The framework of Heath, Jarrow, and Morton (HJM, 1992) is followed for modeling the continuous forward freight rate function that provides the price today for freight at any given point of time in the future. This is derived empirically using a smoothing algorithm for each trading day in the sample. They report a volatility structure that is increasing over a horizon of several weeks and then sharply declining in the time to maturity of the contracts. It is suggested that this is a reflection of the expected short-term positive autocorrelation and long-run mean reversion of tanker spot freight rates. It is further reported that while the volatility of short-term forward freight rates is increasing in the vessel size, the annualized volatility of forward freight rates across sizes is converging, at a maturity of around one year. However, the authors argue that the empirical results must be interpreted with caution, as the freight futures market in general remains illiquid compared to other commodity markets.

11.6.8 Pricing of freight options

Tvedt (1998) estimates an analytical formula for pricing European futures options on BIF-FEX. The following assumptions are made: Due to the possible lay-up of vessels, the underlying index of BIFFEX, namely the BFI, is never close to zero. Therefore, it is assumed that the BFI, and also the futures price process, are restricted downwards by an absorbing level, which is above zero. Further, it is assumed that freight rates are mean reverting, due to frictional capacity adjustments to changes in the demand for shipping services. These properties influence the valuation of options contracts on BIFFEX.

Let λ be an absorbing level for the BFI process that would be the lay-up level for vessels. Assuming that the BFI less the absorbing level λ is log-normally distributed, then the increment of the index is given by the following mean reversion process:

$$dX_t = k[a - \ln(X_t - \lambda)](X_t - \lambda)d_t + \sigma(X_t - \lambda)dZ_t \qquad (11.14)$$

where X_t is the index value (BFI) at time t, dZ_t is the increment of a standard Brownian motion, and k, a and σ are constants. Generally, the futures price at time t (Φ_t) is the expected value at time t of the spot price at the time of settlement T. Following Black (1976), in the case of no risk-premium from investing in the futures market, it is argued that the futures price process is given by the expectation of the spot process at the time of settlement. Therefore, the futures price process is given by:

$$d\Phi_t = e^{-k(T-t)}\sigma(\Phi_t - \lambda)dZ_t \qquad (11.15)$$

where the weight $e^{-k(T-t)}$ determines the degree by which the volatility in the spot rate (the BFI) is transferred over to the futures price process. Tvedt (1998) argues that since BFI is an index of prices of shipping services, and since a service cannot be stored, the cost-of-carry argument does not apply. Consequently, he argues that mean reversion in prices can prevail without being smoothed out by storage and can be explained without referring to changes in inventory costs.

The present value of a European call option on a BIFFEX futures at time t is given by the expectation of the value of the option at settlement date (C_T):

$$C_T = e^{r(T-t)}E[(\Phi_t - \psi)\chi_A] \qquad (11.16)$$

where r is a constant risk-free interest rate, χ_A is the indicator function of the event A (that is, the option is only exercised when it is favourable for the option holder) and ψ is the strike price. Calculating Eq. (11.16), using traditional arbitrage arguments and assuming no transactions costs or taxes, the value of a European option on a futures contract in the BIFFEX market was derived as:

$$C_T = e^{-r(T-t)}[(\Phi_t - \lambda)N(d_1) - (\psi - \lambda)N(d_2)] \qquad (11.17)$$

where,

$$d_1 = \frac{\ln\left(\frac{\Phi_t - \lambda}{\psi - \lambda}\right) + [1/2\,e^{-2k(T-t)}\sigma^2(T-t)]}{e^{-k(T-t)}\sigma\sqrt{T-t}}, \, d_2 = \frac{\ln\left(\frac{\Phi_t - \lambda}{\psi - \lambda}\right) - [1/2\,e^{-2k(T-t)}\sigma^2(T-t)]}{e^{-k(T-t)}\sigma\sqrt{T-t}}$$

Koekebakker et al. (2007) propose a mathematical framework for Asian freight options modeling, which is an extension of the framework put forward in Black (1976). Under this theoretical framework, the spot freight rate at time t, which is a non-traded asset, is denoted $S(t)$. A future arithmetic average of S consists of N fixings at time points $T_1 < T_2 < \ldots < T_N$. An FFA contract with a price $F(t, T_1, T_N)$ can be interpreted as the price set today at time t to deliver at time T_N the value of the arithmetic average of the underlying spot freight rate during the period $[T_1, T_N]$. Moreover, an FFA is a cash-settled contract that gives the difference between this average and the price $F(t, T_1, T_N)$ multiplied by a constant D.[13] They show that the value of an FFA can be found by discounting this cash-flow received at time T_N and taking the conditional expectation under the pricing measure Q. Rearranging and solving for the FFA price, it is simply the expected average spot price under the pricing measure:

$$F(t, T_1, T_N) = \frac{1}{N} \sum_{i=1}^{N} E_t^Q [S(T_i)]. \tag{11.18}$$

It is argued that FFAs are lognormal prior to the settlement period, but this lognormality breaks down in the settlement period. They suggest an approximate dynamics structure in the settlement period for the FFA, leading to closed-form option pricing formulas for Asian call and put options written on the spot freight rate indices. Using Eq. (11.18), the payoff of a call Asian option with strike price K and maturity $T \leqslant T_N$ is derived as:

$$D\left[\frac{1}{N}\sum_{i=1}^{N} S(T_i) - K\right]^+ = D[F(T, T_1, T_N) - K]^+ \tag{11.19}$$

and for a put

$$D\left[K - \frac{1}{N}\sum_{i=1}^{N} S(T_i)\right]^+ = D[K - F(T, T_1, T_N)]^+. \tag{11.20}$$

Given that freight options relate to periods that are non-overlapping multiples of the monthly settlement period, they are caps and floors. Thus, the price at time $t < T_N$ for a call option is derived as:

$$C(t, T_N) = e^{-r(T_N - t)} D(F(t, T_1, T_N) N(d_1) - K N(d_2)) \tag{11.21}$$

where $d_1 = \frac{\ln\left(\frac{F(t,T_1,T_N)}{K}\right) + \frac{1}{2}\sigma_F^2}{\sigma_F}$, $d_2 = d_1 - \sigma_F$, and $N(x)$ is the standard cumulative normal distribution function.

---

[13] The constant D refers to the number of calendar days covered by the FFA contract or an agreed cargo size for time-charter routes and voyage route, respectively.

For the put option, the put-call parity for futures contracts combined with the symmetry property of the normal distribution is used to derive:

$$P(t, T_N) = e^{-r(T_N - t)} D(K\, N(-d_2) - F(t, T_1, T_N)\, N(-d_1)). \qquad (11.22)$$

The authors conclude that other stochastic specifications of the spot freight rate process may be more appropriate. For instance, extensions of this work should incorporate the term-structure of volatility that exists due to mean reversion in the spot freight rate process and the possible existence of seasonal volatility.

11.6.9 Measuring freight market risk

An important question in the sector is when to utilize derivative products to hedge freight rate risks. To that effect, Kavussanos and Dimitrakopoulos (2007) introduce and formalize a market risk measurement and management framework for the shipping business. Two alternative risk metrics are proposed: Value-at-Risk (VaR) and Expected Shortfall (ES). VaR is a single, summary, statistical number that expresses the maximum expected loss over a given time horizon, at a certain confidence interval and for a given position or portfolio of instruments, under normal market conditions.

Defining the continuously compounded return of an asset as $r_t = \ln(P_t/P_{t-1})$ for the period from $t-1$ to t and letting r_t follow the stochastic process $r_t = \mu_t + z_t\, \sigma_t$ (where, $\mu_t = E(r_t)$ is the conditional mean and σ_t^2 is the conditional variance) VaR denotes the maximum loss over a predefined investment horizon (e.g. one day), that can be sustained at a certain confidence level $(1 - \alpha)$. Mathematically:

$$F(VaR_{t+1}^{1-a}) = P(r_t \leqslant VaR_{t+1}^{1-a}) = a. \qquad (11.23)$$

VaR has been criticized for its inability to quantify and express the loss beyond the VaR level and for not being a coherent risk metric.

The ES is defined as the expected value of the loss beyond the VaR level (shortfall), under the condition that a shortfall occurs and fulfils the coherency conditions required for risk metrics:

$$ES = E_t(r_t | r_t < VaR_{t,a}). \qquad (11.24)$$

Kavussanos and Dimitrakopoulos (2007) provide an evaluation assessment of alternative VaR and ES forecasting models for short- and medium-term freight risk exposures for the tanker shipping sector. More specifically, freight market risk exposures corresponding to vessel portfolios, employed to routes of the Baltic Clean Tanker Index (BCTI) and Baltic Dirty Tanker Index (BDTI) or to single vessels employed in individual routes are considered.[14] The alternative modeling approaches include: variance modeling approaches (such as the random walk, the GARCH, and exponentially weighted moving average specifications); simulation based approaches (such as the historical simulation, the exponential historical simulation,

---

[14] Individual routes used include: TD3 (Middle East Gulf to Japan, for vessel sizes of 250 000 dwt), TD5 (West Africa to USAC, for vessel sizes of 130 000 dwt), TD7 (North Sea to Continent, for vessel sizes of 80 000 dwt), and TD9 (Caribbean to US Gulf, for vessel sizes of 70 000 dwt.

the filtered historical simulation and Monte Carlo);[15] and semi-parametric approaches (such as the extreme value methods).[16] Each of the alternative VaR specifications is evaluated in terms of statistical accuracy (or statistical sufficiency in the concept of interval forecast evaluation) and regulatory performance (regulatory loss functions, penalizing large deviations of VaR and ES values from realized losses, are used).

The results indicate that unhedged positions in routes TD3 and TD9 are found to be more risky than positions in the other markets examined (TD5 and TD7). The comparative analysis of the alternative VaR and ES forecasting models indicates that the GARCH and the Historical or the Filtered Historical Simulation approaches perform best for forecasting short-term (daily) risk. On the other hand, the most reliable method for estimating long-term risk exposures is the empirically scaled historical simulation model. Thus, it is suggested that both the VaR and the ES risk metrics, if employed correctly, may contribute to an effective management of freight risk.

Besides the aforementioned study, two other empirical studies try to measure freight market risk with the use of the VaR methodology. Angelidis and Skiadopoulos (2007) apply several parametric and non-parametric VaR methods in dry-bulk (Baltic Dry Index, the 4 Time-Charter Average BPI and the 4 Time-Charter Average BCI) and wet-bulk (Dirty Tanker TD3 route) markets. They argue that the simplest non-parametric methods can be used to measure freight market risk and that the freight rate risk is greater in the wet-bulk market. Lu *et al.* (2007), using index data from the dry-bulk market (BCI, BPI, and BHMI), find the General Error Distribution (GED) Exponential E-GARCH-VaR model to be able to efficiently measure market risk.

11.7   CONCLUSION

This chapter presented how freight derivative instruments, such as futures, forwards and options, can be used to hedge freight rate risks in the dry- and wet-bulk sectors of the shipping industry. It started by presenting the underlying indices of freight rate derivatives, which are constructed by the Baltic Exchange. These indices and their constituent routes provide the underlying commodities for freight rate derivatives to be written upon. Then exchange-traded, OTC and cleared-OTC freight derivatives were analyzed. It can be argued that freight derivatives can provide the flexibility that traditional methods of risk management are not able to provide to shipping companies.

Furthermore, the economics underlying the freight derivatives markets and the empirical research evidence related to them have been outlined. In general, it has been shown that: (i) freight derivatives contracts serve their price discovery function well, as FFA prices are unbiased predictors of future spot rates and FFA markets informationally lead, in terms of returns and volatilities, the underlying spot markets; (ii) FFA contracts serve their risk

---

[15] In the non-parametric **historical simulation**, the next period's returns are well approximated by the empirical distribution of the last m-observations. In the **exponential historical simulation**, heavier weights are assigned to more recent observations in the available historical m-observation data window. In the **filtered historical simulation**, GARCH modelling is combined with the historical simulation method. In the **Monte Carlo simulation**, GARCH modelling is combined with simulation of standardized pseudo-random normal variables that are used in conjunction with volatility forecasts in order to generate price paths.
[16] According to the extreme value method of filtered peaks over threshold, a generalized Pareto distribution is fitted to excesses over a high threshold of standardized residuals by means of a maximum likelihood technique in order to obtain quantile estimators.

management function through hedging; (iii) the existence of freight derivatives markets have reduced spot market volatility and the informational asymmetries in the spot market; (iv) market participants, by collecting and analyzing FFA prices, can obtain "free" information about the future direction of spot freight prices, as FFA prices can assist in forecasting spot prices; (v) VaR and ES methods can be utilized to provide meaningful and accurate risk forecasts, leading to consistent and effective management of freight risk; and (vi) the volatility structure of the forward freight rate function in the freight futures market and pricing formulas for freight options have been examined. Obviously, there is a lot more work that can be carried out in our effort to understand better the fundamentals of freight derivatives markets. However, this chapter can form a basis upon which further work in the area can develop.

11.8 REFERENCES

Adland, R. and K. Cullinane (2005). A Time-varying Risk Premium in the Term Structure of Bulk Shipping Freight Rates. *Journal of Transport Economics and Policy* **39**(2): 191–208.

Adland, R., S. Koekebakker and S. Sodal (2007). Forward Curve Dynamics in the Tanker Futures Market. In: *Conference Proceedings of the 17th International Association of Maritime Economists (IAME)*, Athens, Greece, 4–6 July 2007.

Alizadeh, A.H., R. Adland and S. Koekebakker (2007). Predictive Power and Unbiasedness of Implied Forward Charter Rates. *Journal of Forecasting*, **26**(6), 385–403.

Angelidis, T. and G. Skiadopoulos (2007). Measuring the Market Risk of Freight Rates: A Value-at-Risk Approach. In: *Conference Proceedings of the 17th International Association of Maritime Economists (IAME)*, Athens, Greece, 4–6 July 2007.

Batchelor, R., A.H. Alizadeh and I.D. Visvikis (2005). The Relation between Bid-Ask Spreads and Price Volatility in Forward Markets. *Derivatives Use, Trading & Regulation* **11**(2): 105–125.

Batchelor, R., A.H. Alizadeh and I.D. Visvikis (2007). Forecasting Spot and Forward Prices in the International Freight Market. *International Journal of Forecasting* **23**: 101–114.

Bessembinder, H. and M.L. Lemmon (2002). Equilibrium Pricing and Optimal Hedging in Electricity Forward Markets. *Journal of Finance* **57**: 1347–1382.

Black, F. (1976). The Pricing of Commodity Contracts. *Journal of Financial Economics* **3**: 167–179.

Chang, Y. and H. Chang (1996). Predictability of the Dry-Bulk Shipping Market by BIFFEX. *Maritime Policy and Management* **23**: 103–114.

Cullinane, K.P.B. (1991). Who's Using BIFFEX? Results from a Survey of Shipowners. *Maritime Policy and Management* **18**: 79–91.

Cullinane, K.P.B. (1992). A Short-Term Adaptive Forecasting Model for BIFFEX Speculation: A Box-Jenkins Approach. *Maritime Policy and Management* **19**: 91–114.

Dinwoodie, J. and J. Morris (2003). Tanker Forward Freight Agreements: The Future for Freight Futures. *Maritime Policy and Management* **30**(1): 45–58.

Ederington, L. (1979). The Hedging Performance of the New Futures Markets. *Journal of Finance*. 157–170.

Eydeland, A. and H. Geman (1998). Pricing Power Derivatives. *RISK* **11**, October: 71–73.

Geman, H. and O. Vasicek (2001). Plugging into Electricity. *RISK* **14**, August: 93–97.

Glosten, L.R., R. Jagannathan and D. Runkle (1993). On the Relation between the Expected Value and the Volatility of the Nominal Excess Return on Stocks. *Journal of Finance* **48**: 1779–1801.

Haigh, M.S. (2000). Cointegration, Unbiased Expectations and Forecasting in the BIFFEX Freight Futures Market. *Journal of Futures Markets* **20**(6): 545–571.

Haigh, M.S. and M.T. Holt (2002). Hedging Foreign Currency, Freight and Commodity Futures Portfolios. *Journal of Futures Markets* **22**(12): 1205–1221.

Haralambides, H.E. (1992). Freight Futures Trading and Shipowners Expectations. Conference Proceedings, *6th World Conference on Transport Research*, Lyon, France. Les Presses de L'Imprimerie Chirat 2: 1411–1422.

Heath, D., R. Jarrow and A. Morton (1992). Bond Pricing and the Term Structure of Interest Rates: A New Methodology for Contingent Claim Valuation. *Econometrica* **60**(1): 77–105.

Ishizaka, M., K. Tezuka and M. Ishii (2007). A Study on Shipping Freight Futures Curves in an Equilibrium Market Model. In: *Conference Proceedings of the 17th International Association of Maritime Economists (IAME)*. Athens, Greece, 4–6 July 2007.

Johansen, S. (1988). Statistical Analysis of Cointegration Vectors. *Journal of Economic Dynamics and Control* **12**: 231–254.

Johnson, L.L. (1960). The Theory of Hedging and Speculation in Commodity Futures. *Review of Economic Studies* **27**: 139–151.

Kavussanos, M.G. (2002). Business Risk Measurement and Management in the Cargo Carrying Sector of the Shipping Industry. In: *The Handbook of Maritime Economics and Business*, Lloyds of London Press, Chapter 30: 661–692.

Kavussanos, M.G. and A.H. Alizadeh (2002). The Expectations Hypothesis of the Term Structure and Risk-Premia in Dry-Bulk Shipping Freight Markets; An EGARCH-M Approach. *Journal of Transport Economics and Policy* **36**(2): 267–304.

Kavussanos, M.G. and D.N. Dimitrakopoulos (2007). Measuring Freight Risk in the Tanker Shipping Sector. In: *Conference Proceedings of the 17th International Association of Maritime Economists (IAME)*. Athens, Greece, 4–6 July 2007.

Kavussanos, M.G. and N.K. Nomikos (1999). The Forward Pricing Function of Shipping, Freight Futures Market. *Journal of Futures Markets* **19**(3): 353–376.

Kavussanos, M.G. and I.D. Visvikis (2003a). Financial Derivative Contracts in the Shipping Industry and the Price Discovery Function of Freight Forward Agreements (FFA). *Lloyd's Shipping Economist (LSE)*, February.

Kavussanos, M.G. and I.D. Visvikis (2003b). FFAs can Stabilize Revenue. *Lloyd's Shipping Economist (LSE)*, July.

Kavussanos, M.G. and I.D. Visvikis (2004). Market Interactions in Returns and Volatilities between Spot and Forward Shipping Markets. *Journal of Banking and Finance* **28**(8): 2015–2049.

Kavussanos, M.G. and I.D. Visvikis (2005). The Hedging Performance of Over-The-Counter Forward Shipping Freight Markets. In: *Conference Proceedings of the 14th International Association of Maritime Economists (IAME)*, Izmir, Turkey, 30 June – 2 July 2004.

Kavussanos, M.G. and I.D. Visvikis (2006a). *Derivatives and Risk Management in Shipping*. 1st edition, Witherbys Publishing London.

Kavussanos, M.G. and I.D. Visvikis (2006b). Shipping Freight Derivatives: A Survey of Recent Evidence. *Maritime Policy and Management* **33**(3): 233–255.

Kavussanos, M.G. and I.D. Visvikis (2007). Derivatives in Freight Markets. *Special Report Commissioned by Lloyd's Shipping Economist*, A Lloyd's MIU Publication, Informa Business, London, November 2007.

Kavussanos, M.G., I.D. Visvikis and R. Batchelor (2004). Over-The-Counter Forward Contracts and Spot Price Volatility in Shipping. *Transportation Research – Part E, Logistics and Transportation Review* **40**(4): 273–296.

Kavussanos, M.G., I.D. Visvikis and M.A. Goulielmou (2007). An Investigation of the Use of Risk Management and Shipping Derivatives: The Case of Greece. *International Journal of Transport Economics* **XXXIV**(1): 49–68.

Kavussanos, M.G., I.D. Visvikis and D.A. Menachof (2004). The Unbiasedness Hypothesis in the Freight Forward Market: Evidence from Cointegration Tests. *Review of Derivatives Research* **7**(3): 241–266.

Koekebakker, S. and R. Adland (2004). Modelling Forward Freight Rate Dynamics – Empirical Evidence from Time Charter Rates. *Maritime Policy and Management* **31**(4): 319–336.

Koekebakker, S., R. Adland and S. Sodal (2007). Pricing Freight Rate Options. *Transportation Research – Part E, Logistics and Transportation Review* **43**(5): 535–548.

Lu, J., F. Wei and H. Want (2007). Value-at-Risk on Dry Bulk Shipping Freight Index. In: *Conference Proceedings of the 17th International Association of Maritime Economists (IAME)*, Athens, Greece, 4–6 July 2007.

Tezuka, K. and M. Ishizaka (2006). Equilibrium Spot and Futures Price Formulae and Numerical Calculation of Biasness in Shipping Markets. *Journal of Logistics and Shipping Economics* (in Japanese), **40**: 115–124.

Thuong, L.T. and S.L. Visscher (1990). The Hedging Effectiveness of Dry-Bulk Freight Rate Futures. *Transportation Journal* **29**: 58–65.

Tvedt, J. (1998). Valuation of a European Futures Option in the BIFFEX Market. *Journal of Futures Markets* **18**(2): 167–175.

Working, H. (1960). Price Effects of Futures Trading. Reprinted in A.E. Peck (Ed.) (1997) *Selected Writings of Holbrook Working*. Chicago: Chicago Board of Trade, 45–75.

Mean-Reversion and Structural Breaks in Crude Oil, Copper, and Shipping

Hélyette Geman and Steve Ohana

12.1 INTRODUCTION

Commodity prices have been rising at an unprecedented pace over the last seven years. As depicted in Fig. 12.2, an investment of $100 made in January 2002 in the global Dow Jones AIG Commodity Index had more than doubled by July 2006 while Fig. 12.3 indicates that these $100 invested in the Dow Jones AIG Energy sub-index had turned into $500 in July 2005.

The increase of prices in the last three years has been even more dramatic, with a huge demand coming from China, India, and developing countries. In the case of commodities like copper and crude oil, the issue of exhaustibility and depleting reserves is certainly one element that contributes to the irresistible ascension of prices displayed in Fig. 12.3. As far as shipping is concerned, the explosion of international trade in iron ore, coal and cereals has greatly outpaced the capacity of shipyards and translated into large spikes in freight indexes such as the Baltic Dry Index described in Section 12.2.

The financial literature on commodity price modeling started with the pioneer paper of Gibson and Schwartz (1990), dedicated to the valuation of options on oil. In the spirit of the Black-Scholes-Merton (1973) model, they chose a geometric Brownian motion for the crude oil price process. Given the behavior of commodity prices during the 1990s depicted in Fig. 12.1, Schwartz (1997) decided to turn to a mean-reverting process for oil prices. Since then, mean-reversion (with or without jumps) has been a central property in the financial literature dedicated to commodity price modeling (e.g. Eydeland and Geman (1998), Miltersen and Schwartz (1998), Geman and Nguyen (2005)).

Unit root testing of commodity prices is quite common: Ardeni (1989) tests for the unit roots in the import/export prices of wheat, wood, beef, sugar, tea, and zinc for four countries, using Augmented-Dickey-Fuller (hereafter ADF) tests with quarterly observations. Babula *et al.* (1995) find that the log corn prices in the US are integrated of order one. Foster *et al.* (1995) could not reject the null of a unit root for the weekly cattle prices at seven locations. Newbold *et al.* (2000) find mixed evidence on the stationarity of deflated wheat and maize prices in the US. Koekebakker *et al.* (2006) analyze the stationarity of freight prices by employing a non-linear version of the ADF (based on an exponentially

Hélyette Geman: Birkbeck, University of London and ESSEC Business School.
Steve Ohana Birkbeck, University of London.

Risk Management in Commodity Markets: From Shipping to Agriculturals and Energy   Edited by Hélyette Geman

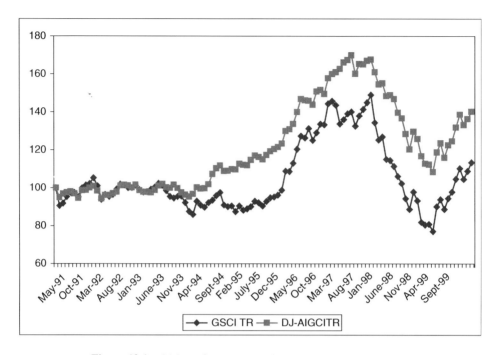

Figure 12.1   GSCI and DJ-AIG Total Return Indexes 1991–1999

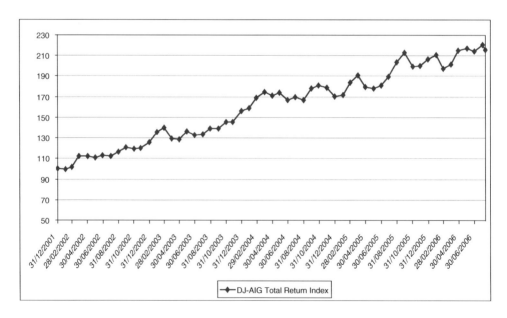

Figure 12.2   DJ-AIG Total return Jan 2002–June 2006

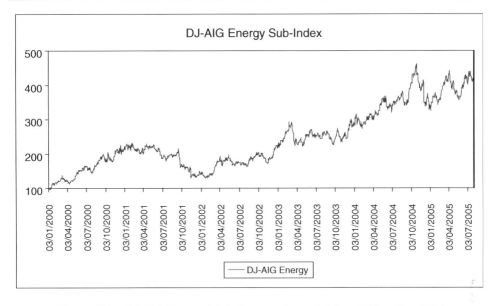

Figure 12.3   DJ-AIG Energy Sub-Index over the period Jan. 2000 to Dec. 2004

smooth-transition autoregressive model) and conclude that dry-bulk freight prices are non-linear stationary. Geman and Ohana (2007) analyze the relations between forward curves slopes and inventories in the US natural gas and crude oil markets: by applying ADF and Phillips-Perron (hereafter PP) tests to the two energy commodities, they reject the null of a unit root for the slopes and inventory deviations to the 'normal' case.

The last 20 years have seen the inclusion of structural breaks in the testing of stationarity. A pioneering piece of work in this respect was that of Perron (1989), which points out the importance of including break points when testing for unit root in macroeconomic time series on a time-horizon of several decades. In particular, he shows that standard unit root tests (ADF and PP) fail to reject the null hypothesis of unit root if the true data generating mechanism is that of stationary fluctuations around a trend with a single break taking place at a known point in time (e.g. the Great Depression or the first crude oil price shock). The reason is that a break is then wrongly interpreted as a permanent shock emanating from the noise component instead of being attributed to a shift in the trend term. He proposed a new unit root test that allows for the presence of a one-time change in the level and slope of the trend function in both the null and the alternative hypotheses. Another test was later on suggested by Zivot and Andrews (1992), to allow for an unknown breaking time; the drawback of this approach is that the existence of a break is only assumed in the alternative hypothesis, not the null of a unit root, which makes the test too sensitive to the break parameters. Lee and Strazicich (2003) propose a Lagrange multiplier test with two unknown break times, and very recently Carrion-i-Silvestre *et al.* (2007) suggested the use of a GLS-based unit root test with multiple break times, occurring at unknown times. A comprehensive survey on structural breaks in the analysis of time series can be found in Perron (2006).

Few papers have, to our knowledge, applied unit root tests with structural breaks to commodity prices. Serletis (1992) performs unit root tests on crude oil, heating oil, and unleaded gas futures prices in the US, comparing the standard ADF test with the test with a break point in level and drift proposed by Zivot and Andrews (1992): his finding is that only the latter test allows one to reject the null of a unit root. Recently, Tomek and Wang (2007) performed a series of different unit root tests (ADF, PP, test in Perron (1990) with one structural change in mean and slope) to the prices of corn, soybeans, barrows and gilts, and milk from 1960 to 2002. They find that, if the test specification does not account for a structural change that shifts the mean of the variable, the results are biased towards concluding that a unit root exists.

The goal of this chapter is to revisit the issue of mean-reversion for three strategic commodities which are making the daily headlines of the actuality, namely crude oil, copper, and shipping. The length of the period chosen is long enough to cover the quiet period of the 1990s and the bull commodity markets of the 2000s. It also allows us to test more subtle forms of mean-reversion such as the possibility of breaks in the trend function as introduced in Perron (1989).

The last seven years have been the stage of major transformations for commodity markets – Chinese growth, geopolitical turmoil in oil producing countries, and the massive rise in speculation activity being some of the most well-known factors. As could be expected, we find that the three prices series under analysis were affected by a structural change in 2001 and 2002, with essentially a change in drift for copper and a change in both drift and level for the West Texas Intermediate (hereafter WTI) and the freight. Using the GLS-based unit root test described in Carrion-i-Silvestre *et al.* (2007), we find that when the trend is subject to one break point under the null and alternative hypothesis, the hypothesis of an integrated noise component can be rejected against the alternative of stationary fluctuations at the 5 % level for the WTI, and at the 10 % level for copper and the shipping index. The same test with two break points allowed us to reject the null of a unit root for the WTI and the freight at the 10 % level, but not for copper. By contrast, none of the standard unit root tests allowed us to reject the null of a unit root, except on the sub-periods Jan. 1983–Jan. 1986 and Feb. 1986–Mar. 2003 in the case of the WTI.

The rest of this chapter is organized as follows. Section 12.2 presents the fundamental qualitative features of crude oil, copper, and shipping. Section 12.3 proposes alternative definitions of mean-reversion. Section 12.4 describes the database, the econometric tests and the results. Section 12.5 contains concluding comments.

12.2   FUNDAMENTALS OF COPPER, CRUDE OIL, AND SHIPPING

12.2.1   Crude oil

Crude oil, also called petroleum, and the most fascinating commodity, was formed million years ago by the remains of dead plants that inhabited the sea and transformed over time into crude oil and natural gas, among other elements. Crude oil is found today, in most cases together with natural gas, in the upper layers of the earth's crust.

Crude oil is made up of hydrocarbons, molecules comprising both hydrogen and carbon atoms, possibly in various configurations. The number of carbon atoms in crude oil determines the amount of CO_2 emissions that will be produced when oil is burnt. There are over 130 grades of crude oil around the world, differing also by the sulfur content and gravity. The highest quality crudes are those with a low sulfur content and high specific gravity. On this basis, the US West Texas Intermediate (WTI) and the Malaysian Tapis represent the highest quality of crude oil. The heavier, sour crudes from the United Arab Emirates and Mexico are of a poorer quality and, consequently, trade at a discount to WTI.

Both the density and distillation curve of a specific crude oil are important to refiners who separate, at higher and higher temperatures, the different components of the crude to make various products like gasoline, heating oil, naphtha, diesel, and jet fuel. The owners of refineries, who today can be veterans of the oil industry as well as private equity funds, have learnt to optimize the "crackspreads" in order to manufacture high value oil distillates depending on the market conditions at different points in the world.

Saudi Arabia is the largest producer (13 % of the world production, i.e. around 11 million barrels (bbls) per day) and exporter of crude oil; the largest reserves are in Saudi Arabia, Canada,[1] Iran and Iraq. On the demand side, the top oil consuming regions are the US, with a consumption of more than 20.8 million bbls per day; then come Europe, China, and Japan respectively consuming 15.2, 7.3, and 5.2 million bbls every day. The transportation and industrial sectors account for the main part of the world oil consumption.

The most common way to produce crude oil is to identify an oil field, then use drilling rigs to create an oil well from which crude oil is extracted. Commercial drilling of oil started in 1859 in Titusville, Pennsylvania. Advances in technology have played a key role in the improvement of oil production. In particular, the recent method of "horizontal drilling" – drilling first vertically into the oil field, then moving horizontally into the reservoir – have represented major steps forward, in particular in the case of older oil wells.

Crude oil prices have exhibited high volatility for a long time. Much of it started in 1973 with the Arab oil embargo which stopped shipments of crude oil to the United States.

The second oil crisis of the 1970s occurred in 1979 during the revolution in Iran when changes in the political regime caused a decline the country's oil production and exports. Another price increase occurred during the years 1990–1991 with Iraq's invasion of Kuwait, creating uncertainty around oil production and exports from both countries. Regarding the downward moves, large price declines occurred when Saudi Arabia noticeably increased production in 1986, then during the Asian crisis of 1997–1999, and again during a short period after 11 September 2001, reflecting concerns about the US and world economy. Figure 12.4(a) shows the impact of these events on the WTI first nearby future price.

But the most remarkable element is the large and steady (except for the year 2006) price increase that started in 2002–2003 and took crude prices at levels approaching $120/bbl in April 2008. This spectacular rise can be explained by several causes:

- a weakening dollar;
- a growth in global oil demand, especially from countries such as China, South Korea, India, and Brazil which have regularly pushed prices up over the last few years;
- a greater world awareness that oil reserves may eventually be depleted (as discussed by Matthew Simmons in his book, *Twilight in the Desert*, 2005) and oil become the first fossil commodity to reach its "peak";
- a significant political uncertainty in oil-producing countries such as Nigeria, Venezuela, Iran and Iraq;
- dramatic weather events such as Hurricane Katrina that in summer 2005 destroyed a number of oil platforms in the Gulf of Mexico; an important one belonging to the oil major BP.

---

[1] Canadian reserves are subject to great uncertainty due to the difficulty of estimating the level of oil sand reserves.

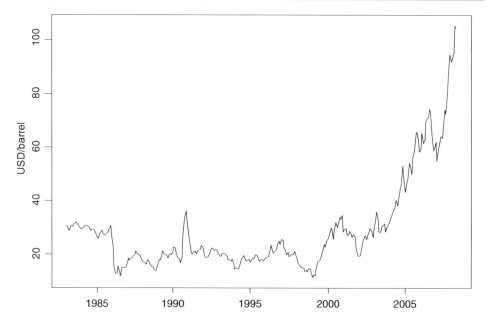

Figure 12.4(a)   Monthly spot prices of WTI

The US Energy Department recently revised its projections and expects crude oil prices to average \$101/bbl in 2008, on the view of expected global demand growth and low surplus production capacity. The Energy Information Administration had previously forecast that the average for the benchmark WTI crude oil would be \$94/bbl. The revision comes as crude prices have spiked over the last two months (at the time of writing), hitting a trading high of \$120/bbl, with more money being poured into crude oil futures and ETFs. "The combination of rising world oil consumption and low surplus production capacity is putting upward pressure on oil prices", the EIA said in a monthly report on petroleum supply and demand. While high prices are damping demand in the US, petroleum consumption remains strong in China, India, Russia, and the Middle East, the EIA said. Demand growth in 2008 is now expected at almost 1.3 million bbl/day, i.e., 1.5 % higher than in 2007.

Global oil supply fell by 100000 bbl/day in March 2008, led by lower supplies from OPEC, the North Sea and non-OPEC African countries. Non-OPEC supply growth in 2008 is trimmed, according to experts, to 815000 bbl/day on a broad swathe of adjustments in the Americas, Africa and Europe. OPEC crude supply fell during the first quarter of 2008 on field maintenance in the Emirates, Nigeria and Venezuela. Pipeline and power outages highlighted the risks to production in Iraq and Nigeria, amid an effective spare capacity of just 2.3 million bbl/day.

12.2.2   Copper

Copper is a reddish-colored metal, malleable and with excellent electrical conductivity. During the Roman Empire, copper was principally mined in Cyprus, hence the origin of its other name as cuprum. The Egyptians found that adding a small amount of tin made the metal easier to cast, leading to the discovery of bronze. The use of bronze, a much harder material with a very low melting point, during the years 2000 BC to 600 BC became so extensive in Europe that this period was named the Bronze Age. Copper has been used as a waterproof roofing material since ancient times, giving many old buildings their greenish roofs and domes. Copper carbonate is highly resistant to corrosion: the Statue of Liberty, for instance, contains more than 81 tons of copper. The use of copper in electronic equipments is gigantic: copper wire, electromagnets, electrical relays and switches, cathode ray tubes, and integrated circuits (where it is increasingly replacing aluminum because of its superior electrical conductivity).

Copper is one of the few metals to appear naturally as an uncompounded mineral, in large open mines that contain 0.4 to 1.0 % of copper. The copper ore dug from the mines is crushed and ground, then skimmed from the top of a water bath. The result is copper concentrate at 20–40 % purity. In order to go into a greater purity, the concentrate copper is smelted to yield a 60–80 % concentrate liquid, in turn heated in the presence of air to produce "blister copper" which is 97–99 % pure. The final procedure is an electrolysis that brings copper deposits at the cathode, with a purity greater than 99.9 %. This grade A copper is the one that trades on the London Metal Exchange (LME) and other major exchanges such as the Shanghai Futures Exchange (SHFE). As is the case for many metals today, recycling plays an important role in copper production, accounting for 10–15 % of total refined copper produced worldwide.

According to the British Geological Survey, Chile is currently the top mine producer of copper, with more than one third of the world's production, through its state-owned company Cameco. Then come the US, Indonesia, Peru, Australia, and China which each contribute 5–8 % of the world's mined copper. In the US, copper is mined in Utah, Nevada, Tennessee and Michigan. Until recently, South America, Australia and Indonesia were the major exporters of concentrate copper, with most of their copper being refined elsewhere. This is currently changing, with mergers and acquisitions leading to mining giants such as BHP Billiton or Rio Tinto which deploy within the firm the whole spectrum of production and refinery activities. Chile and China are the most important refiners and China's production has almost offset the decline in the US. Physical assets such as smelters are now owned worldwide not only by mining companies, but also private equity or hedge funds that are prepared to act as traders by tracking possible arbitrage opportunities between spot prices and refining charges. The price volatility results from physical supply – demand imbalances, as well as political news from copper producing countries or electricity outages such as in South Africa recently.

There are an estimated 61 years of remaining copper reserves, but this number may decrease if the current increase in consumption, more than 3 % since 1995, remains unchanged. After the European Union, China has become the second user of refined copper and accounts for more than 50 % of the increase in consumption since 1995.

Looking at the trajectory depicted in Fig. 12.4(b), we see that copper prices were at $1.320 per ton in June 1999, rose to $8.270 in May 2006 to drop to $5.290 in February 2007 (all these numbers illustrating a very high volatility of prices), rebounded to $7.710 in April 2007 to be again at the time of writing (March 2008) above $8000 per ton. According to the *Wall Street Journal* of 31 March 2008 the year-to-date performance of capital invested in commodities by major pension funds like Calper's was 27.7 % in the case of copper and 10 % in the case of oil, both numbers being very high compared to the current returns in the stock and bond markets.

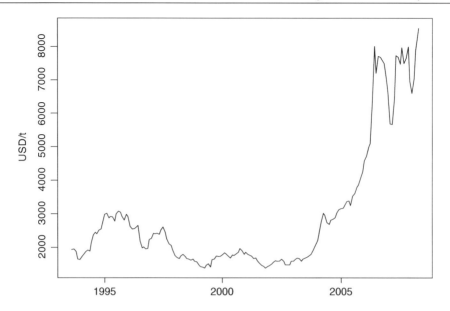

Figure 12.4(b)   Monthly spot prices of copper on the London Metal Exchange

12.2.3   Shipping

The expansion of commodity markets during the years 2000 and the double-digit growth
of the developing countries have contributed to an amazing boom in maritime transport
and shipbuilding. Demand exploded in 2007, with more than 300 million deadweighttons
of new orders (4900 ships) placed. This compares with 94 million in 2005 and 169 million
in 2006. The fleet under construction reached 55 % of the active fleet against 23 % a year
earlier. In fact, 2007 was the fifth consecutive astonishing year for the maritime industry.
All records have been shattered in the dry bulk market and the crude oil market, with
an unprecedented interest in bulk carriers. The order book at the end of 2007 was close
to 530 million deadweighttons (dwt), nearly five times the level of 2000. Annual world
production has now reached about 90 million dwt (2300 ships) compared to 55 million in
2003 and 75 million in 2006. In certain ship categories, the tonnage on order is equal to,
or even in excess of, the fleet in service. Moreover, the quick rise in bunker prices has
persuaded operators to reduce speeds, which in turn requires the addition of more vessels to
maintain the same schedules. Lastly, queues at Panama Canal or some harbors in Australia
are getting longer and more frequent; for instance, the transit time to get through the Canal
of Panama often goes as high as 53 hours when the regular time is 27 to 30 hours.

Korea maintained its ranking as the number one shipbuilder in the world in 2007. The
country's orderbook increased by 60 % during the year, up to 134 million gigatons. China
followed closely, with a portfolio that more than doubled in 2007 to 104 million gigatons
(gt). Japanese shipbuilding has also progressed with a portfolio of nearly 71 million gt (up
from 62 million gt). The orderbook of the European builders remained stable at around
24 million gt.

Exceptional demand, a rise in construction and bunker costs, a depreciating dollar and an
exuberant freight market, in particular for dry bulk, have pushed prices of new vessels to

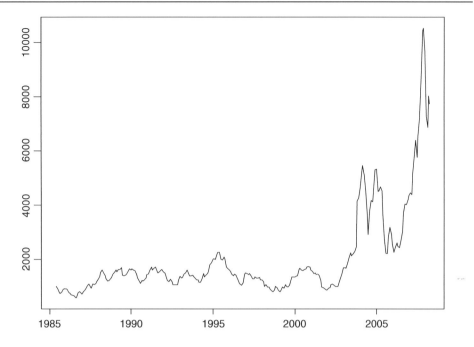

Figure 12.4(c)   Monthly Baltic Dry Index

historic levels and generated spikes in freight indexes, in particular the Baltic Dry Index, the industry main indicator.

The Baltic Dry Index (BDI) is an index covering dry bulk shipping rates and managed by the Baltic Exchange in London. According to the documents published by the Baltic Exchange, the BDI provides "an assessment of the price of moving the major raw materials by sea". Taking into account 26 shipping routes measured on a time charter and voyage basis, the index covers Supramax, Panamax, and Capesize dry bulk carriers transporting a range of commodities including coal, iron ore and grain.

The index is made up of an average of the corresponding Supramax, Panamax, and Capesize indices. Each index is based on professional estimations made by a panel of international shipbroking companies. Since the cost of shipping varies with the amount of cargo that is shipped and dry bulk represents goods like iron ore, coal, or cement, the index is also seen as a good indicator of economic growth for countries like China, India, Korea.

As exhibited in Fig. 12.4(c), the BDI has experienced large spikes over the recent period of booming commodity markets. Within a 12-month period, it went from a level of 4400 points to a high of roughly 11 000 points in mid-November 2007 and is currently (April 2008) at the level of 9250 points, evidence of a very high volatility related to sporadic supply and demand imbalances in the shipping markets.

12.3   DEFINING MEAN-REVERSION

We will start this section by reviewing how mean-reversion has been defined in the financial literature dedicated to the subject in the case of commodities and in the recent period. One perspective is the one adopted by Bessembinder *et al.* (1995). The authors study 11 different commodity markets and, rather than examining time series of asset prices, use futures contracts with various maturities to test whether investors expect prices to revert. They assume that the "Rational Expectations Hypothesis" holds, namely that futures prices are unbiased expectations (under the real probability measure) of spot prices in the future. Hence, the slope of the forward curve – defined as a distant maturity future price minus the first nearby price – should be negatively related to spot prices in the case of mean reversion: when spot prices are high, they are expected to decline and the forward curve should be backwardated (declining). Conversely, it should be in contango in the case of low spot prices. Using this definition of mean reversion, Bessembinder et al. conclude that it does prevail in all 11 commodity markets they study over the period 1982 to December 1991 (a finding consistent with Fig. 12.1). They also exhibit that the magnitude of mean-reversion was large for agricultural commodities and crude oil, and substantially less for metals. Obviously, their conclusions need to be revisited for the decade of the 1990s and, even more so, the last seven years.

Regarding the financial literature dedicated to commodity price modeling, mean-reversion has been essentially translated by the nature of the drift in the stochastic differential equation driving the spot price dynamics. For instance, $X_t = \ln(S_t)$ is supposed to be driven by an Orstein-Uhlenbeck process

$$dX_t = a(b - X_t)dt + \sigma dW_t \tag{12.1}$$

where (W_t) is a standard Brownian motion on a probability space (Ω, F, P), describing the randomness of the economy. Equations similar to Eq. (12.1) can be found in Schwartz (1997), Eydeland and Geman (1998), Miltersen and Schwartz (1998), and many other papers using mean-reverting processes.

Koekebakker et al. (2006) relax the assumption of linear dependence between price returns dX_t and log price X_t and test a model that triggers mean-reversion only when the price hits certain thresholds. Geman (2007) suggests going beyond the mere use of a stochastic differential equation to discuss spot prices and proposes to characterize mean-reversion by the existence of a finite invariant measure for the price process (only assumed to be a Markov process), a property that has the merit of ensuring stationarity.

When the prices exhibit a long-term drift as was the case for crude oil, copper, and freight over the last 20 years, it becomes appropriate to define mean-reversion as station-ary fluctuations around a varying trend. For example, Pindyck (1999) analyzes 127 years (1870–1996) of data on crude oil and bituminous coal obtained from the US Department of Commerce. Using a unit root test, he shows that prices mean revert to stochastically fluctuating trend lines that represent long term marginal costs of the commodities but are unobservable and estimated using the Kalman filter. From an econometric perspective (the one we will adopt in this paper), the log price of a commodity y_t is written under the following general discrete-time form:

$$\begin{aligned} y_t &= d_t + u_t \\ u_t &= \alpha u_{t-1} + v_t \end{aligned} \tag{12.2}$$

In Eq. (12.2), v_t is a moving average term $v_t = \Sigma_{j=0}^{\infty}\delta_j e_{t-j}$, where (e_t) is a sequence of independent and identically distributed (but not necessarily normal) variables.

We therefore model y_t as the sum of a trend d_t and a noise component u_t.

Unit-root tests are designed to discriminate whether u_t is integrated of order one ($\alpha = 1$) (or mean-reverting ($\alpha < 1$)).

In the simplest versions of unit-root tests (Augmented-Dickey-Fuller and Phillips-Perron tests), the trend reduces to a linear function of time:

$$d_t = \mu_0 + \beta_0 t$$

In more recent unit-root tests, like the one introduced in Perron (1989) and later generalized in Carrion-i-Silvestre *et al.* (2007), the trend d_t is assumed to be a linear function of time subject to a sequence of m shifts in level and drift occurring at times $T_1, T_2, \ldots, T_m$, i.e.,

$$d_t = \mu_0 + \beta_0 t + \mu_1 DU_t(T_1) + \beta_1 DT_t^*(T_1) + \cdots + \mu_m DU_t(T_1) + \beta_m DT_t^*(T_m) \quad (12.3)$$

where $DU_t(T_j)$ and $DT_t^*(T_j)$ respectively correspond to breaks in level and drift at time T_j:

$$DU_t(T_j) = 1 \text{ if } t > T_j \text{ and } 0 \text{ otherwise}$$

$$DT_t^*(T_j) = t - T_j \text{ if } t > T_j \text{ and } 0 \text{ otherwise.}$$

If m = 0, then the trend simply reduces to:

$$d_t = \mu_0 + \beta_0 t.$$

12.4   DATASET AND UNIT ROOT TESTS

12.4.1   Dataset

- For crude oil, our dataset consists of the monthly WTI spot prices (in US dollars per barrel) from January 1983 to April 2008.
- Regarding copper, we use monthly copper spot prices (in US dollars per ton) on the London Metal Exchange from July 1993 to April 2008.
- Finally, the dataset for shipping is composed of the monthly Baltic Dry Index from May 1985 to April 2008 downloaded from Datastream.

The three corresponding time series are plotted in Fig. 12.4.

All the analysis that follows will be performed on the price logarithms, rather than the original prices, that are depicted in Fig. 12.5.

12.4.2   First estimate of the break dates

Bai and Perron (2003) provide a simple methodology to position structural breaks for weakly *stationary time series*. As a first analysis, we apply here their methodology to the clearly *non-stationary* log prices of WTI, copper, and shipping.

The method consists in performing an OLS regression of y_t on the set of variables $(t, DU_t(T_1), DT_t^*(T_1))$ for varying T_1, and selecting the break time T_1 which minimizes the sum of squared residuals. Then, the same method is applied on the two subsets $[1; T_1]$ and $[T_1 + 1; T]$, yielding two potential break points $T_2^* < T_1$ and $T_3^* > T_1$.

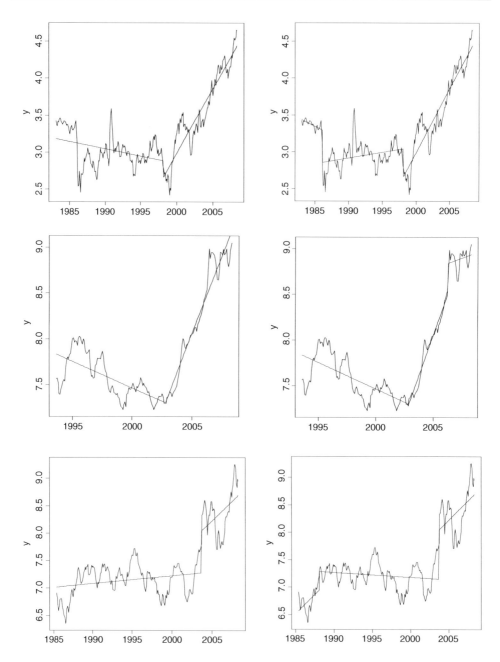

Figure 12.5   Left: fit of the log price with one break point; Right: fit of the log price with two break points; Top: WTI, Middle: Copper, Bottom: Baltic Dry Index

Table 12.1 Estimation of T1 and T2 for the WTI, copper, and the Baltic Dry Index. The star indicates the dominant break date, i.e., the first date detected in the break detection procedure described in the text

	WTI	Copper	BDI
1st break date	Jan 1986	Sep 2002*	Jan 1988
2nd break date	Jan 1998*	Mar 2006	Aug 2003*

T_2 is selected among T_2^* and T_3^* as the one which minimizes the sum of squared residuals in the OLS regression of y_t on $(t, DU_t(T_1), DT_t^*(T_1), DU_t(T_2), DT_t^*(T_2))$. T_1 and T_2 are then relabeled so that $T_1 < T_2$. $T_3, \ldots, T_m$ are defined in a similar manner.

In the rest of this chapter, we will assume that either one or two break points occurred in the WTI, copper, and shipping prices.

Figure 12.5 and Table 12.1 present the results obtained for the WTI, copper, and the Baltic Dry Index with m = 1 and 2. Some of the detected breaking points correspond to well-identified macroeconomic events affecting the worldwide supply and demand of crude oil, copper, and freight.

The first WTI breaking point (Jan 1986) corresponds to a change in Saudi Arabia quota policy. From 1982 to 1985, Saudi Arabia acted as the swing producer cutting its production in an attempt to cut the free fall in prices. In August 1985, the Saudis became tired of this role and by early 1986 increased production from two to five million barrels per day. As a consequence, crude oil prices plummeted below $10 per barrel by mid-1986.

The second break date for the WTI (Feb 1998) is certainly due to the Asian crisis and the increase in Iraqi oil exports consecutive to the oil-for-food program. In 1998, Asian Pacific oil consumption declined for the first time since 1982. The combination of lower consumption and higher OPEC production sent prices in a downward spiral. As regards the freight rates, the second break point (Aug 2003) is largely the product of the Chinese growth which started accelerating in 2003: the tight and inelastic supply of cargo could hardly meet the increased demand for freight resulting from the massive exports of raw materials (iron ore, coal, and agriculturals alike) to China. As a consequence, the Baltic Dry Index more than doubled within a few months.

12.4.3   ADF and PP unit-root tests

The Augmented-Dickey-Fuller test (with a constant and a trend) tests the null that $\alpha = 0$ against the alternative that $\alpha < 0$ in the following model:

$$\Delta y_t = \mu + \beta t + \alpha y_{t-1} + \sum_{i=1}^{k} \delta_i \Delta y_{t-i} + \varepsilon_t$$

The statistics of the test is the t-stat of the coefficient α in the OLS regression of Δy_t on $t, y_{t-1}, \Delta y_{t-1}, \ldots, \Delta y_{t-k}$.

The choice of the truncation lag parameter k is known to have important effects on the size and power of the test (see e.g., Hall (1994)); here, as in Tomek and Williams (2007), we choose k as the minimal lag such that we obtain white noise residuals ε_t while the last lag is statistically significant.

Table 12.2 Results of the ADF tests on the whole period

	WTI	Copper	Baltic Dry Index
k	1	1	1
α	−0.0228	−0.00789	−0.029
t-stat	−1.930	−0.759	−2.253
Critical value 1%, 5%, 10%	−3.96, −3.41, −3.12		

k is the truncation lag parameter, α the regression coefficient on y_{t-1} and t-stat the statistic of the test
*Indicates rejection of the null of a unit root at the 10% level
**Indicates rejection of the null of a unit root at the 5% level
***Indicates rejection of the null of a unit root at the 1% level

Table 12.3 Results of the ADF tests on each sub-period

	WTI	Copper	Baltic Dry Index
Period I t-stat	−4.329***	−2.393	−1.885
Period II t-stat	−4.234***	−2.807	−2.469
Period III t-stat	−2.373	−2.435	−2.087
Period I+II t-stat	−3.754**	−0.167	−2.708
Period II+III t-stat	−1.858	−2.609	−2.098

Only the t-stat of the test is reported
*Indicates rejection of the null of a unit root at the 10% level
**Indicates rejection of the null of a unit root at the 5% level
***Indicates rejection of the null of a unit root at the 1% level

The 1%, 5%, and 10% critical values of the test are provided in McKinnon (1991).

Therefore we cannot reject the null of a unit root at the 10% level for any of the three series. We now perform the ADF test on the three sub-periods: $t \in [1; T_1]$ (denoted period I), $t \in [T_1 + 1; T_2]$ (denoted period II), and $t \in [T_2 + 1; T]$ (denoted period III), where T_1 and T_2 are the break dates determined previously.

Even though the t-stats rise in absolute value compared to the ones displayed in Table 12.2, the null of a unit root is only rejected for the WTI in periods I and II and in periods I + II. Note the important decrease in the t-stat when calculated in period I + II for copper and in period II + III for the WTI. This demonstrates the importance of the structural breaks occurring in Jan. 1998 for the WTI and in Sept. 2002 for copper.

The Phillips-Perron (1988) test (including a time trend) consists in testing the null of $\rho = 1$ against $\rho < 1$ in the following model:

$$y_t = \mu + \beta t + \rho y_{t-1} + \varepsilon_t.$$

The PP t-statistic is the t-stat of parameter $\rho - 1$ in the OLS regression of y_t on t and y_{t-1}, adjusted for the serial correlation in the residuals ε_t.

The PP test was performed on the whole data set and on each sub-sample separately, yielding the results presented in Table 12.4.

Hence, the null of a unit root can only be rejected at the 10% level for the WTI in periods II and I + II.

Table 12.4 Results of the PP tests on the whole period and on each sub-period

	WTI	Copper	Baltic Dry Index
Whole period t-stat	−1.6048	−0.5845	−1.8247
Period I t-stat	−2.013	−2.2898	−1.7843
Period II t-stat	−3.2925*	−2.0909	−2.2074
Period III t-stat	−2.3676	−2.5299	−1.7932
Period I+II t-stat	−3.1415*	0.0439	−2.3632
Period II+III t-stat	−1.5585	−2.2136	−1.6474
Critical value 1%, 5%, 10%	−4.00, −3.42, −3.14		

Only the t-stat of the test is reported
*Indicates rejection of the null of a unit root at the 10% level
**Indicates rejection of the null of a unit root at the 5% level
***Indicates rejection of the null of a unit root at the 1% level

12.4.4 Extended ADF regressions with one and two structural breaks

An alternative way to test for a unit root is inspired from Zivot and Andrews (1992) and Tomek and Wang (2007). It consists, in the spirit of the ADF test, in testing the significance of the coefficient α in the model:

$$\Delta y_t = \Delta d_t + \alpha(y_{t-1} - d_t) + \sum_{i=1}^{k} \delta_i \Delta y_{t-i} + \varepsilon_t$$

where d_t is a linear trend with one or two level and slope shifts occurring at times T1 and T2. This is done by computing the t-statistics of the coefficient α in the following OLS regression:

$$\Delta y_t = \mu_0 + \beta_0 t + \sum_{i=1}^{m} [\mu_i 1_{t=T_i+1} + \beta_i DU_t(T_i) + \gamma_i DT_t^*(T_i)]$$

$$+ \alpha y_{t-1} + \sum_{i=1}^{k} \delta_i \Delta y_{t-i} + \varepsilon_t \tag{12.4}$$

with m = 1 or m = 2 and where the break dates T1 and T2 have been determined previously.

Because the limiting distribution for the t-stat of α in regression (12.4) under the null hypothesis that $\alpha = 1$ in the model (12.2) is in general unknown, the results in Tables 12.5 and 12.6 should not be viewed as a formal rejection of the null of a unit root, but instead as a qualitative indication of the relevance of the inclusion of structural breaks in the ADF regression. Observe in particular the rise in the t-stat compared with the constant trend ADF regressions of Table 12.2.

12.4.5 The GLS-based unit-root test with one and two structural breaks

We finally apply the tests recently proposed by Carrion-i-Silvestre *et al.* (2007), who adapt the test originally proposed by Elliott *et al.* (1996) to the situation of a trend including an arbitrary (but supposedly known) number m of level and drift break points.

Table 12.5   ADF regressions with the dominant structural break on the whole period

	WTI	Copper	Baltic Dry Index
k	1	1	1
α	−0.0967***	−0.0914***	−0.0698***
t-stat	−4.446	−3.412	−3.751
Critical value 1 %, 5 %, 10 %	−2.58, −1.95, −1.62		

k is the truncation lag parameter, α the regression coefficient on y_{t-1} and t-stat the t-statistic of α
Note: the limiting distribution of the t-stat is not specified under the null of a unit root with
one break point; the critical values correspond here to the 0.5 %, 2.5 %, and 5 % quantiles of the
normal distribution
*Indicates significance at the 10 % level
**Indicates significance at the 5 % level
***Indicates significance at the 1 % level

Table 12.6   ADF regressions with two structural breaks on the whole period

	WTI	Copper	Baltic Dry Index
k	1	1	1
α	−0.131***	−0.104***	−0.0867***
t-stat	−5.015	−3.648	−3.844
Critical value 1 %, 5 %, 10 %	−2.58, −1.95, −1.62		

k is the truncation lag parameter, α the regression coefficient on y_{t-1} and t-stat the t-statistic
of α
Note: the limiting distribution of the t-stat is not specified under the null of a unit root with
two break points; the critical values correspond here to the 0.5 %, 2.5 %, and 5 % quantiles of
the normal distribution
*Indicates significance at the 10 % level
**Indicates significance at the 5 % level
***Indicates significance at the 1 % level

We consider a time series y_t, $t = 1, 2, .., T$, assumed to follow a model of the type (12.2),
where $T_1, T_2, \ldots, T_m$, are known break dates.

We want to test the null of $\alpha = 1$ against the alternative that $\alpha = \overline{\alpha}$ in model (12.2),
where $\overline{\alpha}$ is a parameter defined below.

We introduce, for t $= 2, \ldots, T$, the quasi-differenced variables $y_t^{\overline{\alpha}} = y_t - \overline{\alpha} y_{t-1}$ and $z_t^{\overline{\alpha}} = z_t - \overline{\alpha} z_{t-1}$, with $z_t = (1, t, DU_t(T_1), DT_t^*(T_1), DU_t(T_2), DT_t^*(T_2))$.

Introducing the break fraction vector $\lambda = \left(\frac{T_i}{T}, \ldots, \frac{T_m}{T} \right)$, we call

$$S(\overline{\alpha}, \lambda) = \min_{\psi} \sum_{t=2}^{T} (y_t^{\overline{\alpha}} - \psi' z_t^{\overline{\alpha}})^2$$

the sum of squared residuals of the OLS regression of $y_t^{\overline{\alpha}}$ on $z_t^{\overline{\alpha}}$.

The statistics of the test is then constructed as follows:

$$P_T^{GLS}(\lambda) = \frac{S(\overline{\alpha}, \lambda) - \overline{\alpha} S(1, \lambda)}{s^2(\lambda)}$$

The quantity $s^2(\lambda)$ is estimated via:

$$s^2(\lambda) = \frac{s_{sk}^2}{[1 - b(1)]^2}$$

$$s_{sk}^2 = \frac{1}{T - k} \sum_{t=k+1}^{T} \widehat{e_{t,k}}^2$$

$$b(1) = \sum_{j=1}^{k} \hat{b},$$

where $\hat{b}_1$ and $\widehat{e_{t,k}}$ are obtained from the OLS estimation of

$$\Delta \tilde{y}_t = b_0 \tilde{y}_{t-1} + \sum_{i=1}^{k} b_i \Delta \tilde{y}_{t-i} + e_{t,k}$$

and $\tilde{y}_t = y_t - \psi' z_t$, where ψ is the vector of regression coefficients from the OLS regression of $y_t^{\bar{\alpha}}$ on $z_t^{\bar{\alpha}}$. As in Carrion-i-Silvestre *et al.* (2007), we choose the lag parameter k which minimizes the modified Akaike information criterion introduced in Ng and Perron (2001).

Following Elliott *et al.* (1996) we introduce $\bar{\alpha} = 1 + \bar{c}/T$, where $\bar{c}$ is a non-centrality parameter, chosen such that the asymptotic power of the test is 50 %. In the case of a model with structural breaks, $\bar{c}$ depends on the position of the break points; a general functional form depending on λ is provided in Carrion-i-Silvestre *et al.* (2007), who also provide a functional form depending on λ to compute the 1 %, 5 %, and 10 % quantiles of the limiting distribution of $P_T^{GLS}(\lambda)$ under the null hypothesis.

The interest of the above approach is that the convergence of $P_T^{GLS}(\lambda)$ still holds when the breaking points $T_1, T_2, \ldots, T_m$ are derived from the data instead of being known *a priori*.

In this case, the statistics of the test is replaced by:

$$P_T^{GLS}(\hat{\lambda}) = \min_{\lambda \in \Lambda} P_T^{GLS}(\lambda)$$

where Λ is the set of break fraction vectors such that $\lambda_1 \geqslant \varepsilon$, $\lambda_m \geqslant \varepsilon$, and $\forall i \geqslant 1, \lambda_{i+1} - \lambda_i \geqslant \varepsilon$; ε is a trimming parameter that dictates the minimum length of a segment (a standard choice in applications being $\varepsilon = 0.15$).

The estimated break fractions $\hat{\lambda}$ converge to the actual break fractions λ faster than 1/T. Note that the non-centrality parameter $\bar{c}$ and the limiting distribution of $P_T^{GLS}(\hat{\lambda})$ now depend on the *estimated* breaking points $\hat{\lambda}$.

A crucial property is that the convergence of the test does not depend on the magnitude of the shifts. However, the size and power of the test *do* depend on whether the number of break points m correspond to the actual number of structural shifts present in the data. For example, Nelson *et al.* (2001) have shown that unit root tests with single breaks have difficulties distinguishing between a I(0) process with Markov-switching breaks from a I(1) process. This is likely due to the fact that the Markov-switching trend breaks add a unit root to the otherwise I(0) process; hence unit root tests with the wrong number of breaks are ill-equipped to distinguish whether permanent shocks in a process are coming from innovations at each period or infrequent shocks to the trend function. Also, Carrion-i-Silvestre *et al.* (2007) report size distortions when the unit root test with m $= 1$ is applied to a data generating process presenting no break points.

Therefore, selecting the appropriate m is an important task that should be performed before testing for unit roots. The recent paper of Perron and Yabu (2007) provides a rigorous framework to test the null of no break points against the alternative of m break points in a model of type (12.2). An essential feature of this test is that it works whether the noise component is stationary or integrated of order one. To our knowledge, no procedure exists to test the null of m break points against the alternative of m+1 break points in the model (2).

Testing for the existence and number of break points is beyond the scope of this chapter and we instead conduct the GLS-based test successively with m $= 1$ and m $= 2$ for the three time series. The results of the test are displayed in Tables 12.7 and 12.8. For comparison, the results of the GLS-based tests with only a constant linear time trend (whose critical values are found in Ng and Perron 2001) are presented in Table 12.9.

For the WTI crude oil, the dominant break points estimated by the GLS-based unit root test (i.e. Mar 2002 for the one-break test and Jan 2002 for the two-breaks test) differ significantly from the one estimated by minimization of the sum of squared residuals (i.e. Jan 1998). The interpretation of 2002 as a turning point in the oil markets is natural. In the

Table 12.7 Results of the GLS-based test on the WTI, copper, and dry-bulk freight rates with one structural break at an unknown time

	WTI	Copper	Baltic Dry Index
Statistic of the test P_gls	3.34***	5.72*	5.95*
Estimated T_1	Mar 2002	Oct 2002	Sep 2002
Date T_1 recalled from Table 12.1	Jan 1998	Sep 2002	Aug 2003
Critical value 1 %,5 %, 10 %	4.80, 5.75, 6.23	4.74, 5.65, 6.42	4.80, 5.74, 6.24

P_gls is the statistic of the test, T1 the estimated break date
*Indicates rejection of the null of a unit root at the 10 % level
**Indicates rejection of the null of a unit root at the 5 % level
***Indicates rejection of the null of a unit root at the 1 % level

Table 12.8 Results of the GLS-based test on the WTI, copper, and dry-bulk freight rates with two structural breaks at unknown times

	WTI	Copper	Baltic Dry Index
Statistics of the test P_gls	4.57*	12.25	4.03*
Estimated T_1	Mar 1986	Oct 2002	Feb 1988
Date T_1 recalled from Table 12.1	Jan 1986	Sep 2002	Jan 1988
Estimated T_2	Jan 2002	Mar 2006	Aug 2002
Date T_2 recalled from Table 12.1	Jan 1998	Mar 2006	Aug 2003
Critical value 1 %,5 %, 10 %	0.074, 3.96, 5.73	4.6, 6.55, 8.51	−0.046, 3.88, 5.65

P_gls is the statistics of the test, T1 and T2 the estimated break dates
*Indicates rejection of the null of a unit root at the 10 % level
**Indicates rejection of the null of a unit root at the 5 % level
***Indicates rejection of the null of a unit root at the 1 % level

Table 12.9   Results of the GLS-based test with only a constant linear time trend on the WTI, copper and dry-bulk freight rates

	WTI	Copper	Baltic Dry Index
Statistic of the test P_gls	13.22	55.49	15.80
Critical value 1 %,5 %, 10 %	4.03, 5.48, 6.67		

P_gls is the statistics of the test
*Indicates rejection of the null of a unit root at the 10 % level
**Indicates rejection of the null of a unit root at the 5 % level
***Indicates rejection of the null of a unit root at the 1 % level

wake of the 11 September 2001 attack, crude oil prices plummeted. Spot prices for the WTI were down 35 % by the middle of November. Under normal circumstances a drop in price of this magnitude would have resulted in another round of quota reductions but, given the world political climate, OPEC delayed additional cuts until January 2002. It then reduced its quota by 1.5 million barrels per day and was joined by several non-OPEC producers, including Russia, who promised combined production cuts of an additional 462 500 barrels. This had the desired effect since oil prices moved into the $25 range by March 2002. The continuous rise of oil prices from 2002 onwards is due to a combination of factors, including the massive increase in Asian demand for oil, the uninterrupted geopolitical turmoil in oil-producing countries (Middle East, Venezuela, and Nigeria in particular), the declining reserve numbers reported by oil majors and the decreasing value of dollar over the period.

Also, note the distance between the newly and previously calibrated dominant breaking points for the Baltic Dry Index.

The three commodities under analysis appear to have experienced a major structural change in 2002, the break point in copper following the WTI crude oil and freight index ones. Figures 12.6 and 12.7 illustrate the new fits of the WTI and the Baltic Dry Index to the shifting trend.

The null of an integrated noise component around a trend with one break point is rejected at the 1 % level for the WTI and at the 10 % level for the Baltic Dry Index and copper. Interestingly, the null of an integrated noise component around a trend with two break points is rejected at the 10 % level for the WTI crude and the Baltic Dry Index but not for copper. By contrast, the null of an integrated noise around a constant linear trend cannot be rejected at the 10 % level for any time series. These results show the importance of the specification of the nature of the trend when testing for a unit root. The fact that the null of a unit root is more easily rejected with one break point than with two supports the hypothesis of stationary fluctuations around a trend with a major shift in the year 2002.

12.4.6   Implications for commodity risk management

In the light of our analysis, a possible model for the logarithm y_t of the spot price of a commodity is:

$$y_t = \mathrm{d}_t + u_t$$

$$u_t = \alpha u_{t-1} + v_t$$

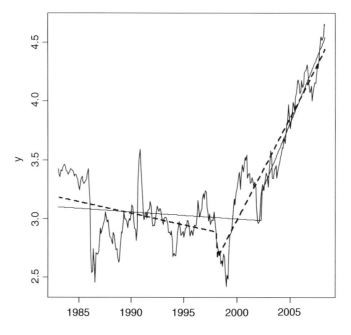

Figure 12.6 WTI fit with one break point
Dotted line: OLS fit with one break point estimated by minimization of squared residuals; solid line:
OLS fit with one break point estimated by the GLS-based unit root test.

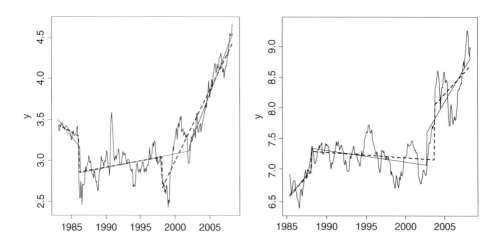

Figure 12.7 Dotted lines: OLS fit with two break points estimated by minimization of squared
residuals; solid line: OLS fit with two break points estimated by the GLS-based unit root test.
Left: WTI crude oil; Right: Baltic Dry Index

where $\alpha < 1v_t$ is a noise process and d_t is a stochastic trend subject to level and slope shifts, occurring at random times T_i:

$$d_t = \mu + \beta t + J_t$$

$$J_t = \sum_{i=1}^{N_t} [\mu_i DU_t(T_i) + \beta_i DT_t^*(T_i)]$$

$$N_t = \sum_i 1_{T_i \leqslant t}.$$

We can assume, for instance, that the intervals $T_{i+1} - T_i$ between the jump times T_i are independent and exponentially distributed with parameter λ, hence the number $N_t = \Sigma_i 1_{T_i \leqslant t}$ of jumps before time t is a Poisson process with intensity λ.

The level and drift discontinuities (μ_i) and (β_i) at break dates (T_i) can be modeled either as independent and identically distributed variables with respective densities $L(\mu)$ and $L(\beta)$ or as Markov processes in the spirit of Pindyck (1999).

The precise calibration of λ, $L(\mu)$, and $L(\beta)$ is a difficult task because very few jumps have been historically observed. They can be chosen instead from economic considerations relative to the perceived probability of observing a structural shift in the future and the possible direction and magnitude of this shift.

Our model is close to the one proposed in Pindyck (1999), where the log price is assumed to randomly oscillate around a linear time trend, whose level and slope are modeled as stationary processes. The difference with our framework lies in the continuous versus discretely shifting pattern of the trend term.

12.5 CONCLUSION

By applying new unit root tests allowing for structural breaks in the trend under both the null and the alternative hypothesis, we have shown that, at a level of at least 10%, the hypothesis of an integrated noise component around a trend with one structural break could be rejected for the WTI crude oil, copper, and shipping. By contrast, none of the standard unit root tests allowed us to reject the null of a unit root, except during the sub-periods Jan. 1983–Jan. 1986 and Feb. 1986–Mar. 2003 in the case of the WTI. The break points detected for the three prices under analysis correspond to well-identified events which altered the supply/demand fundamentals.

An important extension of our paper concerns the "on-line" estimation of a structural break, in the spirit of the filter introduced in Hamilton (1989): can the decision maker assess at any time t the probability of the price having switched to a new regime? This question is particularly important when looking at the paths of the WTI crude, copper, and freight rates in 2002–2003: at what date can we know with a sufficient level of confidence that a break occurred? This problem can for example be solved by using cutting-edge Bayesian techniques such as Gibbs sampling (see e.g. McCulloch and Tsay (1993), where the Gibbs sampler, introduced in Geman and Geman (1984), is applied to estimate a random level/variance shift model on the price of unleaded gasoline in the US).

Other extensions concern the detection of breaks in mean-reversion speed and volatility as well as seasonality.

12.6   REFERENCES

Ardeni, P. (1989). Does the Law of One Price Really Hold for Commodity Prices? *American Journal of Agricultural Prices* **71**, 661–669.

Babula, R.A., F.J. Ruppel and D.A. Bessler (1995). US Corn Exports: the Role of the Exchange Rate. *Agricultural Economics* **13**, 75–88.

Bai, J. and P. Perron (2003). Computation and Analysis of Multiple Structural Change Models. *Journal of Applied Econometrics* **18**, 1–22.

Bessembinder, H., J. Coughenour, P. Seguin and M. Smoller (1995). Mean Reversion in Equilibrium Asset Prices: Evidence from the Futures Term Structure. *The Journal of Finance* **50**(1), 361–375.

Black, F. and M. Scholes (1973). The Pricing of Options and Corporate Liabilities. *Journal of Political Economy* **81**(3), 637–654.

Carrion-i-Silvestre, J.L., D. Kim and P. Perron (2007). GLS-based Unit Root Tests with Multiple Structural Breaks both under the Null and the Alternative Hypotheses. Working Paper, Boston University.

Elliott, G., T. Rothenberg and J. Stock (1996). Efficient Tests for an Autoregressive Unit Root. *Econometrica* **64**, 813–836.

Eydeland, A. and H. Geman (1998). Pricing Power Derivatives, *Risk*, October.

Foster, K.A., Havenner A.M. and A.M. Walburger (1995). System Theoretic Time-Series Forecasts for Weekly Live Cattle Prices. *American Journal of Agricultural Economics* **77**, 1012–1023.

Geman, H. (2007). Reexamining Mean-reversion in Energy Markets: In M.C. Fu *et al.* (Eds) *Advances in Mathematical Finance*, Birkhauser Verlag AG.

Geman, S. and D. Geman (1984). Stochastic Relaxation, Gibbs Distributions, and the Bayesian Restoration of images. *IEEE Trans. Pattern Analysis and Machine Intelligence* **6**, 721–741.

Geman, H. and V. Nguyen (2005). Soybean Inventory and Forward Curve Dynamics. *Management Science* **51**(7), 1076–1091.

Geman, H. and S. Ohana (2007). Forward Curves, Scarcity, and Price Volatility in Oil and Natural Gas Markets. Working Paper, Birkbeck, University of London.

Gibson, R. and E. Schwartz (1990). Stochastic Convenience Yield and the Pricing of Oil Contingent Claims. *The Journal of Finance* **45**(3), 959–976.

Hall, A. (1994). Testing for a Unit Root in Time Series with Pretest Data-Based Model Selection. *Journal of Business and Economic Statistics* **12**, 461–470.

Hamilton, J. (1989). A New Approach to the Economic Analysis of Nonstationary Time Series and the Business Cycle. *Econometrica* **57**, 357–384.

Koekebakker, S., Å. Roar and S. Sigbjørn (2006). Are Spot Freight Rates Stationary? *Journal of Transport Economics and Policy* **40**(3), 449–472.

Lee, J. and M. Strazicich (2003). Minimum Lagrange Multiplier Unit Root Test with Two Structural Breaks. *The Review of Economics and Statistics* **85**, 1082–1089.

McCulloch, R. and R. Tsay (1993). Bayesian Inference and Prediction for Mean and Variance Shifts in Autoregressive Time Series. *Journal of the American Statistical Association* **88**(423), 968–978.

McKinnon, J. (1991). Critical Values for Cointegration Tests. In: R.F. Engle and C.W.J. Granger (Eds) *Long-Run Economic Relationships: Readings in Cointegration*. New York: Oxford University Press, 266–276.

Miltersen, K. and E. Schwartz (1998). Pricing of Options on Commodity Futures with Stochastic Term Structures of Convenience Yields and Interest Rates. *Journal of Financial and Quantitative Analysis* **33**(1), 33–59.

Nelson, C., J. Piger, and E. Zivot (2001), Markov Regime Switching and Unit-Root Tests, *Journal of Business & Economic Statistics* **19**(4), pp. 404–415.

Newbold, P., T. Rayner and N. Kellard (2000). Long-Run Drift, Co-Movement and Persistence in Real Wheat and Maize Prices. *Journal of Agricultural Economics* **51**, 106–121.

Ng, S. and P. Perron (2001). Lag Length Selection and the Construction of Unit Root Tests with Good Size and Power. *Econometrica* **69**, 1519–1554.

Perron, P. (1989). The Great Crash, the Oil Price Shock and the Unit Root Hypothesis. *Econometrica* **57**, 1361–1401.

Perron, P. (1990). Testing for a Unit Root in a Time Series with a Changing Mean. *Journal of Business and Economic Statistics* **8**, 153–162.

Perron, P. (2006). Dealing with Structural Breaks. In: K. Patterson and T.C. Mills (Eds) *Palgrave Handbook of Econometrics, Vol. 1: Econometric Theory* Palgrave Macmillan, 278–352.

Perron, P. and T. Yabu (2007). Testing for Shifts in Trend with an Integrated or Stationary Noise Component. Working Paper, Boston University.

Phillips, P. and P. Perron (1988). Testing for a Unit Root in Time Series Regression. *Biometrika* **75**, 335–346.

Pindyck, R. (1999). The Long-Run Evolution of Energy Prices. *The Energy Journal* **20**(2), 1–27.

Schwartz, E.S. (1997). The Stochastic Behavior of Commodity Prices: Implications for Valuation and Hedging. *The Journal of Finance* **52**(3), 923–973.

Serletis, A. (1992). Unit Root Behavior in Energy Futures Prices. *The Energy Journal* **2**(13), 119–128.

Simmons, M. (2005). *Twilight in the Desert: The Coming Sandi Oil Shock and the World Economy*. John Wiley & Sons Ltd.: Chichester.

Tomek, W. and Wang D. (2007). Commodity Prices and Unit Root Tests. *American Journal of Agricultural Economics* **89**(4), 873–889.

Zivot, E. and D. Andrews (1992). Further Evidence on the Great Crash, the Oil Price Shock and the Unit Root Hypothesis. *Journal of Business and Economic Statistics* **10**, 251–270.

13

Managing Agricultural Price Risk in Developing Countries*

Julie Dana and Christopher L. Gilbert

13.1 THE LIBERALIZATION CONTEXT

Agricultural commodity prices are volatile because short term production and consumption elasticities are low. Production responsiveness is low for annual crop commodities because planting decisions are made before prices for the new crop are known. These decisions depend on expected prices and not price realizations. Price outcomes are seldom so disastrous as to result in the harvest being abandoned. For tree crop commodities, production responsiveness is low because the stock of productive trees takes between two and five years to respond to price increases, because input application generally gives only a modest increase in yield and because prices are seldom so low as to make it worthwhile to cut down trees which still have a productive future. Short-term demand elasticities are low because the actual commodity price will seldom be a large component of the overall value of the final product (examples are cocoa in chocolate and coffee beans in soluble coffee powder – see Gilbert, 2007a) and because substitutability between different raw materials is seldom large. Elasticities may be higher for subsistence crops in poor economies where high prices may force families to try to get by on less.

Throughout the twentieth century, the variability of agricultural prices induced both developed and developing country governments to seek to prevent or offset these movements. By the 1980s unilateral and multilateral interventions in agricultural commodity markets had become the norm. The United States used support prices and inventories to manage domestic prices. The EU had a similar scheme, but also operated a special set of commodity-specific exchange rates ("green rates") for trade among EU members. For those commodities produced predominantly in developing countries, interventions were either multilateral, for example through buffer stock or export control agreements under the auspices of international commodity agreements (cocoa, coffee, natural rubber and sugar – see Gilbert, 1987,

*This chapter draws on the experience of the Commodity Risk Management Group (CRMG) of the World Bank with which both authors have been associated. However, the views expressed are those of the authors and not the World Bank nor its members. We thank other current and past members of CRMG on whose work we have drawn, specifically Erin Bryla, Guido Fernandes, Euna Shim, Joanna Syroka, Pauline Tiffen, Roy Parizat, and Panos Varangis. The authors remain responsible for all errors.
Julie Dana: Commodity Risk Management Group, The World Bank, Washington DC: jdana@worldbank.org.
Christopher Gilbert: Department of Economics, University of Trento, Italy and Department of Economics, Birkbeck, University of London, UK: cgilbert@economia.unitn.it and c.gilbert@bbk.ac.uk.

1996) or through domestic agencies. Marketing boards and stabilization funds were common in both developed and developing countries. There were buffer stock schemes in Bangladesh, India, Indonesia, Mexico, the Philippines and South Korea; buffer funds in Côte d'Ivoire, Papua New Guinea, and South Korea; marketing boards with monopolies on trade in much of Africa and parts of Latin America and Asia; and variable tariff schemes in Chile, Malaysia, and Venezuela (Knudsen and Nash, 1990).

Many of the developing country schemes (national and multinational) encountered serious problems during the 1980s. Producers and producing country governments became over-optimistic about the prices they could obtain in what were generally weak market conditions. At the same time, the inefficiency costs associated with controls became higher over time as rent-seeking activities became increasingly entrenched. In coffee, high prices induced expansion of area in a number of countries with relatively high production costs (mainly in Africa), while quota restrictions held down production in lower-cost origins such as Brazil. Marketing board bureaucracies, such as the Instituto Brasiliero do Café in Brazil and Cocobod in Ghana, multiplied in size and absorbed much of the benefit of higher prices, and other forms of rent extraction were established (Bohman et al., 1996). The consequence was that, as prices weakened through the 1980s, almost all previously successful national intervention schemes succumbed to financial difficulties. In turn, the international commodity agreements were unable to adapt to changes in the market, and by 1996 the economic clauses in them had all lapsed or failed, victims of politics and economics (Gilbert, 1987, 1996).

In many cases, donors were called upon to rescue or restructure national stabilization agencies of funds which found themselves in distress. Market liberalization, in particular the abolition of monopsony-monopoly marketing arrangements and radical reduction in the size of bureaucracies, was often a precondition for such assistance. Thus, a series of reforms aimed at liberalizing developing country agricultural markets was launched in the 1980s and 1990s, largely at the urging of multilateral lenders such as the European Union, USAID, and the World Bank. Akiyama et al. (2001) illustrate the rapid pace of these reforms for Africa. With only a few exceptions, marketing boards and stabilization agencies were either abolished or restructured so that their activities were confined to those of general oversight, regulation and collection and dissemination of market data. A major objective of the liberalization policies was to ensure that farmers received a higher share of world prices. National and regional monopsonies were largely abolished (an exception being cotton through francophone West and Central Africa) and pan-national pricing was dropped. At the same time, export taxes tended to be reduced. Many of these changes encountered strong opposition from market incumbents and entrenched governmental interest groups.

As a consequence, since the mid-1990s agricultural products in developing countries have been produced and marketed under much more competitive conditions than at any time since (or during) the colonial period. Lower taxation and greater competition in the supply chain have helped farmers achieve higher shares of world prices, and the price pass-through process has become faster. On the negative side, liberalization may also have resulted in lower world prices, to the benefit of consumers rather than producers (see Gilbert and Varangis, 2004), and more rapid pass-through has resulted in more variable producer (farmgate) prices. This has been particularly true in Africa, where markets had previously been highly controlled, and also to a large extent in Latin America. It has been less true in central Asia where important prices remain controlled by government.

More complete and more rapid pass-through of world to farmgate prices has increased the exposure of developing country farmers and supply chain intermediaries to price variability.

This was an unintended consequence of market liberalization (sometimes referred to as a "second generation problem") which has had particularly serious implications in developing countries where banks often have poor outreach to the agricultural sector, financial markets are poorly developed and access to international markets is limited. Management of this risk becomes a problem and is the focus of this contribution. For previous literature see Claessens and Duncan (1993), ITF (1999), and Gilbert (2002).

In the developed "market" economies, change has been less marked, particularly where agriculture remains largely protected. Farmers in the United States, the EU, Japan and many other developed economies continue to receive prices well above world market levels. Because much of this support is delivered through price guarantees, the gap is particularly large in periods when world prices are low. High prices are therefore passed through to developed country farmers who nevertheless still remain partially insulated from low world prices.

Section 13.2 discusses price exposure in the developing country agricultural supply chain. Section 13.3 looks at the available risk management instruments, and the challenges to which they give rise. Section 13.4 discusses application of these instruments in the developing country context. Section 13.5 concludes.

13.2   INCIDENCE OF RISK EXPOSURE

Agents in the agricultural value chain are exposed but to differing extents and to differing risks. In this chapter, we will be concerned predominantly with price risk. However, it is important to emphasize that this is not the only, and not necessarily the most important, risk faced by market actors. For many agricultural commodities, weather-related quantity risk may be problematic. For exporters in developing countries, political risk – in particular risks associated with the availability and terms of export permits – may be dominant. For exporters and banks, currency risks can be quite serious, as has been demonstrated most recently in countries such as Zambia and Tanzania which have experienced currency appreciation relative to the US dollar to the detriment of exporters selling commodities in US dollar terms. The justification for compartmentalizing risk into different categories (price, yield, political, currency, etc.) and analyzing these separately is that agents need to adopt different strategies to manage different types of risk.

13.2.1   Farmers

Taking a simple example of price risk in the coffee supply chain, we start with farmers, who are naturally "long" the crop. They benefit when prices rise and lose when they fall. Because intermediation costs are largely independent of the price level and because export and other taxes are normally constant in absolute rather than in percentage terms, price variations at the fob stage are attenuated at the farmgate level. Farmers obtain the residual of the price after all other agents in the value chain have taken their cut. As an example, suppose the fob price of a commodity is $1/kg and price variability measured as the coefficient of variation is 15 %, so that a one standard deviation price movement is 15c/kg. If intermediation costs are 50c/kg and are constant, the same 15c/kg price movement amounts to a farmgate coefficient of variation of 30 %.

Farmers are primarily interested in net revenues. Net revenues are gross revenues less production costs. Gross revenues are based on price multiplied by quantity (yield), and both

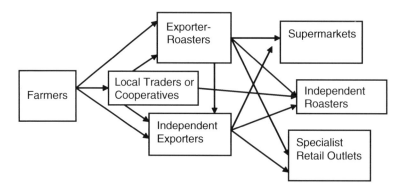

Figure 13.1 The coffee supply chain
Source: Gilbert (2007a).

are subject to volatility. Variation in these may be partially offset if, for example, adverse weather affects many producers at the same time (as, for example, in the possible effects of El Niño). In such a case, the farmer is somewhat self-insured since although yield has decreased, prices have increased. This situation, however, is exceptional and in a competitive market with geographically dispersed production it is more plausible that yield and price risk are uncorrelated.

We can identify two sets of impacts resulting from farmgate price variability. First, revenue variability is likely to transfer into variability of consumption, and also investment, including investment in new technologies. Second, price uncertainty will lead farmers to be cautious in the application of costly inputs and this will tend to reduce yields.

First, consider the impact on consumption and investment. Farmers in developed economies, and possibly also the richer farmers in developing countries, can smooth consumption by saving and dissaving to maintain consumption equal to permanent income. Farmers in developing countries typically have low or zero savings and little collateral. The rural areas of many developing countries are virtually unbanked and this inhibits the accumulation of savings in good times. Even if farm households have managed to save in the form of agricultural capital, e.g. animals, it may be difficult to realize these savings in the event of an adverse shock which affects the entire community. In such circumstances adverse price or yield shocks will force poorer farmers to adopt other strategies. These include reduction of consumption but also, in countries where other labor market opportunities are available, one or more family members taking an additional off-farm job or even migrating. In both cases, this may involve withdrawal of a child from school resulting in an irreversible loss of potential human capital (Duryea *et al.*, 2007). See also Section 13.4.7 below.

Periods of low prices can therefore impose substantial utility costs on developing country farmers. Because adverse shocks are likely to impact investment as well as consumption, these effects can be long term and can endure after prices have recovered (Raddatz, 2005). The irreversibility of investment decisions implies that the effects may be asymmetric between positive and negative shocks and may be permanent (Collier, 2005).

We now turn to the cost side of the equation. Production costs comprise capital, labor and input (fertilizer, insecticide, etc.) costs. The balance between these varies from one crop to another. Some costs, particularly labor costs, depend on the quantity harvested. Other costs, particularly input costs, are incurred earlier in the crop year and, in the case of annual crops, at the time of planting. Short-term supply responsiveness arises out of the ability of farmers to adjust input decisions in relation to their expectations of likely prices. Risk aversion will lead farmers to reduce inputs to the extent that harvest prices are subject to uncertainty. Price uncertainty therefore tends to reduce yields and hence revenues.

The importance of these yield impacts varies from commodity to commodity. In general, we should expect the effects to be highest for annual crops where planting decisions can be very sensitive to expected prices. It is relatively easy, for example, for farmers to substitute between alternative grains. For other crops, such as cotton, which are typically highly fertilizer-intensive, the crucial decision is how much fertilizer to apply (and hence purchase). For tree crops, such as cocoa and coffee, yield responsiveness will depend on the extent to which production is input-intensive. Fertilizer is used in only modest quantities in cocoa production but insecticide application can be important. The fertilizer-intensity of coffee production varies from region to region but modern, fast-growing varieties tend to require more fertilizer than traditional trees.

Farmers therefore face two distinct price risk problems. The first relates to price uncertainty over the crop year: farmers commit time and material inputs based on their expectations at the start of the crop year. If prices turn out lower than they expected, they may fail to cover input costs, while if they are higher, they will have failed to take advantage of market opportunities. Managing this price risk can increase productive efficiency and, in the case of sharp price falls, protect against the risk of financial loss. The second problem is that of sustained low prices. Such periods typically result from global excess supply and, if they persist over a number of years, may not involve significant intra-annual uncertainty – indeed, prices are often less volatile when they are low. Prolonged periods of low prices undermine livelihoods. This is an income maintenance issue and not a risk management issue. The balance in importance between these two factors varies from commodity to commodity depending on the extent of discretion in input decisions and the length and amplitude of price cycles.

13.2.2 Intermediaries, exporters, stockholders, and banks

Intermediaries buy from farmers and sell either to exporters or to other intermediaries. They include low level traders and traitants, who tour producing areas with trucks and purchase from farmers, producer groups, cooperatives, intermediate aggregators such as transport companies, and intermediate processors such as cotton ginners, millers, etc. The common feature across all market intermediaries is that they both buy and sell at market-determined prices and operate on a margin between the two.

Like farmers, intermediaries are generally long the commodity, but they have much shorter price horizons. They will typically not be concerned by the overall level of prices, since this will affect both purchase and sale prices. (High prices will increase financing requirements and may therefore constrain operations.) However, they will be concerned by price variability over the period (generally short) over which they hold a position. Even a small price fall over this period can easily completely wipe out profit margins and there is the danger that such trading losses can consume a significant proportion of the intermediary's capital.

From time to time, some intermediaries also operate by shorting the commodity through forward sales to end buyers. In these cases, since the intermediary has not yet covered the short sale by buying the raw material, the risk is that prices will move higher.

Exporters are in a similar position to intermediaries but their holding period will typically be longer, reflecting transport times from the producing to the consuming market. Exporters may be locally-based companies, cooperatives, companies based in consuming countries or local affiliates of such companies. Liberalization has resulted in many industries coming to be dominated, directly or indirectly, by major multinational companies – see Section 13.4.1. This is true, for example, both of coffee and cocoa. Exporters will normally be long the commodity, although it can also happen that they are short if they sell to consumers prior to purchasing the product at origin.

Stockholders are a particular category of intermediary, and they generally hold long positions in the market. Stocks may be held in the producing country, a consuming country or a third location. For many tropical commodities, there is advantage in holding stocks in a temperate climate. Often financing will be easier if stocks are held in warehouses designated for exchange delivery. These warehouses tend to be in consuming countries to allow consumers to take delivery for purposes of immediate consumption. Stockholders may buy and sell at market prices, or may simply earn a fee for storage and collateral management services. Stockholders in the former category, who are trading the commodity profit either from expected price appreciation or from the opportunity to consume (or sell to a consumer) should the need arise (the "convenience yield" of stock).

Banks are a final category of intermediary with exposure. In their case, the exposure is indirect and results from default risk associated with lending to intermediaries with specific price exposures. A fall in the commodity price can result in inability to repay on the part of an intermediary who is long the commodity and has borrowed in order to finance operations in the supply chain. Once banks have experienced such defaults, they become unwilling to advance credit to the sector and prefer to retreat to safer activities such as lending on urban real estate where collateral is available. Diminished access to credit in the supply chain and increased cost of credit where it is available thus become direct results of poorly managed price risk.

13.2.3 Producing country governments

Governments may have direct or indirect exposure to agricultural commodity prices. Direct exposure arises when tax revenues or fiscal subsidies depend on the level of prices. Price dependence of tax revenues is much less acute now than a few decades ago. In part, this is the consequence of an extended period of low agricultural prices which has obliged governments to look elsewhere for tax revenues. Also, in many countries there has been a move to taxes which are independent of values, since quantities are more easily monitored than values. Direct price exposure therefore tends to be small for export crops.

Food crops may give rise to more complicated exposure patterns. This is most obviously the case in countries in which government imports food, typically grains, for off-market distribution (e.g. for use in schools and hospitals or for subsidized distribution to poor households as a form of social security). The same situation arises in which governments are committed to cap food price rises and manage strategic grain reserves. As current (2008) developments in food markets show, these commitments will often be implicit. In such circumstances, government has a short exposure: it will have an increased financial liability as food prices rise.

Exposure also arises indirectly when governments act, either implicitly or explicitly, as guarantors of stabilization funds and parastatal organizations. This has happened most obviously in the case of stabilization agencies, such as *caisses de stabilisation*. Financial difficulties can arise either if the stabilization agency fails to reduce prices sufficiently in the face of prolonged periods of low prices or if it fails to hedge a price guarantee given to farmers at the start of the crop year and the price then falls through the crop year. These circumstances have both arisen in the Central and West African cotton sectors where this form of market intervention is standard – see Box 13.1 which illustrates this for Burkina Faso.

Box 13.1 Governmental exposure to the cotton price in Burkina Faso

Market liberalization has resulted in three cotton ginning-exporting companies in Burkina Faso, each with a regional monopsony. The largest is SOFITEX, the ex-state ginner which accounts for 80% of Burkina production. Subsequent to liberalization, SOFITEX was owned 35% by the Burkina government, 34% by a multinational trading company and 30% by the cotton farmers through a producers' association. In conjunction with producers, ginners fix a pan-national initial price to be paid to farmers at the start of the season. This price was set at over-optimistic levels in both 2004–05 and 2005–06, resulting in substantial losses to SOFITEX, which was unhedged. The following paragraph is a quote from the Letter of Intent to the IMF signed by Finance Minister Jean-Baptiste Compaouré on 11 April 2007. It makes clear that the incidence of SOFITEX's stabilization losses fell directly on the Burkina Faso government. Much of this incidence was subsequently passed through to donors.

"After sizable losses in two consecutive campaigns (2004/05 and 2005/06), the net worth of Burkina Faso's main cotton company SOFITEX was reduced to below zero. The main reasons behind the loss, based on audited accounts, were the low world cotton prices, the appreciation of the CFAF, and high prices paid to farmers, reflecting slow adjustment to the external shocks. The recapitalization was complicated by the fact that ultimately SOFITEX's main private shareholder decided not to participate. In this context, the government had offered to extend a guarantee of CFAF 50 billion for the outstanding loans from the 2005/06 campaign so that domestic banks would release the funds to pay farmers. The recapitalization need for SOFITEX is currently estimated at CFAF 38 billion. The actual amount will be confirmed in an extraordinary general assembly meeting of shareholders in June 2007. Shareholders must contribute at least 75 percent of the recapitalization amount by end-2007. The final phase, expected after 2007, would bring the company's net worth back to a level compatible with regional business regulations (OHADA). The government's 35% share in SOFITEX could temporarily increase as a result of the recapitalization."

Source: IMF http://www.imf.org/external/np/loi/2007/bfs/041107.pdf (paragraph 22, part) CFAF 38 billion was equivalent to $79m at 2007 exchange rates.

A frequent consequence of financial problems in stabilization funds is that governments turn to donors to assist in the refinancing. This was the case in Burkina Faso (Box 13.1). Similarly, when parastatal organizations incur large trading losses, as a result either of not recognizing or mismanaging price exposure, local banks and governments are often called upon to bail out programs. This can take the form of debt forgiveness or debt rescheduling.

One of the objectives of market liberalization was to reduce the likelihood of such calls for ex post financial support by transferring responsibility for stabilization to the sector, in particular to so-called industry representative organizations. In practice, governments have difficulty in standing aside and letting a major institution fail. When industry participants know that this type of bailout is likely to be available if there is a problem, this can lead to reckless behavior. More fundamentally, because many actors in the supply chain do not have the skills to properly assess risk in an ongoing way, and manage it throughout the season, unhedged price exposures can lead to trading losses at every level of the chain. Implicit guarantees of the sort described here result in a long exposure on the part of government, although the imprecise nature of the guarantee makes quantification of the exposure problematic.

13.2.4 Consumers

By consumers, we mean the companies who purchase the commodity in the final market. Often, the commodity will be processed before being sold at the retail level. Converters, often large multinational trading companies, import cocoa beans and grind ("convert") them to obtain cocoa liquor, cocoa butter and cocoa powder which are inputs into the manufacture of chocolate and confectionary products. Many of these products, including standard retail chocolate, will contain more milk and sugar than cocoa. The cocoa value chain therefore effectively ends at the conversion stage. By contrast, coffee is roasted and packed (if soluble, roast, processed and packed) but is then sold on the retail market as coffee or as a coffee drink. Here the value chain continues to the retail stage. In this respect, cotton is more akin to cocoa and sugar to coffee.

The price exposure of consuming companies depends on how they sell the end product. Cocoa products are generally sold to the chocolate and confectionery industry at prices which closely follow exchange cocoa prices. The converters are therefore in a similar position to that of the producing country intermediaries. They will be long cocoa for the period in which they hold the cocoa for conversion. Coffee roasters buy coffee at market prices and sell at prices which are typically fixed over some period of time (often only a few weeks). They are often short coffee since they will sell first, and then focus on procurement. A rise in the input price, given fixed retail prices, will erode profits, and a fall will enhance them. Chocolate manufacturers are in a similar position relative to cocoa – a rise in the price of their cocoa ingredients will erode their chocolate margins. In their case, the problem is exacerbated by the fact that it is costly to change vending machine prices.

Final (retail) consumers are, of course, short all commodities. In developed countries, unlike agents in the commodity value chains, consumers are highly diversified. Gasoline is a large item in consumer budgets, but price rises for other commodities are irritating rather than painful, except when they move together. This implies that final consumers will not suffer a serious decline in their standard of living if a poor harvest leads to a rise in the price of a particular commodity, but they will be worse off if a rise in demand (perhaps in China) results in an across-the-board rise in prices. In developing countries, particularly in countries with one or two main staple foods, consumers are not diversified and are highly exposed to the risk of price increases. As we have seen recently (in 2008), when consumers of food staple commodities are affected by severe price shocks, the call for government intervention can be strong.

13.2.5 The overall supply chain

Overall, the value chain is long the commodity. Final consumers, and those consuming companies which sell part or all of their output at fixed (list) prices, will be short. The more links there are in the chain, the greater the number of agents who will have long exposure, but the shorter the duration of their exposure will be. And because most supply chains are fragmented at least to some extent, we should expect an excess of agents with long exposure to those with short exposure.

It follows that the supply chain gains if prices rise and loses if they fall. However, because holding periods differ, different agents will be interested in price variability over different horizons. Farmers have the longest horizons. The time between planting (or input application) and harvesting is typically around six months. Farmers are vulnerable to price falls over this period. Cooperatives who offer guaranteed prices at the start of the crop year also have long duration exposures. By contrast, most other intermediaries, such as transport companies, have much shorter holding periods.

Farmers' exposure to short term price variability is more complex. High prices at the tail end of the old crop year bring no benefit to a farmer who can only sell once the new crop is harvested. Farmers have no exposure to variability at this stage of the crop year. However, once the crop is harvested the farmer needs to decide when to sell. It is often alleged that intermediaries extract higher margins at the peak of the harvest (perhaps consistently with rising marginal costs of intermediation), giving farmers an incentive either to harvest early or to hold back on their sales. Discretion with respect to the time of marketing generates a short-term exposure.

Capital investment, either in trees or in equipment, such as in a cooperative gin, gives rise to a very long-term exposure, extending possibly over decades. This is more akin to an equity investment issue rather than a risk management problem.

These are the general categories of price exposure faced by actors in the supply chain. Specific risk assessment is necessary to identify and quantify the specific exposure faced at a particular time. Price risk assessment should be an ongoing exercise for all supply chain actors since the costs of not appropriately identifying, monitoring, and managing price exposure can be severe.

13.3   INSTRUMENTS AND PROBLEMS

Price risks can be managed in a number of different ways. Different agents in the supply chain will find different choices to be appropriate. Some developing country agents may find that none of these risk management methods are feasible and they may thus simply have to bear the exposure. Others may not be aware either of the available management methods or, more fundamentally, of their exposure. They may also end up bearing the exposure even in cases in which risk management is feasible. We discuss the instruments in Section 13.3.1 and review access problems in Section 13.3.2. Section 13.3.3 looks at basis risk, which may reduce the contribution of these instruments. Section 13.3.4 looks at the potential offered by developing country futures exchanges.

13.3.1   Instruments

In the developed market economies commodity price risk within a commodity chain is generally offset using exchange-traded financial products, such as futures and options. (Swaps are potentially important but have not yet played a major role in agriculture.) Typically, these instruments are used to mitigate short-term price risks, say 3–8 months forward.

A futures contract obliges the seller, who is said to be "short" the future, to deliver a specified quantity of the commodity, satisfying a specified range of quality conditions (generally including origin) in one of a range of a specified locations at or by a specified date. The buyer, who is said to be "long" the future, has the obligation to take delivery under the same terms. In the majority of cases, neither of these events will take place, and both shorts and longs will take exactly offsetting positions in the same futures contract prior to the specified delivery date. These offsetting positions cancel the physical delivery obligations but secure the financial purpose of taking futures positions, which was that of locking into the quoted futures prices at the time of the original contract when it was not possible to manage the price exposure through an immediate back-to-back physical contract. The futures contract thus achieves a "hedging" function, operating as a financial risk management tool in parallel with physical trades.

In a well-functioning futures market, futures prices correlate closely with the prices in the physical market, and indeed generally form the benchmark prices for pricing commercial transactions. This correlation allows a futures position to lock in an as yet unknown future cash market transaction. Suppose I sell at the current futures price of $100 to fix the price in a pending sale of the physical in one month's time. If both the futures and the cash price fall over the month to $90, I will obtain only $90 on my cash sale but will profit $10 by buying back the futures contract at $90 against the $100 I have paid. My net price is the $100 I locked in through the futures sale. In Section 13.3.3 we look at reasons why actual outcomes may not be so clear.

Whereas futures contracts allow transactors to lock into current futures prices, options allow transactors to guarantee minimum or maximum prices. A minimum price is guaranteed by purchase of a put option which gives the holder the right (but not the obligation) to sell the physical at a specified strike price. A maximum price is guaranteed by purchase of a call option which gives the holder the right (but not the obligation) to buy the physical at a specified strike price.

As in the case of futures, these positions will normally be purely financial and will not result in the contracted purchase or sale of the physical commodity. To continue with the previous example, consider a put option with a strike price of $95. If the futures price falls from $100 to $90 over the contract period, the put option is $5 in the money and can be closed out for this amount. I sell my physical for $90 but make $5 on the put giving me a net price of $95 which is the floor price I had locked in when purchasing the option. On the other hand, if the futures price remained at $100, the put would expire worthless and I would simply obtain the cash price of $100. The call operates in the same way but allows a purchase price to be capped.

Both futures and options may be exchange instruments (i.e., instruments traded on the originating exchange) or over-the-counter (OTC) instruments. In the latter case, they may either be exchange-look-alikes or specifically designed to suit client requirements.

The price exposures in the developing country agricultural value chains, discussed in Section 13.2, establish the potential for application of price risk management instruments. Two sets of factors reduce the extent to which this potential can be realized in developing countries. The first, access problems, discussed in Section 13.3.2, reduce the supply of risk management instruments to developing country agents. The second, basis risk problems, discussed in Section 13.3.3, reduce the value of risk management instruments in developing countries, and hence the demand for these instruments.

13.3.2 Access problems

Not everyone can simply walk into a futures broker and establish a futures or options account. There are three major factors which can limit access:

1. **Size:** Contract sizes are often much larger than the exposure of many developing country actors. Furthermore, brokers incur fixed costs of trading – there is little cost difference between selling one contract and ten contracts. Both considerations require smaller developing country agents to aggregate their positions.
2. **Credit:** Futures trading requires credit lines, which can be sizeable because commodity exchanges require daily monitoring and management of the overall financial liabilities of all market actors. This is done through a process of marking to market all open positions and then making margin calls. The mark-to-market process involves comparing the net value of open positions to the current market price to establish a dollar value of open liabilities. Futures brokers, and the exchange as a whole, then limit the overall financial liability of the positions by "calling" the margins of these open liabilities. This is done, on an individual customer basis, by requiring either a cash deposit to cover a percentage of the overall liability, or using a credit line to establish coverage for that liability. This credit line will need to be in dollars or an equivalent freely convertible currency. Since many developing country actors lack access to credit facilities needed to cover these liabilities, hedging with futures on international exchanges is typically infeasible. As an alternative, developing country actors can hedge with options which can be purchased by payment of an up-front options premium, thus avoiding the need to manage a credit line and margin calls.
3. **Regulation:** Post 9/11, regulatory authorities have become increasingly vigilant about the possibility that financial markets, including those for commodity futures and options, can be used for money laundering purposes, possibly extending to funding terrorism. Developing country institutions are obvious candidates to front such illegal activities. Developed country regulators now impose very substantial obligations on brokers before they can trade with developed country entities. These requirements relate to any type of business done between developed country financial institutions and developing country market actors. It implies a high start-up cost for developed country actors wishing to expand business in developing country markets. If the business volumes do not appear to be high enough to offset these costs, brokers based in developed countries will simply choose not to invest in these new markets. (In certain developing countries, exchange regulations may also prohibit hedging on international exchanges.)

Overcoming these access problems is a challenge to bridging the market gap between unhedged commodity price risk, and the use of instruments that can mitigate that risk.

13.3.3 Basis risk problems

Basis risk arises where the price of a traded instrument, such as a futures price, is imperfectly correlated with the price that is relevant to the exposure in the supply chain. The prices of most exchange-traded agricultural products relate to transactions in the developed countries, often on the eastern seaboard of the United States and in North Sea ports in northern

Europe. Price movements in commodity producing countries will not always correlate well with these exchange prices. The resulting basis risk is therefore likely to be more acute for agents in the developing country sections of the agricultural value chains than for those in the developed country sections of the same chain for which the US and northern European prices will be directly relevant.

Consider an intermediary who buys the commodity on a particular date, say 7 November, and who expects to hold this position for 14 days. He is vulnerable to adverse movements in the price over this two-week period. He can offset this exposure by selling a nearby futures contract in the commodity in question with the consequence that he is now long the commodity and short the future. Provided the commodity price in the origin country moves closely with the futures market price, any fall in price which would result in a loss in his physical position is offset by a corresponding gain on his futures position. On 21 November, when he sells the intermediated product, he buys back his futures position to close out the original hedge. This leaves him with zero net exposure.

The hedge quality (i.e., the extent to which the hedge does eliminate price exposure) depends on the correlation of changes in the local price and the futures price over this two-week period. If the correlation is unity, the price exposure is completely eliminated. In practice, hedge quality is always imperfect since the price at origin reflects local as well as global market conditions. The difference between the local price and the futures price is known as a "basis" and the risk associated with movements in this basis (i.e., the price relativity) is known as "basis risk". Once the correlation falls beneath around 0.8, basis risk becomes large and offsetting via futures contracts ceases to be highly effective. Box 13.2 provides illustrative figures for Tanzanian arabica coffee.

Basis risk is lowest for commodities which conform closely to the specification for delivery against the futures contract, and specifically for those that conform to the "cheapest to deliver" specification since this is the specification which the futures price will most closely reflect. Ivorian and Ugandan robusta have low basis risk relative to the Euronext-LIFFE robusta coffee contract, Ivorian cocoa has low basis risk against the Euronext-LIFFE cocoa contract and central American arabicas have low basis risk relative to the NYBOT arabica coffee contract. By contrast, the NYBOT arabica basis risk is less good for Kenyan and Tanzanian mild arabicas (see Box 13.2) and for Brazilian and Ethiopian unwashed arabicas. Similarly, West African cotton has a high basis risk relative to the NYBOT cotton contract.

Box 13.2   Coffee basis risk in Tanzania

Tanzanian arabica coffee is priced relative to the NYBOT Coffee "C" arabica price. Most coffees delivered against this contract are central American mild arabicas. The NYBOT price is therefore most appropriate for those coffees rather than Tanzanian coffee which is largely sold in Japan and northern Europe. This creates the potential for basis risk for Tanzanian intermediaries.

Tanzania requires coffee to be sold at auctions held in Moshi at the centre of the coffee producing area. "Segregation" requires that exporters can buy only at auction. Auctions are held weekly from September to April, with occasional gaps for holidays, and biweekly at the end of the season. Cooperatives and other intermediaries purchase coffee from farmers, transport it to Moshi and warehouse it there until auctioned. The consequence is that they bear a long price exposure for between two weeks and perhaps two months.

Basis risk can vary with coffee grade, holding period and also from one year to another. We look at basis risk for the major grades over the seasons 2001–02 to 2006–07 for holding periods of 2, 4, 6, 8, 10, and 12 weeks. We consider hedges which, when closed out (i.e., at the end of the holding period) will be in the second nearby contract. Basis risk was broadly constant over this six-year period. The correlation between NYBOT price changes and those in Moshi was generally highest for the six- and eight-week holding periods and for the A, B and PB (peaberry) grades which are also the most important in terms of volume, where it approached 0.8. It was lower for short holding periods and for the speciality AA and poorer quality C grades (in the range of 0.5–0.6). See Figure 13.2 which averages the six annual correlations for each grade and holding period. A basis correlation of 0.8 implies a 64 % variance reduction whereas a correlation of 0.5 reduced this to 25 %. The basis correlations therefore vary from acceptable to poor, and are stronger for the higher grades.

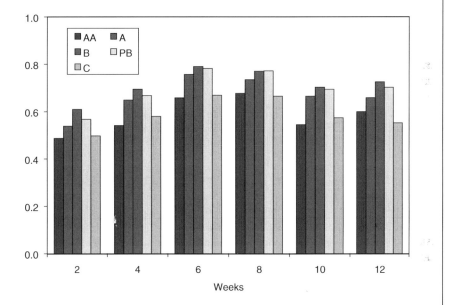

Figure 13.2   Six annual correlations for coffee grades and holding periods
Data sources: DfID (Tanzanian coffee prices), ICE (NYBOT "C" prices).
Based on work by Christopher Gilbert.

There must always be an element of judgment as to whether it is worthwhile for an intermediary to hedge. The vast majority of agents in developing country agricultural supply chains lacks basis price risk management knowledge and also often only have a weak understanding of the price risks to which they are exposed. It follows that they are often not well-equipped for implementing improved risk management approaches.

13.3.4   Developing country exchanges

Historically, the major agricultural futures markets have been concentrated in a small number of developed economies, of which Britain and the United States were the most important. Markets have also been active in Australia, Canada, France, Germany, Japan and the Netherlands. More recently, futures exchanges with agricultural contracts have been established in a number of liberalized developing and transition economies, including Brazil, China, Hungary, India, Indonesia, Malaysia, Poland, Singapore, South Africa and Turkey.

Viable futures trading in developing countries reduces basis risk and improves access for those actors in the supply chain located in the country in question. Developing country futures exchanges therefore have the potential to facilitate risk management in the developing world. UNCTAD has played a leading role in advising on these issues – see UNCTAD (2005a, b). However, at the same time, they can prove controversial when politicians find it convenient to attack futures market speculators for price changes which impact adversely in sections of the population, for example low coffee prices from 1999 to 2002 and the 2008 increases in food prices.

The most dramatic increases in agricultural futures changes that have taken place over the past decade are in China and India. It is probably not coincidental that these are the two countries with the largest domestic agricultural sectors. The majority of the active contracts in China and India are in products which are primarily consumed domestically rather than traded internationally. Neither country has enjoyed the same success in developing futures contracts for agricultural products which are already traded on a developed country exchange.

Successful futures trading requires liquidity. Unless markets can ensure liquidity, potential market participants will be reluctant to trade for fear of being unable to liquidate their positions except at substantial cost. This generates a classic "chicken and egg" problem. Further, if two or more exchanges compete for the same business, traders will generally opt for the exchange with the highest liquidity and hence the lowest spread. Exchanges compete for liquidity and it is difficult for an entrant to attract liquidity from a successful incumbent's contracts. This generates "first mover advantage". Taken to an extreme, it can imply the principle "one product, one contract".

In the case that a developing country exchange introduces a contract which competes with a contract on a developed country exchange, hedgers will compare the costs and benefits of hedging with the new contract relative to the existing contract. Market liquidity is a major determinant of the cost of hedging – the less liquid the market, the higher the likely spread and the more expensive it may be to close out a position. The new contract will have lower liquidity than the existing contract, at least initially, implying that choice of the new contract will raise costs. Against this, the new contract will be more appropriate, in terms either of product specification or of delivery location, for local and regional hedgers and so will have lower basis risk. Hedging with the new contract will therefore be associated with both higher costs and higher potential benefits than use of the existing contract. The balance between these two factors will determine whether the contract is attractive.

Examples of successful competition by developing country exchanges include the arabica coffee contract on the São Paulo exchange (the Brazilian Mercantile and Futures Exchange, BM&F), and the white maize contract on the Johannesburg exchange (the South African Futures Exchange, SAFEX). The BM&F arabica contract competes with the NYBOT contract which effectively defines the reference price for arabica coffee in world trade, while the SAFEX white maize contract competes with the CBOT corn contract which is the reference price for world maize. However, product specifications differ in important respects. NYBOT specifies delivery of washed arabica, suitable for mild coffees, while Brazil predominantly produces the more bitter unwashed arabica. Brazilian coffee therefore has a poor basis with respect to NYBOT. The SAFEX contract is for white maize while the CBOT contract is for yellow maize. Again, there is substantial basis risk, in this exacerbated by transport costs between North America and southern Africa, which can drive a significant wedge between prices in the two continents. Where basis risk is less serious, contracts in the same exchanges have performed less well (soybeans and sugar on the BM&F, yellow maize on SAFEX). Box 13.4 (Section 13.4.6) discusses a hedging application which makes use of the BM&F arabica coffee contract and Box 13.6 (Section 13.4.8) discusses use of the SAFEX white maize contracts for capping food security costs.

These examples show that futures exchanges in developing countries can play a significant role in facilitating risk management in developing country supply chains. However, they will do this only if they can change the benefits between the costs and benefits of hedging. The additional liquidity costs of trading a new contract, which gives existing developed country exchanges "first mover advantage", imply that developing country exchanges are likely to be successful in contracts for domestically consumed commodities and for those internationally traded commodities where basis risk on existing contracts is large.

13.4   PRICE RISK MANAGEMENT IN THE DEVELOPING COUNTRY SUPPLY CHAIN

First, in Section 13.4.1, we consider problems faced by developing country intermediaries. Then, in Sections 13.4.2–13.4.7, we consider the issues arising in intermediating risk management to farmers. Finally, in Section 13.4.8, we discuss risk management on the part of governments.

13.4.1   Developing country intermediaries

Exporters and consumer-importers have mirror-image problems. The exporter sells the commodity to the importer but, because of distance, the transaction takes time to complete. They face a choice between contracting at the price at the time of the transaction, at the time of delivery or at some intermediate date. Typically, the price will be fixed formulaically at the time of the transaction against the price of the relevant futures contract at the time of delivery.

To be concrete, consider the case of a Kampala (Uganda) exporter selling robusta coffee to an importer, a roasting company in Hamburg (Germany). It takes two months to transport the commodity from the Kampala railhead to Hamburg. In a back-to-back sale for his own account, the importer manages the price risk by contracting the purchase (from the exporter) and the sale (to his end consumer) at the same time. He offers the exporter a price based on the current futures market quotation for a month close after the expected delivery, e.g. March for a February delivery, plus a negotiated quality premium or discount. He then immediately contracts the sale of the processed coffee with a similar price basis, i.e. March futures price for a February delivery, plus a negotiated premium. The importer has eliminated his exposure but the exporter bears the price risk between the transaction date and the delivery date.

Large exporters or importers, in particular multinationals, will monitor a portfolio of transactions on a regular basis and will be able to quantify, to the dollar, the exact price exposure of the overall position. They will typically use futures markets to hedge only their net positions since they can benefit from internally offsetting long and short positions. Relative size is therefore one component in comparative advantage. A second component is access to finance, required for margin payments – in the event that the futures price rises, the short party will need to pay margin into the exchange to maintain his position. As discussed above in Section 13.3.2, this will be difficult for a small exporter located in a developing country.

These factors place developing country exporters, particularly small exporters, at a disadvantage relative to multinational exporters, or local companies affiliated to multinationals. At the time of the push for market liberalization, there was a widespread hope that national monopsony-monopoly exporters would be replaced by a competitive export sector. This has not happened. Instead, after an initial burst of competition, exporting has generally tended to become quite concentrated and to be dominated by multinationals. It was also imagined that cooperatives would be able to export directly. Again, this has proved difficult except in niche markets (such as those for organic produce) and in the concessional trade (such as "fair trade"). Locally-based traders naturally ask why they cannot be involved as principals in the export of their own crops. The answer is that, in the absence of financial institutions which can provide credit and finance risk management, liberalization has allowed local firms the right to compete but has failed to level the playing field such that they can compete effectively.

Stockholders have a long exposure, analogously with exporters, and can hedge in the same way. Once they have bought, or contracted to buy, the commodity, they sell futures. If the stockholder intends a long holding period, he will choose a distant future, subject to it being sufficiently liquid. By so doing, he has locked in the market "contango" – the difference between the long-dated futures and the cash price he has paid for his physical. When, eventually, he sells the inventory, he unwinds the futures position by purchasing the same contract. The complication is that, if he chooses to hold his physical position beyond the maturity date of his short futures contract, he will need to roll this position forward, buying back the future as it comes to maturity and selling a further longer-dated contract. If the contango increases, this will be profitable, but if it declines he will lose money. Management of "roll risk" provides opportunities for profitable trading and has the potential to reduce hedging costs. However, when roll risk is mismanaged, this can increase costs and reduce hedge effectiveness.

Commodity futures markets function well for the export and import trade – hardly surprising, since this was the function they evolved to serve. They also facilitate stockholding. As financial instruments, futures can in principle provide the same benefits to a developing country supply chain that they currently provide in developed economies. However, the consequence of uneven access is that they are instrumental in shifting the balance of advantage in commodity exporting towards multinationals and against locally based traders.

Other developing country intermediaries, such as traitants and transport companies, also have long exposure albeit over relatively short periods of time. In principle, they might also hedge their exposure. In practice, this proves difficult for reasons both of market access, discussed in Section 13.3.2, and because of basis risk, discussed in Section 13.3.3. Basis risk makes hedging less effective and access problems make it more difficult. The result is that the majority of developing country supply chain intermediaries generally manage their risk by minimizing holding times. This strategy is reasonably effective provided there are no sharp falls in prices. The strategy becomes dangerous if holding periods are long. This can happen if the intermediary undertakes substantial processing, as is the case with cotton ginners, if it is inefficient (true of many cooperatives) or if it decides to speculate, waiting on a possible price rise (also a common practice among cooperatives).

13.4.2   Farmers: risk management *versus* price stabilization

Farmers are always long the commodity. However, as discussed in Section 13.2.1, they have two distinct time horizons. The shorter horizon is the crop year. To commit inputs, they need to be assured of the price at harvest. The longer horizon relates to investment, either in trees (cocoa, coffee, etc.), in capital equipment or in cooperative facilities. The relative importance of these two horizons differs across commodities.

Hedging is, in principle, possible with respect to the shorter horizon but will never be effective in relation to the longer-term problem. One of the misconceptions of the liberalization agenda was that "market-based risk management" could substitute price stabilization – in fact the two approaches address price variability at different horizons. Importantly, stabilization does not eliminate, and may exacerbate, risk management problems. Marketing boards and like organizations hoped that, by stabilizing prices, they would be able to commit on harvest prices at the start of the crop year. That transferred the short-term price exposure from the farmers to the board. The risk still needed to be managed.

The distinction between price stabilization and price risk management is fundamental – see Gilbert (2007b). This is because the relative importance of the two activities differs across different agricultural commodities, and because, if both problems are to be addressed, it will in general be appropriate for this to be undertaken by different institutions. Risk management is concerned with locking in prices, and hence profits, at the time decisions are made while stabilization addresses the level of prices, and hence profits, that can be locked in. Put another way, risk management is a contracting activity while stabilization is an activity which relates to saving.

13.4.3   Intermediation via cooperatives

Even in the developed economies, very few farmers directly hedge using futures markets. In the developing countries, even fewer farmers are able to do this, even if they understand what it would be to hedge. This was always recognized by the advocates of market-based risk management, who looked for intermediaries which might function as "transmission mechanisms" – see ITF (1999). The analogy was to elevator companies in the North American grains sector which offer a variety of contractual price fixing arrangements to farmers. Once a farmer chooses to lock in a price, thereby passing the price exposure to the elevator company, the elevator, which benefits from aggregation and from superior access to credit, hedges the position on a net basis. Possible developing country transmission intermediaries include cooperatives, banks, and exporters.

Cooperatives have the size to aggregate. They buy the commodity from farmers and sell to exporters, perhaps after some processing. They may also export directly, but in many markets, they will lack the scale and specialized expertise to do this efficiently. They may also supply inputs to farmers at the start of the crop year, generally on a credit basis with repayment taken as a rebate on the eventual purchase price. In principle, cooperatives might sell the product forward or establish a short futures position enabling them to offer farmers a fixed price at the start of the crop year. This would give the farmers the security they require in deciding what quantities of inputs to purchase and how much labor time to supply.

This is a pure risk management activity and does not involve any element of stabilization. With storage, futures prices are only very slightly less variable than cash prices – see Newbery and Stiglitz (1981). In a year in which prices start low, a futures sale will lock the cooperative into this low price. The advantage that this gives is that farmers do not unwittingly purchase inputs which the sales price will not justify. However, they may well remain highly discontented with the price that has been fixed and doubt the wisdom of the forward or futures sale.

Similarly to other intermediaries in the commodity supply chain, developing country cooperatives lack the foreign currency credit to organize margin finance, but also because of regulatory concerns with regard to money laundering – see Section 13.3.2. If they are to hedge this must therefore be through purchase of puts. This will give them an approximate minimum price but not fix their price absolutely. The requirement to pay an up-front premium, often seen as a disadvantage of non-margined options relative to futures, forces cooperatives to put a value on price security. With futures sales, these costs only become explicit if there is a price rise during the course of the crop year.

The institutional structure of cooperatives allows them to manage minimum prices relatively easily by utilizing a two stage payment structure. The initial payment, guaranteed to the cooperative's members at the start of the crop year, is based on the minimum price locked in either through the purchase of the put, less the premium cost, or on the basis of fixed price forward sales contracted prior to the crop year. If, at harvest, the cooperative achieves a higher price than that promised at the start of the crop year, a second payment can be made. This structure is widespread in the cotton sector.

As discussed in Section 13.3.2, it is not feasible for developing country cooperatives to access international commodity futures markets. Few major banks and brokers are willing to invest in building up relationships with developing country cooperatives and to work with them to overcome regulatory hurdles. There are also practical problems at the level of the cooperatives themselves, particularly in Africa where cooperatives have often become inefficient and over-politicized. Many have proved insufficiently sophisticated from a financial and accounting standpoint to use financial markets. Democratic decision-making results in hedge quotes becoming stale, and cooperatives have not always been willing to delegate the power to contract. It has been observed that while cooperatives often welcome technical assistance and apparently benefit from the improved contracting that this generates, they have seldom been able to continue to manage risks with the same competence once the assistance in relation to programs terminate.

One should not be too negative about this experience: farmer cooperatives work well in certain regions of the world (the Netherlands and parts of northern Italy, for example) and less well in others. It is important to understand what leads to success and what inhibits it so that developing country cooperatives can be reinforced wherever circumstances are propitious. If this can happen, these cooperatives may yet be able to securely offer farmers some element of price guarantee at the start of the harvest year.

13.4.4 Intermediation via exporters

Exporters might in principle offer farmers or cooperatives fixed prices or minimum prices. They have an incentive to do this if the pre-announced prices increase output sufficiently such that the resulting increased revenue outweighs the costs of making these commitments.

Moreover, multinational exporters, or local exporters affiliated to multinationals, have the capacity to manage the credit and regulatory constraints that confront local organizations, such as cooperatives, in operating on international futures markets.

To some extent, exporters do operate in this way. The main practical limitation they face is that of contract enforcement. Where farmers have a choice of to whom they will deliver, fixed price contracts become free options – if the market offers a higher price than the contracted price, many will choose to deliver at most only a part of their output against the contract, whereas if the contracted price exceeds the market price, the exporter will find he obtains 100 % of the contracted output. The same logic makes it difficult for exporters to offer input credit financed through a rebate on the eventual purchase price – this simply gives an incentive to farmers to deliver to alternative purchasers, a common problem known as "side-selling".

Competition therefore undermines the ability and willingness of exporters to provide risk management services. The liberalization agenda failed to appreciate this difficulty. The consequence is that it is only in the relatively less liberalized markets that exporters are able to transmit risk management (i.e. guaranteed prices) to farmers. Coffee and cocoa both tend to be very competitive. Traitants and small traders tour round farming communities offering farmers multiple opportunities to sell and hence also to break previous contractual commitments. By contrast, the cotton sector, particularly in francophone Africa, has tended to preserve regional monopsonies reflecting the high fertilizer intensity of most cotton production and the costliness of transporting bulky unprocessed seed cotton over significant distances. In cotton, economic efficiency appears to be best served through a collaborative or symbiotic relationship between regional ginners (often cooperatives) and the farmers who supply them, even though this results in less competitive pressure. The same type of dependency arises in both the cane sugar and the palm oil industries. In these circumstances, exporters are in a position to offer price security without worrying to the same extent whether they will subsequently be undercut by competitors provided that they can manage the price risk that they thereby assume. Facilitation of risk management at the export stage allows the benefits of price security to be transmitted down the supply chain.

13.4.5 Intermediation via banks

Banks form a further set of potential candidates for intermediation of price risk management to farmers, either directly or via cooperatives, but only to the extent that they are active in the sector in question. This excludes many of the poorest countries of the world where banks have seen little profit in an (until recently) stagnant agricultural sector and have thus tended to eschew both the agricultural sector in general and lending to farmers and agricultural cooperatives in particular.

The potential for banking involvement arises from their concern to avoid default in loans to farmers or farm cooperatives. Such defaults are most likely in periods in which prices are low or, even if not low in absolute terms, have fallen during the course of the crop year. Two alternative strategies are available to banks. The first is to hedge their exposure directly by, for example, purchase of puts which pay off in precisely the circumstances that defaults become more likely. The second possibility is to gear the repayment terms on agricultural lending to the commodity price in question so that lower repayments are required if prices turn out to be poor. These lower repayments would need to be compensated by higher repayments in other circumstances, but the lower default risk may yet allow them to offer attractive loan contracts to borrowers. This mechanism would create price exposure for the bank, which would then need to hedge itself.

Box 13.3 illustrates intermediation of this sort in the context of Tanzanian cotton and coffee sectors. In the current more buoyant context, it is possible that there will be an increased appetite for agricultural lending, and these ideas may become more widely exploited. Box 13.4 discusses the innovative Brazilian *Cedula Produto Rural* instrument in which commercial bank financing for coffee exports is facilitated by the locally traded arabica coffee contract. This is an interesting model for other developing countries wishing to increase the availability of export finance.

Box 13.3   Risk management intermediation by a Tanzanian Agricultural Bank

CRDB Bank Ltd is one of two Tanzanian commercial banks with a significant role in coffee and cotton financing. In 2001, CRDB was faced with default issues in the coffee and cotton sector, both of which were experiencing exceptionally low prices. Rather than pulling out of these sectors, the bank chose to implement a collateral management program which would help it to exert tighter control on lending to these high risk sectors. The process begins when the client brings the goods to the certified warehouse or curing company. Once the collateral manager has evaluated the quality and the quantity of the product, it sends a report to the bank. The bank values the inventory based on then current market prices and advances 65 % of the cash value to the client.

This leaves CRDB Bank bearing a long price exposure. It can either hedge the overall portfolio to the coffee and cotton price by using risk management instruments to manage price volatility on its financing flows, or hedge its own exposure through that of individual clients by offering to act as a market intermediary in carrying out hedging transactions on behalf of borrowers. It chose the second option because it wished to expand services to agricultural borrowers and because it was concerned about adding on costs that were not entirely understood by customers and ran the risk of being perceived as "hidden".

CRDB Bank adopted the Swahili term "Kinga Ya Bei" (roughly translated as commodity price protection). The program was introduced at the annual borrower workshops for coffee and cotton in 2004. Since that time coffee prices have recovered and cotton is also somewhat higher. Attention has now shifted to currency risk. The bank continues to provide assistance to borrowers in the assessment of price risk throughout the season by helping them to analyze their positions against the market, assess break-even price levels and mark positions to market. Based on material provided by Erin Bryla, Julie Dana, Roy Parizat and Pauline Tiffen.

13.4.6   Insurance as an alternative?

From time to time, well-meaning commentators suggest that insurance might be a mechanism by which developing country farmers and intermediaries might manage agricultural price risk. In fact, insurance is ineffective in dealing with agricultural price risks although it can be used for weather risk.

Box 13.4   The Brazilian *Cedula Produto Rural*

The Cedula Produto Rural (CPR) is an innovative instrument designed for the agricultural sector. It is essentially a commodity-backed bond, issued by a farmer or cooperative and discounted by a bank. It is used extensively to finance coffee exports.

The CPR structure has three features:

- Stabilization: It guarantees farmers a minimum, local currency, cost-based price which varies only moderately from year to year.
- Risk management: It gives farmers protection against movements in prices and exchange rates over the course of the crop year.
- Finance: It provides producers with low cost finance at an early stage in the crop year.

There are four important sets of actors in the structure:

1. The Bolsa Brasiliera de Marcadorias (BBM) started out as a market for physical agricultural crop products. It has now evolved into an internet-based market for financial products for the agribusiness sector. It issues CPRs, organizes a secondary market in these instruments and is responsible for implementation of government minimum price policies. The CPR requires the farmer to deliver a specified quantity of coffee of specified minimum quality to one of a number of designated BBM warehouses by a specified date. The value of the CPR is the greater of the minimum price and the current BM&F futures price (at the delivery date), translated into local currency at the forward exchange rate.
2. Commercial banks discount CPRs from coffee farmers with good credit histories. This provides relatively low cost finance for the important coffee export business. The Banco do Brasil plays a dominant role in this provision. The Banco do Brasil is a public-private partnership in which government maintains a large influence and which has an extensive branch network in the coffee-producing areas.
3. Private investment institutions buy discounted CPRs on the BBM secondary markets. If the price is too low (i.e. the futures price is below the support price), the CPRs are retained by the Banco do Brasil which may therefore be seen as a market maker in CPRs.
4. The Brazilian Mercantile and Futures Exchange (BM&F) trades dollar-based futures contracts in arabica coffee and contracts on the Brazilian rais exchange rate. Importantly, the BM&F contract specifies delivery is to BBM warehouses, eliminating basis risk for institutions hedging CPRs on the BM&F. This increases the attractiveness of hedging on the BM&F relative to NYBOT, despite NYBOT's greater liquidity. When investment institutions buy CPRs, they typically take on an offsetting short position in BM&F futures and a long position in dollars.

In summary, the structure involves a government agency (the BBM), commercial banks of which one acts as a market maker, private sector investment institutions and a local futures market (the BM&F).
Based on work by Christopher Gilbert.

Economists tend to discuss the failure of insurance markets in terms of moral hazard (not locking your front door because you have full contents insurance) and adverse selection (couples who wish to purchase insurance against the birth of twins disproportionately have twins in their family histories). Neither of these issues arises with price insurance. Instead, there are two other problems. First, the entire supply chain experiences price falls at the same time, so there is no risk pooling. Second, the price distribution varies over time making it difficult to calculate probabilities on an actuarial basis.

Risk pooling arises when individual risks are largely uncorrelated across a population. The fact that one person dies from a heart attack does not change the risk for any of the other persons insured. In the absence of moral hazard and adverse selection, this lack of correlation allows the insurance company to rely on the Central Limit Theorem which states, loosely, that the average incidence of a particular problem in a given sample will tend, as the sample size increases, to be normally distributed with variance inversely proportional to the sample size. If probabilities remain constant over time, this fundamental result allows insurance companies to predict their average payout per policy with considerable accuracy even though they have no means of predicting the payout on a particular policy.

The Central Limit Theorem relies on independence. It fails when all or a large group of insureds suffer at the same time. An example is a disaster such as an earthquake in Los Angeles. A fall in a commodity price is similar – most agents in the supply chain have a long exposure and all of them will lose when prices fall. Lack of risk pooling makes insurance unattractive to the provider.

Non-constancy of probabilities makes it difficult for insurers to offer price insurance. Like many economic events, commodity price changes depend in a complicated way on history. Suppose we believe price changes to be log-normal, i.e. the changes in the logarithms of prices are normal. In the presence of a futures market for the commodity, statistical arbitrage will ensure that the futures price is a near unbiased estimate of the mean of the distribution. However, the variance of the distribution will depend on stock levels, on the price itself (governments often impose export restrictions when prices are high) and on the likely variability of production and consumption, which will also be time-varying. We might attempt to estimate these variances from the implied volatilities on options markets but, in agriculture, these are seldom sufficiently accurate to be reliable. If we cannot characterize the variance, estimation of tail probabilities (which is what will be insured) becomes impractical.

In practice, an insurance company wishing to offer price insurance would very probably choose to offset its position on an organized futures market. It is possible that this may be an efficient way to intermediate access to futures markets but, since insurance companies are currently absent from the agricultural supply chain, it is more likely that this will simply incur an additional level of costs. The two different markets – insurance and commodity futures markets – have different regulatory structures as well, and the regulatory implications make it difficult to offer products structured through some combination of the two.

Contrast price insurance with yield insurance, which is practical. Insurance companies will not offer insurance on the yield from a particular farm since this generates a clear incentive to the farmer to reduce effort (moral hazard). However, it is practical to offer insurance on the yield in a well-defined administrative area, if this can be measured, since an individual farmer will have a negligible impact on overall yield. Where yield variability arises from adverse weather conditions, one can define the payout in terms of the weather at a specified (secure) weather station, or in terms of an index over a number of such stations. Weather is generally fairly local, so insurance companies can pool across a range of geographically separate areas, and probabilities, even if not completely constant, tend to evolve slowly over time. Weather insurance is already extending from the developed to the developing world – see Box 13.5.

Box 13.5 Weather insurance in Malawi

Approximately 50 000 small-scale farmers in Malawi receive agricultural credit for purchasing seed, fertilizer or related agricultural inputs each year. While banks profess an interest in expanding agricultural credit to small-scale farmers, in practice agricultural loan portfolios are declining. A major reason is defaults arising out of crop loss through either inadequate rainfall or flooding.

Rainfall risk is endemic in Malawi. In 2004–05, the country experienced a devastating drought throwing 40 % of the smallholder population into dependence on food aid. Subsequent harvests have been better but in each year there have been pockets of drought in a few areas. Other areas have been affected by flooding.

An index-based weather insurance policy provides a means to offset the weather-related risks of providing credit to a farmer. The policy links possible insurance payouts with a rainfall index calibrated with the rainfall needs of the crop being insured. The main advantage of this index-based approach is that the payout is not based on the condition of the crop *per se*, but on the indisputable rainfall record. A limiting factor, however, is that it requires that farmers are situated close (in practice within 20 km) to a rainfall station with reliable communications and good historical data.

In 2005, the Insurance Association of Malawi (IAM) agreed to offer an index-based weather insurance policy, linked with credit supply, to small-scale farmers. Two banks agreed to offer the insurance backed loans to groundnut producers operating under the auspices of the National Association of Small Farmers of Malawi (NASFAM). The Malawi Meteorological Services Department agreed to provide daily historical rainfall data and daily data from the forthcoming rainfall seasons. Together with a rainfall-based groundnut crop model the historical data was used to design the index-based insurance contracts. The World Bank provided technical assistance in developing the rainfall index and contracts, drafting the index-based insurance policy, monitoring the pilot and brokering the full array of partnerships.

The index-based insurance contracts piloted so far in Malawi cover the value of the input loan, not the crop. If there is a drought, the insurance payout repays part or all of the costs of the loan. Insofar as the risks of loan default are reduced, the costs of credit should decline and banks should be willing to extend larger quantities of credit to more farmers. In 2007 and 2008 the program scaled up to include excess as well as deficit rainfall risk for tobacco, paprika, tea and coffee farmers working with several agribusinesses, contract farming companies and banks in Malawi.

Based on work by Erin Bryla, David Rohrbach and Joanna Syroka.

13.4.7 Risk-coping strategies

Developing country farmers have developed their own mechanisms to deal with hardships. It is useful to distinguish here between ex ante risk management strategies and ex post "risk coping" strategies. The most important ex ante strategy is income diversification, including crop diversification. Ex post strategies include borrowing, sale of assets, risk pooling through informal insurance arrangements between individuals and entire communities, increasing labor supply to the market and possibly even migration.

Risk management and risk coping strategies both impose costs. First consider ex ante risk management strategies. The challenges and preconditions for successful diversification programs have been thoroughly investigated (see, for example, Jaffee (1993) and Barghouti *et al.* (1990)). Poor households are inhibited from entering into riskier higher return activities because the downside risks are simply too great in the event of a crisis. Crop diversification increases security in the face of possible price and weather shocks but at the expense of allowing farmers to benefit from scale and specialization. The choice of safe but less profitable choices can result in negative long-term consequences (Morduch, 1994; Alderman and Paxson, 1994; Rosenzweig and Wolpin, 1993).

Turning to ex post risk coping strategies, richer households can borrow more easily in periods of low prices because they have assets that are available as collateral. If credit is not available, they can smooth their income by selling assets. In contrast, poorer households need to adopt low risk, low return strategies. Informal insurance arrangements appear effective in relation to demographic shocks, such as illness and death, but are less effective with price in coping with risks since low prices will impact all the farmers in a monoculture community. The problem of shock-induced inefficient choices can arise also with ex post strategies that deal with the consequences of shock; for example, requiring children to drop out of school or to work may have long-term consequences and be socially inefficient (de Janvry *et al.*, 2006). Sale of productive assets to maintain consumption may result in lower future incomes. Short run income maintenance may therefore be at the expense of longer-term well-being.

The fact that farmers are already diversified reduces their demand for more formal price risk management tools – effectively, they have already eliminated a large part of the price risk that market methods seek to address. However, if reliable price risk management tools were available to farmers at low cost, this would allow them to specialize, i.e., undiversify, since the price risk would now be sustainable. It follows that if successful intermediation does become possible, for example through strengthened cooperatives, one should expect the take-up to be gradual with farmers moving towards more specialized and larger scale production as the perceived familiarity of the market-based structures increases with use.

13.4.8 Governments

We saw in Section 13.2.4 that governments may have either a long or a short exposure depending on the crop, the tax system and the nature of the explicit and implicit commitments into which they have entered. First and foremost, it is important that governments make themselves aware of their exposure so as to avoid unpleasant surprises – there is always a tendency to hope that things work out and an unwillingness to confront problems until they become serious. Risk management is the antithesis of this approach.

In the case of tax revenues where the exposure is to export prices, governments have a long exposure which they can, in principle, hedge by selling futures. Governments are, of course, always subject to tax and expenditure shocks. They will normally retain a reserve to deal with these. Active risk management becomes necessary when the size of the shocks is large relative to other shocks and the size of the reserve. Typically, governmental exposure to export prices is not of this order of magnitude. In the event that they do decide to hedge, governments of poor countries may face many of the same difficulties in accessing futures as intermediaries in the local supply chain. In particular, they may find that credit issues oblige them to buy options rather than hedge with futures.

The short exposure arising out of commitments on staple food crops can give rise to more substantial exposure, in particular in the event that food prices spike up very sharply, as has happened in 2008. Government often finds itself offering a more or less explicit price cap. Traditionally, food security has tended to be underwritten by food reserves. However, this approach is costly in terms of the capital tied up in the reserve, deterioration and bureaucracy. Currently many governments are subsidizing the price of food staples for consumers. These policies are also costly, and may not be sustainable over time.

The alternative approach is to use financial risk management instruments. Prices caps of this sort are naturally hedged by purchase of out-of-the-money call options which, ignoring basis risk issues, pay off in exactly the circumstances that the government's guarantee is required. By purchasing a call, government is essentially asking the market to store on its behalf. This should result in savings if food shortages are imperfectly correlated across countries, so that the same stock can be available for the entire market, and if international markets can store more cheaply. Dana *et al.* (2006) discuss policies of this sort in relation to Malawi and Zambia.

The disadvantage of the market approach is that stocks are distant from the point of consumption and it will be expensive in terms of time and transport costs to bring them to the consumers. Transport facilities may be quite limited in landlocked countries, and ports may be congested in other countries. A large jump in transport requirements is likely to result in a corresponding jump in transport costs, which will not easily be hedged. Box 13.6 looks at a contingent food security import contract backed by an OTC call option which secured both the grain price and the transport facilities in order to ensure timely delivery of grain at a capped price. This approach to food security has enormous potential. If it had been widely implemented in 2007–08, many of the food price and availability problems currently afflicting poor food-importing countries could have been avoided at quite modest cost.

Box 13.6 Use of call options for contingent food security imports

In 2005–06, Southern Africa experienced a severe drought-related food shortage. Affected countries included Malawi, Mozambique, Zambia, and Zimbabwe. During a food shortage maize prices rise exacerbating the risk of hunger. In the past, governments have attempted to manage this problem by subsidizing the price of maize but such responses have a large cost both financially and in terms of negative impact on local and regional trade.

In June 2005, the Government of Malawi announced that it would take an innovative approach to management of the food shortage by using a SAFEX white maize put option contract. (SAFEX is the South Africa Exchange Market.) In response to a direct request from the Government, the World Bank provided technical assistance to support this operation.

Because the Government was concerned not only about price increases but also about logistics constraints and delivery performance, the call option contract was customized as an OTC contract which would give more flexibility than a standard financial instrument. First, price protection was provided on a delivered basis, thus combining the SAFEX price for white maize plus transport costs to Malawi. Second, the option contract carefully specified terms for physical settlement so that it could be used as a contingent import strategy if needed. Uncertainty about the extent of the food shortage, levels of commercial imports, transportation constraints, performance of local traders, the humanitarian response, and efficiency of procurement processes made the contingent import aspect of the contract very attractive to the Government.

In September 2005, the Government of Malawi concluded an agreement with a commercial bank to provide risk management using the OTC call option structure. The contract represented one of the first-ever instances of macro level hedging by an African government. It covered imports of 60 000 tons of white maize, had a total value of approximately $17 million, and a premium payment of $1.53 million. The UK development agency DfID provided budget support to the Government of Malawi for purchase of the contract.

Throughout November and December 2005, as prices increased and the food shortage grew more severe, the government exercised the call option, elected for physical settlement, and allocated the majority of the maize to humanitarian operations. The maize purchased through the option contract had a superior delivery performance to that of other procurement procedures. Over the delivery period spot prices rose $50–90/ton above the ceiling price of the contract following increases in the SAFEX white maize price and increases in transport costs.

Currently (2008) the Government of Malawi is evaluating proposals to replicate this approach. Since Malawi is facing a surplus year this year but is uncertain about exports, the idea is to create a second layer of strategic grain reserves held in the country, financed and managed by the private sector. The Government will have the option to buy stocks if needed during the lean season. If stocks are not needed in the country they will be exported by the private sector. This material is based on the work of Craig Baker, Julie Dana, Christopher Gilbert, and David Rohrbach.

Exposure to possible losses by stabilization agencies gives rise to a further set of issues. One approach is to argue that problems of this sort are inevitable with such agencies and that governments should therefore avoid stabilization commitments. This certainly solves the consequential risk management problems but, when this approach is advocated by developed country governments, it runs up against the problem of "coherence", since developed countries clearly do support their own agricultural sectors by offering high and stable prices. If developing countries are to follow the same approach, they need to structure stabilization schemes in terms of collective savings programs which would operate according to the principle that disbursements would be constrained by the level of accumulated savings from previous years. They should also examine the potential to hedge exposure of stabilization schemes. Hedged stabilization schemes are more likely to be financially sustainable than unhedged stabilization schemes. Box 13.7 discusses a recent proposal for the West and Central African cotton sector, set out in Rajadhyaksha *et al.* (2007), which goes in this direction.

Box 13.7   Cotton price stabilization and smoothing in West Africa

Cotton is the major (often only) export crop in the arid areas bordering the Sahara. Major producers are Benin, Burkina Faso, Chad, Cameroon, Côte d'Ivoire, Mali, and Togo (all francophone countries). Cotton is input intensive and bulky to transport prior to processing. The francophone countries have traditionally operated the sectors through parastatal monopsonies. They operated in the following way:

- Panterritorial producer prices were announced at the start of the crop year (around February). These were often kept constant over long periods of time or moved only modestly with changes in world prices.
- Ginners provided fertilizer to farmers' groups, the cost of which was deducted from eventual sales revenues.
- They also sold forward to customers, including prior to the announcement of the producer price, with volumes depending on market conditions.
- In the event of high prices, part of the revenue was paid into a *fond de soutien*. In the event of low prices, funds was transferred to the ginner from the *fond*.
- If the price outcome was good, farmers would also be due a second payment. This was paid as a supplement to the following year's producer price.

Cotton prices declined steadily over the 1990s. With producer prices slow to adapt and political pressure to maintain purchasing power, the *fonds de soutien* became exhausted. Refinancing was required if the system was to continue. Donors were unhappy with repeated calls for replenishment of the *fonds*. The French development agency *Agence Française de Developpement* (AFD) proposed that the EU should launch a pilot project based on a "new" concept of *fonds de lissage* (smoothing funds) which would start in 2007 to be piloted in Burkina Faso. In the end, the Burkinabe adopted their own variant of the smoothing scheme.

The structure proposed by AFD differed from the previous arrangements in the following ways:

- Producer prices would be set on a formulaic (and therefore non-political) basis based on prices over recent years (an exponentially smoothed average) and the contemporary forward price.
- Contributions to and support from the *fonds* would be determined formulaically.
- The *fonds* would aim to use market instruments (OTC puts) to ensure that ginners can offer a producer price above the level of production costs.
- The *fonds* would not aim to protect against catastrophically low prices. Instead, donors would be asked to step in if such events occur.
- The *fonds* would have low initial financing, but a regional *fond*, perhaps the West African Development Bank, would provide second level support for the national *fonds*.

The AFD objective was to smooth prices but not to stabilize at any absolute level. The suggestion that market instruments (effectively OTC puts) might be used to keep prices above production costs might be viewed as optimistic given liquidity in the OTC cotton options market and the substantial basis risk between West African cotton and NYBOT cotton prices, but is worth testing in the market. At the same time, price smoothing would not eliminate the requirement for ginners to manage residual intra-annual price exposure, not covered by likely payments from the *fonds*, arising out of their commitment to pay the agreed formulaic producer price. The extent of this residual exposure depends on when and how contributions from the *fonds* are decided and the extent to which the *fonds* can guarantee to compensate ginners for shortfalls in the price relative to that underlying the formulaic producer price.

13.5   CONCLUDING COMMENTS

The market approach to commodity price management was born as a response both to the difficulties encountered by international and national price stabilization schemes and to problems perceived to have arisen out of the liberalization of agricultural market supply chains, which was in part itself a response to those difficulties. Liberalization had the effect of increasing the extent and speed of pass-through. The effects of volatility amplification have been felt throughout the supply chain but, given that farmers are the residual claimants on commodity revenues, most acutely at the farmgate. This volatility generates risk management problems. Failure to address these problems can have serious consequences.

Different agents in the supply chain have evolved different responses to volatility. Intermediaries aim to hold the commodity for as short a time as possible to keep exposure to a minimum. Independent exporters often aim to market on a back-to-back basis. This eliminates price exposure at the cost of limiting the exporter's flexibility in marketing and can often force these exporters to sell at a disadvantage relative to multinational exporters. Cooperatives have been among those intermediaries which have coped least well with both the increases in competition and price volatility. Many lack the expertise to evaluate and manage their risks, a problem which is exacerbated by cumbersome decision-making processes which permit insufficient delegation for prompt response to market signals.

Supply chain actors located in developed countries offset commodity price risk using commodity futures. Access to these instruments is more difficult for actors located in developing countries. An adequate line of margin credit in a convertible currency is a prerequisite for taking futures positions on a developed country exchange. Many developing country intermediaries, including some governments, lack this credit. In such cases, they are restricted to non-margined options-based hedges with full up-front payment. While options are well suited to hedging certain types of exposure – out-of-the-money puts for cooperatives wishing to offer guaranteed minimum prices and out-of-the-money calls for governments (or their agencies) wishing to cap the prices of imported food staples – they are less suited to other types of exposure, in particular the need of intermediaries and exporters to lock in sale–purchase margins.

Access is further impaired by regulatory requirements, which have increased as the result of post 9/11 money laundering concerns, and which impose a high fixed cost on brokers wishing to do business with developing country entities. Often, the value of the business will be insufficient to justify these fixed costs. Finally, in some countries exchange regulations may actually prohibit use of financial instruments for hedging. Together, these credit and regulatory access problems give multinational supply chain actors, and their developing country affiliates, a clear competitive advantage relative to intermediaries located in the producing countries themselves. This is an important unintended consequence of market liberalization.

Finally, basis risk, resulting from imperfect pass-through of world to local prices, implies that in some cases hedging will deliver a lower degree of risk reduction to developing country supply chain actors than to those in the developed economies. The combination of poor access and sometimes only modest benefits has implied that, with important exceptions, developing country entities typically make only limited use of developed country risk management markets. This is particularly true of farmers, since efforts to transmit the favorable impacts of risk management to the farmgate face very considerable difficulties. The poorest farmers, and these include most of the African agricultural community, continue to rely on crop diversification together with informal family and community-based risk sharing mechanisms in the event of serious adverse shocks – what Dercon (2005) calls risk-coping behavior.

The consequence of access limitations varies from commodity to commodity. Farmers are concerned both about the possible intra-year variability of prices, in particular the possibility that the price may fall over the course of the crop year, and the absolute level of prices. The risk management tools discussed in this chapter deal with the former problem but not the latter – locking in a low export price, or a high food import price, eliminates uncertainty but does not impinge on the distress caused by a cyclically low price level. The intra-annual price risk problem is most serious for annual crops, where farmers must decide how much to plant, and for commodities which are highly input intensive, where farmers must decide how much input to purchase on credit. Cotton and maize are commodities which fall into this category. At the other extreme, tree crop commodities do not require annual decisions on planting and in many cases production requires only low levels of inputs (often insecticides to control disease). In this type of environment, although farmers would prefer price certainty, it is the level of the price that is their major concern. Issues of this sort are addressed through the stabilization or "price smoothing" agenda. Stabilization should be seen as a saving and dissaving activity and addressed as such. This is different from price risk management and may even exacerbate the risk management problem faced by supply chain intermediaries. To the extent that potential losses of stabilization authorities fall onto governments or donors, they compound these risk management problems.

Price risk management techniques have the potential to improve the functioning of the agricultural supply chain in developing economies. Many countries still lack expertise on market-based approaches to managing risk. An important first step, which is simple, is to apply modern financial techniques for identifying and quantifying risk, and monitoring price exposure throughout the course of the season. A second step is to establish the type of risk management monitoring and reporting functions which are standard to profitable commodity trading businesses and the banks that lend to them. The third step is managing price risk and, as we have seen, solutions will vary and will need to be highly customized to specific market conditions, which change. Finally, improved access to risk management instruments is necessary, and this in turn needs to be more appropriate to developing country requirements. The experience accumulated over the past two decades of liberalized markets in developing country export crops allows us to see the directions which are likely to generate the greatest returns.

Intermediaries based in many of the poorest countries, including much of Africa, will continue to experience difficulties for the foreseeable future. In a discussion of these issues some years ago one of us wrote that risk management and credit issues are inextricably intertwined: "My belief is that, in the context of developing-country farmers, commodity risk management techniques will, in the main, come to be seen as part of the means in which rural credit can be developed and extended, rather than as a stand alone panacea" (Gilbert, 2002, p. 67) That judgment remains valid and can be extended throughout the entire developing commodity country supply chains.

At the same time, it has become clear that market liberalization and privatization of parastatal operatives does not eliminate government exposure to price risk. This is acutely evident in the current (2008) food crisis. Price risk management becomes an important tool for governments who wish to avoid the adverse budgetary impact of interventions either to support export prices or cap import prices.

13.6   REFERENCES

Akiyama, T., J. Baffes, D. Larson and P. Varangis (2001). Market Reforms: Lessons from Country and Commodity Experiences. In: T. Akiyama, J. Baffes, D. Larson, and P. Varangis (Eds), *Commodity Market Reforms: Lessons from Two Decades*. Washington, D.C., World Bank.

Alderman, H. and C. Paxson (1994). Do the Poor Insure? A Synthesis of the Literature on Risk and Consumption in Developing Countries. In: E.L. Bacha (Ed.), *Economics in a Changing World*, Vol. 4, "Development, Trade, and Environment". London: Macmillan.

Barghouti, S., C. Timmer and P. Siegel (1990). Rural Diversification: Lessons from East Asia. Technical Paper #117, World Bank, Washington, D.C.

Bohman, M., L. Jarvis and R. Barichello (1996). Rent Seeking and International Commodity Agreements: The Case of Coffee. *Economic Development and Cultural Change* **44**, 379–404.

Claessens, S. and R.C. Duncan (1993) *Managing Commodity Price Risk in Developing Countries*. Baltimore: Johns Hopkins Press for the World Bank.

Collier, P. (2005). The Macroeconomic Consequences of Agricultural Shocks and their Implications for Insurance. In: S. Dercon (Ed.), *Insurance against Poverty*. Oxford: Oxford University Press for WIDER.

Dana, J., C.L. Gilbert and E. Shim (2006). Hedging Grain Price Risk in the SADC: Case Studies of Malawi and Zambia. *Food Policy* **31** (2006), 357–371.

de Janvry A., F. Finan and E. Sadoulet (2006). Can Conditional Cash Transfers Serve as Safety Nets to Keep Children at School and out of the Labor Market? *Journal of Development Economics* **79**, 349–373.

Dercon, S. (2005). Risk, Vulnerability and Poverty in Africa. *Journal of African Economies* **14**, 483–488.

Duryea, S., D. Lam and D. Levison (2007). Effects of Economic Shocks on Children's Employment and Schooling in Brazil. *Journal of Development Economics*. **84**, 188–214.

Gilbert, C.L. (1987). International Commodity Agreements: Design and Performance. *World Development* **15**, 591–616.

Gilbert, C.L. (1996). International Commodity Agreements: An Obituary Notice. *World Development* **24**, 1–19.

Gilbert, C.L. (2002). Commodity Risk Management: Preliminary Lessons from the International Task Force. In: R. Garnault (Ed.), *Resource Management in Asia Pacific Developing Countries*. (Essays in Honor of Ron Duncan), Canberra; Asia Pacific Press.

Gilbert, C.L. (2007a). Value Chain Analysis and Market Power in Commodity Processing with Application to the Cocoa and Coffee Sectors. FAO *Commodity and Trade Proceedings* **2**, *Governance, Coordination and Distribution along Commodity Value Chains*, 267–297.

Gilbert, C.L. (2007b). Prix des Matières Premières: Gestion des Risques *versus* Stabilization. In: J.M. Boussard and H. Delorme (Eds), *La Régulation des Marchés Agricoles Internationaux*. Paris, L'Harmattan.

Gilbert, C.L. and P. Varangis (2004). Globalization and International Commodity Trade with Specific Reference to the West African Cocoa Producers. In: R.E. Baldwin and L.A. Winters (Eds), *Challenges to Globalization*. Chicago: University of Chicago Press (for the National Bureau of Economic Research).

ITF (International Task Force on Commodity Risk Management in Developing Countries) (1999). *Dealing with Commodity Price Volatility in Developing Countries: A Proposal for a Market-Based Approach*. Washington, D.C., World Bank.

Jaffee, S. (1993). *Exporting High-Value Food Commodities: Success Stories from Developing Countries*. World Bank Discussion Paper #198, Washington, D.C.

Knudsen, O. and J. Nash (1990). Domestic Price Stabilization Schemes in Developing Countries. *Economic Development and Cultural Change* **38**, 539–558.

Morduch, J. (1994). Poverty and Vulnerability. *American Economic Review* **84**, 221–225.

Newbery, D.M.G. and J.E. Stiglitz (1981). *The Theory of Commodity Price Stabilization*. Oxford: Clarendon Press.

Raddatz, C.E. (2005). Are External Shocks Responsible for the Instability of Output in Low-income Countries? *Policy Research Working Paper* **3680**, Washington, D.C., World Bank.

Rajadhyaksha, G.S., J. Baffes, S. Mink and L. Goreux (2007). Burkina Faso: Analyse du Fond de Lissage des Prix du Coton. Washington D.C., World Bank.

Rosenzweig, M.R. and K.I. Wolpin (1993). Credit Market Constraints, Consumption Smoothing, and the Accumulation of Durable Production Assets in Low-income Countries: Investments in Bullocks in India. *Journal of Political Economy* **101**, 223–244.

UNCTAD (2005a). *Overview of the World's Commodity Exchanges, 2004*. UNCTAD/DITC/COM/ 2005/8, Geneva, UNCTAD.

UNCTAD (2005b). *Progress in the Development of African Commodity Exchanges*. UNCTAD/DITC/ COM/2005/9, Geneva, UNCTAD.

14

Gaining Exposure to Emerging Markets in Institutional Portfolios: The Role of Commodities

George A. Martin and Richard Spurgin

14.1 INTRODUCTION

Two significant investment themes in the past decade have been the growing importance of physical commodities in the workings of the global economy (hereafter, the "Commodity" theme), and the increasing importance of "developing" nations such as Brazil, Russia, China and India as sources of economic growth and poles of wealth accumulation (the "Emerging Markets" or "EM" theme). Because these and other developing countries are either major exporters of commodities such as oil, or primary sources of demand for physical commodities for domestic consumption or inputs in export production, it is not surprising that these two investment themes are linked. However, outside of these casual observations, there is relatively little research that explores the possible linkages between these two investment themes.

This chapter sets out to explore some of those possible linkages, and correspondingly the extent to which investments in commodity assets and emerging-markets assets are overlapping bets on the same or similar economic trends. Our goal is to offer plan sponsors and other long-term institutional investors information that could be useful elements for the efficient formulation of investment strategy. A question of particular interest is whether a well-designed portfolio of EM investments can replace the role of commodities in a diversified portfolio. Alternatively, it may be that a well-designed commodity portfolio makes EM investments redundant. Neither of these hypotheses is supported by the empirical data, however. Instead, we find that commodity and emerging-markets investments are interrelated, but are not redundant.

14.2 ASSET MARKETS AND ECONOMIC GROWTH

One way to visualize the significance of both the EM and Commodity themes on a standalone basis is simply to view the returns to long-only investments in these asset classes

George Martin: Alternative Investment Analytics LLC and CISDM, University of Massachusetts at Amherst.
Richard Spurgin: Clark University and Alternative Investment Analytics LLC.
Contact: Alternative Investment Analytics, LLC, 29 S. Pleasant St., Amherst, MA 01002. P: 413-253-4601. E: [lastname][at]alternativeanalytics.com

Risk Management in Commodity Markets: From Shipping to Agriculturals and Energy   Edited by Hélyette Geman
© 2008 John Wiley & Sons, Ltd

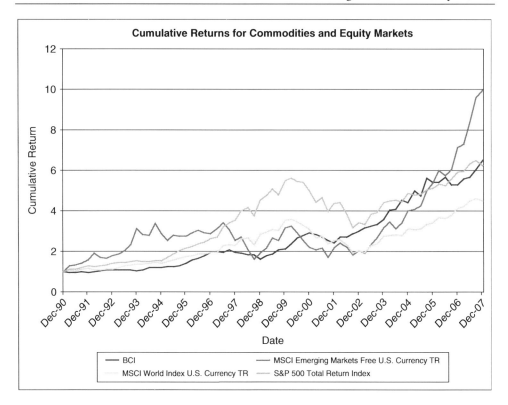

Figure 14.1   Cumulative returns for commodities and equity markets
Source of data: Bloomberg.

(see Fig. 14.1). Here we use the Bache Commodity Index[1] (BCI) as a proxy for commodity returns, MSCI Emerging Markets and MSCI World equity indices for international exposure, and the S&P 500 index for US exposure. We can see that since 1990, both emerging-markets equities and commodities have outperformed US and global equities. This performance has been much more pronounced since 2000.

Coincident with the performance of emerging-markets equities has been the accelerating growth rates in emerging-markets economies, particularly when compared against the less-dynamic growth rates of advanced economies. Figure 14.2 shows that, prior to 2000, global growth rates were relatively similar and synchronized. Since 2000, there has been substantial change in the level of certain individual growth rates, but still some synchronization.

We can see that this growth has not been evenly distributed across sectors of emerging-markets economies, particularly export-oriented sectors that provide cycles of reinvestment and wealth accumulation. Two charts demonstrate this (see Figs 14.3 and 14.4) in absolute terms by plotting the percentage of world exports made up of exports from the reporting country. For China, most growth has come in the manufacturing sector ("MA"); while in Russia, most growth has come from the export of fuels and minerals ("MI"). We can also

[1] See further public information and research regarding the Bache Commodity Index at www.alternativeanalytics.com. Returns and other information are available via Bloomberg.

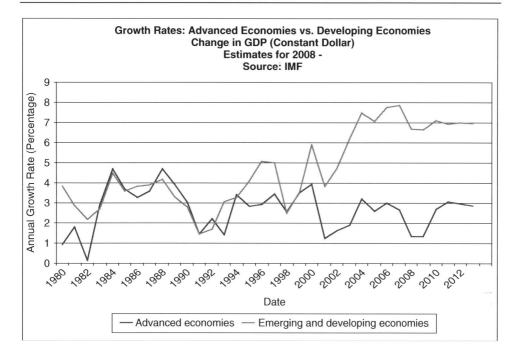

Figure 14.2   Growth rates: advanced economies vs. developing economies
Source of data: International Monetary Fund.

Table 14.1   Export growth by sector

Export Growth by Sector

Country	Sector	Increase 2000–2006
Brazil	Agricultural products	156 %
Brazil	Fuels and mining products	307 %
Brazil	Manufactures	115 %
China	Agricultural products	99 %
China	Fuels and mining products	210 %
China	Manufactures	307 %
India	Agricultural products	125 %
India	Fuels and mining products	638 %
India	Manufactures	142 %
Russian Federation	Agricultural products	120 %
Russian Federation	Fuels and mining products	193 %
Russian Federation	Manufactures	137 %
World	Agricultural products	71 %
World	Fuels and mining products	163 %
World	Manufactures	76 %

Source of data: World Trade Organization.

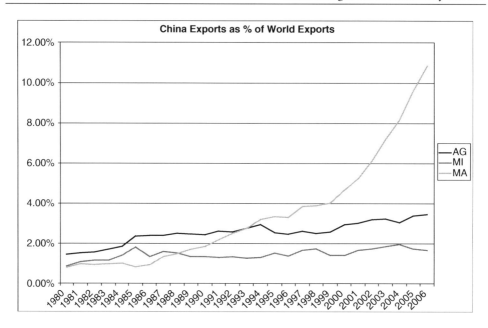

Figure 14.3   China exports as percentage of world exports
Source of data: World Trade Organization.

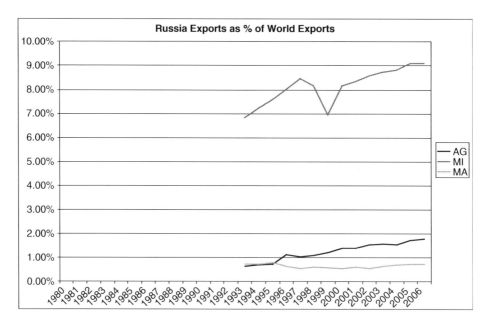

Figure 14.4   Russia exports as percentage of world exports
Source of data: World Trade Organization.

see this in relative terms in Table 14.1, which gives the percentage increase in sector exports over the period 2000–2006.[2]

As we can see from Table 14.2, coincident with the recent growth of emerging-markets economies has been the current boom in commodity prices. However, the commodity-price boom has been:

1. Far more broad-based: Fuels, metals and agricultural products are simultaneously in "boom" phase, which is rare;
2. Longer in duration: Typical booms last 20–24 months, whereas almost all commodities have been booming for 36 months or more;

Table 14.2 Properties of commodity price booms 1960–2007
Source: IMF (2008)

Properties of Commodity Price Booms 1960–2007 (IMF 2008)

	Current phase	Latest turning point[2]		From latest turning point	Average of past booms	From latest turning point	Average of past booms[4]	Synchroni-zation with industrial production[5]
				Price Changes (percent)		Duration (months)		
Crude oil (IMF APSP)[6]	Boom	December-01	T	210.1	54.0	73	18	0.189***
Metals	Boom	March-03	T	104.8	43.0	58	22	0.236***
Aluminum	Boom	April-03	T	29	41.0	57	22	0.025
Copper	Boom	October-01	T	212.5	61.0	75	21	0.259***
Nickel	Boom	October-05	T	74.9	84.0	19	29	0.301***
Food	Boom	November-04	T	30.4	21.0	38	18	0.103
Maize (corn)	Boom	November-04	T	62.2	39.0	38	19	−0.139
Wheat	Boom	April-05	T	124.1	38.0	32	20	−0.103
Soybeans	Boom	January-05	T	83.9	42.0	36	18	0.11
Palm oil	Boom	January-05	T	116.8	61.0	36	20	−0.015
Soybean oil	Boom	January-05	T	100.9	50.0	36	18	0.066
Beef	Slump	September-04	P	−25.1	35.0	...	20	0.091
Beverages	Slump	February-06	P	0.0	47.0	...	19	0.109
Agricultural Raw Materials	Boom	December-04	T	2.2	28.0	37	20	0.128
Rubber	Boom	January-05	T	77.2	56.0	36	21	0.07

Source of data: International Monetary Fund.
Sources of Table and Notes: IMF commodity price database; and current IMF staff calculations.
[1]See text for details.
[2]T stands for trough, P for peak.
[3]Average price increase during past booms (excluding the current boom).
[4]Average duration of past booms (excluding the current boom).
[5]Coefficient of a regression of the cyclical state in the commodity price on the cyclical state in global industrial production (see Harding and Pagan, 2006, for details); ***denotes significance at the 1 percent level.
[6]IMF average petroleum spot price.

---

[2] All quantities are authors' calculations based on WTO data.

3. Greater in magnitude than previous commodity booms: Current price appreciation has been 100 % or more for many assets, compared to an average price appreciation of 40 % from previous booms; and,
4. Synchronized with global industrial production.[3]

From the above information, we can see that certain emerging-markets countries have a substantial exposure to commodity markets, and that fuel and mineral producers especially have been in a position to generate substantial capital inflows. We also raise the possibility that larger emerging-markets economies that concentrate on international manufacturing and/or domestic consumption growth may actually have negative exposure to international commodity markets. The question is: To what extent are emerging-markets asset prices integrated with international commodity prices?

14.3   ARE EMERGING MARKETS EQUITY MARKETS AND COMMODITY MARKETS INTEGRATED?

An initial look at the correlation between the BCI and MSCI country indices for Brazil, China, India and Russia, as well as EM and the world (Table 14.3), indicates that for the period 1995–2007, the correlation between commodity markets and equity indices has been uniformly near zero. Correspondingly, the correlation of equity markets has been relatively high across diverse indices.

We can take a more granular look at the correlation structure of these markets with commodity prices through correlations estimated over a rolling 5-year window (Fig. 14.5).

Interestingly, we see that correlations with commodity markets for all countries, save India, rose substantially from the beginning of the latest commodity boom. However, since the first quarter of 2006, those correlations have diverged, with commodity-exporting economies like Brazil and Russia maintaining or elevating their positive relationships with commodity prices, and the commodity-importing economies of China and India experiencing substantial declines in their correlation. Not surprisingly, our broad-based index of

Table 14.3   Correlation of quarterly returns 1995–2007

Correlation of Quarterly Returns

	RUSSIA	MSCIW	INDIA	EM_E01	CHINA	BRAZIL	BCI
RUSSIA	100 %	43 %	39 %	61 %	24 %	55 %	7 %
MSCIW	43 %	100 %	50 %	73 %	40 %	68 %	−11 %
INDIA	39 %	50 %	100 %	74 %	43 %	69 %	12 %
EM_E01	61 %	73 %	74 %	100 %	63 %	84 %	7 %
CHINA	24 %	40 %	43 %	63 %	100 %	48 %	12 %
BRAZIL	55 %	68 %	69 %	84 %	48 %	100 %	17 %
BCI	7 %	−11 %	12 %	7 %	12 %	17 %	100 %

common sample 1995–2007

Source of data: Bloomberg.

---

[3] IMF (2008).

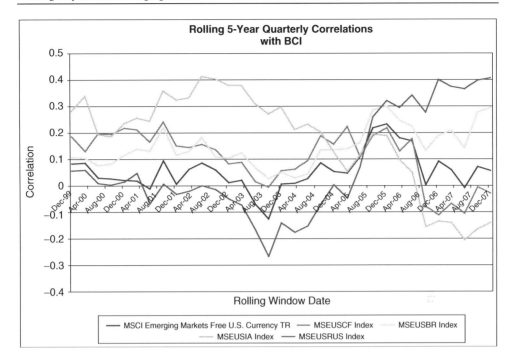

Figure 14.5   Rolling 5–year quarterly correlations with BCI
Source of data: Bloomberg.

EM equities as a partial average of our individual equity indices has become relatively uncorrelated.

To further examine the importance of equity-market factors and commodity-market factors, we conduct a principal components analysis of returns, 1995–2007 (Table 14.4).

From the principal components analysis, we can see that the bulk of contemporaneous-return variation (55%) is explained by a common equity-market factor, while a commodity-market factor explains roughly 15% of total return variation.

However, given the nature of market dynamics, one might be dissatisfied with analyses, like correlation and principal components, that assume that all interrelationships between asset markets are contemporaneous. Rather, given that we are investigating longer-horizon interactions, we can and should be concerned with lead-lag type relationships. We begin by testing whether commodities, as proxied by the BCI, are "co-integrated" with the emerging-markets equities, as proxied by the MSCI EM index. Co-integration between economic quantities suggests that there is a long-run equilibrium relationship, such that short-term departures from that relationship tend to induce mean-reversion back to that equilibrium.

As indicated in Table 14.5, standard test statistics for the presence of co-integration indicate that there is no long-run equilibrium relationship between commodity *returns* and equity market *returns;* nor is there a relationship between commodity price *levels* and equity market *levels*.

Lack of co-integration, however, does not mean that there are not lead-lag relationships in variables. We can evaluate the range of possible linear lead-lag relationships using a very

Table 14.4 Principal components analysis of returns 1995–2007

	BCI	BRAZIL	CHINA	EM_E01	MSCIW	INDIA	RUSSIA
Mean	3.5 %	5.1 %	2.2 %	3.2 %	2.5 %	4.1 %	11.8 %
Median	3.6 %	4.8 %	−0.4 %	4.2 %	2.7 %	6.4 %	5.9 %
Maximum	18.3 %	53.9 %	80.7 %	26.6 %	21.1 %	31.3 %	171.4 %
Minimum	−10.7 %	−39.4 %	−35.2 %	−23.6 %	−18.4 %	−21.8 %	−75.2 %
Std.Dev.	6.3 %	19.5 %	20.2 %	12.8 %	7.8 %	15.0 %	39.1 %
Skewness	0.036	−0.079	1.093	−0.239	−0.204	−0.017	1.448
Kurtosis	2.442	2.980	6.080	2.330	3.646	1.727	7.602
Jarque-Bera	0.685	0.055	30.912	1.468	1.265	3.512	64.048
Probability	0.710	0.973	0.000	0.480	0.531	0.173	0.000

	Comp 1	Comp 2	Comp 3	Comp 4	Comp 5	Comp 6	Comp 7
Eigenvalue	3.8707	1.0689	0.7628	0.5432	0.4409	0.2126	0.1008
Variance Prop.	0.5530	0.1527	0.1090	0.0776	0.0630	0.0304	0.0144
Cumulative Prop.	0.5530	0.7057	0.8146	0.8922	0.9552	0.9856	1.0000

Eigenvectors:	Vector 1	Vector 2	Vector 3	Vector 4	Vector 5	Vector 6	Vector 7
BCI	0.0634	−0.9316	−0.1398	0.0661	0.2768	0.1638	−0.0287
BRAZIL	0.4590	−0.0549	−0.0932	0.1989	0.1223	−0.8112	0.2550
CHINA	0.3308	−0.1464	0.6992	−0.5621	−0.0810	0.0411	0.2367
EM_E01	0.4874	0.0395	0.0406	−0.0364	−0.0290	−0.0183	−0.8699
MSCIW	0.3991	0.3157	0.0037	0.1693	0.7078	0.4147	0.1987
INDIA	0.4059	−0.0677	0.0789	0.5565	−0.5928	0.3406	0.2174
RUSSIA	0.3380	0.0441	−0.6892	−0.5481	−0.2206	0.1584	0.1862

Source of data: Bloomberg.

general, but standard, unrestricted Vector Autoregression (VAR) model, which is a standard tool of macroeconomists.[4] In essence, in a VAR model, each return series is modeled as a function of lagged realizations of itself and all other series in the model. In Table 14.6, for reasons of space, we only present t-statistics for each parameter in the VAR, estimated on commodities and equity indices. Our models for the behavior of China equities, commodities, and EM equities, respectively are the most significant.

Using the VAR, we can test if there are any lead-lag relationships between equity markets and commodities. Specifically, we use a Granger causality test (Table 14.7) to test the null hypothesis of no Granger causality.[5] The results indicate that emerging-markets equity prices *lead* commodity prices, as well as exhibit contemporaneous correlation, and that this effect has increased over time when comparing the period of 1995–2007 versus 1999–2007. We can visualize this relationship via the "impulse response function" of our VAR model, which tells us how a shock to one variable influences other variables through time, all other things held constant. From the impulse response analysis, we can see that shocks

---

[4] See, for example, Hamilton (1994) or Lutkepohl (2005).
[5] A Granger causality test is designed to identify those variables which "lead" others in time, by determining the extent to which one variable or variables can forecast another. Specifically, we calculate the Wald statistic associated with a test of exogeneity of BCI.

Table 14.5 Unrestricted cointegration rank tests

Unrestricted Cointegration Rank Test					Unrestricted Cointegration Rank Test				
in RETURNS					*in LEVELS*				
Hypothesized No. of CE(s)	Eigenvalue	Trace Statistic	5 Percent Critical Value	1 Percent Critical Value	Hypothesized No. of CE(s)	Eigenvalue	Trace Statistic	5 Percent Critical Value	1 Percent Critical Value
None	0.201436	11.6971	15.41	20.04	None	0.188763	10.881	15.41	20.04
At most 1	2.48E-06	0.00013	3.76	6.65	At most 1	6.03E-05	0.0031	3.76	6.65

*(**) denotes rejection of the hypothesis at the 5 %(1 %) level

Trace test indicates no cointegration at both 5 % and 1 % levels

*(**) denotes rejection of the hypothesis at the 5 %(1 %) level

Trace test indicates no cointegration at both 5 % and 1 % levels

Hypothesized No. of CE(s)	Eigenvalue	Max-Eigen Statistic	5 Percent Critical Value	1 Percent Critical Value	Hypothesized No. of CE(s)	Eigenvalue	Max-Eigen Statistic	5 Percent Critical Value	1 Percent Critical Value
None	0.201436	11.6969	14.07	18.63	None	0.188763	10.878	14.07	18.63
At most 1	2.48E-06	0.00013	3.76	6.65	At most 1	6.03E-05	0.0031	3.76	6.65

*(**) denotes rejection of the hypothesis at the 5 %(1 %) level

Max-eigenvalue test indicates no cointegration at both 5 % and 1 % levels

*(**) denotes rejection of the hypothesis at the 5 %(1 %) level

Max-eigenvalue test indicates no cointegration at both 5 % and 1 % levels

Source of data: Bloomberg.

coming from emerging-markets equities to commodities decay slower than the other way around (Table 14.8). We can see that commodity prices are positively led by global and emerging-markets equities.

The result that commodity prices lag, rather than lead, emerging-markets equity prices suggests that the typical narratives about the role of increased commodity prices in explaining the process of wealth creation and re-investment in emerging economies demand reconsideration.[6]

14.4 IMPLICATIONS FOR THE INVESTMENT POLICY OF INSTITUTIONAL INVESTORS

The above analysis has suggested that there is a strong, but somewhat complicated, interrelationship between commodity prices and the performance of emerging-markets equities and that, while there is some relationship between a "bet" on commodities and a "bet" on emerging markets, these investments are not completely correlated. In this section, we review results relevant to portfolio construction programs that wish to incorporate commodity

---

[6] For example, IMF (2008), which argues that sustained elevation in commodity prices has had a substantially positive follow impact on trade, development and institutional reform. Our result does not stand directly at odds with this general hypothesis, though for it to be directly valid one would like to see commodity prices lead domestic equity prices, which are most sensitive to trade, currency, financial and other local factors that are explored by the study.

Table 14.6 Vector autoregression estimates

Vector Autoregression Estimates
Sample(adjusted): 1996:1 2007:4
Included observations: 48 after adjusting endpoints

	RUSSIA	MSCIW	INDIA	EM_E01	CHINA	BRAZIL	BCI
RUSSIA(−1)	[−0.25203]	[−0.99818]	[−1.07173]	[−1.07075]	[0.13259]	[−0.76950]	[−0.87993]
RUSSIA(−2)	[−0.53676]	[0.57680]	[−0.69550]	[−0.59491]	[0.95896]	[0.26245]	[0.68973]
RUSSIA(−3)	[−0.14748]	[0.57113]	[−0.77215]	[−0.12315]	[−1.37977]	[0.10778]	[−0.05793]
RUSSIA(−4)	[−0.33697]	[−1.29685]	[−1.72954]	[−3.23495]	[−2.87226]	[−2.33906]	[−1.55985]
MSCIW(−1)	[−0.47616]	[−0.77532]	[0.07787]	[−1.18120]	[−2.12734]	[−0.49040]	[1.25373]
MSCIW(−2)	[1.25573]	[2.09964]	[2.43912]	[2.56460]	[2.95600]	[2.10609]	[1.13138]
MSCIW(−3)	[−0.06295]	[0.84658]	[0.03851]	[0.69380]	[−0.05506]	[0.14881]	[0.86545]
MSCIW(−4)	[−0.08031]	[−0.65844]	[−1.50482]	[−1.43103]	[−0.05925]	[−1.13446]	[−1.45894]
INDIA(−1)	[0.63021]	[0.51296]	[−1.84587]	[−0.20966]	[−0.13260]	[−0.09969]	[−1.19275]
INDIA(−2)	[−0.67777]	[0.13562]	[−1.95518]	[−1.61632]	[−2.43375]	[−1.48963]	[−0.64176]
INDIA(−3)	[−0.34379]	[0.14314]	[−1.23821]	[−0.01301]	[0.76054]	[−0.38334]	[−1.43971]
INDIA(−4)	[−1.46765]	[0.41897]	[0.21631]	[0.53082]	[−0.06769]	[0.31833]	[−1.30741]
EM_E01(−1)	[−0.03970]	[1.18532]	[1.75113]	[1.76878]	[1.24269]	[1.00609]	[1.19396]
EM_E01(−2)	[−0.08296]	[−2.20731]	[−0.22482]	[−1.09084]	[−0.42422]	[−0.65763]	[0.94614]
EM_E01(−3)	[−0.43749]	[0.01365]	[1.02719]	[0.14636]	[−0.49544]	[0.25645]	[1.51263]
EM_E01(−4)	[1.20331]	[0.22412]	[1.10277]	[1.35535]	[1.49227]	[1.35275]	[1.53177]
CHINA(−1)	[0.61475]	[−1.00122]	[0.03037]	[−0.99558]	[−0.24372]	[−0.36484]	[−0.92809]
CHINA(−2)	[0.74183]	[2.35318]	[2.74070]	[3.44134]	[1.22546]	[3.17751]	[−0.30544]
CHINA(−3)	[0.35939]	[−0.28988]	[0.22714]	[0.10653]	[0.07522]	[0.03953]	[−1.24655]
CHINA(−4)	[−0.31207]	[−0.06649]	[0.06270]	[−0.50618]	[−0.79587]	[0.19555]	[−0.07674]
BRAZIL(−1)	[0.11695]	[0.06793]	[−0.08750]	[0.31151]	[1.22164]	[0.06372]	[0.08009]
BRAZIL(−2)	[−1.23670]	[0.31541]	[−0.90434]	[−0.47034]	[−0.01258]	[−1.19610]	[−1.35461]
BRAZIL(−3)	[0.66024]	[−0.93729]	[−0.80106]	[−1.00648]	[0.68892]	[−0.46175]	[−1.60985]
BRAZIL(−4)	[−0.97593]	[−0.00067]	[−0.26966]	[−0.82307]	[−1.35807]	[−0.78398]	[0.06490]
BCI(−1)	[0.08673]	[−0.52262]	[−0.74051]	[−0.82998]	[−1.32172]	[−0.79259]	[−0.82524]
BCI(−2)	[0.90018]	[0.20053]	[0.53242]	[0.04195]	[−0.13014]	[0.75655]	[2.00155]
BCI(−3)	[−0.09361]	[0.81853]	[0.45808]	[0.76949]	[−0.45320]	[1.05477]	[1.30771]
BCI(−4)	[0.28542]	[−0.19905]	[0.15695]	[0.45403]	[0.93776]	[0.49513]	[−0.94291]
C	[0.94364]	[0.79645]	[2.16623]	[2.20874]	[1.33324]	[1.25422]	[1.17175]
R-squared	0.410275	0.514539	0.593268	0.684149	0.747709	0.624671	0.693042
Adj. R-squared	−0.45879	−0.20088	−0.00613	0.218684	0.375912	0.071555	0.240683
F-statistic	0.472086	0.719216	0.989778	1.469819	2.011068	1.129367	1.532061
Akaike AIC	1.643816	−1.7163	−0.66849	−1.19035	−0.4949	−0.2442	−2.61784

Source of data: Bloomberg.

Table 14.7 Granger causality tests

Granger Causality Test Dependent variable BCI 1999–2007				Granger Causality Test Dependent variable BCI 1995–2007			
Exclude	Chi-sq	df	Prob.	Exclude	Chi-sq	df	Prob.
BRAZIL	14.11095	4	0.0069	RUSSIA	3.093971	4	0.5422
CHINA	8.136453	4	0.0867	MSCIW	5.198797	4	0.2675
EM_E01	0.875533	4	0.928	INDIA	3.588944	4	0.4645
INDIA	3.983581	4	0.4082	EM_E01	7.536969	4	0.1101
RUSSIA	2.769229	4	0.5972	CHINA	2.246107	4	0.6906
MSCIW	12.37687	4	0.0148	BRAZIL	4.68206	4	0.3215
All	52.87	24	0.0006	All	30.59286	24	0.1659

Source of data: Bloomberg.

Table 14.8 Response to nonfactorized one unit innovations ±2 S.E.

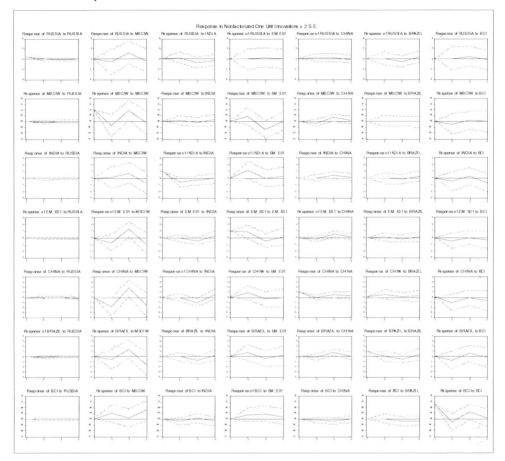

Source of data: Bloomberg.

assets into the same general bucket as emerging markets. In brief, we have seen that commodity prices are related to emerging-markets equity markets, that those correlations are time-varying and, because of lag relationship with emerging-markets equities, have some element of time diversification when compared to the risk associated with immediate and contemporaneous transmission of shocks. We make the additional observation, but do not investigate it further, that commodity exposure, especially via index products, as a proxy mechanism for garnering emerging markets exposure, may have additional benefits, such as lower transactions costs than direct or index emerging-markets equity investment.

We consider the set of portfolio choices of a typical institutional investor with meaningful international exposure to the following benchmarks (Table 14.9).

From a principal components analysis, we see that the bulk of asset risk is derived from equity market exposure (Table 14.10).

We can investigate further the portfolio and risk properties of the assets in question and impose the restrictions on capital allocations shown in Table 14.11.

Table 14.9   Analysis of international benchmarks

1999–2007 Asset Class	Proxy	avg	stdev	skew	kurt	min	max	maxdd	sharp
Commodities	BCI	3.4%	6.5%	0.049	−0.600	−10.7%	18.3%	−21.5%	0.736
China Equities	MSCI MSEUSCF Index	2.9%	20.8%	1.039	3.170	−35.2%	80.7%	−83.0%	0.180
Brazil Equities	MSCI MSEUSBR Index	5.8%	19.3%	−0.032	0.191	−39.4%	53.9%	−76.6%	0.502
India Equities	MSCI MSEUSIA Index	5.1%	15.0%	−0.162	−1.225	−21.8%	31.3%	−56.0%	0.552
Russia Equities	MSCI MSEUSRUS Index	13.1%	39.6%	1.491	5.265	−75.2%	171.4%	−91.8%	0.614
EM Equities	MSCI Emerging Markets Free US Cur	3.6%	13.1%	−0.301	−0.626	−23.6%	26.6%	−52.5%	0.393
EM Bonds	Global Emerging Markets	3.1%	4.6%	0.504	0.354	−4.5%	14.3%	−5.1%	0.913
US Equities	S&P 500 Total Return Index	2.6%	8.1%	−0.284	0.493	−17.3%	21.3%	−43.8%	0.388
World Equities	MSCI World Index US Currency TR	2.3%	8.1%	−0.133	0.583	−18.4%	21.1%	−46.8%	0.324
World Bonds	Lehman Global Aggregate	1.5%	2.9%	0.404	−0.088	−3.2%	8.9%	−6.1%	0.319
Hedge Funds	HFR Composite	2.1%	3.5%	−0.078	3.960	−10.0%	13.5%	−10.5%	0.660
Real Estate	NCREIF National	3.1%	1.0%	0.265	−0.161	0.7%	5.4%	0.0%	3.933
Private Equity	Cambridge Associates PE	4.0%	5.4%	−0.357	−0.255	−8.3%	14.9%	−26.1%	1.134

Source of data: Bloomberg, Hedge Fund Research, Inc. (HFR), National Council of Real Estate Investment Fiduciaries (NCREIF), Cambridge Associates LLC.

Using standard mean-variance analysis, with expected returns and co-variances estimated from quarterly historical data 1996–2007, we find the following optimal weighting scheme shown in Fig. 14.6.

We can see that mean-variance optimization favors a full allocation to commodities in the emerging-markets bucket. This result is driven in part by the diversification benefits that commodities offer relative to emerging-markets equity exposure, as well as improved returns relative to emerging-markets bonds.

More generally, we can generate two efficient frontiers: one that includes allocation to commodities and one that does not, all other restrictions on weights held constant.

We can see that the efficient frontier that includes an allocation to commodities in the emerging-markets bucket dominates that without the allocation (see Fig. 14.7). However, it

Table 14.10 Principal components analysis of international benchmarks

Principal Components Loadings

	Comp.1	Comp.2	Comp.3	Comp.4	Comp.5	Comp.6	Comp.7	Comp.8	Comp.9	Comp.10	Comp.11	Comp.12	Comp.13
BCI	−0.227	−0.487											
MSEUSCF		−0.111		0.575	−0.473	0.287	0.243	0.161	0.276	0.18	0.103		
MSEUSBR	−0.363	−0.135		0.396	0.649	0.377	−0.289	−0.258	−0.316	−0.575	−0.14	0.14	
MSEUSIA	−0.297		−0.229	0.2	−0.123	−0.719		0.231	0.121	0.319	−0.55	0.332	
MSEUSRUS	−0.268	−0.293	0.224	−0.348	0.269	−0.117	0.241	−0.539	0.518				
MSCLEM	−0.371	−0.137			−0.31	−0.168				−0.161	−0.15	−0.563	−0.207
Leh.EM	−0.21		−0.566	−0.16		0.167	−0.285	−0.371	−0.238	0.415	0.589		0.136
SP500	−0.351	0.23		−0.227		0.34	−0.207	0.207	0.226	0.11	0.109	0.216	−0.671
MSCIWorld	−0.365	0.21		−0.139		0.199	−0.14	0.291	0.279	−0.232	−0.103	0.241	0.643
LehGlobAgg	0.121	0.11	−0.7	−0.106	−0.257		0.522		0.187	−0.379	0.232		
HFRFundCom	−0.327		0.217	0.456	−0.18		0.481	−0.49	−0.554	−0.181	0.287	0.355	−0.155
NCREIFNational		0.612		0.153							0.171	0.158	
CA.PE	−0.306	0.354	0.119		−0.254	−0.147	0.366	0.231		0.293	−0.322	−0.53	0.137

Importance of components

	Comp.1	Comp.2	Comp.3	Comp.4	Comp.5	Comp.6	Comp.7	Comp.8	Comp.9	Comp.10	Comp.11	Comp.12	Comp.13
Standard devis	2.4451	1.2793	1.2104	1.0129	0.9198	0.7389	0.6945	0.6175	0.5147	0.4344	0.3155	0.2794	0.0826
Proportion of V	0.4599	0.1259	0.1127	0.0789	0.0651	0.0420	0.0371	0.0293	0.0204	0.0145	0.0077	0.0060	0.0005
Cumulative Prt	0.4599	0.5858	0.6985	0.7774	0.8425	0.8844	0.9215	0.9509	0.9713	0.9858	0.9935	0.9995	1.0000

Source of data: Bloomberg, Hedge Fund Research, Inc. (HFR), National Council of Real Estate Investment Fiduciaries (NCREIF), Cambridge Associates LLC.

Table 14.11 Allocation constraints

Allocation Constraints	min	max	Asset Class
BCI	0 %	5 %	EM
MSEUSCF Index	0 %	5 %	EM
MSEUSBR Index	0 %	5 %	EM
MSEUSIA Index	0 %	5 %	EM
MSEUSRUS Index	0 %	5 %	EM
MSCI Emerging Markets Fn	0 %	15 %	EM
Global Emerging Markets	0 %	15 %	EM
S&P 500 Total Return Index	10 %	25 %	
MSCI World Index US Cur	25 %	50 %	
Lehman Global Aggregate	25 %	50 %	
HFR Composite	0 %	8 %	alt
NCREIF National	0 %	8 %	alt
CA PE	0 %	8 %	alt
total alt	0 %	15 %	
total EM	0 %	20 %	

Source of data: Bloomberg, Hedge Fund Research, Inc. (HFR), National Council of Real Estate Investment Fiduciaries (NCREIF), Cambridge Associates LLC.

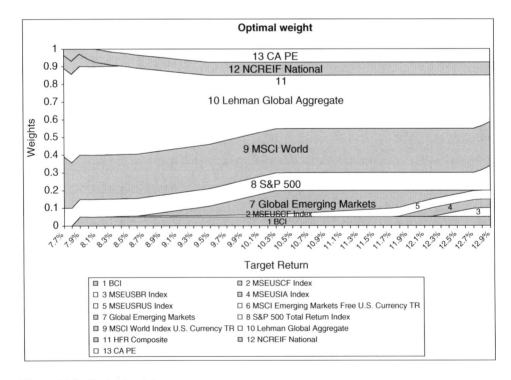

Figure 14.6 Optimal weights
Source of data: Bloomberg, Hedge Fund Research, Inc. (HFR), National Council of Real Estate Investment Fiduciaries (NCREIF), Cambridge Associates LLC.

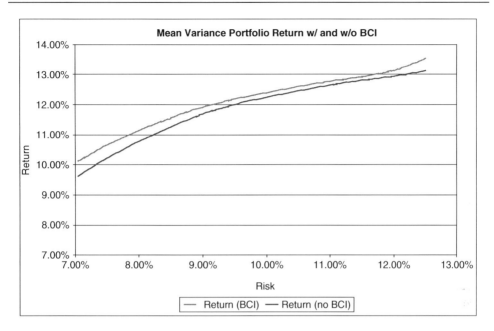

Figure 14.7   Mean variance portfolio return with and without BCI
Source of data: Bloomberg, Hedge Fund Research, Inc. (HFR), National Council of Real Estate Investment Fiduciaries (NCREIF), Cambridge Associates LLC.

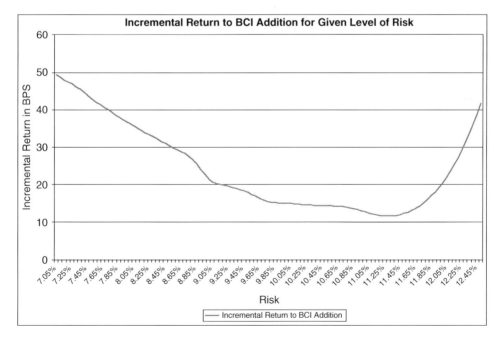

Figure 14.8   Incremental return to BCI addition for given level of risk
Source of data: Bloomberg, Hedge Fund Research, Inc. (HFR), National Council of Real Estate Investment Fiduciaries (NCREIF), Cambridge Associates LLC.

may be useful to look at this at a more granular level: We can compare the results of the efficient-frontier analysis to determine the incremental return available for a predetermined level of risk, once commodities are added to the emerging-markets risk bucket. Depending on the risk level, we can see that adding commodity exposure allows the investor to realize between 10 and 50 bps of additional return for the given risk (see Fig. 14.8).

14.5 CONCLUSION

In this brief analysis, we have examined the interaction between two important themes in investing: the growing importance of emerging markets, and the sustained boom in commodity prices. Given the important role commodity prices play in emerging economies, we have investigated the extent to which commodities and emerging-markets equities are related, and the extent to which their differences are sufficient to warrant inclusion of commodity assets in an optimal portfolio that includes emerging-markets assets. While there is a mild amount of correlation to the investments in commodities and emerging markets, we find that inclusion of commodities offers a substantial amount of risk reduction to an overall portfolio that includes core assets.

14.6 REFERENCES

Hamilton, J. (1994). *Time Series Analysis*. Princeton: Princeton University Press.
Lutkepohl, H. (2005). *A New Introduction to Time Series Analysis*. Berlin: Springer-Verlag.
International Monetary Fund (2008). *World Economic Outlook*. Washington DC: IMF.

Case Studies and Risk Management in Commodity Derivatives Trading

Hilary Till

15.1 INTRODUCTION

Risk management in commodity futures trading takes two different forms, depending on whether trading is done as a commercial or a purely speculative enterprise.

In a commercial enterprise, the rationale for trading activity is usually to "optimize the value of physical assets"; and the returns and risks from this activity would be expected to be a small fraction of the enterprise's overall profits and losses. One would include BP's trading activity in this category, for example.

Commercial and investment banks also engage in commodity derivatives trading, historically to facilitate their overall business in financing natural-resource producers. This is arguably the case historically with Canadian commercial banks.

For commercial enterprises, the important aspects of risk management are in adhering to regulatory rules and laws, and in establishing strict operational policies and procedures over every facet of risk-taking activity.

For a purely speculative participant, the emphasis is almost entirely on market risk-management. The barriers to entry in futures trading are remarkably low: strictly speaking, a participant solely needs a quote device to track the markets and a Futures Commission Merchant (FCM) to execute and clear one's trades. Arguably, the tail risk on a futures trading position is ultimately the responsibility of an FCM.

It is ingrained in the minds of financial-market participants that should fixed-income or equity markets ever have extreme dislocations, they can ultimately rely on a "central-bank put" underwritten by either the Federal Reserve Board (Fed) or the European Central Bank. On 12 December 2007, for example, the Fed unveiled the Term Auction Facility (TAF) to enable depository institutions in the US (and indirectly in Europe) to acquire short-term funds against a wide variety of capital. Further on 11 March 2008, the Fed created the Term Securities Lending Facility (TSLF) whereby primary dealers, including investment banks, could borrow Treasury securities against a wide variety of mortgage-related securities. With these and other actions, financial-market participants were again assured that the too-big-to-fail doctrine still held.

For commodity speculators, though, there is no TCAF ("Term Commodity Arbitrageur Facility"). Instead, commodity speculators are forced to rely on disciplined risk management.

Premia Capital Management, LLC and EDHEC Risk and Asset Management Research Centre
Contact: Hilary Till, Premia Capital Management, LLC, 53 W. Jackson Blvd., Suite 724, Chicago, IL 60604 USA.

Risk Management in Commodity Markets: From Shipping to Agriculturals and Energy Edited by Hélyette Geman

The financial writer, Ralph Vince, goes so far as to recommend that before studying the mathematics of money management, one should consider what would happen if the prospective trader suffered a cataclysmic loss:

Take some time and try to imagine how you are going to feel in such a situation. Next, try to determine what you will do in such an instance. Now write down on a sheet of paper exactly what you will do, who you can call for legal help ... Do it now ... . Vince (1992)

Many experienced traders have noted how ephemeral trading strategies are, or at least, how all strategies have life-cycles: "Just when you think you found the key to the market, they change the locks," declared the late Gerald Loeb, who was a highly successful financier and founding partner of E.F. Hutton, as quoted in Cashin (2008).

As a matter of fact, Weisman *et al.* (2007) have quantified one of the consequences of Loeb's observation. The expected draw-down for a strategy is positively related to how consistently profitable a strategy is, *if a threshold of returns is constantly demanded*. In the words of Weisman *et al.*, the markets have "periodic market efficiency", which is another way of saying all strategies have a limited lifespan. The "tail loss", when a strategy finally (and inevitably) outlives its usefulness, can be found to be:

$$\text{Loss} = [(\text{Demanded Returns}) * \text{Probability of the Strategy Succeeding}/$$

$$\text{Probability of the Strategy Failing}].$$

For strategies that target an absolute level of return, the natural consequences of this demand are that (1) losses are proportional to wins; and (2) losses are inversely proportional to their probability of occurrence, as explained by Weisman and his colleagues.

Ethical issues do not arise when Weisman *et al.*'s analysis is applied to proprietary trading firms since in this case it is the partners' capital at risk. The partners accept that draw-downs are endogenous to the trading strategy. As a result, they may not target absolute returns, knowing that trading strategies are fleeting. As Eagleeye (2007) wrote, "One can manage risk ... [but] one can't demand a threshold return from the market". Enduring proprietary trading firms instead typically target risk.

Now, there are severe consequences to Weisman's analysis for investors in hedge funds, who historically have based their investment decisions on past historical track records which may not be predictive of future results; and who pay hedge-fund traders based on short-term results, with no claw-backs of fees if the strategy suffers disastrous results.

We can take an example from the natural gas futures markets to illustrate the negative consequences to Weisman's observation of the "dangerous attraction" to absolute-return targeting.

Figure 15.1 illustrates how consistent a strategy of trading natural gas bear calendar spreads was in the spring of 2004 through the spring of 2006. A "calendar spread" consists of taking offsetting positions during the different delivery months of a particular futures contract. A "bear calendar spread" consists of taking a short position in a nearer-month futures contract while simultaneously taking a long position in a later-delivery contract of the same futures market.

By early summer 2006, the profitability of this strategy had declined by about half of the performance of the previous two years. If the commodity futures trader had responded by doubling up his or her position size (to try to maintain an absolute-return target), then

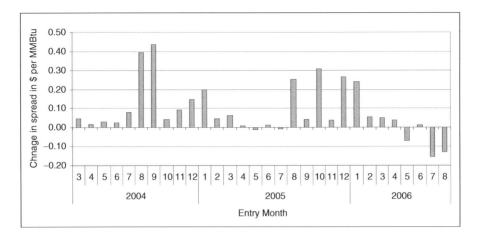

Figure 15.1   Natural gas bear-calendar spread P/L, 1-month horizon, January 2004 through August 2006
Source of Data: Bloomberg.

in July and August of 2006, that trader would have sustained losses about twice the size of the trader's year-to-date profits. The significance of such a loss is that when a trader's risk-and-return results differ dramatically from client and/or prime-broker expectations, this can set off a "critical liquidation cycle" where client redemptions and/or additional demands for collateral from creditors cause a trader to liquidate positions in a distressed manner, which can then cause further losses that imperil a fund's survival, as both the fund's investors and creditors lose faith in the manager. This process is mathematically modeled in De Souza and Smirnov (2004) as being like a short barrier put option.

Keeping Weisman's and De Souza and Smirnov's analyses in mind, perhaps one should accept that individual trading strategies may not be enduring. But perhaps a trader's risk-management methodology can be enduring, instead.

A number of studies have indirectly verified this latter point. The fund-of-hedge-funds investor, David Gordon, found that while pre-investment returns for managers had *no* predictive value, as discussed in Gordon (2003a), it was different for risk:

Historical standard deviation tends to be somewhat helpful in predicting future risk. The correlation between pre-investment standard deviation ... [versus] downside deviation and maximum drawdown during the subsequent period of investment *is* [statistically] significant. (Italics added.) Gordon (2003b).

Further Kat and Menexe (2003) found that the historical value of a hedge-fund manager's track record is precisely in its risk characteristics; they found that the standard deviation of a manager's returns (and the manager's correlation to the stock market) was what persisted across time, but *not* manager performance itself.

Interestingly, for institutionally-scaled hedge funds, the publicly available information on these funds is precisely in the quality of their risk-management-and-monitoring infrastructure. This was the message from the extensive Moody's operational reports on Chicago-based Citadel Investments and London-based Brevan Howard, which are both $15-billion-plus hedge-fund institutions. These reports were made available on Moody's website in 2007 for accredited investors, and are listed in this chapter's references section under Gains (2007) and Lahav (2007).

So perhaps it is not controversial, after all, to state that risk management is the most important aspect of a futures trading operation. In this chapter, we will discuss the risk-management lessons from a number of recent trading debacles with the hope that the reader will thereby be able to avoid such mishaps in their own professional lives.

In the following, we will briefly discuss the apparent risk-management lapses at three large institutions involved in commodity derivatives trading; these lapses were mainly operational in nature rather than market-risk problems *per se*. This section will then be followed by a discussion of the market-risk lessons garnered from trading debacles that have occurred from 2005 through the spring of 2008.

15.2 INSTITUTIONAL RISK MANAGEMENT

15.2.1 Regulatory and legal risk

In 2007, BP ran foul of market-conduct laws and rules, as enforced by the Commodity Futures Trading Commission (CFTC) and the US Department of Justice (DOJ), for trading activities of the previous five years. In one particular case, the civil and criminal fines *far* exceeded the market-risk of the activities, illustrating where the risk-management priorities need to be for large participants in the commodity markets.

There is a strict body of law prohibiting market manipulation by commodity traders, especially when retail customers are put at risk. According to the CFTC (2006a, 2006b, 2007b), during the spring of 2004 traders at BP Products North America cornered the February 2004 physical propane market at a particular delivery location in Texas. This delivery location ultimately serves customers throughout the Midwest and Northeast via pipeline. The largest users of propane in the US are from the residential and commercial heating sector as well as from the petrochemical industry, which uses propane for creating plastics.

A 28 June 2006 CFTC complaint specifically cites recorded telephone conversations where a senior BP trader discusses whether BP could "control ... [a particular propane] market at will". To find out whether they could accomplish a corner, "BP employees purchased enormous quantities of propane to establish a dominant and controlling long position" in physical propane, notes the CFTC (2006a). The CFTC complaint also notes how senior management at BP consented to the strategy. For example, in the CFTC (2006b) complaint, the compliance manager at the BP business unit responsible for propane trading is quoted as approving the propane-purchasing strategy, but told the traders "to refrain from using certain words in conjunction with ... the strategy, including the word 'squeeze'".

From a careful reading of the CFTC complaint, the actual trade construction of BP's speculative trading strategy appears to be one of being long propane for physical delivery by the end of February 2004 while also being short propane for physical delivery by the end of March 2004. BP had also attempted a similar strategy, in what appears to be a smaller scale, in April 2003, again according to the CFTC complaint.

According to an internal BP document that is posted to the CFTC website, BP actually lost $10 million from their speculative propane strategy. The BP traders were only able to sell a relatively small fraction of their February 2004 position at the elevated price levels that prevailed at the end of February, meaning that they had to close out their remaining February longs at much lower prices prevailing in March 2004.

Because of this trading loss, the BP trading bench had put together a Powerpoint presentation, "NGL Feb Value Trade[:] Lessons Learned". This presentation is publicly available on the CFTC's website as Exhibit F of the 28 June 2006 complaint; each page of the presentation is stamped "BP Confidential". Based on past historical relationships, the propane traders had expected their trading strategy's performance to be in the range of $-\$5$ *million to* $+ \$15$ *million*. The document details the controls that were in place, and those which needed to be put in place going forward to avert unexpected trading losses in the future. The report documents the Market Value-at-Risk limits; limits on calendar spreads; and plans for improved communications across BP trading units for better information-sharing. Table 15.1 summarizes the key compliance risks from the internal BP presentation.

Table 15.1 Compliance: key risks as excerpted from internal BP presentation: "NGL Feb Value Trade Lessons Learned"

- Regulatory - No violations under current framework, but could increase the risk of regulatory intervention;
- Legal/credit – No specific legal concerns identified, but could increase the risk of an "aggrieved short" failing to make payment or filing a claim for damages;
- Reputational – Primary risk.

Source: Exhibit F of CFTC (2006b).

Amongst the "actions going forward" are a request for the trading unit to have training in compliance and regulatory matters.

On 25 October 2007, the CFTC announced the entry of a consent order in the United States District Court in Northern Illinois, which settled civil charges against BP. "In a related filing, the Criminal Division, Fraud Section of the United States Department of Justice also announced the simultaneous filing of an information and entry into a deferred prosecution agreement with BP America Inc. based upon the same underlying conduct," stated CFTC (2007b). The total monetary sanction against BP was approximately $303 million; "the largest manipulation settlement in CFTC history," according to the CFTC (2007b), which included both civil and criminal penalties. The order found that BP employees had "violated the Commodity Exchange Act's prohibitions against manipulating the price of a commodity and cornering a commodity market".

The key risk-management lesson from this debacle is to have a clear-cut compliance and ethics program, not just for the trading staff but also for senior management, given how the regulatory and legal risks can outweigh market risks when engaged in large-scale commodities trading. In fact, the 25 October 2007 consent order required BP to "establish a compliance and ethics program, and install a monitor to oversee BP's trading activities in the commodity markets".

On 25 October 2007, the CFTC also announced an additional settlement against an *individual* BP trader. In this case, the CFTC found that a BP gasoline trader had attempted "to manipulate the price spread between the November and December 2002 unleaded gasoline futures contract traded on the New York Mercantile Exchange ... on 31 October 2002, the last day of trading for the November 2002 unleaded gasoline futures contract", according to CFTC (2007c).

The order found that even though BP had 52 more gasoline contracts than were stated as commercially needed, the individual gasoline trader had "bought an additional 720 November 2002 unleaded gasoline contracts throughout the course of the day on 31 October 2002" in order to influence the spread between the November and December contracts.

The individual trader was personally fined $400 000 and was prohibited from any employment activity that required registration with the CFTC.

Again, in this case, the key risk-management lesson is operational. One would conclude that a large-scale trading operation should have systems in place which monitor position sizes versus limits, particularly on the last trading date for a physically-settled contract.

As will be discussed later in this chapter, US regulators are now more active in fining traders *personally* rather than just fining their place of employment. This would lead one to the conclusion that prospective traders entering into large-scale derivatives trading operations should be as (or more) knowledgeable about regulatory rules and laws as they are with sophisticated market risk-management techniques.

15.2.2   Valuation risk[1]

Bank of Montreal was temporarily in the headlines in 2007 for an energy trading debacle. This case received a lot of attention in the specialty commodity press in the spring of 2007, but then quickly faded from the headlines, as the subprime-credit-related crisis picked up steam in the early summer of 2007.

At the end of April 2007, the Bank of Montreal, which is also known as BMO, announced trading losses of about C$400 million. These losses were later revised upwards to C$680 million. This sum was higher than the bank's revenue from trading during the previous year, according to *The Desk* (2007b). Unfortunately, BMO's auditors had found that the bank's over-the-counter (OTC) natural gas book had been seriously "mismarked".

The bank's auditors reported that they had never seen such a large discrepancy between the marks that were used, and market value, according to Mavin (2007). Another way of framing the significance of BMO's natural gas trading loss was that in its filings with the US Securities and Exchange Commission (SEC), BMO had stated that its average one-day Value-at-Risk in its commodity book was only C$8.8 million during the quarter that ended on 31 January 2007 (see Table 15.2).

Figure 15.2 excerpts from a presentation by BMO's chief risk officer that has been available on the Bank of Montreal's website. This presentation is listed in this chapter's references section under McGlashan (2007). Figure 15.2 shows a relatively modest frequency distribution of daily trading profits-and-losses (p/l) for the bank. Clearly, the quantitative method of summarizing BMO's trading risk had fallen short.

A key reason that there has not been more communications from BMO on this unexpected loss is because the bank has had to focus on a number of inquiries from securities, commodities, banking, and law enforcement authorities, according to an SEC filing by the bank. The bank "is cooperating with all of these authorities", noted Bank of Montreal (2007b).

Based on publicly available reports, can we say anything about how BMO's trading loss amounted to about 100 times its average VaR reported for fiscal year 2006? One cannot say conclusively since litigation involving the bank's outsized trading loss was still ongoing, as of the writing of this chapter, but a number of press reports and lawsuit allegations

---

[1] This section is based on Till (2008a).

Table 15.2 Total trading and underwriting MVE summary ($ millions)*

	For the quarter ended January 31, 2007				As at October 31, 2006
(Pre-tax Canadian equivalent)	Quarter-end	Average	High	Low	Quarter-end
Commodities Risk	(16.8)	(8.8)	(16.8)	(4.6)	(8.4)
Equity Risk	(8.6)	(7.5)	(10.8)	(5.1)	(9.8)
Foreign exchange Risk	(1.0)	(2.7)	(5.6)	(0.8)	(3.3)
Interest rate Risk (Mark-to-Market)	(7.6)	(5.3)	(10.2)	(2.7)	(7.1)
Correlation	11.1	8.7	11.9	5.1	10.4
Comprehensive Risk	(22.9)	(15.6)	(22.9)	(11.3)	(18.2)
Interest rate Risk (accrual)	(24.7)	(16.1)	(25.0)	(10.3)	(12.0)
Issuer Risk	(3.6)	(4.5)	(5.7)	(3.5)	(5.8)
Total MVE	(51.2)	(36.2)	(51.2)	(28.1)	(36.0)

*Explanatory Notes:
- MVE means "Market Value Exposure."
- MVE is a one-day measure using a 99 % confidence interval. Losses are in brackets and benefits are presented as positive numbers.

Source: Bank of Montreal (2007a).

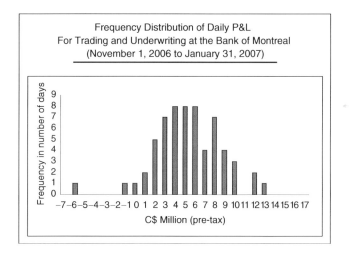

Figure 15.2 Histogram of trading P/L, as excerpted from BMO Financial Group's presentation: "Q1 2007 Risk Review"
Source: McGlashan (2007).

provide some indication of what may have gone wrong. Because a number of the facts and allegations in this case are quite incendiary, this section of the chapter will carefully document the source of each statement.

- Apparently, in the over-the-counter natural gas markets, it "is highly prevalent ... [for] the front office/trading ... [staff to] mark curves for a) implied volatility and b) illiquid basis locations," noted a chief risk officer in *The Desk* (2007d).

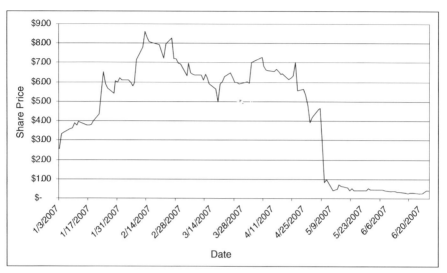

"Optionable, Inc., doing business as OPEX, operates a real-time electronic trade matching and brokerage system. The company provides trading and brokerage services to brokerage firms, financial institutions, energy traders, and hedge funds nationwide."

Figure 15.3   Optionable (OPBL) share price
Source of data: Bloomberg.

- "The Deloitte report [on BMO's OTC energy valuation] ...   indicated that some of the prices used in BMO's mismarked book of trades were provided by Valhalla-NY-based Optionable, Inc.," reported Mavin (2007).
- Optionable is "a brokerage [that] specialized in OTC derivatives for long maturities," stated Blanco and Mark (2007). The firm is a public company with its stock trading on an OTC Bulletin Board, which trades under the ticker OPBL.
- BMO was Optionable's largest customer for a long time, according to *The Desk* (2007c).
- And, correspondingly, Optionable was BMO's principal options broker, again according to *The Desk* (2007a).
- " ... . Optionable made private offers of stocks or warrants to traders in exchange for volume guarantees," reported *The Desk* (2007a).
- The lead natural gas options trader at BMO, who was regarded as the "biggest national-gas options trader in the market, had a close personal relationship with the senior management of Optionable," wrote Mavin (2007).
- BMO may have been directly connected to over 80 % of Optionable's revenues, according to a lawsuit filed in the US District Court of Southern New York (2007).
- The Optionable CEO's past included being sentenced to 30 months for a felony conviction on credit card fraud in 1997, and six months for income tax evasion in 1993, reported Leising (2007a).
- As shown in Fig. 15.3, Optionable's share price precipitously declined after the revelations of BMO's unexpected losses and associated fraud allegations. As Richard Oldfield said in his book on investing, *Simple But Not Easy*, "Ethics is not just a county to the east of London.[2] Markets are particularly intolerant of seriously unethical behavior by

---

[2] Explanation of Richard Oldfield's quote: Essex is a county in the East of England.

management, and the revelation of scandal is something which can be relied upon to cause a collapse in share price."

Blanco and Mark (2007) conclude the following about the BMO fiasco:

- "Insufficient checks and balances in the mark-to-market process" appear to be the main reason for this debacle.
- A contributing factor may have been "deficiencies in the bank's pricing and risk models in terms of incorporating the impact of implied volatility changes".
- "The bank started experiencing heavy losses as implied volatilities came down in the first months of 2007."
- BMO's "chief risk officer noticed [then] that the risk models had some deficiencies in measuring the risk of *long positions in [deep] out-of-the-money ... natural gas OTC options*". (Italics added.)

Figure 15.4 illustrates the dramatic swings in implied volatility that are inherent to the natural gas options market.

According to *The Desk* (2007c), the lessons thus far for energy-trading participants are as follows:

- " ... [A]lways get your marks from ... [large,] legitimate, established brokers, publishers, or exchanges."
- " ... [M]ake sure that one's code-of-conduct document for traders is ... [sufficient,] and that ... [all traders] have signed it."

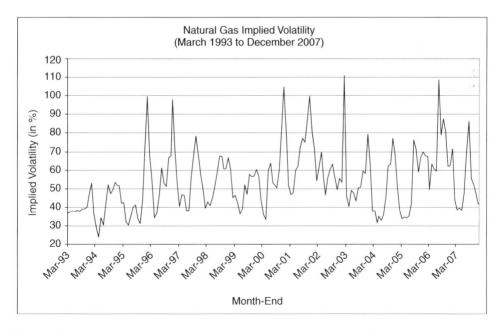

Figure 15.4 Natural gas implied volatility (March 1993 to December 2007); monthly data implied from call prices
Source of data: Bloomberg.

- Include in the code-of-conduct document what sort of broker "perks" are unacceptable for traders, and "let nothing be left to common sense".
- Ensure that one's trading activity is diversified across more than one broker.

Again, like the two BP case studies, we have to conclude that for large-scale commodity-trading efforts the complexity may not be in market-risk monitoring, but in relatively simply described operational controls, which must be rigorously applied throughout a large organization.

15.2.3 Position Limits

On 28 February 2008, the FCM, MF Global, Inc., revealed an unexpectedly large $141.5-million loss from a wheat-futures trading position taken by one of its registered representatives in Memphis, Tennessee for the representative's proprietary (own) account. The MF representative had amassed more than 15 000 futures contracts covering 75 million bushels of wheat on the Chicago Board of Trade, between midnight and 6 am on 27 February reported Smith and Scheer (2008). According to Cameron and Lucchetti (2008), "the futures brokerage blamed the loss on a failure in its systems". Apparently, the clearing firm did not have automatic limits in the sizing of futures trades executed electronically, when the operator was a registered representative of the firm.

Dowd (2007) wrote about the potential downside of electronic trading:

The downside of all this speed is that it can now take milliseconds for an 'out trade' to go horribly wrong. We often hear the 'fat-finger' trade cited as one of the drawbacks of electronic trading. (The term *fat finger* is trading jargon to describe electronic trades that were entered incorrectly.) For example, there is the story of the trader who spilled his coffee on the keyboard and mistakenly sold 10,000 Japanese Government Bond futures.

As a consequence of the wheat loss, MF Global's CEO stated that "the company would introduce limits on positions taken by all customers and traders," reported Cameron and Lucchetti (2008).

The FCM also took other remedial actions to restore customer and shareholder confidence in its risk-management infrastructure. According to MF Global (2008), the firm increased "the number of on-site risk specialists in every company center around the world, assigning additional staff to duty in each center overnight and ensuring that all centers operating in daytime hours back up nighttime centers". The firm also commenced the search for a "new chief risk officer to be in charge of all risk areas of the company and to report directly to MF Global's CEO".

As of late April 2008, the marketplace affirmed these risk-management improvements by MF Global, as shown by the FCM's share-price recovering by a substantial margin from its mid-March 2008 low.

In this case, a corollary to Oldfield's previously-cited maxim held: because the firm's financial loss had not been due to an ethical lapse by the company's management, MF Global was successful in retaining the market's confidence.

15.2.4 Summary of risk-management lessons for large institutions

None of the three case studies described above involve complex mathematical issues, and can be summarized briefly and simply as fundamental control problems. That said, this statement is admittedly not fair to individuals at large organizations, who operate in *extremely* complex social environments. Frequently, for individuals working at large companies, one can liken employment to a sumo-wrestling match. From the outside, it does not look like anything much is getting done, but just staying in the ring is actually the accomplishment.

The real conclusion from this section might be an insight from a textbook, which is not considered a risk-management primer: *Good to Great* (Collins, 2001). In the main, a large organization can only do well when it implements a handful of simple concepts, which it consistently applies in scale, and across time, by individuals who all share common business values. In the case of large commodity derivatives trading companies, an emphasis on:

1. complying with regulatory rules and laws;
2. valuing instruments based on pricing sources genuinely independent of the trading team; and
3. imposing strict position limits in all electronic trading systems;

are clearly core principles that all stakeholders in institutionally-sized commodity trading firms should embrace.

15.3 PROPRIETARY-TRADING RISK MANAGEMENT

In contrast, in a proprietary trading firm one is not dealing with the complex external world of clients, distribution agents, and enhanced regulatory scrutiny, so complexity in the trading process is much more acceptable (and possible). In addition, there is no agency-versus-principal problem of struggling to come up with the right incentives so that agents handle client or shareholder obligations responsibly. At a proprietary trading firm, the principals have their own capital at risk so a complex system of controls and incentives becomes a moot point: the possibility of facing personal bankruptcy is usually a sufficient disciplining mechanism in carrying out business operations responsibly.

Quite simply, a proprietary trading firm exploits some empirical regularity in the futures markets. There are two main risks to this business model. A strategy might have arisen because there was enormous commercial demand for some exposure, and there was not sufficient speculative capital to offset this demand, creating abnormal economic profits for speculators. The risk is then that what had once been one-sided flow becomes two-sided flow as more speculators enter a "too-good-to-be-true" strategy.

Another risk for proprietary traders is that there are structural breaks. A signature example is that prior to the current business cycle, the US could safely be said to be the dominant participant in a number of commodity markets, especially on the demand side. This created numerous empirical regularities, particularly in the energy and grain futures markets. This is now a questionable proposition in the face of the historic Chinese industrial revolution. Another way of saying this is that strategies, which relied on the continuation of the US as the dominant factor in commodity demand, may no longer work.

These two risks can best be explained by understanding that the fundamental nature of speculative commodity trading is "flow trading". Kins explained this in Akey *et al.* (2006). The following are excerpts from Kins' text:

- "Many traders in sizeable organizations benefit from extensive information flow, and many of these traders do not even realize the degree of their dependence on such information.

- Once removed from the deep information channels, many formerly successful traders may become incapable of trading profitably.
- In other instances, the . . . effects of reduced information flow are more difficult to detect. In these scenarios, it appears at first that a trader is unaffected by his or her new situation and is able to perform as well as he or she had historically.
- After a period of time, [however,] . . . the trader's performance dissipates dramatically.
- This phenomenon is often caused by the fact that when an individual leaves an institution, they may be able to maintain several key relationships with former colleagues, clients, or counterparties who are still in a position to provide valuable information flow for some while. As time passes, however, this information flow . . . often . . . dwindle[s], . . . thereby leaving these traders unable to perform as they had historically.
- In order to avoid such a situation, flow traders either need to find new return drivers or become large enough so that they can obtain similar information themselves before their relationships expire."

Kins' observations help us to understand how temporary any individual trader's capacity to be profitable can be, once they leave the employment of institutionally-sized firms.

15.4   HEDGE-FUND RISK MANAGEMENT

Hedge funds are a hybrid of an institutional asset-management firm and a proprietary trading company. Whether a hedge fund is more like an institutional firm versus a proprietary trading firm depends on how much of the principals' wealth is at risk. Historically, hedge funds were operated by traders who were successful in their own right, and then consented to allow a limited number of investors into their fund. This made them like proprietary trading firms until relatively recently. But now that firms such as JP Morgan, Morgan Stanley, the Man Group, and Goldman Sachs are buying (or taking stakes in) hedge-fund firms, and with sovereign wealth funds becoming large-scale investors in hedge funds, this historical description is no longer accurate. For a number of large-scale hedge funds, we have to think of them as more like institutional firms where the operational issues are what are paramount in risk management.

In support of this latter assertion, Christory *et al*. (2006) cite a 2003 study by Giraud, which found that:

in the case of blowups, operational risk greatly exceeds the risk related to the investment strategy, with more than half of hedge fund collapses directly related to a failure of one or several operational processes.

Also, arguably once a hedge fund becomes sufficiently large, the only opportunities that exist in the required scale are either traditional or alternative betas (which are also known as risk premia), so the complexity in risk management is typically not in market-risk management since it is the fund's clients who are assuming the market risk.

15.5   FUND-OF-HEDGE-FUNDS DIVERSIFICATION

A key way that commodity investors can choose to diversify the idiosyncratic operational risk of individual commodity hedge funds is through a natural-resources fund-of-funds, as explained in Akey *et al.* (2006). Because the opportunity set for commodity investments is so diverse, a fund-of-funds can potentially dampen the sharp peaks-and-troughs of individual managers, as demonstrated in Akey (2005, 2006). Even with this in mind, each individual manager should take steps to keep their market risk within well-understood bounds, which is covered in the next section.

15.6 MARKET RISK MANAGEMENT

No matter what the scale of an individual trading operation is, the management of market risk is still necessary (but not sufficient, as the previous case studies showed). The five basic elements of commodity risk management are as follows:

- Trade construction,
- Sizing,
- Exit strategy,
- Scenario analyses, and
- Choice of leverage level.

We will take the reader through recent trading mishaps and show how losses might have been lessened with a more judicious application of these elements of risk management.

15.6.1 Trade Construction

Futures traders typically aim for a long-option-like payoff profile. Grant (2004) notes, for example, that global macro traders typically have an additional objective besides a return threshold. He provides a benchmark objective for the "performance ratio", which is the ratio of average daily gains divided by average daily losses. Based on Grant's experience, a performance objective "in the range of 125 % is entirely achievable ... [although some traders can exceed that], consistently achieving 200 %+ in this regard".

That said, some opportunities in the commodity futures markets have short-option-like payoff profiles. One example is weather-fear premia strategies. In these trades, which can be found in the grain, tropical, and natural gas futures markets, a future price is systematically priced too high relative to where it eventually matures. This occurs before a time of unpredictable weather such as the Brazilian winter or summer time in the US Midwest and Northeast. In the case of the Brazilian winter, an extreme frost can damage Brazil's coffee trees. In the case of the US summertime, an exceptional heat-wave can impair corn pollination prospects as well as stress the delivery of adequate natural gas supplies for peak air-conditioning demand.

Over long periods of time, it has been profitable to be short these commodity markets during the time of maximum weather uncertainty. But during rare instances, these strategies can have very large losses, which create classic short-option-like profiles.

If one includes short-option-like strategies in a futures program, then the sizing of these trades needs to be reduced compared to the sizing of trades with long-option-like profiles in order to preserve the program's overall long optionality.

Bear-calendar spreads in physically-settled commodity futures markets typically have short-options-like payoff profiles. In times of scarcity for a commodity, market participants will pay extremely high prices for the immediately deliverable contract, meaning that a rally will only substantially benefit the front-month price rather than later-month maturities. In extreme cases of scarcity, the front-month contract's price can become disconnected from the values of the rest of the commodity's futures curve. If a trader is short the front-month contract and long a later-month maturity, then that trader is at risk to this scenario. In other words, a bear-calendar spread puts one at risk to extreme losses. Therefore, if one is aiming to have a sustainable trading career, then one should devote limited risk capital to trades that have this type of construction.

Collins (2007) noted how during 2006, wheat futures traders at the Chicago Board of Trade had assumed there was "free money" in establishing bear-calendar spreads prior to commodity-index roll dates. Unlike an equity index, one unique aspect of a commodity futures index is that its precise rules need to specify on what dates each of its contracts have to be rolled before the maturity of each contract. These rules are known as "roll rules". The rules specify when a particular index constituent should be sold and a further-maturity contract should be bought. In advance of such a procedure, wheat speculators had historically sold the front-month while buying the next-month contract, establishing a bear-calendar spread. They would then unwind this position during index roll dates. Collins (2007) wrote that this strategy suffered during the fall of 2006 "when a [wheat] supply disruption in Australia caused sharp reversals in wheat spreads[;] ... certain calendar wheat spreads moved [substantially against the speculative spreaders] ... in a week".

Collins (2007) reported that "the use of bear calendars this way [can be compared] to an options writing strategy, which can offer consistent profits until one huge spike in volatility can wipe out months of profits and more".

15.6.2 Sizing

Natural gas seems to be at the center of a lot of trading debacles. Natural gas derivatives trading has offered hedge funds a potentially alluring combination of scalability and volatility and also, at times, pockets of predictability. This faith has continued unabated. For example, even in the aftermath of Amaranth sustaining the largest hedge-fund loss thus far in history, one of Amaranth's natural gas traders based in London was soon able to obtain a $1 million signing bonus when joining another large-scale global macro hedge fund, according to Harris (2006).

By the spring of 2007, Amaranth's former head natural gas trader had apparently obtained close to $1 billion in investor commitments for a new hedge fund headquartered in Calgary, Alberta, reported Herbst-Bayliss (2007). A July 2007 US regulatory action against the head trader himself (and not just against his former employer, Amaranth) appeared to put an end to these particular plans.

There are two main publicly known hedge-fund natural gas trading mishaps: that of MotherRock and Amaranth in 2006. More recently, in February 2008 the Houston-based energy hedge fund, Saracen, was reported to have had difficulties with natural gas trading positions, too. That said, in each of these cases, the losses in the US and European banking system are so massive that the losses by these hedge funds seem very small in the rear-view mirror. (According to Tett (2008), the Western banking system may eventually suffer $500 billion or more in write-downs during the "credit crunch".)

But then again, even if a firm's losses are small compared to what the global banking system is capable of losing, this is not much comfort for a firm's principals or its clients.

The key to understanding the 2006–2008 natural gas trading losses seems to be one of *sizing*. The commodity markets do not have natural two-sided flow. For experienced traders in the fixed income, equity, and currency markets, this point may not be obvious. The commodity markets have "nodal liquidity". If a commercial market participant needs to initiate or lift hedges, there will be flow, but such transactions do not occur on demand. Before a trader initiates a position, particularly one that is large compared to the size of the marketplace, one needs a clear understanding of what flow or catalyst will allow the trader out of a position.

A commodity-market observer can readily identify when a massively-sized distressed liquidation is occurring, particularly in a spread market. If there is no economic or weather news regarding a market, and a spread relationship changes by many standard deviations relative to recent history, this is a clear signal that a market participant is unwinding a position in a distressed fashion.

Therefore, a key risk-management objective in (speculative) commodity futures trading is to keep sizing within a relatively small fraction of daily trading volume and open interest.

The following is a discussion of three commodity hedge-fund case studies, based on publicly available information, which may admittedly be incomplete.

15.6.2.1 MotherRock

According to Leising (2006), MotherRock was a hedge fund that was founded in December 2004, which "invest[ed] in [natural] gas futures, seeking to exploit price differences based on the delivery month of the contracts". As of early 2006, the fund "had more than $400 million in customer funds". The New York-based fund also traded option contracts on natural gas, according to MarketWatch (2006). As of the end of June 2006, the fund had about $280 million in assets under management, reported Goldstein *et al.* (2006).

On 3 August 2006, Leising and Burton (2006) broke the story that MotherRock was "preparing to shut down because of 'terrible performance'", based on a letter to the fund's investors from the hedge fund's founder. According to Boyd (2006), by mid-September 2006 "investors in . . . MotherRock . . . lost their last chance to recover any of their stake in the ill-fated operation".

Further, according to MarketWatch (2006), MotherRock had left its clearing firm, ABN Amro, with up to $100 million in losses. This is an illustration of how an FCM can ultimately be responsible for the tail risk of a customer's strategies. MotherRock's clients had no further liability for their losses beyond their investment.

The summary thus far contains information that became known *after* MotherRock's founder announced the fund's plans to shut down. Market participants, though, were already alerted to a distressed liquidation on 2 August, 2006, the day before MotherRock's announcement.

A near-month calendar spread in natural gas experienced a 4.5 standard-deviation move intraday before the spread market normalized by the close of trading on 2 August, 2006. Figure 15.5 illustrates the intraday and three-month behavior of the September vs. October Natural Gas (NG U-V) spread.

We might assume that MotherRock had on a position that was correlated to being short the NG U-V (September October) spread. Why make this assumption? The brief intense rally in this spread on 2 August 2006 is consistent with the temporary effects of a forced liquidation, involving a position related to this spread.

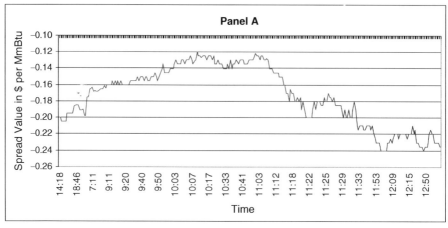

The intraday peak-to-trough move in the NG U-V spread was 12c on 8/2/06.

Trading in the NG U-V spread was discontinuous, so there are gaps in the graph when the spread did not trade.

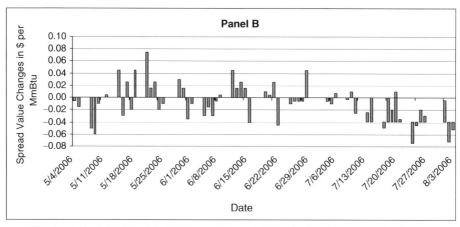

As of 8/1/06, the daily standard deviation of the NG U-V spread had been 2.67c based on the previous three months of data.
Therefore, the spread's intraday move, which is illustrated in panel A, was 4.5 (=12/2.67) standard devitations (based on the last three
months of daily data).

Figure 15.5   Panel A: Natural gas September–October spread. Panel B: Daily changes in natural gas September–October spread
Source: Till (2006b).

As it turned out, the scale of MotherRock's losses, which may have been up to $300 million, was small compared to Amaranth's experience the following month. According to Boyd (2006), Amaranth "was a buyer of many of the positions [of MotherRock.]".

15.6.2.2 Amaranth[3]

Amaranth Advisors, LLC was a multi-strategy hedge fund, which was founded in 2000 and was headquartered in Greenwich, Connecticut. The founder's original expertise was in

---

[3] This section is partially excerpted from Till (2008c). Copyright © Institutional Investor Journals.

convertible bonds. The fund later became involved in merger arbitrage, long-short equity, leveraged loans, blank-check companies, and in energy trading. As of 30 June 2006, energy trades accounted for about half of the fund's capital and generated about 75 percent of its profits, according to Burton and Leising (2006).

Davis (2006) has provided the best overview thus far on Amaranth's energy trading. The following account largely draws from her article.

Davis reported that Amaranth's head energy trader sometimes held "open positions to buy or sell tens of billions of dollars of commodities". Amaranth's energy trading operation was based in Calgary, Alberta. "[Amaranth's head energy trader] saw that a surplus of [natural] gas ... [in the] summer [in the US] could lead to low prices, but he also made bets that would pay off if, say, a hurricane or cold winter sharply reduced supplies by the end of winter. He was also willing to buy gas in even further-away years, as part of complex strategies."

"Buying what is known as 'winter' gas years into the future is a risky proposition because that market has many fewer traders than do contracts for months close at hand."

"Unlike oil, [natural] gas can't readily be moved about the globe to fill local shortages or relieve local supplies."

"[Natural gas] traders ... make complex wagers on gas at multiple points in the future, betting, say, that it will be cheap in the summer if there is a lot of supply, but expensive by a certain point in the winter. [Amaranth's head trader would] closely watch how weather affects prices and whether conditions will lead to more, or less, gas in a finite number of underground storage caverns."

Amaranth's structural position-taking may have assisted energy companies in their need to hedge their far-forward production, including through 2010.

"[Amaranth's energy book] was up for the year roughly $2 billion by April [2006], scoring a return of 11% to 13% that month alone, say investors in the Amaranth fund. Then ... [the energy strategies] ... had a loss of nearly $1 billion in May [2006] when prices of gas for delivery far in the future suddenly collapsed, investors add. [The energy traders] won back the $1 billion over the summer ... "

As of 31 August 2006, the fund had about $9.2 billion in assets under management.

On Monday 18 September 2006, market participants were made aware of Amaranth's distress. The founder had issued a letter to investors, informing them that the fund had lost an estimated 50% of their assets since its end-August value. Additionally, the fund had lost −$560 million on Thursday 14 September 2006 alone, according to *Reuters* (2006).

According to Davis *et al.* (2007), the fund had scrambled to transfer its positions to third-party financial institutions during the weekend of 16 and 17 September. Merrill Lynch had agreed to take on 25% of the fund's natural gas positions for a payment of about $250 million. The fund then lost a further $800 million through Tuesday 19 September 2006, due to the natural gas market moving severely against its positions. On Wednesday 20 September 2006, the fund succeeded in transferring its remaining energy positions to Citadel Investment Group and to its clearing broker, JP Morgan Chase, at a −$2.15 billion discount to their 19 September 2006 mark-to-market value. Apparently, the two firms equally shared the risk of Amaranth's positions. On Thursday 21 September 2006, the natural gas curve stabilized.

The hedge fund's losses ultimately totalled $6.6 billion, according to O'Reilly (2007).

On 25 June 2007, the US Senate Permanent Subcommittee on Investigations (PSI) released a report on the Amaranth debacle, entitled, "Excessive Speculation in the Natural Gas Market".

The 135-page report (and its further 345 pages of appendices) provided a wealth of detail on the Amaranth case. In carrying out their forensic analysis, the Senate subcommittee examined several million individual trades. The subcommittee obtained this information by subpoenaing records from the New York Mercantile Exchange (NYMEX), the Interconti-nental Exchange (ICE), Amaranth, and other traders.

Amaranth's spread trading strategy involved taking long positions in winter contract deliveries and short positions in non-winter contract deliveries. These positions would have benefited from potential weather events such as hurricanes and cold-shocks from 2006 through 2010. Although one can justify the economic rationale for Amaranth's strategy, both trade-sizing *and* value matter even more so.

The US Senate PSI found that in late July 2006, Amaranth's natural gas positions for delivery in January 2007 represented "a volume of natural gas that equaled the entire amount of natural gas eventually used in that month by US residential consumers nationwide".

Drawing from the US Senate's report, Table 15.3 summarizes the scale of Amaranth's natural gas trading activity. Figure 15.6 draws from the report's appendix to show the positioning of the fund through May 2009, as of the end of August 2006. The US Senate report does not include similar charts for the fund's positions past the May 2009 maturity date. The report also does not include the fund's miscellaneous commodity investments.

Table 15.3 Scale of Amaranth's natural gas trading: excerpted from US Senate Report of 25 June 2007

At times Amaranth controlled up to 40 % of all the open interest on NYMEX for the winter months (October 2006 through March 2007).	pp. 51–52
In late July 2006, Amaranth held a total of more than 80,000 NYMEX and ICE contracts for January 2007, representing a volume of natural gas that equaled the entire amount of natural gas eventually used in that month by US residential consumers nationwide.	p. 52
On July 31st, 2006, Amaranth's trading in the March and April 2007 contracts represented almost 70 % of the total NYMEX trading volume in each of these contracts on that date.	p. 52
Amaranth held large positions in winter and summer months spanning the five-year period from 2006-2010.	p. 52
For example, Amaranth held 60 % of the outstanding contracts (open interest) in all NYMEX natural gas futures contracts for 2010.	p. 52
On 7/24/06, Amaranth's futures position as a % of NYMEX futures open interest in the December 2007 contract was 81 %.	p. 94
On 8/28/06, Amaranth accounted for over 40 % of the total volume on the ICE, and over 25 % of the entire volume of exchange-traded futures and swaps on NYMEX and on ICE on that date.	p. 101
NYMEX: New York Mercantile Exchange	
ICE: Intercontinental Exchange	

Source: Excerpted from Staff Report (2007). The right-hand column shows on what page of the Staff Report each point is derived from.

Amaranth's position sizes were obviously too large for a financial entity that had *no* phys-ical energy assets. If a financial firm cannot make or take physical delivery of a commodity, then that firm's exit strategy is *very* constrained. Also, the fund had entered into these vast positions at exceedingly wide levels for these spreads.

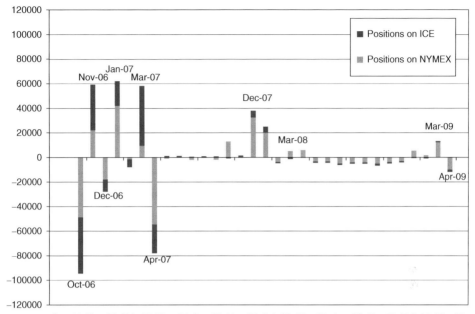

Figure 15.6   Amaranth's forward curve on 31 August 2006. Natural gas contracts on NYMEX and ICE
Source: Based on Staff Report (2007), Appendix V, p. 38.

Using the Senate report's documented positions for Amaranth as of 31 August 2006, we find that two spreads were 93 % correlated to Amaranth's natural gas book: the November 2006 vs. October 2006 (NGX-V6) spread; and the March 2007 vs. April 2007 (NGH-J7) spread.

In our analysis, we examined the past spread values for the November vs. October 2006 spread and the March vs. April 2007 spread in order to understand the riskiness of Amaranth's documented 31 August 2006 portfolio.

If these two spreads had reverted to levels that had prevailed at the end of August during the previous six years, one could have seen that up to −36 % could have been lost under *normal* conditions. This is illustrated in Table 15.4.

This was two weeks before the fund's implosion.

One caveat with this analysis is that it is based solely on the positions that were documented in the 25 June US Senate report's graphical appendix. This analysis may therefore be incomplete, to the extent that Amaranth held other sizeable positions *not* documented in the Senate report, *or* if the Senate report oversimplified Amaranth's natural gas position-taking, which included options.

In the middle of September 2006, the fund had lost more than $2 billion month-to-date. It was at this point that the critical-liquidation-cycle was initiated for the fund, as illustrated in Fig. 15.7. Figure 15.7's framework appears to be quite appropriate for the Amaranth case.

In the case of Amaranth, there was no natural (financial) counterparty who could entirely take on their positions during a very short space of time when the fund became distressed

Table 15.4 Scenario analysis of Amaranth's key risk positions as of 31.08.06

Number of Contracts (105,620) 59,543	Spread Symbol	Natural Gas Spread	8/31/06 Level
	NGV-X	October–November	−2.18
	NGH-J	March–April	2.14

Scenario Analysis if Winter vs. Non-Winter Spreads Reverted to Past Relationships

Date	NGV-X	NGH-J	Losses due to V-X	Losses due to H-J	Total Losses	Portfolio Loss
8/31/2000	−0.058	0.26	$(2,241,256,400)	$(1,119,408,400)	$(3,360,664,800)	−36.5 %
8/31/2001	−0.33	0.09	$(1,953,970,000)	$(1,220,631,500)	$(3,174,601,500)	−34.5 %
8/31/2002	−0.33	0.113	$(1,953,970,000)	$(1,206,936,610)	$(3,160,906,610)	−34.4 %
8/31/2003	−0.25	0.44	$(2,038,466,000)	$(1,012,231,000)	$(3,050,697,000)	−33.2 %
8/30/2004	−0.643	0.57	$(1,623,379,400)	$(934,825,100)	$(2,558,204,500)	−27.8 %
8/31/2005	−0.185	2.24	$(2,107,119,000)	$59,543,000	$(2,047,576,000)	−22.3 %

Source: Till (2008c). Copyright © Institutional Investor Journals.

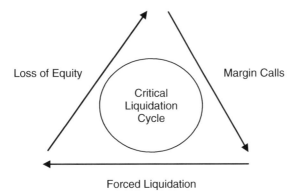

Figure 15.7   The critical liquidation cycle
Source: De Souza and Smirnov (2004). Copyright (c) Institutional Investor Journals.

in mid-September 2006. The natural counterparties to Amaranth's trades were the physical-market participants who had either locked in the value of forward production or storage. The physical-market participants would likely have had physical assets against their derivatives positions so would have had little pressing economic need to unwind these trades at Amaranth's convenience.

We can infer how long it may have taken to unwind the Amaranth positions by seeing if there were any footprints in natural gas price patterns from 20 September 2006 onwards.[4]

Figure 15.10 shows the evolution of natural gas spreads in which the long legs are the winter contracts, and the short legs are summer and spring contracts, which in turn are collectively correlated to Amaranth's actual positions. This graph is from 1 September 2006 through 31 December 2006.

From this graph, we see that the spreads recovered in late September during the immediate aftermath of the portfolio transfer, indicating a (temporary) absence of liquidation pressure. At the end of September 2006, Citadel assumed the entire Amaranth portfolio, taking on JP Morgan's half of Amaranth's positions, by paying JP Morgan $725 million; Citadel also received all the remaining concessionary payments from Amaranth, according to Baer (2006).

Again examining Fig. 15.10, we note that the natural gas spreads smoothly declined throughout October, and in the main bottomed out by the end of October.

At the end of November 2006, there were widespread public reports about the contents of Citadel's bond prospectus, which provided some commentary on the timing of the unwind of Amaranth's trades. According to Baer (2006), the Citadel document said that the firm had reduced the risk of its Amaranth positions by two-thirds during the first two weeks of October. Since the natural gas curve bottomed out at the end of October, we infer that Citadel essentially finished unwinding the risk of the remaining positions during the last two weeks of October.

We expect that commercial-market hedgers were the natural other side to Citadel's orderly unwind of October 2006. Commercial-market participants probably elected to realize their substantial hedging windfall at this time.

---

[4] This section is based on Till (2007b).

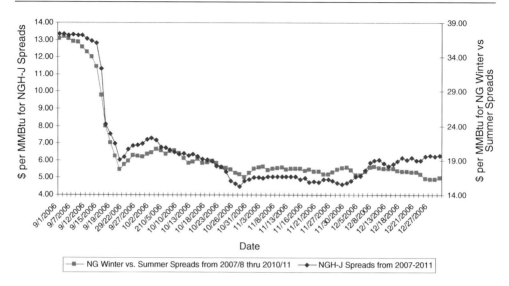

Figure 15.8   Natural gas spreads, 01.09.06–31.12.06
Notes: NG is an abbreviation for natural gas. H and J are symbols for the March and April futures contracts respectively.
Source of Data: Bloomberg.

Figure 15.8 shows that there does not appear to be further liquidation pressure on the natural gas curve in November and December 2006. Given how stable the curve was during this time, this is when normal two-sided flow likely resumed.

Given how orderly Citadel's unwind was during October 2006, the firm probably only sustained relatively small losses during this time. Therefore, it appears that Citadel was able to realize substantial net profits, given the $1.425 billion payment that it ultimately received for agreeing to take on Amaranth's distressed portfolio. [$1.425 billion = $2.15 billion (concessionary payment received by Citadel and JP Morgan) minus the $725 million (that Citadel paid JP Morgan so that Citadel could fully take on the entire Amaranth energy portfolio and all remaining concessionary payments).]

A key lesson from the Amaranth debacle was noted by Greer of PIMCO, as cited in Hougan (2008): " … the market showed that someone can actually be so big that the market will punish them, rather than reward them for their size".

Tying the MotherRock and Amaranth debacles back together, the two firms were on the opposite sides of two natural gas spreads: the NGH-J (March–April) and the NGF-V (January–October) spread,[5] according to Leising (2007b), who quoted the 25 June Senate report on the Amaranth debacle. The Senate report, in turn, cited an unnamed trader. In particular, MotherRock had been short the March–April 2007 spread:

" 'When Amaranth's trading caused a sudden 72-cent jump in the March/April price spread, a number of MotherRock's positions were directly affected, and MotherRock was

---

[5] We had previously noted that Amaranth's positions were very highly correlated to the March–April 2007 spread and the November–October 2006 spread. The November–October 2006 spread, in turn, had been highly correlated to the January (2007)–October (2006) spread.

Panel A

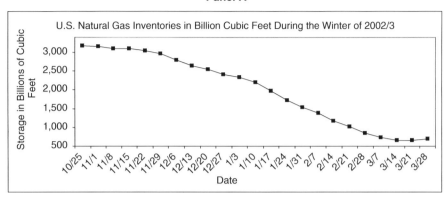

Panel B

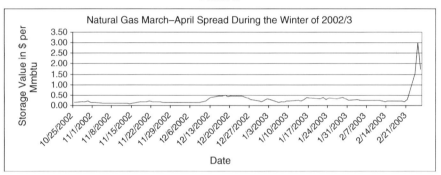

Figure 15.9   Panel A: February 2003 near-stock-out scenario. Panel B: Natural gas March–April spread during the winter of 2002/3
Source: Till (2006b).

unable to' pay its broker, the [Senate] report said. MotherRock 'no longer had sufficient funds to continue operations. The hedge fund folded soon after.' "

In summary, MotherRock shut down after being *short* the March–April natural gas spread. Correspondingly, Amaranth shut down one month later after being *long* the March–April natural gas spread. It is no wonder that traders refer to the March–April natural gas futures spread as the "widow-maker".

What makes this spread so unstable? At the end of the winter, if there is a cold shock and inventories are at their seasonal low, the end-of-winter futures contract's price can explode relative to later-month contracts in order to limit current use of natural gas to absolutely essential activities. This scenario occurred in the winter of 2002/3 and is illustrated in Fig. 15.9. Lammey (2005) quotes a futures trader regarding the extremely cold winter of 2002–2003: "I remember that season well, because we started off the winter with intense cold, and ended the season late with intense cold – and many participants in the industry were seriously worried that there might not be enough gas to get us across the finish line."

Note in particular how extremely positively-skewed the March–April natural gas spread can be, if there is a near-stock-out scenario in natural gas, as shown in Fig. 15.9 Panel B.

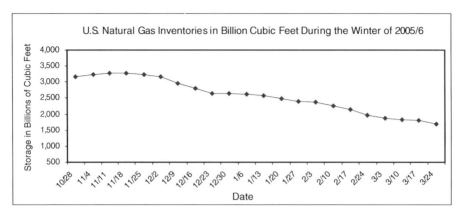

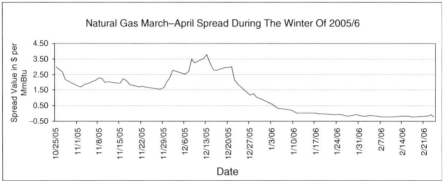

Figure 15.10   Fear-premium-drained-out-of-spread-market scenario
Source of data: Bloomberg.

Instead, if the winter is unexpectedly mild, and there are still massive amounts of natural gas in storage, then the near-month price of natural gas plummets to encourage its current use and the curve trades in contango (that is March trades at a discount to April) in order to provide a return to any storage operator who can store gas. This occurred, for example, during the end-of-the-winter in early 2006. This is illustrated in Fig. 15.10.

As one examines the performance of the March–April spread over the past eight years, it appears that this spread has a binary outcome: either it trades in steep backwardation (with March over April) if there is a sufficiently cold winter *and* insufficient end-of-winter inventories, or it trades at a contango level, representing the returns to storage, if there is a mild-to-normal winter. This observation will help us understand the continual problems that hedge funds (who do not have physical storage capabilities) have with positions in the March–April natural gas spread.

But first we should note that the Amaranth debacle of 2006 was already foreshadowed by the unsuccessful trading experience of BP's propane traders. The CFTC complaint against BP and its propane trading activities shows that BP's propane traders had studied the experience of early spring 2003. The BP traders noted how (1) *propane* inventories had been drawn-down substantially; and they also documented how (2) nearer-month-delivery *propane* had traded at a substantial premium to later-month-delivery propane at the end-of-the-heating season. A chart showing a propane calendar spread during February 2003 in BP's

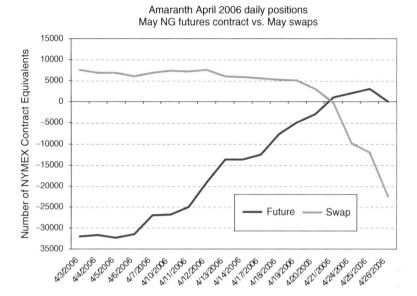

Figure 15.11 Amaranth April 2006 daily positions: May NG futures contract vs. May swaps
Source: Based on Figure 15.10 of FERC (2007).

"Lessons Learned" presentation, which, as noted, is included in the CFTC complaint, qual-itatively looks identical to Fig. 15.11's natural gas spread over the same period. Assuming that 2003's season-ending inventories indicated true scarcity, the BP traders believed they had a fundamental indicator for whether a similar tight situation could develop in 2004, and which they could further profit from, if they established "a dominant position" in end-of-winter-delivery propane.

In fact, physical propane was not scarce in March 2004, and the BP traders lost twice as much as their worst-case scenario in carrying out their speculative strategy. As noted previously, the trading loss was $10 million, at least according to the "Lessons Learned" presentation. Again, though, the greater loss was from the civil and criminal penalties exacted by the CFTC and DOJ for adopting a strategy to corner a commodities market, with the fines totaling $303 million.

One of the unresolved elements of the Amaranth case is what civil penalties may be assessed against the hedge fund and its principals. From the outcome of the BP propane case, as announced on 25 October 2007, one might expect substantial fines could also be potentially levied against Amaranth. Given that the CFTC had also fined a BP gasoline trader as an individual, one might also expect that Amaranth's principals could be at risk as well.

Perhaps it is not a surprise then that both the CFTC and the Federal Energy Regulatory Commission (FERC) have been pursuing actions against the former hedge fund.[6] These actions were announced on 25 and 26 July 2007 in CFTC (2007a) and FERC (2007). That said, as of the writing of this chapter, Amaranth's current and former principals were vigorously countering the regulatory actions against the firm and its former traders.

---

[6] This section is excerpted from Till (2008c). Copyright © Institutional Investor Journals.

While the Senate report focused on whether Amaranth's position-taking pushed *up* the price of forward winter natural gas prices, the CFTC and FERC's (publicly known) investigations were much more narrowly focused on Amaranth's trading activities on several days of 2006.

The CFTC's regulatory authority mainly covers the exchange-traded futures markets, so their investigation narrowly focused on the fund's documented activities on the NYMEX. Correspondingly, the FERC is responsible for overseeing the wholesale natural gas and electricity markets in the US. The monthly settlement price for the expiring NYMEX natural gas futures contract is frequently used in pricing physical natural gas transactions, so the FERC may have oversight jurisdiction if there is an attempted (or actual) manipulation of the NYMEX settlement price for expiring contracts.

Essentially, both the CFTC complaint of 25 July 2007 and the FERC preliminary findings of 26 July 2007 allege that Amaranth and its energy traders attempted to manipulate the settlement price of the expiring NYMEX futures contract *downwards* on several occasions in order to benefit very large over-the-counter Intercontinental Exchange (ICE) swaps that were positioned short.[7] The fund's ICE swaps cash-settled against the NYMEX settlement price and so would benefit from a decline in the NYMEX price.

Figure 15.11, for example, shows the relative positioning of Amaranth's futures and swaps positions going into the 26 April expiry of the May 2006 natural gas futures contract. This figure illustrates how the ICE short position became much larger than the NYMEX long position as of the late-April expiry. The CFTC and FERC cite numerous trading records, showing how the fund concentrated its sales of its long position in NYMEX futures until the very end of the trading day. This strategy may have had a large impact in driving down the price of the expiring contract.

In addition to trading records, both the CFTC and FERC cite voluminous e-mail exchanges, instant messages, and recorded phone conversations to bolster their allegations of an attempted (or actual) price manipulation.

The CFTC also alleged that Amaranth made false statements to the NYMEX when the exchange formally asked the fund about the justification and commercial purpose of its May-contract expiry trading.

The CFTC complaint requests that the US District Court in the Southern District of New York enter an order prohibiting Amaranth and its former head trader from "engaging in any business activities related to commodity interest trading" amongst other prohibitions.

The FERC was granted anti-manipulation authority in the physical natural gas markets by the Congress in 2005, and the Amaranth case is the first such exercise of this authority.

Procedurally, the FERC issued a "show cause order" on 26 July 2007 "after making a preliminary finding of serious manipulation in the natural gas markets". The FERC is "proposing to order disgorgement of unjust profits and civil penalties totaling nearly $300 million", including a penalty of $30 million for Amaranth's former head trader.

The FERC order explains why the commission was calling for very large monetary penalties for Amaranth and two of its natural gas traders:

"There are strong enforcement and deterrence policy bases for setting the civil penalties for individual traders at a high level. The traders in this industry have historically been capable of easily recovering from disastrous performance or misconduct by simply moving to,

---

[7] To be more precise, the CFTC complaint alleges *attempted manipulation*, while the FERC order alleges *actual manipulation*.

or starting up, another trading operation. Even after spectacular failures, a trader can attract capital to start new trading activities or a new fund. ... Under the circumstances, the Commission sends here a clear message that manipulation will have severe personal consequences for individual traders in order to deter them and others from violative behavior."

15.6.2.3 Saracen

We had previously stated that the March–April natural gas spread can have a binary outcome, depending on whether there is an extreme winter or not. For markets with storage, delivery, or processing rigidities, the inter-market or intra-market spreads frequently have binary outcomes. Arguably, this has essentially also become the case for gasoline crack spreads. One either has insufficient refining capacity and the margin of gasoline over crude oil (the gasoline crack spread) becomes $35 per barrel, as in the summer of 2007; or one has sufficient capacity, and the gasoline crack becomes negative, as in March 2008.

In binary markets such as the end-of-winter natural gas calendar spread (and the summer gasoline crack), one can see what probability the market is pricing in for extreme outcomes in the future, and then decide whether those odds make sense for a trading strategy.

The following is an example of this methodology employed by Premia Capital for the March–April (H-J) natural gas spread. If there is a near stock-out at the end of February, the March–April spread can trade to $2.99 per MMBtu, as in the winter of 2003. If there is a mild-to-normal winter, the spread can mature to about −15c per MMBtu, as in the past four winters.

As of 29 December 2006, the forward natural gas spreads with maturities in 2007 through 2011 had the following values:

NGH-J7:	−10c
NGH-J8:	$1.14
NGH-J9:	$1.33
NGH-J0:	$1.30
NGH-J1:	$1.29

Average from 2008 through 2011: $1.265.

Say p is the probability of a stock-out scenario, and (1−p) is the probability of a comfortable winter.

$$\$1.265(\text{forward price of NGH} - \text{J}) = [p^*\$2.99] \mid [(1 - p)^* - \$0.15]. \longrightarrow p = 45\%.$$

As of 29 December 2006, the forward natural gas market was pricing in a continual 45 % chance of stock-out-fears coming to pass over the following four years.

Is this probability a low or a high number? It would depend on one's information on whether sufficient new production, storage, or Liquid Natural Gas (LNG) terminals would come on-line over time to make a stock-out scenario unlikely. In the absence of sufficient new capacity, then the NGH-J spread is purely a bet on Mother Nature, which is rather difficult to risk-manage.

On 16 February 2008, Whitehouse et al. (2008) reported that Houston-based Saracen Energy Partners LP had "posted undisclosed losses on natural gas trading and ... [had]

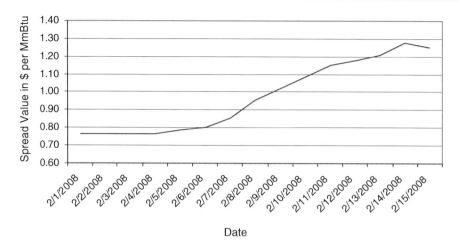

Figure 15.12   Natural gas March–April 2009 spread – 01.02.08–15.02.08
Source of data: Bloomberg.

been forced to liquidate positions". The firm operates in the "energy markets, including those for natural gas, coal, refined products, and electricity. Natural gas traders said the fund incurred losses betting on the difference between March 2009 and April 2009 natural gas contracts."

"The Saracen fund had $1.6 billion in assets under management at the end of January [2008] ...   The fund ...   dropped 31 % year-to-date, as of Thursday [14 February 2008] ...   According to traders, Saracen bet that the spread between the March and April 2009 contracts would decline, when in fact it widened by 41 % in a month," reported Whitehouse *et al*. (2008). Figure 15.12 shows the evolution of the NGH-J 2009 spread during the first two weeks of February 2008.

For market participants, it was noteworthy that the March–April spread appeared to be the culprit in trading losses once again, this time from the short-side, whereas Amaranth's difficulties arose from trading this spread from the long-side. (And arguably, BP's propane strategy was highly correlated to this end-of-winter strategy as well, where they were approaching this situation from the long-side, like Amaranth.)

The five-(business-)day move in the NGH-J9 spread from 7 February 2008 to 14 February 2008 was equal to a 7-standard-deviation move, based on the spread's previous three months of trading history. This is for a spread that matured one year into the future. It is unlikely that expectations on one-year-out storage had changed in a week, so this is a sign of a distressed liquidation.

Based on the binary-outcome model described above, a spread value for NGH-J9 of +85.5c (which was where the spread was trading on 7 February 2008) implies a market forecast of there being a (near-)stock-out of 32 % one-year forward. A spread value of +$1.25 (which was where the spread was trading on 14 February 2008) gives a corresponding probability of 46 %.

Whether fading the possibility of a future stock-out in the natural gas market is a good idea or not, one would definitely conclude that, for short-options-like trades such as this, sizing should be constrained to where an exit would not result in undue liquidation pressure on the market.

When examining an energy trading loss such as Saracen's in light of the diminished liquidity and credit existing during the spring of 2008, one might reasonably assert that we are missing the overall point. If Bear Stearns, the (previously) fifth largest investment bank in the United States, could so completely misjudge its liquidity situation in mid-March 2008 that it nearly went bankrupt, then it might not be unusual that other market participants had temporarily missed that the trading environment had fundamentally changed as well.[8]

To be fair to commodity traders who have been in the press for experiencing 20%-plus losses, investors in commodity funds are conditioned to expect both volatility and drawdowns from individual commodity managers. A large loss does not mean that a commodity fund is no longer viable, as long as the loss is within investor expectations and no fraud is involved. For example, the highly-regarded commodity hedge-fund firm, Ospraie Management LLC, closed one of its hedge funds, the Ospraie Point Fund, after it lost −29% during the first five months of 2006, according to Bentley (2006). The firm's flagship fund also lost −19% over the same period. Since June 2006, this hedge-fund firm has both been profitable for its clients and very successful in increasing assets under management; the firm currently manages $9-billion (as of the end of March 2008), according to Kishan and Batcho-Lino (2008).

While we have focused on the natural gas markets reasonably extensively in this chapter, one should note that the most consistent calendar-spread strategies have historically arisen from inflection points in seasonal build-draw cycles in commodity inventories. The reasoning described in this section for natural gas calendar spreads applies across all storable and quasi-storable commodity markets. This underlying principle was originally described for the grain futures markets in Cootner (1967) and reviewed in Till (2007a).

15.6.3   Exit strategy[9]

Provided that one's sizing in the commodity futures markets is modest enough that liquidating a position does not cause a many standard-deviation move in price, which then causes one's investors and/or creditors to create a further distressed liquidation, we would recommend the following strategy for deciding when to exit a losing strategy.

Using long-term data, one can directly examine the worst performance of a commodity trade under similar circumstances in the past. In practice, we have found that such a measure will sometimes be larger than a Value-at-Risk measure based on recent volatility.

If the loss on a particular commodity futures trade exceeds the historical worst case, this can be an indication of a new regime that is not reflected in the data. This should trigger an exit from a trade since one no longer has a handle on the worst-case scenario.

During the summer of 2005, a very good example of a market undergoing fundamental changes has been the petroleum complex. A historically reliable strategy had been to enter into the gasoline versus heating oil spread. Until 2005, traders had expected gasoline to outperform heating oil coming into the US summer driving season. The market historically

---

[8] Further, Credit Suisse's ex-CEO, Oswald Gruebel stated in late April 2008 that the international financial system had been close to the brink in mid-March 2008, according to Thompson (2008). Fortunately, the Federal Reserve Board and the European Central Bank realized this, and on a *de facto* basis took over the inter-bank market. "We've narrowly escaped a system collapse. This has never happened before," Gruebel said.

[9] This section is excerpted from Till (2006a).

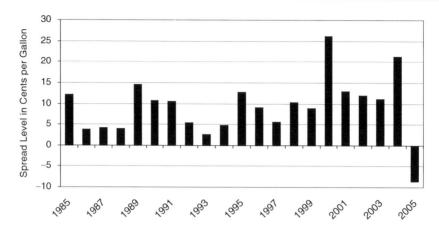

Figure 15.13   July gasoline vs. heating oil spread differential as of the 5th business day of June 1985
through 2005
Source: Till (2006a).

provided large monetary incentives to refiners to maximize the production of gasoline at
the expense of heating oil to sufficiently service US summer gasoline demand.

2005 was different. Fusaro (2005) revealed that in the summer of 2005, "the big Wall
Street houses and some other hedge funds lost many ... hundreds of millions [of dollars]
on gasoline/heating oil spreads. They could not imagine that heating oil would go higher
than gasoline in June. It just never happened before."

Figure 15.13 shows the gasoline versus heating oil spread differential as of the beginning
of June since 1985. Indeed, it had been unprecedented for heating oil to be priced at a
premium to gasoline during that time of year.

What happened? One hypothesis is that Chinese demand patterns have created structural
changes in the commodity markets, as alluded to previously. According to Stein (2005),
"This is the first business cycle where Chinese demand is having a global effect on prices,
notably of energy and other raw materials."

In the specific case of petroleum products, Farivar (2005) stated that "in China, diesel
demand has been rising rapidly, because power shortages have forced many companies to use
stand-alone generators. Diesel accounts for a significant portion of the overall rise in Chinese
oil demand over the past year." Because diesel and heating oil have similar compositions,
heating oil futures are frequently used as a proxy hedge for diesel inventories, which means
that a rise in diesel prices tends to lead to a rise in the value of heating oil futures.

It appears that the Chinese demand for diesel trumped the American consumer's demand
for gasoline, a scenario that was historically unprecedented.

In 2005, once the summer gasoline-versus-heating-oil spread had declined more than had
been the case in previous years, one had a signal that a structural break was occurring, and the
prudent reaction was to exit the strategy before further potentially catastrophic losses ensued.

15.6.4   Scenario analyses

As described in Till and Gunzberg (2006), when designing a risk-management program for
a commodity investment, one needs to address both idiosyncratic risks and macro risks.

Idiosyncratic risks include those unique to a specific commodity market. Examples include simulating the impact of the discovery of Mad Cow disease in the US on live cattle futures positions as well as examining the impact of the New York harbor freezing over on the price of near-month heating oil futures positions. Macro risks include discovering those risks in the portfolio that can create inadvertent correlations amongst seemingly uncorrelated positions. Examples include simulating the impact of a 9/11/01 event on a portfolio that is long economically sensitive commodities as well as examining the impact of surprisingly cold weather at the end of the winter on a portfolio of energy positions.

15.6.5 Leverage level

Another consideration in a commodity futures risk management program is how much leverage to use. Futures trading requires a relatively small amount of margin. Trade sizing is mainly a matter of how much risk one wants to assume. An investor is not very constrained by the amount of initial capital committed to trading.

Since the spring of 2006, the choice of leverage level has become more difficult, given the periodic bouts of de-risking and deleveraging that have occurred as the commodity markets have become more correlated with other risk assets, at least over short time-horizons.

Commodities were clearly not immune from sharp episodes of widespread deleveraging of risky investments during the past two years, as occurred during May and June of 2006; end of February 2007; and again in mid-August 2007, and which was commented upon by the Bank of Japan in "Monitoring Commodity Markets From the Perspective of Understanding Global Financial Market Trends" in Terada and Shimizu (2007).

During the May/June 2006 deleveraging of risky investments, for example, commodities appeared to become the same trade along with other risk assets. This is illustrated in Table 15.5. In observing this correlation, one might temper the amount of leverage applied to long commodity trades, or include other assets in the portfolio that would be expected

Table 15.5 10 May 2006 through 13 June 2006

"Risk Indicator" VIX (Equity Implied Vol)*	12.0 %
"Risk Assets"	Percent Change
Bovespa (IBX50)	−23.5 %
Nasdaq	−10.4 %
S&P 500	−7.3 %
Nikkei	−10.4 %
Silver	−32.4 %
Copper	−18.2 %
Gasoline (RFG)	−3.6 %
"Safe Havens"	Percent Change
Long Bond	1.8 %
Dollar vs. Yen (Long Dollars)	4.5 %

*The VIX increased from 11.78 % on 5/10/06 to 23.81 % on 6/13/06.

Source: Till (2008b).

Table 15.6   Risky asset price changes on 16 August 2007

Global Unwind	16-Aug-07
"Risk Indicator"	
VIX (Equity Implied Vol)*	31 %
"Risk Assets"	Daily Percent Change
Bovespa (IBX50)	−2.11 %
Nasdaq	−1.01 %
Nikkei	−1.99 %
Silver	−8.44 %
Copper	−7.26 %
Gasoline	−1.52 %
NZD vs. Yen	−5.32 %
"Safe Haven"	Percent Change
Long Bond	0.94 %
Crack Spreads (Refinery Margins)	Daily Change
Gasoline Crack	$1.05
Heat Crack	$0.48

*Absolute level of the VIX (and not change in level as in previous figure.)

	DJAIG MOVERS 8/16/2007 10:07 am CST		
Commodity	Price	Change	% Change
LMAHDS03	Aluminum	2543.00y	−9.00	−0.35
NGX7	Natural Gas	7.791	−0.046	−0.59
W Z7	Wheat	688 3/4	−8 1/4	−1.18
LCV7	Live Cattle	94.600	−1.325	−1.38
LHV7	Lean Hogs	67.550	−1.025	−1.49
LMZSDS03	Zinc	3230.00y	−65.00	−1.97
XBX7	RBOB Gasoline	187.43	−3.95	−2.06
GCZ7	Gold	665.20	−14.50	−2.13
CTZ7	Cotton	58.85	−1.33	−2.21
CLX7	Crude Oil	71.10	−1.73	−2.38
HOX7	Heating Oil	201.55	−4.99	−2.42
C Z7	Corn	336 1/2	−8 3/4	−2.53
LMNIDS03	Nickel	26500.0y	−800.0	−2.93
SBV7	Sugar	9.16	−0.29	−3.07
KCZ7	Coffee	119.30	−3.90	−3.17
BOZ7	Soybean Oil	35.27	−1.25	−3.42
SIZ7	Silver	12.290	−0.445	−3.49
S X7	Soybeans	821	−33 1/2	−3.92
HGZ7	Copper	314.80	−17.40	−5.24

Source of data: Bloomberg.
Source: Till (2008b).

to do well during any deleveraging. That said, the risk in the current environment may be more about being careful about the solvency of one's counterparties rather than about being concerned about future episodes of de-risking and deleveraging. According to Delaney *et al*. (2008), the UBS Equity Risk Appetite Indicator was languishing in extreme risk-aversion territory, so the likely problems, as of the spring of 2008, were due to not enough risk capital being devoted to risky trades rather than the other way around.

Another example of simultaneous deleveraging is from 27 February 2007. At the end of the trading day, market participants saw algorithmic strategies simultaneously deleverage across numerous risky investments, including in popular commodity plays. In this unusual environment, the normally illiquid platinum market was more liquid than the gold futures market, as leveraged participants rapidly tried to simultaneously unwind gold positions.

This phenomenon again became of concern on 16 August 2007, the day before the Federal Reserve Board cut the discount rate. On that date, *all* commodity markets in the Dow Jones AIG Commodity Index were down, along with *all* other risky assets; this is illustrated in Table 15.6. The next day, after the announcement of the Fed's action, most risk assets simultaneously rallied, including commodities.

One exception to the "global unwind" of the time was petroleum-complex refining margins, which were underpinned by relatively low product inventories, particularly in gasoline.

Tables 15.5 and 15.6 illustrate how the VIX, the equity-index implied volatility gauge calculated by the Chicago Board Options Exchange, has been a useful early indicator of the market entering into a de-risking environment, that in turn can negatively impact popular commodity plays.

During the week of 17 March 2008, market participants appeared to embrace a "preservation-of-capital" stance in the aftermath of the near collapse of Bear Stearns. Not only did three-month US Treasury Bills (T-Bills) hit a nadir of 39 bps in (annualized) yield, but the commodity markets witnessed a weekly sell-off, the scale of which had not been seen since 1956, according to Carpenter and Munshi (2008). Figure 15.14 shows how the

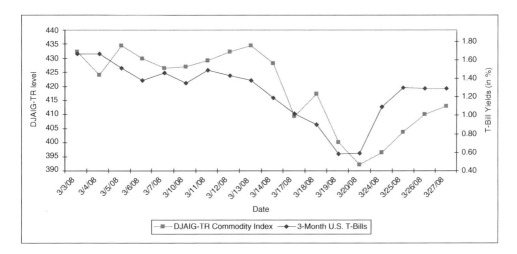

Figure 15.14 Dow Jones AIG Commodity Index: Total Return and 3-Month US Treasury Bills 3/3/08 to 3/27/08
Source of data: Bloomberg.

fortunes of the Dow Jones AIG Commodity Index fluctuated in March 2008, according to the degree to which investors were embracing T-Bills.

As of Spring 2008, T-Bill yields have been the best early indicator of the market entering into a powerful deleveraging environment, which in turn can have a strong adverse effect on leveraged commodity strategies.

15.7 CONCLUSION

Until recently, one could only gain expertise in commodity-derivatives relationships if one had worked in niche commodity-processor companies or in banks that specialized in hedging project risk for natural-resource companies. The contribution of this chapter is to help fill the knowledge gap in the risk management of commodity derivatives trading. The chapter emphasizes the constant challenges to a trader when attempting to navigate the very dynamic flows of both the commodity markets and the prevailing risk environment. The chapter also emphasizes that operational controls are paramount in an age of increasing legal and regulatory risk, particularly for firms involved in large-scale commodity derivatives trading.

15.7.1 Endnotes

The author would like to thank Hendrik Schwarz for helpful comments.

The ideas and opinions expressed in this article are the sole responsibility of the author.

The information contained in this chapter has been assembled from sources believed to be reliable, but is not guaranteed by the author.

15.8 REFERENCES

Akey, R. (2005). Commodities: A Case for Active Management. *Journal of Alternative Investments*, Fall, 8–29.

Akey, R. (2007). Alpha, Beta, and Commodities: Can a Commodities Investment be Both a High-Risk-Adjusted Return Source and a Portfolio Hedge? In H. Till and J. Eagleeye (Eds) *Intelligent Commodity Investing*. London: Risk Books, 377–417; and in *Journal of Wealth Management*, Fall 2006, 63–82.

Akey, R., H. Till and A. Kins (2006). Natural Resources Fund of Funds: Active Management, Risk Management, and Due Diligence. In: G. Gregoriou (Ed.) *Funds of Hedge Funds*. Oxford: Elsevier Finance, 383–399.

Baer, J. (2006). JP Morgan Sold Its Amaranth Energy Trades to Citadel. *Bloomberg News*, November 29.

Bank of Montreal (2007a). CAN 6-K for 5/29/07 Ex-99–1. Securities and Exchange Commission File 1–13354.

Bank of Montreal (2007b). CAN 6-K for 8/29/07. Securities and Exchange Commission File 1–13354.

Bentley, A. (2006). Ospraie Closes $250 Mln Commodity Hedge Fund. *Reuters*, June 8.

Blanco, C. and R. Mark (2007). BMO's Derivatives Blow Up. *The Desk*, June 1.

Boyd, R. (2006). Mother of All Losses. *The New York Post*, September 15, accessed electronically through LexisNexis.

Burton, K. and M. Leising (2006). Amaranth Says Funds Lost 50% on Gas Trades This Month. *Bloomberg News*, September 18.

Cameron, D. and A. Lucchetti (2008). MF Global Takes a Large Loss On Unauthorized Wheat Trades. *Wall Street Journal Online*, February 28.

Carpenter, C. and M. Munshi (2008). Commodity Prices Head for Biggest Weekly Decline Since 1956. *Bloomberg News*, March 20.

Cashin, A. (2008). Market Commentary. UBS Financial Services, March 18.

Christory, C., S. Daul and J.R. Giraud (2006). Quantification of Hedge Fund Default Risk. *Journal of Alternative Investments*; Fall, 71–86.

Collins, D. (2007). Commodity Indexes Getting More Complex. *Futures Magazine*, July, 58–61.

Collins, J. (2001). *Good to Great* New York: HarperBusiness.

Commodity Futures Trading Commission (2006a). US Commodity Futures Trading Commission Charges BP Products North America, Inc. with Cornering the Propane Market and Manipulating the Price of Propane. Release 5193-06, June 28.

Commodity Futures Trading Commission (2006b). Complaint for Injunctive and Other Equitable Relief and Civil Monetary Penalties Under the Commodity Exchange Act. United States District Court, Northern District of Illinois, US CFTC (Plaintiff) v. BP Products North America, Inc. (Defendant), June 28.

Commodity Futures Trading Commission (2007a) Complaint for Injunctive and Other Equitable Relief and Civil Monetary Penalties Under the Commodity Exchange Act, United States District Court, Southern District of New York, US CFTC (Plaintiff) v. Amaranth Advisors, LLC, Amaranth Advisors (Calgary) ULC and Brian Hunter (Defendants), July 25.

Commodity Futures Trading Commission (2007b). BP Agrees to Pay a Total of $303 Million in Sanctions to Settle Charges of Manipulation and Attempted Manipulation in the Propane Market. Release 5405-07, October 25.

Commodity Futures Trading Commission (2007c). Former BP Trader Paul Kelly Agrees to Pay $400,000 Civil Penalty to Settle US Commodity Futures Trading Commission Charges of Attempted Manipulation of the NYMEX Unleaded Gasoline Futures Contract. Release 5402-07, October 25.

Cootner, P. (1967). Speculation and Hedging. *Food Research Institute Studies, Supplement*, **7**, 64–105.

Davis, A. (2006). How Giant Bets on Natural Gas Sank Brash Hedge-Fund Trader. *Wall Street Journal Online*, September 19.

Davis, A., G. Zuckerman and H. Sender (2007). Hedge-Fund Hardball: Amid Amaranth's Crisis, Other Players Profited. *Wall Street Journal Online*, January 30.

Delaney, J., W. Darwin, J. Palma and T. Adolff (2008). Global Risk Radar. UBS Investment Research, February 11.

De Souza, C. and M. Smirnov (2004). Dynamic Leverage. *Journal of Portfolio Management*, Fall, 25–39.

Dowd, G. (2007). The Move to Electronic Trading: What to Expect in the Natural-Resources Markets. In: H. Till and J. Eagleeye (Eds) *Intelligent Commodity Investing*. London: Risk Books, 501–515.

Eagleeye, J. (2007). Risk Management, Strategy Development, and Portfolio Construction in a Commodity Futures Programme. In H. Till and J. Eagleeye (Eds) *Intelligent Commodity Investing*. London: Risk Books, 491–497.

Farivar, M. (2005) Diesel Prices Take on Life of Their Own as Demand Surges. *Dow Jones Newswires*, May 20.

Federal Energy Regulatory Commission (2007). *Amaranth et al.*, Docket No. IN07–26-000, "Order to Show Cause and Notice of Proposed Penalties", July 26.

Fusaro, P. (2005). Energy: An Immature Financial Market. *Energy Hedge*, October 1.

Gains, K. (2007). Citadel Wellington LLC & Citadel Kensington Global Strategies Fund Ltd. Operations Quality Rating Report. Moody's Investors Services, March 23.

Goldstein, M., L.R. Silva, and M. Davis (2006). MotherRock Cries Uncle. TheStreet.com, August 3.

Gordon, D. (2003a). Risk By Any Other Name. Glenwood Capital Investments, LLC. Presentation to Chicago QWAFAFEW, http://www.qwafafew.org/chicago, October 16.

Gordon, D. (2003b). Risk by Any Other Name. *Journal of Alternative Investments*, Fall, 83–86.

Grant, K. (2004). *Trading Risk*. Hoboken: John Wiley & Sons Inc.

Harris, C. (2006). Landing on His Feet. *Financial Times*, November 3, accessed electronically through FT.com.

Herbst-Bayliss, S. (2007). After Huge Hedge Fund Failure, Amaranth Trader Woos Investors For New Fund. *Reuters*, March 23.

Hougan, M. (2008). An Interview with Bob Greer. HardAssetsInvestor.com, March 25.

Kat, H. and F. Menexe (2003). Persistence in Hedge Fund Performance: The True Value of a Track Record. *Journal of Alternative Investments*, Spring, 66–72.

Kishan, S. and S. Batcho-Lino (2008). Ospraie to Buy ConAgra Trading Unit for $2.1 Billion. *Bloomberg News*, March 27.

Lahav, O. (2007). Brevan Howard Master Fund Ltd. Operations Quality Rating Report. Moody's Investors Service, October 16.

Lammey, A. (2005). Choppy Winter Forecasts Suggest Healthy 1 TcF End to Drawdown. *Natural Gas Week*, December 5, 2–3.

Leising, M. (2006). MotherRock Energy Hedge Fund Closing After Losses. *Bloomberg News*, August 3.

Leising, M. (2007a). Nymex Director Quits Optionable Over CEO's Jail Time. *Bloomberg News*, May 15.

Leising, M. (2007b). Amaranth Trading Led to MotherRock Loss, Senate Report Says. *Bloomberg News*, June 25.

Leising, M. and K. Burton (2006). MotherRock Energy Hedge Fund Closing After Losses. *Bloomberg News*, August 3.

MarketWatch (2006). Hedge Fund's Failure May Threaten ABN Amro, UBS Deal: Report. August 9.

Mavin, D. (2007). BMO Moves On Auditors' Report: Source. *National Post*, May 10.

McGlashan, B. (2007). Risk Review: Bank of Montreal Group/Investor Community Conference Call/Q1 2007/Prior to Restatement. March 1.

MF Global (2008). MF Global Expects Record Volumes and Net Revenues for Fiscal Fourth Quarter 2008: Independent Consultants Report Preliminary Risk Review Findings. April 18.

Oldfield, R. (2007). *Simple But Not Easy*. London: Doddington Publishing, as quoted in *HFM Week*, November 22–28, p. 12.

O'Reilly, C. (2007). Ex-Amaranth Trader Sues Agency to Block Enforcement. *Bloomberg News*, July 24.

Reuters (2006). Amaranth Says Determined to Stay in Business. September 22.

Smith, E.B. and D. Scheer (2008). MF Global's Dooley Lost House on Bad Trades Before Bet on Wheat. *Bloomberg News*, March 26.

Staff Report (2007). Permanent Subcommittee on Investigations, Committee on Homeland Security and Government Affairs, United States Senate. Excessive Speculation in the Natural Gas Market. June 25.

Stein, G. (2005). World Oil Demand Revised Down Again. *Lombard Street Research's World Service Daily Note*, September 9.

Terada, T., and T. Shimizu, 2007, Monitoring Commodity Markets: From the Perspective of Understanding Global Financial Market Trends *Bank of Japan Review*, November.

Tett, G. (2008). Western Banks Face Backlash As They Hand Out Begging Bowl. *Financial Times*, February 8, accessed electronically through FT.com.

The Desk (2007a). As the Implosion Turns. www.scudderpublishing.com, May 4.

The Desk (2007b). Trader Surprised by Optionable's Dirty Tricks. May 18.

The Desk (2007c). Optionable Debacle: What Next? May 25.

The Desk (2007d). Desk Chiefs Comment on Marking Your Books. June 1.

Thompson, A. (2008). International Financial System Was Close to the Brink: Credit Suisse Ex-CEO. *Thomson Financial*, April 20, accessed electronically through afxnews.com.

Till, H. (2006a). Portfolio Risk Measurement in Commodity Futures Investments. In: T. Ryan (Ed.) *Portfolio Analysis: Advanced Topics in Performance Measurement, Risk and Attribution*. London: Risk Books, 243–262.

Till, H. (2006b). EDHEC Comments on the Amaranth Case: Early Lessons from the Debacle. *EDHEC-Risk Publication*, http://www.edhec-risk.com, October 2.

Till, H. (2007a). A Long-Term Perspective on Commodity Futures Returns: A Review of the Historical Literature. In: H. Till and J. Eagleeye (Eds) *Intelligent Commodity Investing* London: Risk Books, 39–82.

Till, H. (2007b). Lessons Learned from the 2006 Energy Hedge Fund Debacles. Financial Analysts Seminar: Improving the Investment Decision-Making Process, Hosted by the Chartered Financial Analyst (CFA) Society of Chicago, July 20.

Till, H. (2008a). Lessons from Recent Energy Trading Debacles: The Bank of Montreal Case Study. The Till and Lhabitant Seminar on State-of-the-Art Commodities Investing, EDHEC Asset Management Education, London, January 22.

Till, H (2008b). Intelligent Commodity Investing: Opportunities and Challenges. Presentation to the London Chapter of the Chartered Alternative Investment Analyst Association, January 23.

Till, H. (2008c). Amaranth Lessons Thus Far. *Journal of Alternative Investments*, Spring, 82–98.

Till, H. and J. Gunzberg (2006). Absolute Returns in Commodity (Natural Resource) Futures Investments. In: I. Nelken (Ed.) *Hedge Fund Investment Management*. Oxford: Elsevier Finance, 25–42.

US District Court, Southern District of NY (2007). *Class Action Complaint*. Alexander Fleiss et al. vs. Optionable Inc. et al., May 11.

Vince, R. (1992). *The Mathematics of Money Management*. New York: John Wiley & Sons Inc.

Weisman, A., S. Patel and A. Suri (2007). Chasing Your Tail. Merrill Lynch Draft Paper, March 29; a version of which was presented to the Spring 2007 Seminar of the Institute for Quantitative Research in Finance (Q-Group) in Sea Island, Georgia, March 25–28.

Whitehouse, K., J. Checkler and C. Buurma (2008). Saracen Cites Losses Tied to Natural Gas. *Wall Street Journal Online*, February 16.

Index

Printed and bound by CPI Group (UK) Ltd, Croydon, CR0 4YY

24/04/2025

14661403-0001